Chronicles and Stories

of

OLD BINGLEY.

A FULL ACCOUNT OF THE

History, Antiquities, Natural Productions, Scenery, Customs and Folk-lore

OF THE ANCIENT TOWN AND PARISH OF BINGLEY, IN THE WEST RIDING OF YORKSHIRE.

BY

HARRY SPEIGHT,

AUTHOR OF "THE CRAVEN HIGHLANDS;" "THROUGH AIREDALE;" "NIDDERDALE;" "ROMANTIC RICHMONDSHIRE;" ETC.

NUMEROUS ILLUSTRATIONS.

THIRD EDITION.

LONDON:
ELLIOT STOCK, 62, PATERNOSTER ROW, E.C.
1899.

PREFACE.

THE OLD Saxon town of Bingley, is very pleasantly situated in the valley of the Aire, about twelve miles from Leeds, and six miles from Bradford. At one time consisting of but few houses, clustered round its venerable Parish Church, the little place lay deeply embosomed amidst high craggy hills and embowering woodlands, and well did it deserve its title of "The Throstle Nest of Old England," which it still fondly bears.

In the following pages I have endeavoured to trace the history of the town and parish from the remotest times. The work is divided into four parts; the first embracing the period from the foundation of the rocks to the Ice Age and the advent of man; the second from thence to the Norman invasion; the third conducting to the present time; while the fourth deals with outlying places in the parish. The design and general scope of the work will at once be apparent on turning to the index of Contents on page 5.

Since the prospectus of the work was issued in 1896 a very large amount of additional matter has been received, which accounts not only for the delay in the publication of the volume, but also for its greatly increased size. My thanks are especially due to Mr. Ferrand, of St. Ives, Bingley, the principal landowner in the parish, whose estates and valuable manuscript collections have been open to me in the most generous manner. Mr. Ferrand has also been good enough to revise the proof-sheets relating to his family's possessions, without which help the book could not have been so accurate and complete. To Mr. Arthur C. Benson, son of the late Archbishop of Canterbury, I am indebted for many interesting particulars respecting his family's connections with the parish. The Right Hon. the Earl of Cranbrook has also sent me many interesting notes. To the clergy, ministers, and a large number of others, in the parish and elsewhere, I am likewise indebted for various useful help, and especially to the following :—Mr. W. A. Brigg, Kildwick Hall; Mr. Francis R. Shackleton, Torquay; Messrs. Farrer & Co. (solicitors to Mr. Lane Fox), London; Miss Maud, Seattle, U.S.A.; Mrs. Staffurth, Bognor; Mrs. Le Page, Cheadle; Mr. J. Stephenson, Bath; Mr. Algernon G. Hartley, London; the late Mr. J. Aldam Heaton, London; the Rev. R. V. Taylor, Melbecks; Mr. J. Norton Dickons, Bradford; Mr. J. J. Stead, Heckmondwike; and the following local residents, namely: Messrs. J. E. Preston, John Walker, J. A. Clapham, T. Wilkinson Green, Alfred Platts, N. H. Walbank, Thomas Longbottom, William Green (librarian), Stephen Darlow, and Sydney Waddington.

The numerous illustrations, and the names of those who have supplied the originals, are given on pages 6 and 7. For a large proportion of the photographs engraved I am indebted to the industry and skill of Mr. George Whitaker, of Bingley, who has taken them specially for this work, and has been unremitting in his pains to supply excellent and suitable originals. Mr. T. W. Goodall, of Bingley, has kindly supplied some beautiful pictures, including various views in the Main Street before the alterations. Miss Nannie Preston, of Gilstead, has furnished some original drawings, and her work—too well known to need any comment of mine—will speak for itself. All the blocks have been engraved by Messrs. Armitage and Ibbetson, of Bradford, and printed with the book by Mr. Edward Foulds, of Bingley.

The valuable plate of "Bingley Eighty Years Ago," in the best edition only, depicts the old church, grammar school, canal, and Belbank woods before the railway was made, and the picture was dedicated to the Rev. Richard Hartley, D.D., vicar of Bingley, and published by N. Whitley, of Halifax, in 1822.

To the subscribers and the many friends who have helped to obtain them my thanks are also due. The subscribers' names are printed at the end of the volume.

HARRY SPEIGHT.

Bingley, Yorks.

CONTENTS.

PART I.

PART II.

PART III.

PART IV.

LIST OF ILLUSTRATIONS.

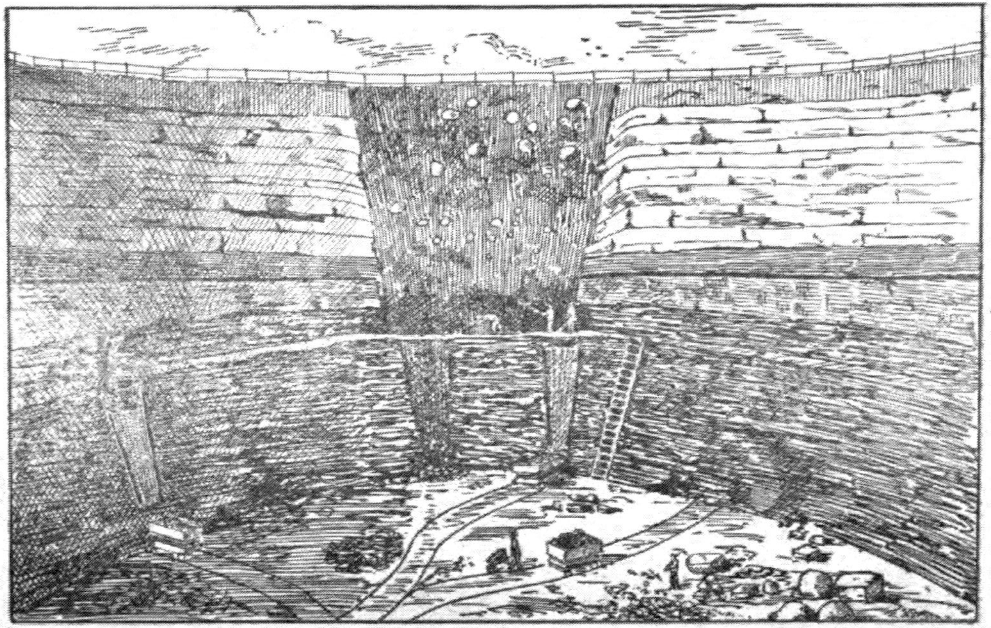

Stream Gully filled with Glacial Debris at Greenhill.

CHRONICLES AND STORIES OF OLD BINGLEY.

PART I.

PRIMEVAL BINGLEY.

"A land wherein thou shalt eat bread without scarceness, thou shalt not lack anything in it; a land whose stones are iron, and out of whose hills thou mayest dig brass. When thou hast eaten and art full, then thou shalt bless the Lord thy God for the good land which he hath given thee."—*Deut. viii, 9, 10.*

IN order to determine the causes which led to the site of Bingley being first chosen as a place of dwelling, it will be necessary to go far back to primeval ages, long before the human epoch. It was then through the wisdom of their infinite Author that the rocks with their mineral treasures were deposited, followed by a wondrous vegetable growth and a beauty of form and mould adapted to man's services and advancement, as implied by the words of the above scriptural text.

As was the case with most ancient centres of population, the spot was unquestionably selected by reason of the physical advantages of rock-structure and surroundings. Moreover, the situation of Bingley at the confluence of two secluded and well-wooded valleys, was one calculated to inspire the early love of meditation and retirement, and even long antecedent to the time when the first fragment of local history was carved in stone, now more than 1100 years ago, the place doubtless was the scene of a happy religious devotion. Ages before then, however, the aboriginal skin-clad native rowed his coracle on the bright waters of the Aire, albeit the full manner and fruition of his life in the district are obscured in the darkness of antiquity.

Yet, again, this man's presence at Bingley is but as of yesterday compared with the time that has elapsed since the rocks on which he first stood and the valley in which he first lived were formed. How came these rocks and this valley, are questions I must now engage to answer. The divers grit rocks and sandstones which constitute the floor and sides of the valley are said to be the result of the decomposition and dispersion of the constituents of granite. Granite consists of an aggregation of felspar, silica or quartz and mica, such materials in fact of which the first solid crust of the earth was made. But how this grit came to be deposited here is a problem that may well arouse enquiry. There appears, however, to be a consensus of opinion that it was derived from the granites of Norway and Sweden, as no other granite resembles so exactly the fluids, gases, and crystals of the grit rocks of this country. As granite decomposes most readily under alternations of great heat and cold, it is conjectured that this took place when the earth was sufficiently cooled to admit of this possibility, and that the particles were borne from the east by hurricanes of wind to find a barrier and stay upon the range of Carboniferous Limestone, at a time when no land existed eastward of the limestone,—all the present land surface in this direction being of more recent formation. The phenomena of wind-borne particles over long distances is not unreasonable when we consider the travelling power and desolating effects, even at this day, of great masses of sand in the desert region of Sahara in Africa and in Central Asia; the sea bottom in many places is covered with a great thickness of sand blown from the desert of Sahara, as was proved by the dredgings brought up by the *Challenger*, often at very considerable distances from the African coast. Yet the wind-bearing theory while it explains many circumstances attending the deposition of the gritstone in England does not explain all. The angularity of the enclosed quartz particles may be accounted for in this way, whilst on the other hand the rock at Bingley is often found to have these pebbles in varying size rounded and smoothed as if by the action of water. The precise determining causes of these variations have never been satisfactorily explained.

Overlying the Rough Rock, which forms the topmost bed of the Millstone Grit series we have the Coal Measures, consisting of alternating beds of sandstone, shale, and thin seams of coal. Bands of ironstone and a stratum of fire-clay are also associated with these measures at Bingley. A valuable sandstone, close-grained and highly silicious, termed galliard, is likewise found in small quantities usually directly beneath the lowest coal seams.

In these upper beds appeared the first vegetable life at Bingley. Also the vegetable origin of coal has long been established. With the gradual cooling and thickening of the earth's crust fresh deposits of mud and sand were formed, and as each successive surface rose above the water it was soon covered with a luxuriant and dense vegetation. The jungles of tropical forests at the present day are mere barrenness in comparison with the extraordinary growth of terrestrial vegetation during this warm period of local history. The giant *lepidodendron*, or fossil tree of our quarries, waved its palm-like branches over a rank and profuse undergrowth of large and magnificent ferns, of which half-a-hundred kinds grew within a few miles' radius of where Bingley now stands. Enormous *calamites*, so called from the reed-like jointings of the stalk, flourished on the muddy banks of these primeval streams; their representatives being the dwindled "horsetails" of our hedge banks and beck sides. Occasionally, as at Gilstead, we find these fossil trees encased in a thin cylinder of coal, formed by the preservation of the bark, the tree having become hollow got filled up with mud or sand, and so took the shape of the trunk. Sometimes, too, we find the sandstone ripple-marked, produced by a gentle flow of water over the surface, which had hardened on the retreat of the wave; likewise the sandstone pitted with small holes caused by rain drops, and we may sometimes tell by the position and form of the holes which way the wind blew when it rained in those far-off days.

Undoubtedly at one time the land within and adjoining the parish was almost one unbroken level surface, but the eye of God alone beheld this. The places which we now know as Greenhill, Druids' Altar, Cottingley Moor, Wrose Hill, Baildon Hill and Gilstead Moor were once joined together by an almost continuous table-land. There happened at this time and also at intervals before, great subsidences in the strata, some taking place suddenly, while others were gentle and protracted. The effects of these subsidences, throws, or "faults," as they are technically termed, we are witnesses of at the present day. An important one extends from near Greenhill, by Gawthorpe Hall, and crossing the town extends the whole length of the Harden valley, throwing out some fine springs in Bell Bank Field and at the back of St. Ives, until its course is stopped by a cross fault through Harden Moor, forming the romantic ravine of Deep Cliff, and passing southwards by Harden Hall towards Wilsden. There is little doubt that the beautiful Harden valley owes its inception to this fault, although so much removed above the present valley bottom.

The Aire valley, where Bingley is situated, is however not directly due to any such faulting as I have described. This dale, like the other great valleys of Yorkshire, owes its origin to the great and much older Penine ridge, which runs in a north and south direction from Derbyshire to the Cheviots. It is noteworthy that most of the great rivers of the world run east or west for similar reasons. The Danube, the Po, and the Tagus in Europe; the Amazon, the Orinoco, and the La Plata in South America; the St. Lawrence, the Ohio, and the Missouri in North America, flow towards the east or west; though the Apennines in Europe, the Andes in South America, and the Alleghany and Rocky Mountains in North America, extend northwards and southwards.

That the Bingley valley is a valley of denudation only is obvious from the corresponding position of the strata on opposite sides of the valley. These strata when not interrupted by faults are perfectly conformable and rise in regular sequence. It is impossible to estimate correctly in point of years how long it has taken to form the valley.

In remote times no doubt the denuding power of water and the actions of heat and frost, have been much more rapid than they are at present, but if we are to accept Dr. Geike's hypothesis that upon an average one-twelfth of an inch is worn out of the valleys in 8½ years, or say one foot in a century, we arrive at the conclusion that it must have taken fully 450,000 years to excavate the Bingley valley, say from the level of the Druids' Altar and Greenhill (650 feet) to the river level at Castlefields (270 feet). This may be an over-estimate, inasmuch as the thickness or depth of the valley is not wholly solid rock, but contains a good proportion of shale, which would wear away much quicker than the sandstone and grit. The trough of Priesthorpe, for example, was excavated out of this softer material, and forms a plateau resting on rock sloping westwards to the valley.

I have spoken of the vegetable life of the local rocks and the earliest evidence of animal life I have met with in the parish is an *annalide* or form of water-worm; petrified castings of which are found in the sandstones of the millstone grits and coal measures. An admirably-preserved specimen is to be seen on a sandstone gate-post at Ravenroyd, and this may be regarded as the oldest representative of animal life extant in the parish. Little or nothing is known of the life-history of these interesting creatures, which occur in varying forms in the rocks long antecedent to the sandstone era, even far down to Cambrian age. Doubtless all our freshwater and terrestrial worms are modern developments of these primitive estuarine and marine forms. Higher up in the series of local rocks we find a more advanced type of animal life in the shape of fossil shells and fish remains. No insects, however, or reptiles are seen, which belong to a later period than is yielded by the local strata. And these facts, by the way, are quite in accord with science and the Bible; the humble forms of life are the oldest, and the most wonderful and complex, viz., man, appears as the consummation or climacteric of life on the earth.

In the coal measures is found a well-preserved mollusc, *Aviculopecten*, accompanied with a goniatite, a univalve shell coiled up like a snail, a form of which occurs in the Carboniferous Limestone of Bolland, Derbyshire, and the Isle of Man, as well as in the limestone and coal measures of Ireland. A higher type still, ranking between the fishes and reptiles, is found in the roof of the Hard Bed coal, including the colossal *Megalicthys Hibberti*, a fine specimen of which is in the Leeds Museum.

The "fossil mussel," hardly distinguishable at sight from the common sea-mussel of the present age, which is found in quantities close above the coal seams on Baildon Moor, is doubtless a descendant of the primeval form occurring in the Carboniferous Limestone, and allied to the freshwater types found in the neighbourhood of Bingley at the present day. I am told on the authority of several old men, still living, that when the railway was made at Bingley in 1846, the stone tippings in the bog caused numerous specimens of black mussel and sea-cockle to ooze to the surface, and in places where they could not possibly have been thrown. That these should appear at Bingley dark coloured, or even black, is easily accounted for by long continuance in stagnant water and subject to the pressure of decayed vegetable matter excluded from the air, precisely in the same way as the vegetable accumulations of coal become black. But the occurrence of the sea-cockle at Bingley, if it be ever proved to be such, is of more than ordinary importance. Until, however, actual specimens are produced from the spot the subject is purely speculative. Possibly the shells were the freshwater helices *(Tellina cornea)* which have been found in peat-moss, but in these forms the stripes are across the shell, from side to side, not in the same directions as the sea-cockle. I have met with but a single mention of the occurrence of sea-cockle in peat-moss in Yorkshire, and this about forty miles from the sea, at a point about two miles from Greta Bridge and about two miles from the river Tees. The cockles were, it is said, found in considerable quantity, and an old farm-house near, called Cocklesbury, is said to have taken its name from the circumstance. But in the *Edinburgh New Philosophical Journal*, vol. II (1827), Sir W. C. Trevelyan doubts that they are native to the place, and asserts that after an actual visit he found some freshwater specimens, the common whelk; and if the sea-cockle (*cardium edule*) has been found there, they have been put there for the purpose of hoaxing the individuals who collected them afterwards. The only shell which I have myself found in the peat at Bingley was obtained during the recent draining in the highroad on the edge of the bog going to Crossflatts. Here at a depth of 16 feet from the present surface I obtained from the peat dead specimens of *Helix rufescens*, a common and still-existing land shell. A marine shell (*Cyprina Islandica*), I may add, has been found in this valley at Greengates, but embedded in glacial drift. In the same material at Bingley, about 8 feet from the surface, there was found, while digging a grave on the east side of the cemetery, in January, 1898, about sixty well-grown specimens of the peculiarly limestone mollusc, *Helix nemoralis*. It is not unusual for this creature to burrow 3 to 4 feet down, but to find it at a depth of 8 feet is very remarkable. Probably they had slipped through an aperture in the gravel. All were dead.

When the conditions which had produced the rocks and strange life above described had ceased, and the hills and valleys were clothed with a tropical growth, there was another and more complex kind of life existing here, of which, however, we know little. Still we are sure there were some strange quadrupeds at Bingley, for the bones of the hippopotamus, the teeth and bones of the mammoth, bear, bison (a tooth was found in forming the fish-pond at Milner Field), and the molars of a single lion, all found in Airedale, constitute undoubted evidence as to the kinds of creatures that infested the local woods and glades in those primeval times. But we have no evidence of the presence of man and his handiwork until after the close of the Ice Age, a comparatively recent event when considering the antiquity of the valley he inhabits, an antiquity that recalls the words of the divine Interrogator to His servant Job: "Where wast thou when I laid the foundations of the earth? Declare if thou hast understanding!" And the man answered: "Behold I am vile; what shall I answer Thee? I will lay mine hand upon my mouth."

Glacial Drift on Sandstone at Seven Arches.

BINGLEY DURING THE ICE AGE.

THE stupendous walls of blue ice that completely filled the gorge at Bingley and had been encroaching upon this district during many centuries, drove away every form of life save that which is peculiar to the frozen regions of the north at the present day, as for example, the bear, Arctic fox and certain species of birds. The huge mammoth (now extinct) seems also to have survived the rigours of this Polar cold in Yorkshire, and doubtless, the hippopotamus too, a denizen of the Bingley swamps, as bones of this thick-skinned sluggish creature, identical with the species now inhabiting African rivers, have been found in glacial clay lower down the Aire valley. About sixty years since while a small tunnel was being made from the river to a well in Mr. Wm. Maud's property on Elm Tree Hill there was found in the glacial drift some fifty or sixty feet from the surface a leg bone of a fowl, but singularly not far from it was a brass pin. But it is very questionable, considering the proximity of the latter, if the bone was of glacial age. Man, however, as I have just said, does not appear to have been present in Yorkshire antecedent to or during this great northern cataclysm. In North Britain, Scandinavia, and indeed throughout Northern Europe paleolithic implements have never been found nor any evidence of pre-glacial man, whilst in the south of England and in France they are abundant. It is moreover now agreed that the supposed human fibula found in glacial debris along with bones of the mammoth and spotted-hyæna in the Victoria Cave, near Settle, is not a human remain, but may be the bone of some inferior order of animal which cannot be determined with certainty. That man may have come northwards and witnessed the *retreat* of the glaciers in the Yorkshire dales is not at all improbable, as I have shewn in my work on Richmondshire. The discovery of a bone brace of very primitive make, along with the remains of reindeer and other evidences of the occupation of Wensleydale during a period of intense cold, seems to point to the belief that man and the reindeer were coeval in Yorkshire when it had an Arctic climate. The reindeer is an animal that subsists on lichens and has a preference for a certain degree of cold; it is a migratory animal upon which one class of mankind—the Laplanders—are mainly dependent for their existence. Is it not likely then that the reindeer followed the retreat of the ice northwards, and that man accompanied it; the present inhabitants of the Arctic regions being the descendants partly of the primeval tenants of the Yorkshire dales? As will be explained in the next chapter, many Arctic plants have survived at Bingley unto this day; among others the old Reindeer Lichen *(C. sylvatica)* still maintains its ground.

In my work on Nidderdale I have expounded the astronomical discovery of General Drayson shewing that "about 23,000 years B.C., the Arctic circles extended about 30 degrees from the Poles, at about 13,500 B.C., they extended nearly 35½ degrees from the Poles, or to be exact to the latitude of 54 degrees, 34 minutes, 13 seconds in both hemispheres. Consequently North Yorkshire was within the Arctic Circle, the dales were filled with glaciers, the land to an altitude in some places of nearly 2000 feet above present sea-level, was submerged in ice and snow and all the appearances of an Arctic climate prevailed." Long after the ice-mantle disappeared from the higher ground, tongues of ice in the shape of local glaciers continued to fill the Yorkshire dales, and in Airedale we have evidence that the glacier extended below Shipley, thinning away in the neighbourhood of Leeds. Ice-groovings have been noted on rock near Apperley Bridge, &c., and at Bingley magnificent evidence is to be seen of the contest which the ice had with the winding sandstone gorge, in forcing through which enormous mounds of moraine matter were deposited. Nowhere in Yorkshire can the strange effects of these ancient glaciers be better studied than in the neighbourhood of Bingley, where the confined valley must have been choked with ice for many hundreds of years. And these singular mounds with their loads of transported limestones, &c., were to prove in after days, as I shall shew by-and-bye, a source of great and exceptional profit to the inhabitants of Bingley.

It was not until 5,600 B.C., that the Arctic Circles had contracted to 30 degrees from the Poles or to the latitude of about south Shetland, and it would not be until about 3000 years B.C., that Yorkshire would possess a climate suitable for habitation by man. The fabulous antiquity so frequently ascribed to certain finds of human remains, and their associated relics in the north, must therefore be received with caution. There is probably not a human bone ever found in Yorkshire that has an age of 5000 years upon it, whilst the first steps in the human history of this parish begin long after this date. Northern Europe, as I have pointed out, was not inhabited until the Neolithic or second Stone Age.

In the long and severe winters of that frozen era, ice and snow covered the hills and valleys in winter, whilst the almost tropical heat of short summers produced enormous floods, accompanied by dense fogs, just as they arise now on the banks of Newfoundland from the same cause. In Airedale these successive annual floods filled the valley in many places to a great depth with water; lakes were formed, traces of which remain to this day. A considerable amount of denudation also took place; many of the stones composing the glacial hummocks were rolled in water and the striations caused by the scratching of one stone against another during the ice pressure were largely removed, whilst upon the hill slopes almost every trace of glacial deposit was obliterated. Ice-scratched limestone pebbles may however still be picked out of the clay on the hill sides surrounding Bingley, as well as from the till and esker-ridges on the moor tops. Perched blocks, galliard resting on millstone grit, were also at one time very numerous on Harden and the surrounding moors. On Gilstead Moor and on Rumbalds Moor these white, flinty rocks have been very numerous in places where no galliard is in situ. Most of them have been used for walling purposes as the moors became enclosed.

The town of Bingley stands on one of these old glacial moraines, the Main Street following its longitudinal apex, whilst the "Old Hills" and Myrtle Pasture (formerly worked for limestone), completes the drift on the south side of the town. At the north end a long mound commences on the north-west side of the church and rises towards the cemetery. This single deposit occupies all the ground between the river on the west and the railway on the east running north-west and south-east for 45 chains (about half-a-mile), and is 20 chains at its broadest part. The maximum depth above normal river level is about 70 feet. Its northern boundary is limited by the river-bend at Ravenroyd to Castlefields Mill, and the reason why the river has not followed a straight and natural course along the valley on the east side of the hill where the railway runs, is owing to the thick spreads of gravel, which rising towards Crossflatts, have baulked the river and compelled it to cut a fresh channel by the lower level on the west side of the town. This extensive mound, called Bailey Hills, was at one time undoubtedly an island and a secure refuge of the early inhabitants (*see* chapter on The Advent of Man). It was bounded on the west by the river and on the east by an extensive lake which continued impassably wet until the making of the railway in 1846. The highroad from the vicarage to Crossflatts rises over the eastern slope of this mound, and the railway cuts through the northern extremity of the gravel at the bridge. Crossflatts is built partly on gravel containing drifted sandstone and limestone pebbles, and it is gravel all along the canal-bank as far as the Five-Rise Locks, where the drift is abruptly terminated. The whole of the expanse below towards the vicarage (which is erected on elm piles) formed a large lake, whilst another wide-spreading lake filled the valley beyond Crossflatts towards Marley. Peat has accumulated to a great thickness in the valley below the vicarage, and during the recent excavations for the main drain I had opportunities of noting that the peat at a depth of 18 feet from the road surface rested on a stratum of tough boulder clay. The valley has moreover nurtured a forest of indigenous growth, and much decayed as well as sound wood has been found here. One trunk of black oak, fully 20 feet long and 2 feet in diameter was dug out, and others of varying dimensions have been also unearthed from time to time whilst digging for foundations in different parts of the valley. Pieces of black oak which an axe could not cut were lately met with while excavating for the foundations of the centre buttresses of the new aqueduct across the Aire near Cottingley Bridge.

One noteworthy feature in connection with these mounds is the very stony character of the deposits at Bingley, where boulders up to half-a-ton in weight are not uncommon. The included boulders consist principally of local grits and sandstones of various kinds, also limestones, white, blue, and encrinital, and now and then I have met with boulders and pebbles of a hard detrital bluish-grey rock—though sometimes found of a greenish tint—which appears identical with the Silurian grits of upper Ribblesdale, of which the magnificent group of erratics at Norber, near Austwick, constitute the most notable existing example of ice-transportation of this rock (*see* my "Craven Highlands," pages 168-170).*

Northwards, nearer Marley and at Sandbeds, the deposits are almost wholly pure sand, forming smooth, rounded lesser hills and beds of fine sand of great thickness. This circumstance may be explained by the fact that at the south end of the town, where the valley makes a sharp curve with the principal declination of the ground towards the west, the glacier has accumulated to an enormous thickness, filling the whole of the gorge, and depositing its burthen of debris, which here attains its greatest thickness. These accumulations have completely stopped the outlet of the water, and the dam so formed has caused the waters to gather into a large lake, the current, or rather conjunction of currents, with the main valley from Morton Glen have tended to form banks of sand by continued attrition. Higher up the dale, opposite Carlton, similar whirlpools have caused deposits of sand, and on the

* A well-rounded boulder of this rock, weighing probably 2 cwt., has lately been dug out of the drift in Priesthorpe Road, at an elevation of about 150 feet above the river. Sandstones have also been found containing fossils, evidently of a Silurian facies.

site of Skipton Cemetery graves are dug through fifteen feet of sand without finding a stone bigger than a pigeon's egg.

An inspection of the ground at Bingley shews that the declension of lateral currents and the increased power of the main current have in course of time forced an outlet near Castlefields Mill, cutting along the west side of the Bailey Hills, thus lowering the level of the old lake, and leaving a sandy shore. The principal mounds of the valley, too, appear to be formed on a neucleus of solid rock. The rock is in evidence near Castlefields; in Myrtle Place and Main Street, and a good section is exposed in the mound at Hirst Wood, close to the Seven Arches, where it has been quarried for sandstone (*see* page 16). The glacier grinding over these strata would smooth and polish them, or it may also have been partially cleft, and crevasses would be formed, causing a more rapid break-up of the ice-mass and consequent deposit of debris.

As I have stated, the tough blue clay forms the floor of the superficial deposits of the valley, and this boulder clay, consisting of clay and stones intermingled, ascends nearly, if not quite, to the summit level of the watersheds of Aire and Wharfe. During the construction of the Shipley reservoir on the moor above Eldwick (750ft.) a good example of this till was come upon in the course of excavating. A similar mass of till extends from Calverley Moor to Eccleshill and Idle, about 600 feet above the sea level. A peculiarity of these beds, observes Mr. Davis in *West Yorkshire*, is that whilst they contain numerous sub-angular boulders of grit and sandstone derived from the Millstone Grits and Lower Coal Measures south of Skipton, no Carboniferous Limestone has been found. But this supposition may be controverted. I have myself obtained well-rounded and beautifully-striated limestones from the blue clay on Greenhill, overlooking the Bingley valley, at a similar elevation (600ft.). The deposit at this spot is of unique interest. In the quarries of the Bingley Sanitary Tube Co. at Greenhill, a section has been bared of an extraordinary character. It consists in descending order as follows :—(1) Top soil 3 to 4 feet; (2) about 20 feet of shale and sandstone of no commercial value; (3) black shale, about 3 feet, from base of which springs of water are pumped into a small reservoir in the quarry; (4) a parting of coal about 1½ inches thick; (5) the coal rests on a bed of fire-clay 3 feet thick, from which the sanitary tubes are made; (6) below the clay, forming the base of the quarry, is about 20 feet of "blue-bind" (shale), from which common bricks are made. The whole series comprises a thickness of about 50 feet. The bed of fire-clay is apparently of no great extent, following a north and south direction towards Greenhill Grange, perhaps 200 yards, when it disappears, being cut off by a fault, which brings up the sandstone of the Millstone Grit series.

But the most remarkable features connected with these measures is the presence of an ancient stream-gully, which at first sight I took to be a breach made by a fault in the strata, but a little investigation showed that the gully was completely filled with the glacial till above described. The till consists of a stiff blue clay with a blackish sandy base, containing rounded and scratched stones. The gully takes a curvilinear direction from north-west to south-east right through the measures, and is about 25 yards wide at the summit (moor) level, maintaining nearly the same width until a depth of over 30 feet is reached, when it narrows to about 9 feet, though originally it maintained a pretty uniform width to the floor level. On the east side the strata along the margin are perceptibly bent by impact of the superincumbent mass; on the west boundary they appear to be less compressed. The illustration prefacing the first chapter shows the main features of the strata, with the till in the gully; the latter has no commercial value, and is now being removed. The limestones found in it are small, and never more than a pound or two in weight, whilst several boulders of local sandstone, some upwards of a ton in weight, have been removed. That the gully primarily originated by the action of water is also evident from the presence of several basin-shaped hollows in the shaly floor (where the rails are laid), which contained hundreds of pebbles, well-rounded by the swirl of waters in these cavities.

A Botanist's Paradise, Seven Arches.

WANDERINGS AMONG WILD FLOWERS.

Honour the Most High for His sweet power,
  The gift of flowers!
The glory and the meekness of the earth,
Telling of years not ours, but time of eld,
Ere wit of man knew aught of the deep truths
That spring from out their secret majesty.—*H. Speight.*

WHEN the babe Nature grew into the perfection of womanhood she girdled the earth with flowers. Her attractions play so prominent a part in the parish of Bingley, and they have done for ages we cannot count, that these must form the next step forward in the sequence of local history. Once on a time the old place lay encircled in leafy and many-coloured luxuriance. Great trees with their spreading arms grew around on all sides, literally embracing the old town; swelling uplands towered above the valley gay with a thousand floral treasures, while many a rill poured forth in musical sweetness its pure flood into the valley below. To the lover of Nature the scene under such purely rustic aspects must have been charming; a "Throstle Nest," truly, as the old folks loved to call it, and a "Throstle Nest," too, that lay deeply hidden as in a huge nosegay!

Let memory go back for a brief space to those happy olden days whilst we wander in thought through the leafy lanes of old Bingley. I am told by aged people still living that sixty or seventy years ago the vernal season was ushered in with such a show of primroses, anemones, and celandines as few other places could boast. From Bingley Bridge to Ravenroyd the river sides were aglow with countless primroses; the same lovely flower starred every hedge bank, and in the pastures at the bottom of Priesthorpe, where now are rows of streets, cowslips and primroses might have been gathered in hundreds. The delicate white flowers of the anemone and the yellow rays of the celandine also covered coppice and wood on the Harden as well as Priesthorpe sides of the town. In the Harden valley primroses are still pretty numerous, but the glory of their profusion, alas ! is gone.

What a welcome flower is the soft-eyed primrose at each return of spring! There is hardly a poet of rank from Chaucer onwards who has not loved it and sung its praises. Its peculiar creamy tint resembles no other British flower, and it is said we must go to the moist banks of tropical countries to find its likeness. Perhaps the primrose is one of those tropical species which has come down to us from very remote ages? It delights in a warm and sheltered soil, and dwindles and perishes in cold and exposed situations. Then there are the curious arums and orchids of our woods, which are said to be descendants of old tropical forms. Have these lain sepulchred for ages under an Arctic ice-blast, until the light and warmth of another era have raised them fresh and sweet into life and beauty, though in an altered form? We know there are certain seeds and roots that have retained their power of germination after preservation through numberless centuries.

There are many plants and flowers peculiar to our district which suggest themes for the studious and inquisitive lover of Nature. Many, doubtless, are the survivors of ancient tropical or sub-tropical forms, whilst others have been brought hither by the great glaciers from the north, described in the last chapter. Take the pretty tuberous moschatel (*Adoxa moschatellina*), which grows in two or three places, but notably about Beck-foot. Here, in the lap of an old glacial moraine, this interesting little plant has flourished in a wild state, probably for several thousand years. It is a characteristic plant of the cold and frozen north. It grows on the summits of Scotland's highest mountains, expanding its pale green blossoms beside the hardy saxifrages; on the Scandinavian ranges, too, and in the treeless deserts of Siberia and Lapland, as well as on the wind-swept shores of Arctic seas it revels in the sun-warmth of the short summer incident to those frigid parts. Singularly, this plant and two or three other northern species are not found in the Calder valley; having their westward range apparently limited by the Airedale spurs of the great Penine Chain.

Some of the saxifrages found in the Bingley area also luxuriate in the far north, and never have I seen finer specimens of the beautiful flower of Parnassus (*Parnassia palustris*) than those which bloom among the mountains of Argyll. I have seen this plant on the edge of Rumbalds Moor, above Bingley, and I have also gathered it lately on the Cornshaw Moors, west of Keighley, at an elevation of near 1,000 feet. The golden saxifrage (*Chrysosplenium*) occurs in Bingley streams, and is found in the Yorkshire highlands up to an altitude of fully 2,000 feet. The little rue-leaved saxifrage (*S. tridactylites*), growing near Cottingley, is very rarely found on grit rock. It is partial to limestone districts, and must have been carried down the valley from the white crags of Craven. Then again, there are here certain Scandinavian insects, and there are those remarkable little insectivorous plants, the butterwort (formerly used for curdling milk, and still so in Lapland) and sundew (described by Darwin), both of which occur in our area but sparingly, though they are abundant in the moorland districts further north. The round-leaved sundew (*Drosera rotundifolia*) is by no means common in Airedale, yet in the Priesthorpe district, almost within a stone-throw of where I write, I have seen at least one hundred specimens in a wild state, as it only will grow. Cultivation out of its own element kills it! In the highlands of Scotland I have seen it redden the streams for miles, and it is found all down the Penine ridge by Blackstone Edge to Derbyshire.

The distribution of plant-life is one of engrossing interest. It must not be supposed that the occurrence of this or that species in a given locality is due entirely to spontaneity or is a gift direct from the Creator. Geological formation and climatic conditions are the great governors of the plant-life of the earth. Ice and water have had a share in the local distribution of plants, and there is no doubt that winds and high gales are important factors in the dissemination of seed, particularly in the case of the minute spores of certain ferns and mosses. How else are we to explain the records of the delicate and rare Killarney Fern (*Trichomanes radicans*) in the Bingley woods except by these means? I have often thought that high south-westerly gales must have prevailed for a long period up to the close of the Ice Age in this district, and that these sweeping winds down the Harden valley may have contributed not only to the transmission of spores, but

A HOME OF THE KILLARNEY FERN, BINGLEY.

to the break-up of the ice in the Bingley valley. This fern, which at one time flourished amazingly about the beautiful Lakes of Killarney, but is now, I regret, through the rapacity of collectors, almost extinct, was first recorded for Bingley by Dillenius in Ray's *Synopsis* (A.D. 1724). It is hardly likely to have been planted here at a time when no interest was taken in ferns, and communication with Ireland was tedious and difficult. The first monograph on British Ferns was, I believe, written by J. Bolton, and published in 1785. In that work the author refers to this fern having been "first discovered by Dr. Richardson in a little dark cavern, under a dripping rock, below the spring of Elm Crag well, in Bell Bank." In the same place Bolton saw it in plenty in 1758, and again when he visited the spot in 1782 he found the cavern had been destroyed, but a single root was discovered under a rock to the left side of the current, and about fifteen yards above the cistern. From this specimen an engraving was made for his book. Dickson and Teesdale (*vide Linn. Trans.*, 1800) likewise record the existence of the fern at the same place. Since this time there is no evidence of its having been seen, and it is known to have been long extinct here.

The length of time covered by these valuable records leaves no room to doubt that the Killarney Fern has been a native of Bingley. But who shall measure the period of its continuance at this spot, so far from its true home? It is, however, well-known to have been observed in some retired glens of North Wales within the last twenty years, and may perhaps be found in other places there and in England yet, whilst in many others it has probably become extinct. The plant is not so much injured by frost as by the direct rays of the sun, and those who know the situation of the recorded habitat at Bingley, which is represented in the accompanying view, must realise that no more likely spot, embracing all the conditions requisite to the life of the plant, could be found in the county of broad acres.*

But a multitude of other gems awaits attention, so now let us wander awhile through our "fortunate fields

* The situation and conditions are identical with those of the lately-discovered Irish hepatic, *Jubula Hutchinsiæ*, near Hebden Bridge, which Mr. Needham describes in the *Naturalist* for 1897 (p. 128): "Found growing on sandstones in a damp wood in a sheltered glen by a small rill, which empties itself into the river Hebden. The wood in which it grows has a westerly aspect, and is well sheltered from the north and east by lofty hills." This is the first record of the plant in Yorkshire; its habitat being principally confined to the sheltered glens of Glengariff and Killarney.

and groves and flowery vales." Upon these things the great limner of Paradise loved to dwell, for Milton was passionately fond of flowers, both wild and cultivated, and in his blindness loved to have their forms described. Burns and Wordsworth leaned to Nature's wildings, and who has written with more soul-affection than Scotia's prince of song in his idyll, *To a Mountain Daisy?* The celandine was Wordsworth's favourite flower, and who does not love to see its golden rays expand and illume the earth like bright stars in the sky after weeks of dull and clouded weather? It is the first real harbinger of spring, and in the genial days of February or early March it may usually be found lighting up the yet bare and brackish gill above Gawthorpe Hall, as well as in other similarly-sheltered places.

But the best haunts of Nature's varied treasures are, of course, on the woodland side of the valley. Going over Bingley Bridge on to the Harden road we soon pass through the stile on the left, and go through Holme House Wood and by the flower-embroidered path over the Hesp Hills to Beckfoot, a favourite walk at any season. Here we shall find the early purple orchis (*O. mascula*), whose tuberous root is said to yield a preparation equal to the finest salep brought from Persia. The bright pink meadow-lychnis, or ragged-robin, is always found plentifully about here; then we drop on to the woody-nightshade (*Solanum Dulcamara*), with its frail branching stems and drooping flowers of deep purple and yellow. It belongs to an order of poisonous plants which includes the deadly nightshade, potato-flower, and tobacco-plant. The enchanter's-nightshade (*Circæa lutetiana*) also grows in these woods. In different places in this neighbourhood appear likewise the various species of stitchwort, including the rare *Stellaria nemorum*, or broad-leaved stitchwort, which fortunately occurs in some profusion. Here, too, is the old medicinal wood-sanicle (*S. europæa*) and the large flowered bitter-cress (*Cardamine amara*). Here also grows the sweet violet (*V. odorata*), which puts forth its fragrant blooms in the early spring. Then there is a solitary patch of the curious fleabane, its scientific name being *Inula dysenterica.* Anciently it was called *Helenium*, the heroine of the Trojan war, and the plant is said to have sprung from her tears. Year after year it appears in the same place.

Walking about Harden and in the Goit Stock valley we have many precious flowering plants, mosses, and ferns, whose localities I dare not name, lest the despoiler lay ruthless hands upon them. The hellebore (*E. latifolia*), one of the rarest of our orchids, grows sparingly in two places. Herb Paris and monk's hood (*Aconitum napellus*) I have seen; the latter, no doubt, a garden escape, though here far away from any garden. Several of the hawkbits also occur here, including *Leontodon hirsutus*, whilst the familiar "mother-of-thousands," or ivy-leaved toad-flax, fringes many an old rock and cottage wall.

Ascending the river to Marley, we have the two geraniums, *sylvatica* and *pratense*, and along the wood bottom, taking the river-side walk, to Ravenroyd is the passion-dock or snake-root (*Polygonum Bistorta*), with its spikes of pale pink flowers. It grows here in profusion, and has also lately got established in the public lane. *Polygonum Hydropiper*, or water-pepper, is also found about here. The frog orchis (*Habenaria viridis*), butterfly orchis (*H. chlorantha*), bog violet (*Hottonia palustris*), water plantain (*Alisma plantago*), water figwort (*S. aquatica*), monkey-flower (*Mimulus lutens*), knotted spurrey (*Sagina nodosa*), and three species of mint, are amongst some noteworthy plants of this district.

Crossing to the heights of Gilstead and Eldwick, we find patches of good king Henry (*Chenopodium Bonus Henricus*) and the pretty scarlet pimpernel (*Anagallis arvensis*) (in my garden at Crow Nest the variety *cærulea* has cropped up among waifs of the common speedwell, dwarf spurge, &c.). We have quite a host of waifs and strays to record in the corn-lands about Glovershaw Beck. Such, for example, as the madder, grey speedwell, shepherd's needle, lamb's lettuce, field woundwort, sun spurge, &c. The butterfly orchis and the beautiful bog pimpernel (*Anagallis tenella*) occur on the edge of Rumbalds Moor. At Morton has been found the sowthistle (*Sonchus oleraceus*), with its succulent leaves and stems, for which pigs have a particular liking, hence its name. Coming down from Gilstead to the canal we find the rare gipsy-wort (*Lycopus europæus*) here growing by the water brink in some quantity. The rare mountain crane's-bill (*G. pyrenæcum*) has also been noted in this locality for many years.

Now we are at the Seven Arches, and truly we may wander far over the big shire before we find a spot where so many objects of interest to the naturalist are crowded into a like space. This is an attractive and never-tiring spot, very well known to members of the Bradford Naturalists' Society, who have made it a special field of investigation. Every foot of ground has been scrutinized, and probably every object recorded. I have deemed it interesting to perpetuate some aspects of this classic ground in the engraving which prefaces this chapter. My friend, Mr. John W. Carter, ex-President of the society named, is introduced into the picture; he is shewn upon the rustic bridge which spans the stream below the Arches. Many happy hours has he and other members of the long-established Bradford Naturalists' Society spent here in fruitful quest of flower and insect and shell. It is unnecessary to enumerate all the records that have been made. It must suffice if I describe one bit of bank close to the scene of the picture. Here within a space of a few yards I have noted the following plants. Beside a spreading sycamore (whose foliage and flowers are no where more luxuriant than at this spot), where a thorn and hazel crop up among trailing brambles, springs the wild hyacinth and red-flowered campion, barren and fruiting strawberry, yellow archangel, and sweet-scented ciceley; the fern-like foliage of the white-flowered earth-nut, rough chervil, ground ivy, and white-flowering cow parsnip; the tender green leaves of the wood sorrel (which some believe is the true shamrock), wood violet, wild garlic, the star-like stitchworts, broad and narrow-leaved, Jack-by-the-edge, herb Robert, and climbing bush-vetch, with the modest little Greenland moschatel half screened from view. The common ivy plant trails its shining leaves in and among this wealth of various plant-life, whilst above and around range the sweet wild roses and stately bell-flowers, as if they would make an Eden's bower. And all this within almost an arm's-breadth of Nature's own garden ground! Of insects and other curious things of God's own giving, each having its wondrous life-history, these are in plenty, too.

But I must stop. May all of them, I pray, continue to harbour the same sweet spot for years yet to come; helping by their manifold beauty and diverse structure to guide us to a nobler appreciation of the best aims of life; to grow wise in the loving and rich in the spirit of His glorious works. Spare thou, therefore, the flowers and the green sod where thou canst! Do not let the cunning of thy hand smite the tree and floral bank for pure lust of gain! If we had all the wealth of Crœsus we should be poor if our woods and fields and flowers were gone. The meek-eyed tender wildings are as angels' looks by the thorny paths of life! Their pure love never ceases, for while cities and temples have fallen and the stones of man's hewing have crumbled to dust, the uninjured flowerets of the field are clothed as with immortality, and shall gladden thy soul for aye! Let us not forget, too, that

> "Other eyes than ours
> Were made to look on flowers;
> Eyes of small birds, and insects small,
>
> . . . .
>
> The tiniest living thing
> That soars on feathered wing,
> Or crawls among the long grass out of sight,
> Has just as good a right
> To its appointed portion of delight
> As any King."

The "Throstle Nest of Old England," Bingley.

WILD BIRDS OF BINGLEY DISTRICT.

FLAP! flap! What is that? Bingley by the sea! No, that cannot be, yet the great white wings of the sea-gull pass close before my window, the birds doubtless making for their old accustomed haunts by the quiet reaches of the river near Marley. I have seen them sometimes, too, in the retired marshy hollows about Beckfoot. Are they instinctively scouring the land in search of some long-lost prehistoric sea? I trow not, although the vagaries of migration are yet but imperfectly understood. In this district it is generally accounted a sign of approaching stormy weather when the gulls are seen; but they do not stay long, merely making this a halting-place in their quick passage from coast to coast. Flocks of wild geese also fly inland, resting in the same spots as the gulls, and I have noticed that their presence here has been followed by sudden storms of wind, rain, or snow. The delicate organisms of birds are, no doubt, more susceptible to atmospherical changes and alterations of season than are the larger animals. This is unquestionably one of the motives for seasonal migration, inasmuch as an equable climate conduces to the comfort and consequent health and maintenance of the species. To trace the complexities of migration to their source, and to explain the reason for the preferences of certain birds to particular climates and surroundings we must again go back to the remote Ice Age. Then there must have been a forcing southwards of certain northern types and a re-installation of certain species on the amelioration of climate as the ice withdrew. The common red-grouse of our moors, for example, possesses a close affinity with the willow-grouse (*Lagopus albus*); the latter, however, is arboreal in its habits, and the differentiation of the species can only be explained by isolation at some remote epoch when the changed aspects altered the food supply. The red-grouse is now strictly confined to the cold, bracing moors of the north, and the theory of its continuance in these latitudes since the Ice Age is very ingeniously set forth in an interesting chapter of Mr. Chas. Dixon's "Migration of British Birds."

Most of our so-called resident birds are more or less migratory, and this is especially applicable to a district like Bingley, where altitudinal range is so marked. It is also noteworthy that in any general migration southwards the female birds of some species greatly preponderate, and this fact did not escape the vigilant eye of Gilbert White, who, writing from Selborne in 1770, remarks upon the vast flocks of hen chaffinches appearing in that neighbourhood in winter time, and Linnæus remarks the same thing. In this district "resident" birds are usually more markedly numerous in summer than in winter, and this is especially the case in high or exposed situations, like, for example, the Park top, whence there is a general exodus of bird-life on the approach of winter's cold. The winter season, however, has its compensations in the appearance of many interesting species driven by the hyperborean cold and insufficient food supply to pass the winter with us; also some moorland types occasionally seek shelter and nutriment in the lowlands. About Crow Nest and in Priesthorpe, the ring-ouzel, which appears to be only a partial migrant, will sometimes come down for a meal to the gardens, and even hop among poultry. Large numbers of these birds are to be found on the Sussex downs in winter, and also in North Africa, and they return to our moors in spring. Harden Moor is one of their early and favourite haunts in this district. Fieldfares and redwings, which belong to the same genus, also visit us in some numbers in winter. Both these interesting species breed in Norway and Sweden, building their nests, which are most like those of the ring-ouzel, against the trunk of the spruce fir or birch, at varying heights from the ground. Flocks of wild ducks also generally pass the winter in one or two places near Bingley, and there are water-hens also to be found.

Among the rarer winter visitors to this district have been noted, principally by Mr. E. P. Butterfield, of Wilsden, the siskin, great crested grebe (*P. cristatus*), green sandpiper (*T. ochropus*), pochard (*F. Ferina*), greenshank (*T. canescens*), common buzzard (*B. vulgaris*), once an abundant resident among the crags of north-west Yorkshire, and hooded crow (*C. cornix*). A handsome specimen of the honey buzzard was shot by Scott, the keeper, in Blakey Wood, Marley, some ten years ago, and is now at Cuckoo Nest. In the severe weather of January, 1895, Mr. Butterfield observed several snow-bunting (*P. nivalis*) in the Main Street, Wilsden. I have seen numbers of these pert little birds about the snow on the summit of Ben Nevis in the warm days of mid-August. Its nest has been found as far north as Grinnel Land, at latitude 82°·88′. In February, 1896, an immature specimen of the great northern diver (*C. glacialis*) was shot on Baildon reservoir. It was sent for preservation to Mr. Fred. R. Kirby, taxidermist, of Bradford. It is a very rare visitor to this district; its nearest home and breeding-place being in the far-away Western Hebrides. The true Canada-goose (*B. canadensis*) is also reported from the Bingley district, and I am assured by the Rev. J. Beanland, of Calverley, that it has nested on the tarn side near St. Ives, in 1887, and that he obtained three eggs from the nest. The nest was very large, and built of twigs, grass, &c., and originally contained six eggs, but three were hatched when the nest was found on June 24th, 1887.

Of all seasons spring is the best time to enjoy the company of the birds, to learn something of their ways, and delight in their varied notes and songs. Who, after the long, dull, winter-time, does not rejoice at the arrival of the first summer migrants, seeking their old accustomed haunts by stream, or moor, or woodland? Who does not welcome the familiar twin notes of the cuckoo as they issue from the depths of the green, awakening woods, or perchance a little later are heard in the solitudes of the far-extending moorlands? In the glistening skies of April the lark, too, keeping tune by the vibration of his wings, floods the air with joyous melody.

"Now rings the woodland loud and long,
The distance takes a lovelier hue,
And drown'd in yonder living blue,
The lark becomes a sightless song.'

As Tennyson hymns the praise of spring. Now is the time when Bingley's woods are fresh and fair, and a thousand feathered choristers have gathered about the "Throstle Nest," and are filling the air with amorous song. Some birds, however, which are with us all the year round, sing at all seasons. Such is the redbreast, whose smart, vivacious airs enliven many a cold and frosty day's walk.

But in Spring, when haunts are "green and bright," with light heart and buoyant step we take to woodland paths, climb the invigorating heights, and join the living voices of wild nature once more. I invite my friend, Mr. E. P. Butterfield, of Wilsden, to join me in some of these pleasant rambles, for to him, more than to anyone else, I think, we owe our best and fullest knowledge of the wild birds of this district. Away, then, we go—one day by Beckfoot, and by the river side to Cottingley; another day up to the heights of Marley; and on another through the lovely Harden valley and by the sequestered shades of Hallas. All these ways are ways of pleasantness, and abound with much and varied interest. Mr. Butterfield is a keen and accurate observer, and has devoted a large portion of his leisure to the study of Nature, and of local birds particularly he has made a special study.

On one occasion I met him by appointment in the neighbourhood of Beckfoot. While we stood discussing some object, "There," said he, "keep your elbow off that wren's nest." I suddenly looked round. "Where, pray, is it?" I asked. "Why, there," he answered, pointing to a very small aperture in the grassy bank, which none but the eye accustomed to such haunts could have detected. I peered in, and there was the curious dome-shaped nest, evidently just completed. The female bird is usually the architect of the home, but the male amuses himself often with nest-building, though he does not give his work the same delicate finish which is peculiar to that of the female. Many of these male nests are to be met with during the breeding season unoccupied, and generally go by the name of "cock nests." Some good people may think these nests had been robbed or deserted, and, doubtless, too many nests are, yet be it remembered with respect to the wren and the robin, who cheer us with song all the year round—

> "Who hunts the robin or the wren
> Will never prosper, sea or land."

Once a robin built its nest in a watering-can suspended from the roof of a greenhouse at Wilsden. This bold little bird makes its home in odd places sometimes.

The Beckfoot district is a good locality for observing many kinds of birds and their ways. In and about the stream the handsome wagtails, both pied and grey, are commonly to be met with, and it is also a favourite haunt of the thrushes. Bingley well deserves its title of the "Throstle Nest of Old England," for these birds were formerly very abundant here, and the throstle's rich and fluent notes could be heard on every hand. Strange to relate, for two or three years after the almost Arctic winter of 1879-80 they were remarkably scarce, but they are now fairly numerous again, and in Spring-time, when the hedgerows are green and the milk-white flowers of the thorn spread a delicious fragrance around, it is a treat to listen to the male bird pouring forth his love-song to his mate from some blossoming bough.

But come, now, let us take a walk, the day is quite perfect! Along the verdant glade we leisurely go, listening to the many gladsome voices, as the golden sunlight streams down among the tall trees upon the moss-velvet of the old walls, also brightening our onward path. Ah! soon we stop and peer into a bush close beside the way. And what do we see? A throstle's nest, with its lovely freight of speckled eggs, snugly laid among flowers, gray lichen, and bowery fern, and screened by full, overhanging trees. A pretty sight, surely! Brush the screen away, and now, my friend, step into the picture, and let us try to commemorate your good work and the

In the Harden Valley.

"Throstle Nest of Old England!" Mr. Butterfield, after some hesitation, meets the wish; a camera is brought, and the *tout ensemble* is transferred to the sensitive glass, eventually to form the illustration prefacing this chapter.

Now, going towards Harden, we notice several sparrow-hawks, whose flight very much resembles that of the cuckoo, and when on the wing the latter is often mistaken for it. Hundreds of cuckoos for this reason are sacrificed to the keeper's gun every season throughout England. The sparrow-hawk, by the way, is not now a common bird in this district, though a few still breed here. In the woods owls are not uncommon, and on a calm night it is impressive to listen to their vehement conversation: "Quotha! tu whit; tu whit! tu whoo! oh-h, h, h!!" ringing on the night air. Mr. Butterfield tells me he once found a tawny owl's nest in a rabbit-hole near Wilsden, a most unusual place. The stockdove also breeds in the woods, and for more than twenty years a colony of jackdaws have reared their sable nestlings here. Some jackdaws have been taught to talk very fairly, but in this respect they do not equal either the magpie or the raven.

Continuing our walk by Bank End, my friend related a singular discovery he once made here. Everyone knows a wasp's nest, made from particles of sound timber, which are kneaded up with the insect's saliva, and then moulded into fine combs. Well, one of these curious structures was found in a hole in the ground, and it was resting partly on the back of a toad, which lay motionless in a state of torpor. The creature had, perhaps, been drawn by the warmth of the nest into its remarkable hiding-place, and had it moved afterwards would, no doubt, have been stung to death.

In the charming Goit Stock valley we meet with a great variety of bird-life. The lanes are alive with redbreasts, chaffinches, throstles, blackbirds, and titmice. It is amusing to watch the great titmouse and blue titmouse pegging away at the bark of some well-crusted elm trees to obtain the larvæ. Here, too, we get a sight of the handsome little gold-crest, whose true home is among the Norwegian pine-forests. He is the smallest of European birds, and remains with us through the severest winters, a few probably remaining to breed in suitable places. In early autumn he may sometimes be seen with the gathering swallows, wheatears, tits, &c., in Bingley Park, and how interesting it is to see some of the birds tossing themselves into every conceivable attitude whilst hunting for food !

The rare hawfinch has also been noted in the Goit Stock valley, and at Manywells a specimen was shot. The lesser white-throat, green and great spotted woodpeckers, kingfisher, and pied flycatcher have likewise nested in the district. The beautiful kingfisher was once numerous in the Bingley becks and about the river, but the rapacity of traders in their plumage has greatly diminished the numbers. Happily, however, an improved taste has brought about a decline in the demand, and the birds, I understand, are everywhere becoming more numerous. Both the kingfisher and the dipper used to nest in the vicinity of Goit Stock waterfall. To get to its nest the wet-loving dipper has sometimes been known to dash through the torrent of the descending cascade. He has been met with far north, even within the Arctic Circle ; a true denizen of mountain and upland streams, and in his lonely hermitage, if not molested, is as happy as the day is long.

But my ramblings after these fairy wights at Bingley must here end. How long some of them may have dwelt here or have come hither, God alone knows. But during those bleak ages, in the very twilight of our history, when the bright moon silvered the wide-sheeted ice, casting a glamour over the lone, frosted wilds ; or the bristling sun at mid-day pierced with his rays the lofty glacier-walls in Bingley's time-wrought vale, the fowl of the air were moved by an irresistible impulse, and came hither at God's bidding. And here, forsooth, they remained until by the beckoning of His hand that bade the ice-storm cease, man once more appeared.

PART II.

THE ADVENT OF MAN.

The Aborigenes.

THE deluge following the Ice Age rendered, as I have said, this immediate district uninhabitable by man for a long period subsequently. In some parts of North England evidences of a post-glacial people are to be found in implements made of the bone of reindeer and in the galleried tombs and dwellings, which are identical with those of the Esquimaux of the present day. Implements and weapons of bone and stone were used at this time, and it was not until the commerce in flint had been established by Neolithic traders that flint was adopted in the manufacture of these articles in this district. The rude flint implements picked up on our moors are probably of more recent date than is generally supposed; mere crudeness of make cannot be accepted as a criterion of antiquity, and the oldest of these articles are, as I hope to shew, not older than the late Goidelic settlers of the great Celtic immigration. Metal, of course, was well-known to the ancient Britons as well as to the Romans, yet stone and flint continued to be used even down to historic times. Not, however, until the Goidelic immigration have we any positive knowledge of man and his work in this district.

The Celt.

On the westward emigration of the Indo-Celtic races the aborigenes were driven further and further north, and that branch denominated the Goidels or Gauls of France and Switzerland overspread Britain, and eventually obliterated the existence of the original inhabitants of the island. Gradually they died out in the remote western isles of Scotland, though in St. Columba's time 1,300 years ago, we are told their language was still living; a few men of rank being found on the mainland opposite the Isle of Skye with whom the great missionary could not converse in the Goidelic tongue.* These Goidels from Gaul were in turn driven to the western and northern mountains on the great Brythonic irruption or second Celtic wave, yet so largely and firmly had the original Goidelic or Gallic tribes established themselves in Britain that their language in this country was almost universal, and even so late as the Roman conquest was spoken by the bulk of the people in the north and west.

It is with both of these Celtic peoples that we are concerned in our district. They have long since gone, but some little knowledge of their mode of life and language has been preserved in our midst even to the present day. In the primitive sheep-scoring numerals, hereafter mentioned, and in such names as *bailey*, *bel*, *beldune*, *cat* or *cath*, *bron* or *brown*, *pen-y-thorn*, *crummach*, and possibly *Dobrudden*, we have evidences of dialectal forms of these old Celtic tongues. An immemorial tradition also exists in this district respecting the Druids' Altar, and in the ancient earthworks, marked stones, and stone circles, single and double-ringed, on the moors, as well as in the tumuli and their contained remains; these all point to the possession of this district by the first as well as by the second family of Celtic invaders.

The best example of a stone circle in the vicinity of Bingley lies on the moor close to the parish boundary, on land belonging to Mr. Fawkes, of Farnley Hall. It is a complete circle, consisting of about twenty stones, placed close together (a very unusual arrangement), from two to four feet high, the circumference being about 35 yards. An excavation was made in the middle of it some years ago, when bits of flint were found, but no trace of burial.

* Cormac, writing in the 9th century, gives us to understand that the Iarn, a non-Aryan language, lingered in Ireland until the 8th century.

It is built on a slight slope of the moor, facing the south, and is now much concealed by heather. It is, doubtless, the oldest known evidence of man's handiwork remaining in the neighbourhood of Bingley, and there is small doubt that it was originally intended to fence a burial, such "Druids' Circles" being primarily meant to enclose places of sepulchre in the same way that walled enclosures came to be adopted round our churchyards. A large flat stone on the top side, about three yards distant, is marked with cups and channels, and probably was in the centre of the circle originally.

The Goidels were Druids, and they worshipped the sun, moon, and stars; the Brythons, so far as is known, were

Ancient Stone Circle, near Bingley.

not under the sway of Druidism, but were polytheists of the Aryan type. Cæsar goes so far as to say that Druidism originated in Britain, but with his limited knowledge of the country, the statement must be doubted. It is more than probable that it was the common religion of the aborigenes of the Continent as well as of this country, although some authorities maintain that it was introduced into Britain by the Phœnicians, and did not entirely disappear until the Roman idolators cut down the sacred groves, and ultimately suppressed the practice. I cannot, however, conceive that Baal worship prevailed at

Baildon because the present name lends itself to that convenient construction. In the oldest records the name is spelled Beldune, which is pure Goidelic for a *ford* (*bel*) at a *hill* (*dune*) (its Irish equivalent *dun*, genitive *dune*), having reference in all probability to the old road which came up the valley, and *forded* the Aire at Baildon Bridge, then ascending the old foot-road up the hill to the Celtic encampment on the common, with its stone circles and tumuli, existing to our own day. *Bel*-bank, Bingley, is another instance of an ancient *ford* or entrance to a Goidelic settlement, which I shall presently show was on the Bailey Hills.

It must not be supposed that the Celtic tribes always clung to the hills. They took refuge there chiefly by stress of conquest. We find them often living in the midst of marshes, in lakes, or upon islands protected by artificial ditches or by natural waters. Both Cæsar and Strabo tell us that they generally chose a place well shut in by woods, with a good supply of water near at hand, and on such a spot they would build their huts and collect their cattle. The prevalence of Brythonic words about the hills within this district seems to me to point more clearly to the Goidelic occupation of the valley, and on the conquest of the latter to a complete Brythonic possession of both hill and dale, rather than to the Brythonic withdrawal on the Anglian irruption. In such places as Brown Hill (Bryth-Celtic, *brón*, a hill-slope), Ive Bridge, Gildas-stead, which are all adjacent to the Bingley valley, we see the Celt; the same names occurring in the ancient Celtic provinces of Britany and Cornwall. I suspect also that Fern Cliff, below Gilstead, has nothing to do with ferns, but betrays its Cymric-Celtic origin in the root *ffynnon*, cognate with the Goidelic *fuaran*, a fountain, well, or gushing water, in allusion to the copious springs which issue from that side of the hill. The old pronunciation of the name was *fearnan* or *fearn*, and I have seen the name in old parish books, to wit in the minutes of the overseers last century, written Fearingcliff.

But to turn to the original settlement. I have said that after the Ice Age the glacial floods converted the

Bailey Hills into an island, and it is very probable they retained this character down to Roman times, and even to our own day the valley side of them through which the railway runs was almost in the condition of a lake. I am persuaded that no better site could possibly have been chosen for habitation, at a time when the district was densely wooded, particularly with mast-bearing trees, and the woods and thickets were the haunts of wild beasts. It is on this site that the traditional "castle" once stood. Now these "castle hills," applied to prehistoric camps and forts, are universal, and many a time as I have wandered over the assumed site of Dodsworth's "castle" on the Bailey Hills it has occurred to me that a tradition existed before Dodsworth's day that the hills had been occupied with some manner of fortification, and that old and perhaps extensive foundations were in Dodsworth's time still pointed out. These proofs of some "castle" of unknown origin would gain credence in the popular mind, which time has not obliterated, but rather strengthened. Such is the prevailing belief that we find the sites of many hills and mounds, now or in past times occupied with ancient earthworks or foundations, still known as "Castle Hills." Fortunately, the name "Bailey Hills" has been preserved, while the name "Castlefields" is merely a later adjunct of the castle theory.

Now, in the absence, so far as I can discover, of any written record or evidence of a castle, or of any reference whatever to such save the tradition mentioned by Dodsworth, I am suspicious that no post-Norman castle ever existed. But even if it can be proved to have existed it will not operate against my deduction that the Bailey Hills was the original home of the Celtic settlers at Bingley. Physically, botanically, philologically, and by the evidence of actual remains it can be proved to have been such. The name Bailey is older than any personal name that can be applied to it, and, if I mistake not its meaning, this word *baile*, *baily*, or *bally* is Goidelic-Celtic for a fortified place, a home, a town or settlement, and is at the root of the words *vallum*, wall, &c. Such, for example, are Ballymore (great town), Ballymena (middle town), Ballycastle, Balmoral, Balachulish, anciently Baile-na-caolish, &c. The name *baile* (pron. baily) is a frequent compound in Goidelic or Gaelic place-names in Scotland and Ireland, and Dr. O'Donovan, a well-known authority, says that the word is frequently used in old Irish to signify a castle or military station. Then again, we have at the most likely approach to the Bailey Hill, namely, at the ancient ford at Ireland Bridge, the name Bel-bank, and this word *bel* signifies, in the same Goidelic dialect, a ford or mouth, or in a secondary sense, as stated in Blackie's "Place Names," *an entrance into any place.* This is, therefore, as I shall shew in discussing the subject of old roads, the most ancient approach to Bingley and to the original British settlement on the Bailey Hills.

On the Hills, in a field next the cemetery (the site of the traditional "castle"), is a camp-like enclosure, occupying a flat hollow of about 1,600 square yards. It is bounded on the north and west sides by a raised fence, that on the north side falling deeply and sharply to the enclosure, and affording capital shelter on that side. In the field beyond, parallel with the wall separating the Grammar School land (now the Show Field) and Mr. Butler's estate, is a rampart-like bank, partly natural, extending from the school buildings right across the hill to the river, and is nearly complete all the way, a length of about 200 yards, in some places being 20 feet above the natural field-level. The north face has, no doubt, sloped naturally, but has been cut back into a precipitous front, while old ash and sycamore trees, with boles four or five feet in circumference, grow upon it, proving, at anyrate, that the hill was scarped or cut back before any house or building was built on the Hills. It is a kind of defence, natural or artificial, that one may expect to find in such a place, being to the north, whence danger came, and appears of similar import to those extensive lines of earth and stones that are found stretching across many of the Yorkshire dales. It is designedly thrown up to a great height above the river, and at the opposite extremity, in Mr. Town's garden, there are some very large mounds, obviously older than any garden-tips, though they may be cast-up mounds of the old kiln-workers. I have not heard that any relics have been discovered at this point, because it has never been dug, but on the south side, where the cemetery is now, a couple of stone querns or hand-mills have been dug up; one of them, a fine and perfect specimen, is now in the Bingley Free Library. It is marked "Roman," but there is no evidence of the Roman occupation of the site; it is more likely to be ancient British or Anglo-Celtic (*see* illustration at the end of this section).*

So far the prehistoric *bailey* or castle. Over the river and above this ancient rampart and enclosure, rises the far-famed Druids' Altar, "a name it has borne of yore, and shall do a thousand more." It is not for me to draw fancy pictures of the traditional rites of the Druids, but will content myself by adducing such *facts* as support the

* Since the above was written I have learnt that this fine quern was found while digging a grave near a Scotch fir-tree, about fifty yards east of the chapel. Near here, I am told, are traces of what looks like an ancient wall. It has been discovered extending in a north and south direction for a distance of about 20 yards, when the gravel walk is reached; then it continues on the opposite side in the same direction, occurring in every grave for a further space of nearly 20 yards. A great many of the stones have been removed, and have been utilised for the walls and steps on the paths leading down to the river; others have been tipped in the heap for the new walk parallel with the river, now in course of formation. The stones are not rounded boulders, but flat and rudely shaped, some of them being 6 to 8 inches thick and from 2 to 3 feet long, and must be from 2 to 3 cwt. in weight. The stones are not mortared, and from the massive character of the work there appears little doubt of its antiquity. In places it is from 7 to 8 feet below the present surface, but owing to the disturbance of the soil by the 17th century lime-burners (*see post*) it is difficult to say what has been the original elevation. Mr. Greaves, the registrar, tells me that another apparent wall has been found extending for some yards north and south on the north side of the main walk, near the church. It runs parallel with the above. Portions of a more recent wall are visible below the main walk above the river. When this path was laid the top of this wall was used for the foundation of the wall supporting the path above. The appearance, character, height, and thickness of these peculiar walls I have had no opportunity of viewing, and in the absence of fuller information, I give these particulars with every reservation. I have thought they might be the wall-stones of old kilns, but am assured the wall is continuous in one direction for the space so far discovered.

popular belief in this romantic spot. The situation of the noble-looking rock is perfect for its purpose; it faces the rising sun, and commands a magnificent prospect of the valley below, while the rosy hues of departing day are often seen reflected on its surface. From the old *bailey* by the ancient road from the ford to the mystic rock, may we not indulge the picture of the tribes in procession, led by the venerable fathers through the sacred groves of oak on the day of sacrifice or thanksgiving? For thanks to God or the all-seeing Power have gone forth from man from the time of our first knowledge of him on earth; and the idols of his worship or temples of his faith are among the earliest relics we possess of his belief in a Creator and in the immortality of the soul. From the Celtic word for the oak, *derw*, the Druids took their name, and the oak has been a conspicuous tree in the neighbourhood of the Altar from time immemorial. The tree or its timber were indispensable at their great festivals, and when living with the mistletoe upon it was held in the highest reverence. The mistletoe is rarely found on the oak, says the Rev. C. A. Johns in *The Forest Trees of Britain*, but when it was discovered the Druids went forth clad in white robes, and cut pieces off with a golden knife. It was always gathered at a particular age of the moon, at the beginning of their year, and should any chance to fall to the ground it was considered an omen of misfortune to the people.

I have endeavoured to ascertain if the mistletoe has ever been found growing on the oak near the Druids' Altar, and I am assured by Miss Maud, of Seattle, U.S.A., that she herself gathered it there when a girl, now nearly seventy years ago. She told me on her recent visit to Bingley that she well remembered the circumstance, and was surprised on reading a book on the subject that stated there were only some dozen places in England where the mistletoe had been observed growing on oak, and Bingley was not mentioned. If the place has produced mistletoe this century, I can see no reason why it should not have done so before the Roman conquest, and in this event it is more than probable it would form an important factor in the selection of a home of the early

Celtic Druids. Oak, moreover, has always grown in plenty around Bingley, and that portion of the town bordering on Chapel Lane and the Dubb has been an old forest or pasture of oak, known in Anglo-Saxon times as *mæst-stæl* now (Mastal), from the oak-mast it yielded in the fattening of swine, and in times of scarcity as food for the people.

The old rites and customs of these early British possessors of Bingley have almost entirely succumbed to newer beliefs, yet I have not the smallest doubt that when they held Bingley the well-known Midsummer fires blazed on the hill-tops, and at what more likely spot than the Druids' Altar? These Beltane fires continued in some parts of Yorkshire down to the present century, but at Giggleswick they were lighted on St. Lawrence's Eve, the 9th of August, yet no one seems to know why that particular day was chosen. At Bingley the preservation of the half-burnt yule-log from one Christmas Eve to the next is the simple survival of the Druids' "perpetual fire," for once every year all the fires of a British town were extinguished, and re-lighted from the sacred fire of the Druids. This sacrifice of fire was the visible thank-offering for the sun's beneficent gifts, and our present harvest-thanksgivings are the survival of these ancient British rites.

It does not appear that Druidism nor the language of its followers survived but in a small measure the Brythonic conquest. With but few exceptions, the Celtic names of places around Bingley apparently belong to the later invaders, and their study and consideration are essential in the proper elucidation of the early history of Bingley. Some of these names have reference also to the Anglo-Saxon and Scandinavian possession of the district, which will be dealt with in chronological sequence. I have already pointed out some Celtic names, and I need at present only refer to the old sheep-scoring numerals which have survived in the district of Bingley to the present time, though probably now known to very few. They are, however, evident in the corrupt jingles of children's games where counting-out is used (*see* FOLK LORE). From Mr. Edward Smith (aged 80), of Cowling (late of Harden), I have taken down the numbers as he remembered hearing them from old men at Harden when a young man. I have not followed the doubtful Celtic orthography, but spell the words exactly as they are pronounced in English:—

1—Era.	6—Southa.	11—Era-dicks.	16—Era-pumpit.
2—Tera.	7—Loutha.	12—Tera-dicks.	17—Tera-pumpit.
3—Tethera.	8—Cobbera.	13—Tethera-dicks.	18—Tethera-pumpit.
4—Fethera.	9—Dobbera.	14—Fethera-dicks.	19—Fethera-pumpit.
5—Pimps.	10—Dicks.	15—Pumpit.	20—Jiggit.

These numerals differ from any I have seen printed, and my aged informant repeated them to me several times, not always in the same sequence, yet always in pentads of five, or by finger arithmetic, being the oldest form of counting. Sometimes he placed the set 16 to 20 before the 11 to 15, but the above is obviously the correct order. It may be noted that 1 and 2 are rendered *era*, *tera*, while in all versions I have seen *n* takes the place of *r*. Thus the Rhode Island Indians say *ene*, *tene*, *tether*, *fether*, *pip*; the Massachusetts Indians *eeni*, *teeni*, *tuderi*, *federi*, *fip*; in Swaledale it is, *yan*, *tean*, *tethera*, *methera*, *mick*; in Nidderdale, *yehn*, *tehn*, *eduru*, *peduru*, *pips*. An old man at Bingley, who was a coal agent in the Midland Goods Yard, used to be called "*Yan* West" because he always counted in these numbers. I am told he came from near Colne.

It is stated that these numbers originated in the Brit-Welsh kingdom of Strathclyde, and that all the versions are but dialectal forms having one common origin; the North American Indians having learnt them from early English or Welsh settlers. That they really sprang from Old Kymric, and are found throughout the Brythonic region from the Dee to the Solway, is evident, because it is only in the Welsh dialect of the Kymry that this method of counting in fives prevails. In Irish, Manx, and other Goidelic provinces the system and language are different, but into these distinctions I cannot here enter.

There is no reason to doubt that the Brythonic element entered largely into the aggregate population of the Bingley district, and that the language of these people prevailed down and beyond the Roman conquest, when the establishment of the Roman station at Ilkley diffused the habits, manners, and language of the Latins among the

Britons of these parts. We have the authority of no less a geographer than Ptolemy (A.D. 150) that Olicana (Ilkley) was one of the chief towns of the Brigantes, and these Brigantes were the later comers, the stronger, privileged, free-men, who drove off the older race, and established themselves on their best lands. The Brigantes, or Brythons, were a hardy and courageous people, and gave the Romans, perhaps, more trouble than any of the other tribes in their conquest of the island. I do not think the Romans troubled Bingley, but directed their energies rather to the greater station at Ilkley, which they ultimately reduced to submission. This I judge to be the case in spite of the Brown Hill entrenchment, which I take to be a later work, for while the name *brown* is derived from a Brigantian term *(brón)* for such a situation as that which it occupies (now the Park), I have many reasons for considering that this post was a refuge for a time on the Anglian or Pictish irruption after the Roman evacuation.

QUERN FOUND ON BAILEY HILLS.

THE ROMANS,

we know, penetrated this romantic district in the time of Agricola, who was appointed legate of Britain in A.D. 78. This great Roman leader, after a very determined effort, beset with unnumbered difficulties, conquered the Brythonic province of the Ordovices in North Wales, and made

Deva (Chester) his headquarters and starting point of his wonderful expedition through the forests and marshes of Lancashire and Yorkshire. Some idea of the extent of these primeval woods and the difficulty of passage may be gathered from the fact that even at the time of the Norman conquest there were not less than 250,000 acres of more or less tangled forests in the single region between the Mersey, Calder, and Ribble. Nearly the whole of Airedale, with its tributary valleys, was one continuous thicket, and the valley bottom was a vast swamp. Above these rose the high moors, which the Romans chose, not only as affording an easier passage, but also for the better observation of the movements of the natives. With them they brought, often by accident, the seeds of various plants and herbs hitherto unknown in England, just as in the same way many kinds of weeds and wayside flowers were introduced into France by the invading armies of Germany during the great war of 1870-71. So, too, with birds and beasts. The domestic cat, for instance, which is mentioned in Egyptian inscriptions as far back as 1680 B.C., was brought from Rome with the conquering legions to England, where it had been hitherto unknown. Likewise the rabbit was undoubtedly an importation from Rome at the same time.

But let us turn to the Roman steps in this district. It is, as I have said, not likely that the Romans made any attack on Bingley, nor can the discovery of the great chest of Roman coins at Morton Banks be interpreted into an attack from this quarter, which rendered, as some suppose, the sudden concealment of the chest necessary. As coins from the time of Nero, A.D. 54, to Pupienus, A.D. 238, were found in the horde it is obvious the chest was buried long after the local Britons were at peace with the Romans and under the Roman power. The road from Aldborough to Manchester, *via* Ilkley, which for several miles passed through the parish of Bingley, was also undoubtedly made during the latter days of the Empire, probably by the Emperor Philip, who reigned A.D. 244-8. Some of the mile-stones on the Roman road from Warrington to Lancaster have his name upon them, and there are good reasons for believing that the roads northwards and eastwards through the hilly regions of the Penines were made about the same period, or after a general restoration of the camps in the time of the Emperor Severus. That they were also assisted in this enterprise by the conquered Brigantes appears evident by the discovery of the well-known valuable Roman altar-stone at Thick Hollins, in Greetland, which is dedicated "to the god of the states of the Brigantes and of the deities of the Emperor [Severus]." This shews that not only were Romans and

ROMAN ROAD ON BLACKSTONE EDGE.

Britons of this district in friendly alliance early in the third century, but that paganism was yet rampant in these parts.

From Manchester the road came over Blackstone Edge, where extensive and perfect remains of it still exist. I present a view of it as it appears on the western slope of the moor—perhaps the finest existing example of a Roman roadway in the North of England—which shews a causeway 16 feet wide, with a central massive pavement about 8 feet wide, furrowed on each side, caused, doubtless, by the abrasion of wheeled vehicles. The entire road is composed of wrought blocks of millstone grit, laid in a foundation of sand and rubble, and the whole appears as sound and almost as perfect as when first laid down more than 1,600 years ago. This road passed between Halifax and Illingworth, continuing thence through Denholme Park, where it was visible as a paved way about 100 yards south of Denholme Gate, and again a little to the east of Denholme Mills. It then went by Cullingworth and Hainworth, but its course here is less certain. Some have supposed that it passed up old Dolphin Lane, which terminates peculiarly, without any further traces of its continuance, on Harden Moor. But Dolphin Lane is too much east of that directness which is a characteristic of Roman roads to lend such assumption in the least degree probable. I have carefully examined the ground many times, and my own impression is that it ran to the *west* of Cullingworth by the old Turf Lane and Benty Lee Lane, on the west side of Catstones. Warburton, (*vide Lansdowne MSS.*), says that the Roman road appears "near to Morton Highgate, from which place it disappears until it comes to Hainsworth Shaw, upon Harding Moor, where it crosses the way that leads from Bingley to Epworth, taking its course inside the Bounder Stones, and so by Ellarcarr; and, crossing the wall, appears again in the field of Thomas Horsfield, near to the Weir Stones, little west of the highroad to Halifax." Dr. Richardson, writing to Ralph Thoresby about 1709, says that the road betwixt Hainworth and Cullingworth, where it appeared bare, was above 12 feet broad, and neatly set of such stones as the place afforded. This corresponds with the character of the excellent remnant of the same line of road yet remaining on Blackstone Edge, of which I append an engraving from a drawing by Miss Bolton.

Some forty years ago, when the moor was enclosed, an old paved road was discovered while breaking up the land in Mr. John Spencer's allotment, behind the Hainworth Shay quarries. It extended for about 50 to 60 yards, and was composed of unhewn calliard boulders, being the characteristic ice-borne stones from the moor. Mr. Thomas Middlebrook, late of Hainworth Shay, tells me that a continuation of this old calliard pavement was laid bare by his father when the present Hog Holes Lane was lowered, about a hundred yards below the well, and on the same side of the road. Most of the stones were quite hollow with long usage. As this was the old road from Keighley to Halifax, it seems likely that this ancient thoroughfare was constructed in this neighbourhood on the line of the old Roman road.

Just below lies Caster, or Kester Wood, with the farm long tenanted by the Ambler family. I am persuaded that this was a *mansion*, post-station, or resting-place *(castra)* of the Roman soldiery on their passage between the several camps. It occupies a spacious and level hollow, with an abundant supply of good water, and commands a wide view over the valley, as well as of the Roman road climbing the hills out of Airedale to Ilkley. It is exactly the spot where one would look for such a camp; the strategical character of the ground being admirable, falling rapidly on all sides save that commanded by the road. Some such resting-place, or fortified barracks, would be necessary, for the Roman leaders invariably sent out scouts before entering woods or descending a valley, in order to ascertain the whereabouts and number of the enemy, or the condition of the river and whether the fords were passable.

The local pronunciation of this name has always been Caster, Kester, or Kesty, and in 1764 I find it written Kersti. During various interrogations I have made there I have learnt that a notion prevails that its real name is Kirkstall, while others assert it is Kestrel, from the supposed occurrence of this bird on the spot. But I venture the opinion, above suggested, that it is the Roman *castra*, which enters into the composition of such names as Lancaster, Ribchester, Manchester, Tadcaster, Doncaster, &c.; these being well-accredited Roman stations. There is at this day a similar place near Colne, called Caster Cliff, where are indications of ancient entrenchments, and where numerous evidences of its Roman occupation have been found, such as coins, pottery, ornaments, &c. There is no doubt that it is the site of the Roman *Colonio*. The Roman road from Ribchester to Ilkley passed through Colne, and in its eastward course through Oxenhope to

Castleford and Doncaster was bisected near Denholme by the road through Hainworth to Ilkley. Unfortunately the Hainworth camp has nothing to shew in the way of relics that may have been found on the site, but many years ago, during a search for coal near the Kester farm-house, a number of antique-looking bricks were come upon three or four feet below the surface, and there were other indications of the ground having been at some time disturbed for building upon.

On the opposite side of the valley, near Upwood, a portion of the continuation of this Roman road was discovered by the late Mr. Busfeild, of Upwood, who was also fortunate in obtaining a number of the Roman coins contained in the copper chest found at Morton, particulars of which were communicated by Mr. Busfeild to Mr. Smith, of Morley, and printed in the first volume of *Old Yorkshire*. Many of the coins are now in the possession of Colonel Busfeild. The road from Morton Church, leading up to four lane ends for Rivock and Upwood, is known as *Street Lane*, suggestive of the Roman *strata*; though if this was on the Roman road it must have left the present road at the bend, and continued straight across the moor by Upwood. Dr. Richardson (A.D. 1709) says that the road points to a place called the Moor House, above Morton.

It was not all peace during the Roman occupation of this district, governed as it was from the camp at Ilkley. Petty insurrections among the Brythonic population against the Roman power continued to harass the late usurpers, which force ultimately quelled, and the two races became united in course of time. Then we hear of raids from the north by

THE PICTS AND SCOTS,

who committed great ravages, and were with difficulty driven back by the united forces of Roman and Briton. On the partial withdrawal of the Roman troops in the year 387, a fresh attack was made by these wild northern hordes; then the hapless Britons petitioned Rome for aid, and a legion was sent to thwart the invaders and garrison the northern wall. In 407 the Emperor Constantine withdrew the Roman troops, which, it should be remembered, included the flower of the native Britons. One of these, a Brython named Gerontios, rebelled against Constantine for his disloyal action, ending in the loss of Britain; and uniting with an army from Germany, he made an unsuccessful attempt to secure Gaul and Britain. The Picts and Scots, however, in conjunction with bands of foreign pirates who descended upon the coasts, were already in conflict with the natives, and the country for a long time after the Roman withdrawal was in a state of complete anarchy. It was not, indeed, if we might trust Father Haigh, until about the year 756 that the King of the Picts, uniting with the Anglian rulers, established something like peace in this district. But the proclamation of this "gracious ban," which is supposed to be recorded on the precious rune-stone preserved at Bingley, I have, as will presently be seen, ventured to dispute.

THE ANGLO-SAXONS,

under the great Hengist and Horsa, landed in Britain in A.D. 449, but it was not until the end of the 6th century that the kingdom of Northumbria, along with the other six Teutonic kingdoms, was formed. Bingley, which had previously been included in the Brit-Welsh kingdom of Strath Clyde, and afterwards in the Roman province of Maxima Cæsariensis, was now under the Anglian sway within the extensive region of Northumbria. These Angles, Saxons, and Jutes from North Germany and Jutland fell upon the British possessors of the soil, driving them from the best lands pretty much in the same way as the English of the present day have seized the fertile riparian lands of the poor aborigenes in Australia. But whilst these Australian aborigenes have been powerless to withstand the recent invasions of their territory, the Britons of Airedale must have been estranged from and at war with the Anglo-Saxons for more than two centuries, making raids from their hill-fortresses, and otherwise harassing the usurpers with great bitterness. This is what we are made to believe the old rune-stone at Bingley tells us, and if we could trust it, such a splendid heritage of graven language would be as a grand beacon-light shedding its clear rays wide over the obscure paths of local history.

Christianity, through the teachings of Paulinus in Northumbria, in the 7th century made surprising headway; converts and churches rose with amazing rapidity all over the country, and in our own district doubtless several were established, of which at this day every trace and tradition has perished. They had the good effect of withdrawing the people from the conflict of war, and so zealous were they in advancing the faith that instead of the constant din of battle the sound of prayer and praise rose from the cloistered woods.

Ever since the great battle of Chester (A.D. 607) the Celtic Brythons, or Welshmen, had been playing a losing game. Eadwin, the first Christian king of Northumbria, captured Loidis and Elmet in 620, and by fresh accessions to the Anglian populations, which still continued to pour in from abroad, the Northumbrian King is said to have annexed the whole of the Kymric country, stretching from the Dee to the forests of Cumberland, and the neighbourhood of the Derwent, an extent of territory, in fact, embraced by the boundaries of the old diocese of Chester. According to Skene's *Ancient Books of Wales*, the bards of the Kymry mourned the departing glory of their nation, and urged the Welsh warriors to rise again in arms and drive the Angle foemen bag and baggage out of the realm which they had so wrongfully seized. Thus it is that we hear of continued dissensions and slaughterous raids made upon the Anglian camps by the Welsh Britons long after the recorded annexation of their territory by the Northumbrian Angles.

How this important annexation came about at Bingley is explained in this way. On Eadberht's coming to the throne of Northumbria, in 737, he set about to still further extend the Anglian frontier, and in this object he found an able compatriot in the well-known veteran, Angus, or Oengus, King of the Picts. In 750 the two armies waged war against the Welshmen of Cumbria, which resulted in the loss of part of their territory to the Angles. In 756 the same confederates took from the Britons their capital town of Alclyd (Dumbarton), after which they appear to have immediately set out on further warlike enterprises. Father Haigh makes them come forthwith to Bingley.

But let me now turn to Simeon of Durham for some light upon this vexed point. He informs us that on the 10th August, 756, Eadberht set out with his army from "Ouoma to Niwanbyrig, * * * all adversaries being either reduced to subjection or vanquished in war; the kings who dwelt on every side, of Angles, Picts, Britons, Scots, not only kept peace with him, but even rejoiced to pay him honour, and the fame of his excellence and of his deeds of valour diffused far and wide, coming even to Pipin, King of France, wherefore united to him in friendship, he sent to him many and different royal gifts." The Rev. Daniel Haigh, who has commendably endeavoured to make history of the Bingley runes, thinks that Ouoma of Simeon's notice was the place where Eadberht assembled his army; Niwanbyrig, *i.e.* the new city, the name of the place whither he had led them in the territory of Oengus. Had this occurred, he observes, independently of its present context, he would have supposed the latter to have been Newbury, adjoining Scarbro', and so called to distinguish it from the old town on the rock. But from the context he is obliged to look for it in Pictland, and identify it with Newburgh, in Aberdeenshire. In Ouama (*m* before *a* becoming *n*) he recognises Hewenden, near Bingley; thus the *dene*, or valley of Ouama (as *Ouana*) or Hewen (pronounced in one syllable *Haioun*), and here, after a nine days' march, Eadberht, he makes no doubt, actually assembled his army, and was joined by Oengus, or Angus, King of the Picts. If, however, we are to accept the literal statements of Simeon of Durham, Dumbarton capitulated on the 1st of August, 756, and the two conquerors left Ouania (so spelled) for Niwanbirig on the 10th of the same month. But I cannot tell on what authority the old chronicler, writing three centuries after the event, got his dates so nicely fixed. Mr. Haigh, moreover, does not appear to have discovered that there is a Loch Ouan, in

Perthshire, at no great distance from Abernethy, once the capital of the Pictish kingdom, and this, I think, is the most likely place referred to by Simeon. At any rate, the spot would agree with the circumstances recorded in point of time. I shall, however, have more to say on this rune-stone in the chapter on the Parish Church, and need only here remark that the two widely-differing meanings of the runes as furnished by Father Haigh and Professor Stephens quite upsets one's faith in either of them.

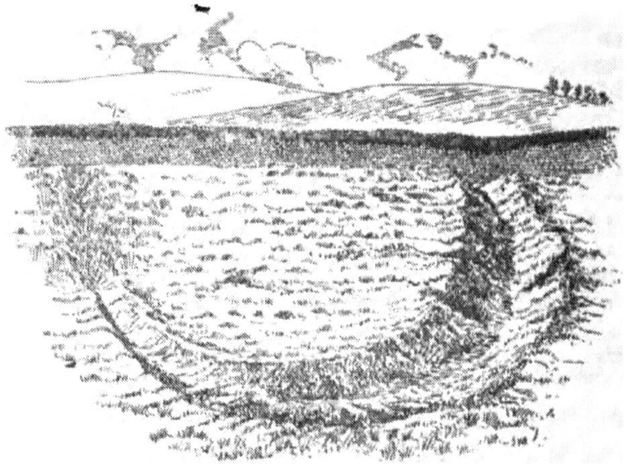

Castlestead Ring, near Cullingworth.

That a war of extermination of the Brython at Bingley by the Anglian incomers did actually take place, I think cannot reasonably be doubted. But dare we fix the site of the final conflict on the evidence of the Bingley runes? Father Haigh has done this. He says the battle actually took place at Hewenden. If a battle were fought in this locality, is it not more likely to have happened on the open plain, between Harden and Cullingworth Moor, between the two camps or redoubts, known as "Cat-stones" and "Castlestead Ring," both of which I hear sometimes called by the neighbouring farmers "Blood Dykes"? Anyone visiting these sites must realise the strategical aspect of the ground with regard to the position of the two camps. Here, mayhap, the last blow was struck at the old Celtic liberty about Bingley; but alas! all the records I can now accept of this important gathering are these two diked enclosures and the few stone-heaps on the moors, which, as in the songs of Ossian, have been left to speak to other years. Dr. Richardson, writing about 1709, says Benjamin Ferrand, Esq., shewed him on Harden Moor a "skirt of stones," much smaller than the two other on the moor he describes, and remarks that "nigh it a row of stones were placed in a line nigh 200 paces in length, but few of them appear above two feet above the heath, and some lie hidden under it." It may be inferred from this that there had not been a double row of stones like the avenue at Maiden Castle, in Swaledale (*see* my "Richmondshire"). These rows of stones connecting places of refuge and sepulture are peculiarities in the work of the ancient Celt that need explaining.

The last strongholds of these Brit-Welsh people in the neighbourhood of Bingley were, on the west Wilsden, Hewenden, and Harden, and on the east Baildon and Eldwick. Wilsden (in *Domesday* written Willesden), I do not doubt, is the Anglo-Saxon *Wealhas-den*, meaning the dene or valley of Welshmen, or "strangers." It was the practice of the Angles after securing a country to themselves to designate its former inhabitants on Celtic ground foreigners, or Welshmen; that is, "We, the Anglo-Saxons, are *the people*;. everybody else is a stranger." The Esquimaux and other primitive people still adopt the same idea.

Above the railway viaduct over the beck which separates Wilsden from Cullingworth is the slope of Brown Hill, reaching towards the camp of Castlestead. This is like the Brown Hill on the Eldwick side of Bingley, a corruption of the Brit-Welsh *brón*, meaning a hill-slope. Cat-stones, associated with the suggested conflict above described, derives its name from the Brythonic or Brit-Welsh *cat*, Irish *cath*, modern Welsh *cad*, which means a battle. Mr. Rhys, Professor of Celtic in the University of Oxford, says it is of the same origin or import as the Anglo-Saxon *heatho*, or *hatho*, meaning war. Athelstan may literally mean war or battle-stone, and there is a Hadel or Hathel-stone on Harden Moor, an ancient boundary-stone mentioned in the charters of the local properties of Rievaulx Abbey. There is an Eddleston and an Early Vale in the Brythonic province of Peebleshire, in Scotland, and I have heard the Hadelstone on Harden Moor called Early, or Arley Stone. The name of Harden may be of the same origin; but see also under ST. IVES. In *Domesday Book* it is written Hatel-tun, because the Norman writers were unaccustomed to the Anglo-Saxon sound of *th*, which it would present; thus Hathel-tun became Hateltun, or battle-town. Probably Adel, or Athell—as it sometimes appears—near Leeds, has the same origin; where a stone was found inscribed to the goddess Brigantia, and in which neighbourhood are evidences of early earthworks, &c.

The want of cohesion among the Celtic tribes, and the lack of any unanimous system of administration, leave us in doubt as to what really were the determinate boundaries of their respective territories. Whilst each community possessed its own laws, manners, and customs, constant internecine war must have greatly interfered with anything like settled lines of jurisdiction. That Bingley, however, formed some sort of territorial limit even at this remote period looks probable, for the parish, which is distinctly an ecclesiastical creation, has its boundary formed on the old Anglo-Celtic division, while the subordinate divisions of the pre-eminently Celtic counties of York and Cornwall retained their distinctive character of *shires*, in contradistinction to the *hundreds* of other places. Craven-shire, for example, appears to have become a definite ecclesiastical division on the Anglian conquest, which marked Bingley as its southern limit. But under the Danelagh we find it included, not within the wapentake of Staincliffe, embraced by the deanery of Craven, but in that of Skyrack, while the dividing line of the wapentakes of Agbrigg and Morley and Skyrack was, as it still is, determined by the parish boundary which separates Bingley from Wilsden. I may even go so far as to suggest that the boundaries were fixed as far back as the Gadhelic or first Celtic occupation, if we may interpret the *Black* Hills, Cottingley, and *Black* Moor, Cullingworth, which bound the parish southwards, as corrupt forms of the Gadhelic *bealach*, a pass or entrance from one district or dominion to another. Places compounded in Black are not uncommon in the Celtic regions of England and Ireland, but in Scotland the word often takes the form of *Balloch* and *Ballagh*, a pass. Such places in *black* that I have found invariably lie on the borders of shires or parishes: Blackstone Edge, between Lancashire and Yorkshire, the Blackwater, between counties Tyrone and Armagh, also Blackwater, between Cork and Kerry, and Black river, between Galway and Mayo, may be cited as examples. Blackburn, in Lancashire, probably has the same significance. In *Domesday* it is *Blacheburn*.

What may have been the determining causes which led to this ancient demarcation we have now no other means of ascertaining. Bingley being taken within Skyrack may have formed, and according to Dr. Whitaker, John James, and other writers actually did form a boundary to the British province of Elmet; * the High Courts for this district were afterwards doubtless held at the capital, Leeds, and as likely at the Shire Oak, Headingley, as anywhere. Wilsden and Hewenden, on the other hand, were, as I have shewn, legally foreign to the civil and ecclesiastical jurisdiction of Bingley in Anglo-Saxon times, whatever they may have been before. They must have had their own place of meeting, or folk-moot, and there is a characteristic eminence called Moot Hill (locally Moit Hill), near Hewenden, which may or may not have been the

* But if this were the case, Bingley must have been included in the conquest of Elmet by Eadwin in the year 620 (*see* p. 60), though the local Britons were in all probability not finally subdued until the defeat and death of the heathen Penda near Doncaster in A.D. 650; whereupon St. Hiev came into Elmet and established her Celtic Christian monastery, *ca.* A.D. 655. But Father Haigh would make the defeat of the Bingley Britons not take place till *ca.* A.D. 756, according to his interpretation of the rune-stone.

accustomed place of assembly. These meeting-places were generally chosen in the vicinity of some famous tree or trees—it was under the oaks of Dartmoor that the Britons and the Saxons held their celebrated conference after the invasion of the latter—or on some hill or eminence sacred by association of some battle or place of sepulture. Such the Moot Hill, at Hewenden, appears to have been, for there still exists upon it, on the still uncultivated portion, a little beyond the north side of the farm-house, very distinct evidences of an ancient burial, in the shape of a circular rampart of earth, nearly 70 yards in circumference, with a mound raised in the centre.

The Anglians continued to hold Bingley with little fear of molestation from the conquered Celts, and although Northumbria was much broken by the rival factions of its bipartite elements, Bernicia and Deira, we hear of no particular disturbance in this district until the arrival of

The Danes

in Northumbria in 867. The savage attack of Ragnar Lodbrog on the Northumbrian coast in 793 met with a check from the English before its terrors had spread far inland. Not until the great army of Vikings had crossed the Humber in 867 did the Angles of this territory realise the danger and full meaning of the invasion. Such fleets and such armies had never been seen in the north before. For a long time it was a merciless battle between heathendom and Christendom. The intrepid rovers captured York, and then with brand and sword they set out all over the country burning, plundering, and killing everything that belonged to the foe. The ravages of the heathen Halfdene, the first Danish King of Northumbria (875-77) completed the subjection of the Angles of Deira, or the modern Yorkshire, which was now under the rule of the Vikings. Yorkshire, in common with fourteen other English shires, which had been conquered by the Danes, became subject to Danish laws, and the Danish influence, both of character and language remains marked among the people of these shires to the present day.

Airedale was strongly Anglian, and great bitterness must have been felt at the sudden and crushing blow given to the English of this district by the new invaders, who proceeded to settle in their midst and "lay down the law." A revolt took place under "Athelstan, the Glorious," as the Angles called him, which resulted in the overthrow of the Danes at the great battle of Brunanburgh, in Yorkshire, in 937. Perhaps the historic boundary-stone, Athelstone, Hadelstone, or Earlystone, on Harden Moor, has something to do with commemorating the victory of the English over the Danes by this Saxon King, just as the Orange Rock, at Wilsden, marks the celebrations of the landing of the Prince of Orange in 1688.* The Saxon triumph, however, was of short duration, for in 940 we find the Dane, Eric Bloodaxe, again raised to the throne. Revolt followed revolt, and nearly all Yorkshire was harried and wasted by contending bands. About the year 975 fresh hordes of Vikings from Denmark and Norway again entered England, and swarmed over the northern parts. Thousands of Anglo-Saxons in the Yorkshire dales, unable to withstand the wild onslaught,

* A field between Ripon and Nunwick is called Athelstane Close because on the adjoining road one of the stone sanctuary crosses stood, ordained by Athelstan in his grant of immunities to the monastery at Ripon.

fled to the north. The Scottish Lowlands were filled with them, and the Celtic-Scots, rather than mingle with their old enemy, took refuge in the western Highlands, while the sturdy Pictish Highlanders were assailed on all sides, both by the Lowland invaders and by Norwegian pirates in the north and west.

The native Angles and Saxons were obliged to levy a tax on the whole land, called Danegelt, in order to meet the expenses consequent upon the Danish invasion, but the money thus raised was frequently expended in purchasing their freedom, or in maintaining the stalwart victors during their sojourn in this country. They came over on special commissions to exact the toll, a large portion of which went back to Norway, Sweden, and Denmark, and the large number of Anglo-Saxon coins (there are 20,000 in the museum at Stockholm) of the reigns of Canute and Harold I., as well as some of William the Conqueror, found in these countries, shews the extent to which the Danegelt was remitted from England even after the Norman conquest.

On the Danish irruption at Bingley, the natives probably abandoned for a time their old haunts, and retired, as the Britons had before them, to the less fertile tracts of Wilsden, Cullingworth, and Hainworth, and there founded Anglian colonies on the deserted, or old British settlements. As we gather that the Saxons, especially where numerous, sometimes purchased the right from the victorious Danes to govern by their own laws, subject to the Danish over-rule, I am disposed to believe that on the Anglian occupation of the ancient British town of "Wealhasden" (Wilsden) some such arrangement was made here on their estrangement from the Danes at Bingley. The name of the hill or mound on the north-east side of Wilsden, called Coplawe, bears some such significance; *cop-lah* being interpreted by Dr. Bosworth, F.R.S., to be in Anglo-Saxon a purchasing of the rights of law. The subject of cop-law is treated by Dr. Maitland in the *Growth of Seignorial Power*. In the absence of written records, a careful study and consideration of local place-names is essential to the proper elucidation of early history, a subject, unfortunately, which has hitherto received but superficial recognition at the hands of most local historians.

I am, moreover, constrained to believe that the Vikings on getting a firm foothold in this parish were first established at Micklethwaite; the Angles having been long previously at Bingley. Bingley is unquestionably the older settlement of the two, and this I shall explain later. Micklethwaite is compounded from two Norse words, *mykel* (great) and *thveit* (a clearing), indicating that a great clearing in the wood at this part had been made for the Scandinavian settlers. This was the first legal union of Bingley with Micklethwaite, which continued ever afterwards to form an integral part of the manor. The isolation of the Danes from the Anglo-Saxon element at Bingley was probably due to deference paid to the latter by virtue of ancient custom, the basis and circumstances of which are pretty well defined by Mr. Keary in his observations on the village and the *gau* in *The Vikings in Western Christendom* (pages 32-35). Thwaites was, no doubt, another similar station, and in the old name of Ravenroyd (mentioned in the Poll Tax of 1378-9), between Thwaites and Bingley, we have still another exposition of a *royd*, or clearing, made for the men of the *raven*, as the Vikings were sometimes called. Often on their marches they carried live ravens, as portents of good luck, and on their battle-flags and banners its image always appeared, in the same way as the eagle was borne as the ensign of the Romans. The raven, indeed, was unknown in Yorkshire before its importation by the Vikings from the cliffs of Norway in the ninth century. To the valleys of Yorkshire they gave the name *dales*, and the streams they called *becks*, and the ravines *gills*.

On the formation of the Danelagh, district "things," or law-places, were established, and at each of them was installed an overseer, chief magistrate, or law-giver, who was known as the *Gótha*, originally a functionary who conducted the sacrificial rites, but who in later days acted as district law-giver, or law-proclaimer to the people within his jurisdiction. His seat, or residence, was generally removed some little distance from the centre of Anglo-Saxon population, just as we find on the Danish settlement the conqueror and conquered did not at once unite. On the Micklethwaite, or Norse, side of Bingley, within half-a-mile of the original Anglian settlement, we have the old homestead of Gawthorpe, which apparently marks the home, or *thorpe*, of the local legal head of the Danelagh. These Gawthorpes are scattered all over England, but thickest where the Anglo-Saxons were most numerous. There are probably a score still known within the two counties of York and Lincoln, and it is questionable whether any are found outside the Danelagh. They seem to be also mostly situated within half-a-mile of the original Anglian or Saxon settlements, and where they are not there may be local circumstances to explain the reason. Around some of them villages have grown, whilst others have retained their original character of single homesteads, because the Norsemen came from a land of isolated homesteads, while the Anglo-Saxons came from a land of villages. The *thorp* meant not so much a collection of cottages as a single house or farm to which some land was attached for cultivation, as the word *torp* signifies in Sweden at this day. Some of the *thorpes*, of course, were not introduced until long after the Danish invasion. Such, for example, as Priesthorpe, which will be explained later. Yet there is no evidence of such assumption regarding the Bingley Gawthorpe. Moreover, we have between Gawthorpe and Micklethwaite an old farm called Laythorpe, and in this word there lurks possibly not only the presence of a law-giver, but the actual spot where the law was delivered. The "thing-stead" may have been on one of the natural drift-mounds at this place, and I have observed on the north side of the farm-house such a mound, which has been evidently levelled and scarped on the west side, fronting Micklethwaite Lane. The south side of the mound appears to have been planted with thorn trees, and to have formed a thick hedge, the line of which is still apparent. Laythorpe means literally *law-thorpe*, or the place of law or judgment, from the Danish *lagh*, Old Norse *log* (law). These *things* were usually held in isolated spots in order to escape any rude surprise. Mr. Holderness, of Driffield, points out that in the parish of Lowthorpe the old Scandinvian rulers of the Burton Hundred held their annual "thing," or folk-moot, and promulgated their enactments. Lowthorpe and Laythorpe are variants of the Scandinvian compound. The Laythorpe mound, I should say, has been cut in two, and bounded by an old road; formerly a narrow, hedged lane, known from time immemorial as Sty Lane. This is an obvious derivation from the Danish *stig*, *sty*, a steep path, also *sti*, a ladder, the word *stee* being still in use in Denmark, as well as in this district, for a ladder or ascent.

It is noteworthy that the Danish, or rather Norse colony, (for there are good reasons for believing that Bingley was not *colonized* until the latter days of the Northumbrian kings) lay on the east side of Bingley, covering the ground about Priesthorpe and Micklethwaite. That such an old and important Anglian settlement as Bingley was over-ruled by such a law-man as I have described is not, I think, to be contraverted, and such being the case, what places are more likely to have been chosen for the residence of the law-man and the spot for the giving of the law than Gawthorpe and Laythorpe, both of them situated within the area named. The chief *Thrithing*, or Riding Court, may have been at Leeds, or, perhaps, at Tingley (Thing-law), near Wakefield, and Bingley may have been one of the smaller district *things*, such as is described by Worsaae. The importance of the district is evidenced by the visits made to it by the Danish Kings of Northumbria, notably of Anlaf, who came to the throne in 949, and who is supposed to have died and been buried at Leeds. Some years ago, whilst undertaking some repairs at the Parish Church there, part of an ancient Christian cross was discovered, bearing in Anglian runes the name of Anlaf, who it is well known became a convert to Christianity in the latter part of his reign. He was the last Danish King of Northumbria.

On the reduction of Northumbria from a kingdom to an earldom, about the year 950, the Deiran portion of Yorkshire, which included Bingley, became a fief of the

Crown of England, and it is about this time that we hear of a considerable recession of the Scandinavian population to the fastnesses of the North-West Yorkshire fells, Westmorland, and Cumberland. The horrible Danish massacre on the festival of St. Brice also drove many northwards, never to return. On the institution of Canute, in 1017, the Vikings were again in possession of Northumbria and of England, but flame and sword had done its worst, and the country was in a deplorable state. A barbarous code of laws was passed, which possessed, however, at least one redeeming feature. It was that the idol and brazen image should be for ever cast aside, and that but one God should be worshipped in the land. The destroyed churches were to be restored, and the people once more were to find true holiness and consolation in the adoration of Him who rules and governs all. Some there were still who believed in the divine power of kings, and to whom honour and worship could rise no higher. Canute himself was a mighty and valorous chief, and a ruler of the most resolute type; but we all know the story of his sitting on the sea-beach, while his courtiers, heaping on flatteries, bade him request the waves to advance no further. At their bidding he commanded the waters to retire, but the wild waves took no heed, and soon drenched him to the skin. Then turning to the gazing crowd, he raised his hand to heaven, saying, "How frivolous and vain is the might of an earthly king compared to the might of that Great Power who rules the elements, and can say to the ocean, 'Thus far shalt thou go, and no further'!" Then taking in his hand the golden crown which he wore he bade a courtier carry it to the cathedral at Winchester, to be placed, as a memorial of the incident, above the plaited thorns of the great crucifix. "There," he added, "is the place for the kingly crown; crown the Lord of Hosts!"

It is during the reign of Canute that we get another glimpse of light on the history of the neighbourhood of Bingley. Archil, a Dane, who was lord of Kildwick, &c., and one of the most powerful chiefs in Yorkshire, was father of Gospatric, lord of Bingley for some years before

1066. Gospatric was grandson of the great Earl Uchtred, who died in 1016. Ardulf, who held the manor of Riddlesden and half Morton at this time, was one of the thanes who marched to York to avenge the murder of his countryman, Gospatric, in 1065. For his rebellious action against the Conqueror he lost his estates. Archil, the father of Gospatric, who lived in the reign of Edward the Confessor, also rebelled against the Conqueror, and was likewise dispossessed. Gospatric took to wife a daughter of Dolphin, son of Thorfin, and one of his sons was named after him. Gospatric, the elder, was the only Englishman in Yorkshire permitted to keep any of his estates after the survey of England completed by the Conqueror in 1086. Gospatric forfeited the manor of Bingley, but retained many others, including the manor of Holden-in-Craven, which he continued to hold as King's thane. He must not be confounded with Gospatric, ancestor of the Earls of Dunbar, who in 1069 had purchased the rule of Northumbria from the Conqueror; but afterwards revolting, was obliged to seek quarter in Scotland under protection of King Malcolm. This Gospatric was son of Maldred, by Algitha, sister of Archil, son of Uchtred, consequently the lord of Bingley was cousin to the great Earl Gospatric of Northumbria. Both were powerful chiefs, whose descendants continued to hold important positions in the northern aristocracy long afterwards. As much confusion has arisen between the various Gospatrics and their families, the accompanying hitherto unpublished pedigree (*see* next page) shews the connections of the pre-Norman lord of Bingley.

The ancient knightly family of Redman, of Harewood, appear identified with the old line of Gospatric, and I find that about 1250 Matthew de Redman was witness to the confirmation of a grant of lands at Preston, &c., by William de Lancaster to Patric, son of Thomas, son of Gospatric. Has the old "Redman Spa," on Rumbalds Moor, anything to do with this, as Gospatric's manor of Bingley extended but a little further westward of this point? The Gascoignes, of Gawthorpe (Harewood), held lands in Morton, *temp.* Henry VIII., when Magdaline, daughter of Henry Redman, married Marmaduke Gascoigne, of Gawthorpe.

Waltheof, 2nd Earl of Northumbria, *ca* A.D. 980.

Uchtred, 3rd Earl of Northumbria; attacked on Stainmoor, A.D. 1013; murdered by Thorbrand in 1016. (There were three families named Thorbrand living at Skipton-in-Craven in 1379.) = (1) Ecgive, dau. of Aldun, 1st Bp. of Durham. (2) Sigen, dau. of Styr. (3) Elfigue, dau. of King Ethelred (*ob.* 1016).

Edwulf succeeded Uchtred in the Earldom of Northumbria; died *ca.* 1020.

Children of Uchtred:

- Aldred succd. his uncle Edwulf to the Earldom of Northumbria.
- Edwulf, Earl of Northumbria; slain by Siward, A.D. 1041.
- Gospatric, 3rd son of Uchtred; treacherously slain at York with Gamel and Ulf, A.D. 1064-5.
- Archil* rebelled against the Conqueror in 1069; fled to Scotland, where King Malcolm granted him lands which afterw'ds constit'd the Earldom of Lennox. = Sigfrida, d. of Kilvert, son of Ligulf.
- Algitha dau. of Uchtred, by his 3rd wife. = Maldred.
  - Gospatric purchased for a large sum of money the Earldom of N'thumbria in 1068. He rebelled against Conqueror in 1072; fled to Scotland. Was ancestor of Earls of Dunbar.

Children of Archil and Sigfrida:

- Gospatric lord of Bingley, &c., before 1066; lord of 32 manors in 1086, incl. Weardley, which had belonged to his mother's grandfather, Ligulf. = dau. of Dolphin, son of Thorfin. (Dolphin, son of Thorfin, had the manors of Appletreewick, &c., in 1086).
- Archil =
  - Alwyne, First Earl of Lennox.

Children of Gospatric:

- Gospatric =
  - Adam =
    - Richard.
  - Dau =
    - Simon de Montalte (living A.D. 1165), lord of Riddlesden.
- Thurstan =
  - Alan.
- Uchtred of Allerston and Cayton, gave lands in Cayton to Prior Serlo (*ob. ca.* 1102) and monks of Whitby.
- Dolphin.

* This Archil has been stated to be the son of Uchtred; also the son of Fridgist; and the son of Ulf. There is no doubt there was more than one Archil at this time. Archil, lord of Ripley, &c., in Nidderdale, is said to be son of Fridgist, son of Vickingr, a Danish sea-king, (*vide* Ordericus). Mr. Ellis, the Domesday authority, says Gospatric, lord of Bingley, &c., was *cousin* to Earl Gospatric, as stated above.

OLD ROADS.

THIS might be made a very long chapter, as the subject is one that extends over a long period, from the time of the first Celtic invasion to the day when the stage-coaches rattled along the Main Street. Doubtless, the original roads in the parish made by Goidel and Brython were mere forest tracks, and no paved ways existed before the Romans came. The Romans were the great pioneers of road-making, and from them the Celts learnt that a paved track was a better means of passage and a safer guide from place to place than a trodden path, often badly defined, through forest and morass.

The oldest road of which we can speak with certainty is that which came up the Aire valley by way of Cottingley and Beckfoot Lane, through Belbank Wood, parallel with the present road, but high up in the wood, where it is still well defined. It entered Bingley by the well-marked depression in the wood bottom opposite Ireland Bridge. This was doubtless the first road across the river on to the original settlement on Bailey Hills (*see* p. 48). This road by Beckfoot Bridge was the old bridle and pack-horse route to and from Bingley for centuries before the Aire bridge was made at Cottingley and the road thence along the Main Street became a public thoroughfare. It was the main highway through Bingley from Scotland and Cumberland through Craven to the south, and doubtless it was along this flower-banked picturesque lane by Beckfoot that the stately cavalcade of Henry, Lord Clifford, the great and gallant Earl of Cumberland, passed on its way from Skipton to London in the sunny May days of 1526.

Probably there was an old track on the north side of the Aire from Leeds, the capital of Elmet, by way of Horsforth, Rawdon (where a British torque of gold was dug up on the Billing), and thence by Baildon to Bingley. The road from Bingley to Eldwick is undoubtedly also of

British antiquity, of which more presently. There was also a foot-track across the Bailey Hills from the church to Crossflatts or Castlefields Mill, and this ancient path continued in use down to the present century. The late Richard Dawson, of Ryshworth Bridge, used to say that in his young days, now nearly a century ago, old inhabitants spoke of this path over the Bailey Hills as "The Bridge of Earth," which seems to recall the time when impassable waters surrounded this long dry bank, making it really what it must have been in ancient days—*a bridge of earth.*

The old cobble-paved road from Bingley Bridge to the Druids' Altar, as well as that diverging through the Middle Hollins to Marley and Keighley, may be safely put down to British origin, as the latter is undoubtedly the original forest route northwards, in use ages before the highway was made through the valley. I present a view of it, showing a portion of the track before the recent felling of the trees there. The pavement, of course, cannot be ascribed to any particular date; its age is unknown. The road must originally have gone forward through the Domesday hamlet of Marley, but as that site in former times must often have been inundated and impassable, another way seems to have been made through Smith Fold, and thence by the lane to Currer Lathe and Long Lee to Keighley. Another old road out of Beckfoot Lane left the Belbank descent to Bingley, and ascended Blind Lane by Cross Gates and White Cote, west of the Altar Crag, and over Transfield Top, joining the same road at Currer Lathe for Keighley.

Coming down to the ford at Bingley Bridge, which existed long before the bridge was built in Norman times, there is some doubt as to the precise direction the road took across the valley. Doubtless, the making of the canal in 1772, and of the railway in 1846, diverted then existing roadways, although the Plan of the Canal kept in the Registry at Wakefield does not unfortunately mark all the roads and footpaths. Before the railway was made, the late Robert Longbottom farmed some land behind the old smithy, now occupied by the site of the Midland Goods

Yard, and at that time a cart-road out of his land crossed the canal in the direction of Beck Lane and Gawthorpe, and when the canal was made his family claimed a right of way for carts along the canal bank, which he himself

ANCIENT BRITISH ROAD THROUGH HOLLINS WOOD.

used in lieu of the old highway. From the ford an old road also crossed the foot of the Main Street, opposite the *White Horse*, and went past some still-remembered thatched cottages in the Goods Yard, skirting the south bank of the canal into the same road past Gawthorpe. As this road lies very low, the probability is in wet weather the river was crossed a little way below the bridge, and old inhabitants say that sixty or seventy years ago several large stepping-stones remained in the bed of the river, opposite Ferrand Lane, which circumstance points to the fact that there was an old crossing here, which continued up Ferrand Lane, and then went "high and dry" across the Main Street, down "Treacle Alley" (now Commercial Street) into Longbottom's land behind the old smithy, as above described. I find also that in 1777 Mr. Ferrand agreed to give up so much land from the side of the Dove Croft as may be wanted to widen the present road leading from the Vicarage House to the gate above to the width of seven yards, provided the township will take the road upon them to widen and keep in repair for the time to come, and also build him a new fence wall of five feet high, and take the present causeway which goes down the side of Dove Croft into the highroad, and hang a gate at the top of the lane. It was agreed that Mr. Ferrand's proposals be accepted, and that the surveyor for Micklethwaite hamlet be desired to proceed upon it without delay.

Bingley Bridge up to 1685 was a narrow wooden structure, available only for horse and foot-passengers. No cart could cross it, nor was it necessary, as wheeled carts were not generally adopted in this district till about this time. In the year named the bridge was re-built of stone, and repaired and widened in 1775; it being then "very ruinous, narrow, and in great decay." Formerly it was the rendezvous of the gossips of the town, for here young and old were wont to congregate and gather news from passing travellers and from the drovers of the pack-horses who regularly crossed this way between Otley, Ilkley, and the villages between here and Halifax. It is generally spoken of as "Ireland Bridge," a name of comparatively recent date, given to it because the river here separated two manors and ownerships, and to cross the water was a facetious comparison with the passage over the channel between England and Ireland. Similarly, when the property on the Mornington Road side of Bingley was built it was called "Little Dublin," because one had to cross the canal to get to it from Bingley.

In the early part of last century the old road through the wood to Harden was abandoned, and the present excellent carriage road made, which during this century has undergone further improvements. The bridge at Harden Beck was then of wood, and, as appears by the following order, which I have copied from the Sessions Records, it was rebuilt of stone in 1711:—

Halifax, July 12, 1711.—Whereas it was ordered last Skipton Sessions that Ten Pounds should be estreated on the severall Wapentakes of Agbrigg and Morley and Skyrack as a grant towards making a stone bridge over Harden Beck (which divides the said wapentakes) instead of an old wood bridge there. And whereas this Court is satisfied that it will be very convenient and advantageous to the public to make it a stone bridge, but being of opinion that it is more convenient the said gratuity should be charged on the whole Riding. It is therefore ordered that the said Order made at Skipton be discharged, and that the sum of Ten Pounds be estreated on the said Riding, and paid to Robert fferrand and Willm Busfield, Esqrs., as a gratuity to the parishes of Bradford and Bingley towards the charge of altering the said wood bridge into a stone bridge.

On the completion of the road and bridge, an upright stone was fixed against the wall, facing the road, near Cockcroft Fold, on which was cut the crest of Ferrand, with this inscription beneath: "The soil and ground of the way from hence to Bingley Bridge belongs to Benjamin Ferrand, Esq., 1718." At this period the old Roman road from Manchester to Ilkley (89 miles) was in evidence, and visible nearly the whole of the way. As already explained, it traversed Bingley parish several miles. The late Mr. F. A. Leyland, of Halifax, says that in 1849 Mr. King, of Luddenden (then in his 80th year) told him that his, Mr. King's, grandfather, who lived to an advanced age, had travelled the whole distance from Luddenden to Ilkley by this old Roman road. In 1884, Mr. Leyland, in company with several gentlemen, including Mr. Watkinson, of Halifax, an aged and interested antiquary, then on the verge of 80, who acted as guide, traversed the same Roman road from Cockhill, in Ovenden, as far as Mount Tabor, in

Warley. So far as it concerns the parish of Bingley, I have defined the direction of this lost Roman iter.

The ancient Dolphin Lane, one of the oldest roads in the parish (called, perhaps, after old Dolphin, son of Gospatric, lord of Bingley before the Conquest; or may be from some later family of that name), leaves the Bingley and Cullingworth highroad to the east of Cowhouse, and runs up to Harden Moor, leading now from nowhere to nowhere else in particular. Whether this old lane has been continuous with the old road from Cullingworth, or whether it has been connected with a thoroughfare from Wilsden, I have been unable to make out. There is a very old stone stoop at the foot of the lane, inscribed—"To Kighley, 2 M."; but the road from Cullingworth to Keighley followed, as I have shewn, the old Roman road west of Ca-tstones through Hainworth Shay. Moreover, the distance from this stoop (assuming it to be in its original position) to Keighley is fully three miles. At the top of Dolphin Lane its continuance is lost on the moor, so that it is doubtful which direction it took.

Some very old roads are mentioned in the early grants of Paganel to Drax Priory. One of these mentions the road from Priesthorpe to Gilstead, a portion of which still exists as a bridle road at Crow Nest. The road was continuous with the one leaving Bingley by Park Road, crossing the wood-yard from Longbottom's smithy, off the east end of Charles Street and up Priesthorpe Road, then a very narrow way, with a stile at the top on to the existing road to Crow Nest, where it turns to the left at the cottages, and goes up to the crag side, behind the Cottage Hospital, joining the present road to Gilstead further on. The road from Cottingley Bridge to Gilstead over Primrose Hill and past Milner Field is also very ancient; at least as old as the Domesday record. Up to the farmhouse at the top it was, in the middle of last century, a narrow hedged way, with deep ruts, subsequently improved, and about thirty years ago widened to its present dimensions. Well may his Majesty's liege subjects in their "coaches, carts, and carriages," have run "great danger of their lives" by attempting the passage of this hedged quagmire in times when highways were mostly left to take care of themselves. Had we records of all the adventures and mishaps of passengers by this lane in former centuries, there would doubtless be some pretty anecdotes to relate. I find by the Sessions Records that in October, 1759, a fine of £40 was to be levied upon the inhabitants of Bingley if they did not repair the road. At the Sessions held at Bradford, 27th July, 1758, the following indictment was made against the inhabitants :—

And that from the time whereof the memory of man is not to the contrary there was and yet is a certain common and antient King's Highway leading from the Village of Ilkley in the West Riding of the County of York to the Village of Halifax in the said Riding used for all the Liege Subjects of our said Lord the King and his predecessors by themselves and with their Horses Coaches Carts and carriages to go return pass ride and labour at their will and pleasure. And that a certain part of the same King's Common Highway at the parish of Bingley in the Riding aforesaid (to wit) for the space of one thousand seven hundred yards in length of a certain Lane there called Cottingley Bridge otherwise Gilstead Lane from a certain Gate situated at the South West side of the Village of Gilstead in the parish aforesaid commonly called the Town Gate [opposite the present Post Office] to the Turnpike Road on the North West end of a certain Bridge called Cottingley Bridge situate upon and over the River Air in the same parish the twenty second day of July in the thirty second year of the reign of our Sovereign Lord George the second now King of Great Britain &c. and continually afterwards until the day of the taking of this Inquisition at the said parish of Bingley was and yet is very ruinous miry deep broken and in such decay for want of the due Reparation and amendment of the same so that the Liege Subjects of our said Lord the King through the same may by themselves and with their Horses Coaches Carts and Carriages could not during the time aforesaid nor yet can go return pass ride and labour without great danger of their Lives and the Loss of their Goods to the great damage and common Nuisance of all the Liege Subjects of our said Lord the King through the same way going returning passing riding and labouring and against the peace of our said Lord the King his Crown and Dignity and that the Inhabitants of the parish of Bingley aforesaid the Common Highway aforesaid (so as aforesaid being in decay) from time whereof the memory of man is not to the contrary have been accustomed and of right ought to repair and amend when and so often as it shall be necessary.

This ancient highway went over the then unenclosed Gilstead Moor (by what is now Warren Lane) to Eldwick, and across Rumbalds Moor to Ilkley. There were also other recognised routes across the moor to Otley and Ilkley before the present moor road was made from "Dick Hudson's." One of the most frequented went by Crossflatts, up Micklethwaite Lane, past the chapel, and on the old Kiln Lane, up the brow, over Drake Hill, passing the present keeper's house, and by the moor-path to the Ashlar Chair, as at present existing. The old road previously mentioned from Ferrand Lane to Beck Houses appears to have led by the Spa Well, near the Pinfold, through Oakwood, almost parallel with the long snicket, on to Lady Lane, then close to the east side of Cross Butts Farm (now Ogden's), where the old causeway was until this year *in situ*. This old farmhouse up to about forty years ago was a "public," called the *Plough Boy Inn*, the last tenants of the inn being a family named Wilkinson. It was a familar resort of the "jagger-men" passing between Otley and Ilkley and Bingley, and many are the stories one might relate of this out-of-the-way "travellers' rest." The road hence went over the Height down to Tewett Farm, and by the well-known "Saddle Loin" past the reservoir, emerging on the carriage-road near Eldwick Hall. Then it turned along the old lane opposite Eldwick Hall, but a "short cut" opposite the "Saddle Loin" crossed the fields, where the old pave-stones have been removed, on to the same old Otley and Ilkley road.

This old road under Eldwick Crag, by Gaping Goose, was formerly a narrow, miry way, like most of the other roads about Eldwick at that time. It had been kept in repair by Joshua Crompton, Esq., of Esholt, who owned considerable property at Eldwick, but in 1786 Mr. Lobley, his agent, at a meeting held in Bingley to discuss the desirability of making a new road at Eldwick, proposed to give up such land as would be wanted for the said road, and also to allow the sum of fifteen guineas provided the inhabitants undertook to maintain the road at Eldwick Crag side in repair. Soon afterwards, in May, 1786, the surveyor was ordered to prepare an estimate for a road from Glovershaw Beck to Knapling; and also another estimate for making a road from Eldwick Hall to Eldwick

High Gate ("Dick Hudson's"). This was intended to divert the old pack-horse road to Otley, which went by the lane, now existing, opposite Eldwick Hall, by Whinney Hill to Robert Atkinson's Gate, on the Otley road, a little beyond the chapel. At first it was intended to utilise this old road, but Mr. Crompton would not consent to it, owing to the sharp angle at Whinney Hill and Bill Nook, so the idea was abandoned, and the narrow, hedged lane up to the High Gate, or "Dick Hudson's," was adopted instead.

This important road up to "Dick Hudson's," which is now travelled by thousands of people every summer making their way between Saltaire and Bingley and Ilkley, was consequently approved, and made in 1787. At a vestry meeting held on January 23rd, 1787, it was agreed as follows :—

FIRST, Mr. Crompton agrees on his part, in case the road be carried up the Old Road from Elwick Hall to the High Gate he will give up his property in the Lane to the Town of Bingley for ever, in consideration of the inhabitants of Bingley taking upon them the making of the roads at all times hereafter to maintain the same and keep the same in repair.

And also of their paying him a valuable consideration for such of his grounds adjoining the same as shall be necessary and wanted for the widening of the same.

And Mr. Crompton further generously offers to give such Consideration Money for the benefit of the Sunday Schools of Bingley to which said proposals the inhabitants have consented.

And also Mr. John Hartley having on his part as proprietor of lands adjoining the said road made the same generous proposal. It is agreed upon the said inhabitants to accept of the same.

N.B.—It was agreed that Fences shall be made all the way on both sides the road equal to the Fences made for Mr. Ferrand and Mr. Sharp.

(Signed) JOSA. CROMPTON, JOHN HARTLEY, BENJN. FERRAND, J. LOBLEY, JAS. MURGATROYD, JOSEPH HEATON, Jun., THO. DOBSON, JOHN OLIVER, JONAS WHITLEY, THOMAS RASTRICK, JOHN ANDERSON, ROBERT ATKINSON.

Mr. Crompton was a generous friend to education and progress of any kind. He started the first Sunday School in his own neighbourhood of Esholt, and his amiable daughters taught it for many years. When the above road was completed, it was decided to transfer the licence from the old Battlebank "public" to the farmhouse at High Gate, then occupied by John Anderson. It was named *Fleece Inn.* A gate was hung across the road, the stoops of which still remain. In 1790, it may be interesting to note, a rate of 9d. in the pound was levied "on all and every occupier of lands, tenements, woods, tythes, and hereditaments" in the townships of Bingley and Morton, for the use and benefit of the highways in these townships.

Thomas Hudson, the Bingley constable and pinder, took the *Fleece* in 1809, and his son "Dick" succeeded on his father's death in 1850, and kept the house until his death in 1878, when he was succeeded by his son John, who died here in 1898. I have heard it said that "Dick Hudson's" must be known to at least a million folks!

Connected with these roads out of Bingley were some branch paths, one of which left the ancient Gilstead road (above described) at a thatched cottage below Mr. Alfred Green's house, at the top of Priesthorpe Road, and took under the quarry (now gardens) to Priesthorpe Green and Beck Houses, as above. Another path ascended to an old barn which stood near the well at Mr. Pickard's garden; it then continued up Stony Lane and along the hillside through Langley (Kennels), and out on the Gilstead Moor road to Eldwick, as above. The road from Eldwick by Glovershaw Lane and Acre Howe to Hawksworth and Baildon is also one of the very oldest in the district; but that portion of it extending from Eldwick Beck to Glovershaw Gate was only widened and improved in the year 1777. At this time application was made to Sir John Goodricke (lord of the manor of Bingley) for as much land as was required for widening Vicarage Lane, leading to the church.

In the year 1778, I may add, the old pack-horse bridge over Hawksworth Beck was replaced by a new and substantial carriage bridge; and at the West Riding Sessions held at Leeds, on October 8th, it was represented that the inhabitants of the several townships of Bingley, Hawksworth, and Baildon were expending large sums of money in the erection of this bridge. Eventually, on the 15th July, 1779, the townships named received £25 as a gratuity out of the Riding stock, and an additional £25 was allowed at the Sessions held at Pontefract, April 3rd, 1780.

When coaches began to run in the time of Charles I., more attention began to be paid to the highways, and in 1662 the first Turnpike Act was passed, and in 1679 the first toll-bar was erected on the London and Harwich Road. But it was nearly a century afterwards before any real headway was made in the improvement of roads in the north. In 1664, a violent flood had partly undermined the foundations of the old wooden bridge over the Aire at Cottingley, and some twenty years later it was re-erected

COTTINGLEY BRIDGE.

in stone, but not widened for some time after the turnpike was made for the coaches (about 1752), which now ran this way through Bingley to the north. The old Beckfoot route,—the scene, doubtless, of many a grand cavalcade, such as the one previously mentioned, became impracticable to any but those on foot or on horseback. When the highroad was completed, some improvements were made in the Main Street, and the fine Market House was erected here (now in the Park), which bears the date 1758. This year is memorable for the terrible riots that followed the completion of the turnpike roads about Leeds, when a shocking tumult prevailed; the military being called out, and on one day, in Briggate, eight persons were shot dead, and fifty more or less badly wounded. After the bars were erected, it was usual to offer for public competition the letting of the tolls throughout the country. An advertisement stated what the tolls had realised on each particular road in the year previous. In 1797, I find that on the road from Bradford to Keighley the turnpike-gate at Stock Bridge yielded £210; at Cottingley Bridge, £180; and at Toller Lane, £112, after deducting expenses of collection. These items afford some idea of the amount of traffic a century ago between Bingley and Keighley, as compared with the traffic between Bingley and Bradford.

Doubtless the ancient British ways through the Hollins and over the Bailey Hills were less frequented on the Norman settlement, when the present main road through Crossflatts existed as a bridle-way. The road is mentioned in grants to Drax Priory in the 12th and 13th centuries. It was widened by Act of Parliament in 1752, when the Keighley and Kendal Turnpike Trust was granted. Although an Act had been passed for repairing the highways as early as the reign of Queen Mary (1556-7), the roads throughout the kingdom remained in a deplorable condition for nearly two centuries afterwards. The statute, as old Harrison tells us, was constantly being evaded; parish surveyors taking care to have good roads to their own fields, but neglected those which led from market to market. At Bingley, for example, I find that in 1710 one John Skirrow was overseer of the highways, and, as appears by his account presented March 2nd, 1710, he had disbursed the magnificent sum of £1 12s. 10d. in keeping the highways in repair for two years! He had a balance of £3 11s. 8d. in hand, of which £3 was ordered to be paid to Dr. Swain for amputating and curing the leg of one Christopher Colton. How the said Colton came to injure his leg is not recorded, but it is not at all unlikely it was by accident on the beautiful highways of the period.

At any rate, the accident (if it were such) cost the parish nearly four years' price of maintaining the highways. Happily we are wiser in these days, and know it is cheaper to the community to keep the roads in good repair.

The road out of Bingley to Cottingley Bridge was called Leeds Lane, and I find that at a meeting of the Bingley overseers, held on December 2nd, 1782, it was ordered that James Hudson do apply to Mr. Moore for the different admeasurements of the land taken from each proprietor for the purpose of widening the said Leeds Lane, beginning at the Nab Gate, and ending at the township road at Cottingley Wells. He was also to make a just estimate of such new fences as have been built by each proprietor of land in consequence of widening the said road. This action arose out of a charge preferred against the inhabitants of Bingley in 1776-7 for neglecting the repairs, and consequently five or six years elapsed before they were finally completed. It appears that the expenses incurred by the town for this improvement in widening Leeds Lane reached the modest total of £69 10s. 5d. The items of expenditure are interesting, as shewing the price of land and labour about a century ago :—

					Town Paid.		
GROUND TAKEN FROM MR. WICKHAM'S LAND.							
1294 yards of land at 3½d... ..	£18	17	5	½	£9	8	8½
165½ roods of walling at 5/- ..	41	7	6	½	20	13	9
80 roods of road-making at 8/6..	34	0	0	¼	8	10	0
GROUND TAKEN FROM MR. HOLLING'S LAND.							
641 yards of land at 3½d... ..	£9	6	11	½	£4	13	5¾
58 roods of walling at 5/-	14	10	0	½	7	5	0
Road-making	17	11	6	¼	4	7	10½
GROUND TAKEN FROM MR. ISAAC SMITH'S LAND.							
33 yards of land at 3½d.	£0	9	7½	½	£0	4	7¾
11 roods of walling at 5/-	2	15	0	½	1	7	6
5½ roods of road-making at 8/6..	2	6	9	¼	0	11	8¼
Mr. Lobley's Bill	23	0	0	½	11	10	0
Mr. John Moore's Bill for planning	0	17	6		0	8	9
James Hudson's Bill for setting out, &c...	0	18	0		0	9	0
Total					£69	10	5

Bingley Bridge, as I have said, was not widened until 1777, and Cottingley Bridge, on the coach road, a year or two later. Great difficulty was experienced in getting proper foundations for the piers of Cottingley Bridge, owing to the great thickness of loose gravel overlying the boulder-clay in this part of the valley. The contractor, Barnabas Morvill, who was one of the contractors, in 1770, for the mason-work at the Three-Rise and Five-Rise Locks on the Canal, and apparently an able and conscientious workman, was considerably out of pocket by the Cottingley Bridge contract, and on laying his case before the West Riding Justices at Pontefract, on April 3rd, 1780, it was ordered that a gratuity of £40 be given to Mr. Morvill in respect of the extraordinary expense he had suffered in the proper execution of the work. The Morvills (an old West Riding family) were living at Beckfoot in 1620.

All the principal wooden bridges in the district were now giving way to more durable erections in stone. The stream at Beckfoot, which had been spanned by rickety wooden structures from at least the time of the Crusades, being on the chief highway into Bingley, was in the year 1723 supplied with a serviceable one of stone. As this bridge lies in one of the most visited and picturesque nooks in the vicinity of Bingley, I give the particulars of its erection in full, as they appear in the parish books. A view of it is also presented from a photograph by Mr. G. Whitaker.

THE BUILDING OF BECKFOOT BRIDGE.

7th, 2nd, 1723.—Whereas the Constablery or Township of Bingley have this day paid by Willm. Ellison, the p'sent constable, to Benja. Craven and Josa. Scott, masons, ye sum of Ten Pounds, for building a Stone Bridge ovr Harden Beck at Beckfoot. In consideracon whereof ye said Benja. Craven and Joshua Scott doe hereby promise joyfully and severally to uphold and keep the sd Bridge in good and sufficient repair during the terme of seaven years from the day hereof, as witness our hands the day and year above sd.

Test:	BEN CRAVEN
WILLM. ELLISON,	The mark of
JOSHUA SMITH,	JOSHUA X SCOTT.

This is interesting. Imagine a couple of contractors at the present day building a serviceable stone bridge and keeping it in good repair for seven years for a five-pound note apiece, and withal thankfully rejoicing at the job!

I regret that the space at disposal prevents me from dwelling on many of the old roads in the outlying parts of the parish. One of the most frequented of these in the old days was that which led into Bingley from Haworth and the west country, and it was a sight to see the strings of pack-horses and drovers meeting those from Halifax and Otley, as sometimes they did, at Bingley Bridge. The

Beckfoot Bridge.

Haworth road came by Cross Roads, and ascended the moor-side by an old bridle-way, still known as Bell-horse Lane, emerging in Goff Lane, near the old Goff Well. This was a famous resort of gipsies before the moor was enclosed in 1861. The road went then over Harden Moor, by the Harley, or Early Stone, and above the Altar down to Bingley. The descent intersected the old British track-way through the Hollins, and was by a rough cobble-stone pavement, which old inhabitants tell me was one of the best "bone-shakers" in the district. Had anyone attempted the descent of this road with a load of pots they, the pots, would have been smashed into a thousand fragments. Yet this is the way that funerals came from the high moors in olden times. The coffin was borne on a hearse-litter, suspended between two horses, and the cortege proceeded, by way of the bridge, to the Parish Church. The litter continued in use in this district long after the introduction of wheeled vehicles, as owing to the narrowness and condition of the lanes no other means, save pole-carriage by hand, was practicable. The last time the hearse-litter was employed in the parish was probably when the body of old Mr. Wm. Garnett, of Lane Head, Eldwick, was conveyed to the Parish Church for interment, now about seventy years ago. Old Mr. Wildman, of High Crag Farm, Eldwick, tells me he remembers following the cortege in this manner when a boy. Gilstead Moor was then, of course, unenclosed. I may here also record the interesting fact that Mrs. Martha Moulding (aged 80), of Gilstead, who is a granddaughter of the above Wm. Garnett, is one of the very few persons still living in Bingley who took part in the local celebrations of the Queen's coronation in 1837, and who lived also to participate in the local rejoicings on the completion in 1897 of Her Majesty's sixty years' reign. One of her surviving sisters is Mrs. Waddington (aged 76), now of Beck houses, Bingley.

Mr. Wildman informs me that the tinkling of the bells suspended to the necks of the pack-horses was a familiar sound along the road which crossed the moor from Morton to Otley, and in the early part of the century, when the house he now occupies at Eldwick Crag Side was built, all the lime used for mortar was brought in sacks by saddle-back out of the then distant solitudes of Lothersdale.

OLD DYKES AND BOUNDARIES.

OF prehistoric tribal dykes the parish of Bingley retains but scant evidences. A word upon them, however, is here necessary in pursuing the sequence of the handiworks of man. The subject of these early landmarks has been little dealt with, and nowhere that I can discover has it been broadly or comprehensively taken up. One must turn here and there to local topographical productions for any allusions to them, and when found there is by no means a concensus of opinion with regard to their origin or design. So far as our present knowledge of the subject will enable us to decide, there seems little doubt but that they are pre-Roman works, not intended as military defences, but as defining lines separating one tribe from another. In my "Richmondshire" I have described in some detail one of these remarkable excavations, known as "Scots' Dyke," which extends through Richmondshire in a northerly direction to the borders of Scotland, a distance of over 70 miles. The so-called "Danes' Dyke," at Flamborough is another Yorkshire example, which it is now safe to affirm has nothing to do with the Danes, but must be classed as coeval with the above and other similar lines of entrenchment which are to be found in various parts of the country, and especially in those tracts peopled by the ancient Celts.

By the term "tribal dykes," I do not include the various earthen enclosures on Baildon, Harden, and Cullingworth Moors, which are distinctively "camps," or fortifications intended for defensive purposes only. I allude to the continuous entrenchments, traces of which are here and there apparent, and such as can have served only as boundary lines, and in places even where natural *impedimenta* might, but have not been so utilised or regarded.

One of these entrenched lines seems to have extended in a north-west and south-east direction over Cullingworth Black Moor, a little to the west of "Castlestead Ring," or "Blood Dyke," as it is locally called; thence to have taken in the direction of Denholme and Queensbury, and so towards Bradford. Perhaps Black Dike, at Queensbury, and Laister-dyke, to the east of Bradford, may be parts of the same line, although the Queensbury Dyke is believed to derive its name from an old water-course in the peat, which formerly ran near the old Black Dike farmhouse, the site of which is now occupied by the mills. But the source of the stream and extent of the dike are uncertain. A portion of the Scots' Dyke, near Housesteads, by the way, is known as Black Dyke, and this word Black, which is commonly met with in out-of-the-way districts in Celtic territory, appears to be as distinctly Celtic as the word Brown, already explained, and occurring in similar solitary and waste places (*see* page 58).

On the opposite side of the valley, on Gilstead Moor, near Eldwick, we have, or rather had, another of these ancient dykes, which no one seems to have regarded as anything very particular. Old inhabitants tell me it was locally known as the "Old Dyke Cam," but why so called they cannot explain. But *cam* is used both by the Gaelic and Cymric Celts to indicate anything crooked or bent; as for example Morecambe, anciently *mor-cam*, which may mean the *great bend*, as applied to the bay. *Cambus* is a creek or inlet of the sea; *Mor*, cognate with the Latin *mare*, Teut. *meer*, also means *the sea*, so that "Morecambe" may be either the great bend or the crooked sea, as its contour shews. The Eldwick, or Gilstead *cam* was likewise a crooked dyke. It extended from the west of Eldwick Beck, on the top side of Eldwick Church, in the direction of Sheriff Farm, where it made a marked turn, but why is not obvious, as the ground did not necessitate such a curve; it then continued in a pretty straight line across Gilstead Moor towards Stubbin House, whence its continuance is not remembered. It is noteworthy that this dyke ran almost parallel with the Bingley parish boundary, now formed by Glovershaw Beck and Eldwick Beck, past Load Pit (or Loopit) Bridge, down to the Hurst; Trench Wood lying to the east, and the old homestead, Trench Farm, just over the boundary, but whether this word, "Trench," has anything to do with the dyke I cannot say.

Many of these ancient dykes constitute parish and township boundaries to the present day. We need not go very far away for evidence of this kind, as Thoresby in his *Duc. Leod.* mentions a dike that divides the manor of Leeds from that of Hunslet, as well as the wapentake of *Skire-ake* (Skyrack) from that of *Ake-bride* (Agbrigg) and Morley. Is it possible that the name of the present Sheriff Lane, on Gilstead Moor, which is almost coextensive with this dyke, is as old as the Anglo-Saxon occupation of Bingley? The ancient farmstead here appears to have been known from time immemorial as Sheriff House. Was this, then, at one time the limit of the local Anglo-Saxon jurisdiction at Bingley, of the ward of the *scire-reeve*, or sheriff, while the land beyond was held by the Cymric Celts? But the *cam*, as I have said, was no doubt originally a British tribal boundary, made upon the irruption and undoubted settlement, as I have sufficiently shewn in a preceding chapter, of the Brythonic Celts at Bingley, when the Druidical Goidels were driven to the moors, and ultimately as a distinct tribe wholly exterminated in this district.

If we take a map and pair of compasses and fix one point at Bingley, then with the other strike a radius of say three miles, we should describe a circle embracing all the higher ground occupied by the two classes of Celts, while the lower lands between bear the strong impress of Anglo-Saxon possession. This sweep of the compass would take in Rivock, Faweather, Baildon Common, Cottingley Moor, Stony Ridge, Old Allen, Burn Moor, Hewenden, Black Moor, Crummach, Castlestead Ring, Harden Moor, Cat-stones, Druids' Altar, &c. To define the Celtic occupation southwards and eastwards from its chief stronghold (Wilsden) in Brythonic times we should take in Burn Moor (of which more anon) and Old Allen; thence at the same elevation by Black Dike Lane and Bell Dean top over Storrs Heights towards Allerton, or southwards along the tops to Queensbury and Clews Moor. The well-known picturesque opening of the sea on the west coast of Ireland, known as Clew Bay, seems to point to a Goidelic or earliest Celtic occupation of this similarly-named portion of high land.

To quit, however, the region of speculation with regard to these ancient Celtic boundaries, let us consider the lines of demarcation taken over or adopted by the Anglian conquerors here. From what I have said in a previous chapter, there is little doubt that the boundary was already fixed which defines the limits of the parish to this day. Take the Anglian word Mytholm, or Myth-holm, the name of a small district, extending from near old St. Ives to Harden Beck Bridge, which tract separates the ancient parishes of Bingley and Bradford, as well as marks the dividing-line of the deaneries of Craven and Bradford. Dr. Bosworth defines *mythas* as *bounds*, *limits*; and *holm*, a green plot of land environed with water, which exactly suits the situation of Mytholm, lying as it does on the limits of the two parishes, and on low land between Mytholm and Harden Becks. There are other Mytholms in Yorkshire, which are similarly situated on the boundaries of parishes. Thus in this one word we have confirmatory evidence of the limits of the parish in this direction having been accepted in Anglo-Saxon times, and an investigation of places at other points would doubtless establish equally interesting conclusions.

But not to dwell longer on these definitions, let me now record the boundaries of the parish as they have undoubtedly existed from its original formation. Starting on the west from where the Carr Clough Beck enters the Aire, the boundary follows the river past Stock Bridge to a short distance beyond East Riddlesden Hall, when at the boundary-stone, opposite the causeway end, it turns southwards close to the Keighley Gasworks (which are in Bingley); then east of Thwaites Houses, up Thwaites Bank, where the wall on the left side of the road separates it from Keighley; then passing close by the west side of Jackfield Farm and Currer Lathe, it continues southwards over Harden Moor to Harden Gate, thence westward to the Harley Stone; then northwards to the beck at Long Lee, which flowing down through Hog Holes to Woodhouse Bottom it enters the river Worth. The latter stream defines the parish boundary forward by Ingrow Bridge (Ingrow Station being in Bingley) for nearly two miles to the Vale Mill (Bingley parish including the populous districts of Cross Roads, New Road Side, Hermit Hole, and part of Ingrow, which are now taken into Keighley); then it turns up west of Mytholme Mill, following Lees Sike above Ebor Mill, near Cross Roads, within 500 yards north-east of Haworth station, whence it passes through Lees Mill Dam, and pursues the water-course up to Brow Moor, near Flappit Springs. Hence southwards three furlongs west of the cross roads at Laverock Hall, crossing

HARDEN BECK BRIDGE.

(On the boundary of the parish, deanery, and wapentake).

the Allotments south of Castlestead Ring, and then by the Manywells Beck that flows eastward under Ive-stone Bridge (on the Halifax and Haworth road), and down Brown Hill, under the railway viaduct at Cullingworth Gate, where this stream marks the boundary of the parish, deanery, and wapentake. The same stream then continues through Cullingworth, and in perambulating the boundary it was necessary to creep along the beck under Cullingworth

Mills, following the beck to Cow House Bridge, where the Eller Carr Beck joins the main stream. The united waters then form the boundary to Goit Stock Mill, where the Hewenden Beck enters it from the famous Goit Stock waterfall (which is not in Bingley parish). Hence the combined waters are known as Harden Beck, which flowing through the Harden valley, by Harden Beck Bridge, form the parish boundary, as well as that of the deanery and wapentake, to its junction with the Mytholme Beck below Harden Grange. Then it takes a sharp turn up Ruin Bank Wood, and southwards by the long wall over the Black Hills, keeping a little west of March Cote (which is in Bingley) to Stocker Gate. Then it continues over Cottingley Moor, crossing Cottingley Beck close to Stoker House, which is the farthest point it reaches southward. Then keeping west of the Moor Road and Moor Dike, the boundary is by the field-wall for more than a mile in a north-west direction, passing Cottingley village a little to the east, on to the Bingley highroad at Nab Wood end. Then it strikes north to where the railway crosses the river, and the river hence on its west side to Seven Arches, and forward by the north bank to the Loopit or Eldwick Glen Beck, which enters the Aire opposite Hirst Mill, forms the parish boundary towards Saltaire. The above beck now forms the boundary up to its junction with the Glovershaw Beck at Spring Wood, Eldwick, whence it follows the Glovershaw Beck by Golcar Side to the old boundary-stone, and thence eastward past Sconce to the Gill Beck at Hawksworth Spring; Sconce, Hollins House, and Low Spring being all in Bingley parish. It then turns back north-west up the Gill Beck a little east of Faweather, over Knapley Ing, following the beck up to its source, close to the west side of Horncliffe House, where the boundaries of Burley and Hawksworth meet. Then two miles over Rumbalds Moor to the Ashlar Chair,* north of Redman Spa; thence to the

* The Ashlar Chair has been stated to be a relic of Druidism; in shape it is like a couch or chair, and bears numerous cups and grooves. It is the boundary of the four lordships of Bingley, Burley, Morton, and Ilkley Moors, and upon it are the initials: M.M.; B.T.P.; I.S.P.; I.W.; and I.G., 1826.

West Buck Stones, in a south-westerly direction over Rivock Edge, down the west side of Elam Wood, by the beck course to the Aire and point of starting. The circuit of the parish by the bounds thus defined is 28 miles, its greatest extension from east to west being nearly 8 miles, and from north to south 5½ miles.

At the time of the Norman Conquest Baildon was also included within the bounds of the soke of Bingley, and its exclusion at this day seems a physiographical anomaly. But ethnologically considered, the anomaly disappears, for it presents a wedge of Celtic ground in the midst of Anglo-Saxon territory, or, to employ a common illustration, it is like an apple held in the mouth of a boar; the apple representing Celtic Baildon, while the jaws define the protrusion of the Anglian boundaries as now existing. On the west the line of demarcation is strongly marked, and it must have existed from a very remote period. I concur with the authorities named a few pages back that it formed the westernmost boundary of the British kingdom of Elmet, though I do not believe the province embraced the large extent of country usually ascribed to it. I take its bounds to have been very nearly coextensive with the old wapentake of Skyrack, with Leeds as its capital, and the Shire Oak, Headingley, as the headquarters of the wapentake courts in Anglian times. By this demarcation we should have Burn Moor and the Hadelstone, or Early Stone, Harden Moor, on the west, passing eastwards over part of the parish of Otley, including Baildon, where, by the way, is another of these remarkable memorial stones, called Harley or Early Stone; thence northwards, embracing the parishes of Guiseley and Adel and the township of Bramhope, and eastward including the parishes of Barwick-in-Elmet and Kippax, as far east, perhaps, as Haddleston, adjoining Sherburn-in-Elmet on the west. Its southern limit would be defined by the Aire by Allerton-Bywater to the parish boundary north of Bingley, above described. This, roughly, embraces the wapentake of Skyrack, and includes an area of little more than 90,000 acres, and I consider it to have formed the small Celtic province of Elmet, which so long maintained its independence of the Anglian authority. The area agrees almost exactly with old Camden's statement from an ancient MS. that Elmed-Setna (that is the inhabitants of Elmet) possessed or occupied 600 hides of land. Wight Gora (Isle of Wight) is stated in the same MS. to contain 600 hides of land, and as the area of that island is about 86,000 acres, it agrees very nearly with the area I have defined of the province of Elmet. Although the area implied by this tribal hidage was not the same in all localities (and it does seem to have been an areal measurement, not like the fiscal hide of Domesday); yet considering the importance and strength of Elmet, and its population in British and Anglo-Saxon times, when the moors were as valuable as the richest pastures (a sheep for its wool was worth as much as a cow), does it not seem likely that the average hide of land in this locality maintained as many people and was worth as much as that in the Isle of Wight at the same period?

The riding of the boundaries in the old days was at Bingley attended with considerable animation. The parties usually assembled at the *King's Head*, when, accompanied by the lord's steward, they went up to Eldwick, and walking up the beck, followed the line I have defined by Hawksworth Springs, and past the *Gaping Goose* across Rumbalds Moor. Thomas Hudson, father of "Dick," who lived over sixty years at the well-known "pub." on the moor edge, used to come up about noon with a cart laden with cheese and bread and ale; then each would find a seat among the rocks and heather, and thoroughly enjoy the ample repast provided at the lord's expense. Sometimes fifty or sixty men and boys would attend on these perambulations, and it may be imagined with what gusto they sat down to this welcome provision after the scrambling, joking, and antics that took place during a long morning in the bracing air of this high moor. Two centuries ago the parish made a substantial gratuity on the occasion of these perambulations, and in 1704 it was agreed that the sum of 10s. be allowed at each gathering. The "meets" were looked forward to with the most pleasurable anticipations, both by young and old, and many a youngster would be "up with the lark" on the morning appointed for the ramble, calling upon his comrades to be up early on the moors, and then to join in the fun of the throng :—

> "Come! will you not go where the bilberries grow
> On their beautiful bushes of green;
> Whose ruby bells smiled, in the desolate wild,
> On the far-away moorland scene?
> We are up and away, at the dawn of the day,
> Young cottagers moving in scores,
> Ere the dawn of the day we are up and away—
> Away to the bilberry moors."

And here on the "bilberry moors" many a youth would have cause to remember the gathering, for it was usual to take one or two and give them a good-humoured "ducking" or drenching in some stream or ditch that lay on the line of march, that the boundary might be "well-remembered unto the next generation."*

It is now, I understand, more than forty years since the last perambulation, which arose out of a dispute between the boundaries of the Bingley and Burley lordships, when Mr. Kell (Mr. Fox's steward) and over one hundred followers traversed the bounds from Glovershaw Beck forward until darkness came on, and its completion was postponed to another day. But they never came again, and the question of the boundary was settled without a visit. The boundaries of the manor of Bradford were, I believe, last traversed in 1823.

* The Bingley moors were famous for their abundance of bilberries and cranberries, but for some cause or other they are not now so plentiful. Old William Greenwood, of Eldwick, who was born early in the century, used to say that he could gather plenty of cranberries on the site of Ben Preston's garden when a boy.

RIVER-SIDE VIEW OF "OLD BINGLEY."

PART III.

MANORIAL HISTORY.

Antiquity of the Boundaries.

WITH the advent of William the Conqueror and the absorption of the old Anglo-Norse population in a new element and under a new code of laws, we reach a great revolution in the progress of local history, yet one that did not immediately violate a pre-existing order of government to the extent generally supposed. Customs as old, may be, as the first Anglian settlers continued to direct local affairs long after the Conquest (*vide Dom. Book*, I. 298 b). The boundaries, too, were fixed and immutable, and with the exception of the loss of Baildon (probably at De Burun's forfeiture, though it did not go to the Archbishops till 1222), the dominion of the parish from the Conquest forward has retained the same strong demarcation which I have explained belonged to it from at least the Brythonic or Welsh conquest—even antecedent to the Christian era—and down through the Anglian and Norse occupation. It is probably to the Anglians that Bingley owes its name. Let me now endeavour to explain

The Meaning of Bingley.

It is usually accounted the *field* of *Bing*, but before pronouncing on the origin of a name we should trace it back through the various changes it has undergone. Literally there was originally no such person as Bing. This name is really composed of two words: B-ing, signifying the *sons* of or *descendants* of some settler, probably called *Bui*, which means a dweller, as in Norse *nah-bui*, German *nach-bar*, Danish *nye-bœ*, a neighbour. It afterwards became a personal name, and *Bui-ing*, a family name, now seen in Boyen, Bowen, Bing, &c., which are English and Danish proper names at the present time. Bingley was therefore the *ley*, field or possession, of the descendants of Bui. It enters into the name of Bingham, in Notts., and perhaps in Bingen-on-the-Rhine, and Bingendorf-on-the-Nied, in Lorraine, the first of which, like the Yorkshire Bingley, came to William Paganel from Roger de Buinley, or Builli. So far as Bingley is concerned, the original settlers were undoubtedly kinsmen. The Anglo-Saxon *ing* is equivalent to the Scotch *Mac*, the Irish *O'*, and the English *son*. We have other examples of its occurrence in this district, such as Cott-*ing*-ley (field of the sons or descendants of Gotti, as in Gottingen); Cull-*ing*-worth (descendants of Coll, or Culle), Fris-*ing*-hall (hall of the sons of the tribe of Fries, which manor had its pleas in the lord's hall), Mann-*ing*-ham (home of the sons of Manan); all these being indicative of old Anglian or Norse clan stations. Without travelling the wide realm of England for comparisons, we have in the single county of Worcester a group of Domesday names almost the exact counterpart of those in the parish of Bingley; thus Buington (Bui-ing-ley), Mortune (Morton), Colingvic (Cullingworth), Hageleia (Hagenwurde, Hainworth), Hatete (Hateltun, Harden), Merlie and Mertelai (Marthelai, Marley). In Domesday we find again the name of Bingley written *Bingheleia*, which spelling seems to denote that the old Anglian compound was pronounced or handed in by a Danish or Norse inhabitant to the Norman compiler of Domesday. In the final *leia* we have a close affinity with the Norse and Icelandic *ljá*, equivalent to the Anglo-Saxon *ley*. Likewise the recorded *carucates* of Domesday support the same idea of Scandinavian occupancy.

The Coming of the Norman.

I have said that under the Viking rule a stiff tax was imposed on the Anglo-Saxon people, and in a hard-wrought (by this I mean a rather backward than a very fertile) and comparatively populous district like Bingley such a levy must have rancoured like a sore in the midst of the community, and many a murmur must have gone forth. To make matters worse for the home people, much of the spoil was remitted by these insatiable money-robbers to their poorer kinsfolk abroad. In 1040 Hardicanute wrested £32,000 of good Saxon money from the people of England, a large portion of which was shipped out of the country. Well may the water of delicious expectancy have dripped from the mouth of the future Conqueror when he heard of the strife between Saxon and Dane, and of the golden flow from the shores of England to the barren *dals* of Norway. He resolved on invasion, ostensibly to assist the Confessor against the potent Godwin, but really to crush for ever the Saxon power. It was in truth to be no half-hearted effort, but flame and steel were to do their very worst, and death or victory was to be the watchword of every archer and pikeman who set foot on English soil under the Norman flag. The fact that a compact was made *before* the invasion deciding that in case of victory the land was to be partitioned out among the Conqueror's counsellors and leaders, affords some indication of the determined character of the intended conflict, and reminds us of the events I shall describe hereafter, when, during the great Crusade to the Holy Land, the infidel Saracens trailed clanging chains with them on to the field of battle in order to carry away the Christians captive, so certain were they of victory. The first decisive blow was struck at Hastings; the south soon yielded, but in the north matters were not so easily settled. The old sturdiness and grit of the Anglo-Saxon and the old fierceness of the Viking pirate mingled to withstand the terrible onslaught of the Norman warriors. The great chief Archil, father of Gospatric, lord of Bingley, fought for very life and country, but eventually was obliged to flee (*see* page 78). York fell, and the whole country was harried and wasted in a manner such as hardly any other part of England had been. It is plain from the testimony of Domesday that there was not a man in Bingley who had the strength who did not in one way or another participate in the great struggle. The whole parish was utterly laid waste; that is to say, the

1,400 acres, or thereabouts, comprised within the manor and soke of Bingley, which had been in a profitable state of cultivation in 1066, were before 1086 utterly abandoned. The old church went to decay, the inhabitants were killed or had fled. There were no oxen to plough the land, and what people were left here, or how on earth they were living, God only knows. Let us now turn to

THE DOMESDAY RECORD,

from which there is more to be learnt than it is possible for me to describe in these pages. Briefly, there were four carucates for geld within this manor, and twelve if we include the soke. But these carucates were to be tilled by only half the number of ploughs; that is, one plough managed every two carucates of land. Now "land for one plough" means as much land as one plough will till in the course of a year, while the "carucate for geld" is the amount of land which one plough tills in one field in the course of a year. It is therefore obvious that in Bingley the manor was a two-course manor, and lay in two common-fields. If we accept the carucate as containing 120 acres, and this appears to be the unit after a great many comparisons in the carucated counties of England, we find there were 480 acres of ploughed land within the manor of Bingley before the Conquest. It was then valued at £4 annually, or £1 per carucate, if we exclude the soke, showing how greatly over-rated Bingley was, but it also shews that the land was as valuable here as the average of England in 1066, although the general deduction from Domesday is that land decreased in value going from east to west. In the west also the population was thinnest, but this does not appear to have been the case at Bingley. The number of people and comparative affluence of this district was doubtless in some measure owing to its distinguished ownership before the Conquest. I have spoken of Gospatric, and of the power and influence this noble proprietor of Bingley exercised in English affairs. It was a grand thing, indeed a splendid privilege, in that day to have so great a noble as Gospatric at the head of the estate, because the greater the influence of the lord of the manor and the more freedom and advantages the people really enjoyed, as we learn from the laws of Æthelred and Edward the Confessor. Indeed, this lordly influence continued to the advantage of Bingley for several centuries after the Conquest.

But to continue the Domesday record. We find that within the soke of Bingley were the following carucates :— Beldune (Baildon), two; Cotingelei (Cottingley), two; Helguic (Eldwick), one; Muceltuoit (Micklethwaite), one; Mardelei (Marley), one; and Hateltun (Harden), one; together eight carucates. The demarcation of this judicial area is fixed and certain, yet from the wording of the record we are unable to state the precise nature or manner of the soke, which is not the same everywhere, being affected often by local circumstances. It is safe, however, to conclude that the men of Baildon, Cottingley, &c., were answerable in all pleas of court and other undefined service to their lord, who by the acknowledgment of soke had the right to keep a court and exact suit within the province described. There was in Bingley a considerable area of wood pasture; in fact, one-fourth of the whole manor was woodland, affording pasture for numerous swine, and providing for the people in times of scarcity oak-mast, &c., for food. The venerable Norman rate-book—the oldest rate-book Bingley has to show—does not specify, as in the case of many other places, the number of swine these woods will fatten; but we may be sure that the people of Bingley in 1066 would have a plentiful supply, at any rate, of bacon and bread, not to mention a copious flow of beer, which was consumed in almost every arable parish. Indeed, it has been computed that one-third of the sown land in England contributed to the manufacture of beer. Everybody drank beer; it was for ages the provision of every meal to everyone but the poorest. In the 13th century we read that the canons of St. Paul's had a weekly allowance of 30 gallons of beer each, and they were by no means a privileged class in the matter of drink. Even so far back as Saxon times, we gather from the laws of Wihtred (A.D. 696) that excessive drinking was so common among clerics that special allusion is made to the fact by the law requiring any priest who is so drunk that he cannot properly perform the rites of baptism to desist from doing so until the Bishop should judge his case (*see Boniface Ep. to Cuthbert*, 10).

On the partition of lands, Erneis de Burun got Gospatric's manor of Bingley, as he also got his manor of Masham. Bingley, however, can have yielded precious little revenue to Burun, as long after the Conquest the district was in a deplorable state. From the earliest Pipe Roll (A.D. 1131) we learn that the whole of Yorkshire had yielded a geld of but £160, or not half the amount of such counties as Wiltshire and Norfolk, though it is obvious from the *donum* of 2nd Henry II. that Yorkshire was then recovering. Burun was ancestor of the noble house of Byron, which was settled in Lancashire in the reign of King John, on the marriage of the heiress of Clayton, of Clayton. In the *Black Book of Clayton* there are said to be upwards of 300 charters of the Byron family. The family, failing direct heirs early in the reign of Henry I., lost the manor of Bingley, which, along with many other Burun estates, was given by the Crown to William Paganel, who died about A.D. 1135. He was the founder of Drax Priory, to which he gave the church at Bingley. His brother Elias was Abbott of the neighbouring monastery at Selby. William Paganel, lord of Bingley, had married into the powerful family of Romille, who, according to the "Castle Evidences" at Skipton, gave name to the "great mountain, Rumels Moor." Cecily, daughter of Robert de Romille, married William de Meschines (founder of Embsay Priory), brother to Ranulph, Earl of Chester, who died *ca.* 1129. William Paganel's daughter Alicia, who was heiress of her mother, Avicia, daughter and co-heir of William de Meschines, became the second wife of Sir Robert de Gaunt, Lord High Chancellor of England, and owner of no fewer than 12½ Knights' Fees.* He owed £6 10s. for scutage in 1190. This Robert de Gaunt was lineal ancestor of Matilda, the wife of Thomas, son of Geoffery Chaucer, the distinguished

* *See* "Glossary of Historical Terms" in the author's *Romantic Richmondshire.*

poet, and author of the grand old *Canterbury Tales*. His son, Maurice de Gaunt, inherited Leeds and Bingley; the latter he raised to the status of a burgh†, borough, or market town, and obtained from King John in 1212 a charter to hold a weekly market. The said Maurice had concord with the Knights Templars in the same year. (*See Surtees Soc. Pub.* vol. 94, page 158; also the second volume of the *Thoresby Soc. Pub.*, pages 135 to 141; also the fourth volume, containing pedigree of Paganel, of Leeds, showing ancestry of the said Maurice de Gaunt.) The Bingley charter is as follows, and is a copy from the original Charter Rolls, 14th John :—

GRANT OF MARKET TO BINGLEY.

J dei gratia &c. Sciatis nos concessimus et hac carta nostra confirmavimus Maurico de Gant quod habeat unum mercatum apud manerium suum de Bingelay singulis septimanis per diem Dominicam, ita tamen quod mercatum illud non sit ad nocunnentum vicinorum mercatorum Quare volumus firmiter precipimus quod predictus Mauricus et heredes sui habeant predictum mercatum in predicto manerio de Bingely in perpetuum bene et in pace libere et quiete cum omnibus libertatibus et liberis consuetudinibus ad hujusmodi mercatum pertinentibus sicut predictum est T. domino P. Winton episcopo W. Comite Sarrum fratre nostro W. Comite Arundell Willielmo Brimerr Hugone de Neuill Johanne filio Hugonis Datum per manum magistri R. de Marisco archidiaconi Northumbr apud Turri Londoniensi xix die May anno regni nostri xiiii.

[TRANSLATION.]

John by the Grace of God &c. Know ye that we have granted and by this our Charter confirmed to Maurice de Gant that he have one market at his manor of Bingley every week on Sunday. So nevertheless that the same Market be not to the injury of neighbouring markets. Wherefore we will and firmly command that the aforesaid Maurice and his heirs have the aforesaid market in the aforesaid Manor of Bingley for ever well and in peace freely and quietly with all the liberties and free customs to such market pertaining as is aforesaid. Witness the Lord P. Bishop of Winchester W. Earl of Salisbury our brother W. Earl of Arundel William Brimerr Hugh de Nevill John Fitz Hugh. Given by the hand of Master R. de Marisco Archdeacon of Northumberland at the Tower of London the 19th day of May in the 14th year of our reign [A.D. 1212].

This important grant affords another instance of social development under a great manorial owner. Bingley

† For an explanation of this term *see* BOROUGH in Buchanan's *Dictionary of Science and Technical Terms.*

Market House and Butter Cross, Main Street, Bingley.

subsequently possessed the right, a very important one at that time, of sending two members to Parliament, although there appears to be no record of the fact until the 11th year of King Edward I. (1282), when it was ordered that four knights be sent from each county, and two men from each borough and market town. The Parliament then met at York for counties north of the Trent; but unfortunately the returns of its constituents have not been discovered.

The monks of Drax owned the church, and it is not improbable that the markets were originally held in the churchyard, a custom that was abolished by Act of Parliament, 13th Edward I. (1284). But the old practice, in spite of this enactment, prevailed long afterwards. The Sabbath, too, was the most convenient day for holding the markets in many parishes, where a number of villages lay remote from the church; and the ways being rough and difficult, there was the great advantage of being able to attend divine service and dispose of produce or make any purchases at one and the same time. The market-day was subsequently altered to Tuesday, but an epidemic of fever, locally known as the "Black Plague," which broke out in Bingley in 1789, sent a great many regular frequenters to Otley, and the Bingley market never afterwards recovered its former importance. The Market House was erected in 1753.

Maurice de Gaunt being deprived in 1216, Bingley was retained by the Earl of Chester, who held the manor of the King *in capite* for the service of half a Knight's Fee. In 1229 it was granted to William de Cantelupe in the terms of the following charter :—

Henry King &c. greeting. We have inspected the charter of Randolph Earl of Chester and Lincoln in these words Randolph Earl of Chester and Lincoln to all present and to come who shall see or hear this present charter greeting know ye that I have given and granted and by this my present charter have confirmed to William de Cantelupe junior for his homage and service the whole vill of Bingelay with all its appurtenances and demesnes services and free [customs] and countrymen with all liberties and easements to the same as well within the vill as without belonging. To have and to hold of me and my heirs to him and his heirs as freely fully and quietly as I the same fully freely and quietly ever had or held the same Saving to me and my heirs the knight's fees which are without to the aforesaid land belonging doing therefore to me and my heirs from him and his heirs service of half a knight for all service and exaction to me and my heirs from the aforesaid land belonging. And I and my heirs to the said William and his heirs the said land against all men and women will warrant. In witness whereof this present charter strengthened with my seal I have caused him to have These being witnesses Philip de Orreby then justice of Chester Hugh Despencer Walter de Dayuill Emeric de Lacy Richard Fitun William de Vernun Eudo Kalecot Ralph de Carevill, Philip de Orreby junior Ralph de Say, Richard de Coventry William de Benigsworth his clerk and many others. We having ratified this grant have confirmed the same for us and our heirs. These being witnesses H. de burg &c. H. Earl of Hereford Philip de Albin Hugh de Neuill Stephen de Sedgrave Ralph son of Nicholas John son of Philip and others. Given &c. at Westminster xxvi. day of February.

In 1252, Robert de Cantelupe obtained the right of Free Warren at Bingley, and in the same year his son George was born at the Castle of Abergavenny, which had been the inheritance of his mother. These Cantelupes were of Norman origin, but the English family was undoubtedly named after the manor of Cantalupe, in Shropshire. Robert de Cantelupe was a Crusader in 1096, and bore for arms lozengy, or and sable. Walter de Cantelupe occurs in the oldest Pipe Roll, A.D. 1131. The family was settled in Yorkshire at an early period, but does not appear to have had any residence in Bingley. (*See* my *Nidderdale*, pages 135, 139, &c.) William de Cantelupe died in 1254, when his son George, the next lord of Bingley, was only two years old. The latter died when he was a young man of 21, and by an inquisition *post-mortem*, taken in 1273, we obtain an interesting glimpse of the prosperous state of Bingley at this time.

BINGELE. EXTENT OF THE LAND, &C., OF GEORGE DE CANTELUPE, made by Robert Vileyn, Hugh de Hannewrth, Simon Vileyn, Hugh de Ledes, John de Kihele, John son of Walter of the same, John de Marthele, Hugh de Leyes, Richard de Marthele, Walter de Harnewrthe, Lovetot de Bingele, John Vileyn, William de Helewike, and John de Gildestede, who say that

There is no capital messuage.

There is a water-mill worth yearly £8.

Formerly there were 30 acres of land in demesne let to farm, which yield with meadow by the year 36/-.

A certain meadow there is worth by the year 10/-.

Toll with the oven is worth yearly 15/-.

There are 21 free tenants who pay yearly £4 0s. 8d., of whom eight do suit at the Court of Bingele from three weeks to three weeks.

Richard de Kihele holds 2 carucates of land in Kihele at 8d. rent, and owes suit to the court.

There are in Bingele burgesses who pay yearly 36/5 at Martinmas and Whitsuntide, and bondmen who hold 27 bovates of land with 9 assarts, and they pay yearly at the said terms £4 18s. 9d. The Court of Bingele is worth in common years one marc. Pannage with wood thrown down by the wind is worth in common years one marc.

Milisand, wife of Ivo la Suche, and John, son of Henry de Hastings, are heirs of George de Cantilupe; Milisand of full age, and John aged 15 years.

There is no advowson because the Prior of Drax has the church in his own use, and there is not a knight's fee. The jurors know not of whom the said tenements are held.

Sum Total ... £23 2s. 9d.

A considerable dissertation might be written on the economic facts pertaining to this inquisition, and from it might be drawn an instructive picture of the social and civil life of the parish six centuries ago. In the first place, we are told there was no capital messuage in 1273, although there had been thirty acres of land in demesne, which fact knocks on the head any theory regarding the existence of a tenantable castle or capital mansion-house at this important period. There was a valuable mill (doubtless on the site of the present mill at Bingley Bridge), which must have enforced mulcture from the whole soke, and a good investment it was, surely, to its owner, as its value was equal to a full third of the profits of the whole parish. The lord, too, it will be noted, had a public oven, whereat the tenants were obliged to take their bread, and pay a certain toll called *furnage*.* Bingley had then its own manor court, which, though the outcome of the feudal system, marked a certain social advance, advantageous to both lord and tenant, and possessing powers not wholly obsolete even at the present day. As there was no *aula*, or capital messuage, these early courts were doubtless held at an inn. There were both free tenants and tenants in bondage within the manor, and it

* There was a public bakehouse in Leeds, at the top of Kirkgate, which in 1609 was worth £120 per annum. It was abolished in Thoresby's time. There was also a similarly ancient bakehouse at Skipton, known recently as "Seddon's House."

was at the Court Baron the freeholders only were bound to attend. The bondmen, though paying rent, were mere slaves, held as chattels, like the stock of a farm, and might be bought or sold any time as part or parcel of the estate. This species of servile tenure prevailed in Airedale to a late period, and was not actually abolished by statute till the reign of Charles II. (*see* my *Airedale*, page 200, &c.).

To continue. George de Cantilupe being dead in 1273, his sister Milisent, who married John de Montalto, inherited Bingley; but on the death of Montalto, *s.p.*, she married, secondly, Eudo la Zouche of Ashby, co. Leicester, who died in 1289. (William la Zouche was Archbishop of York in 1342.) The manor of Bingley next passed to Alianore la Zuche (*see Kirkby's Inquest*, A.D. 1284), and in 1302 John de Harcourt, who had married the heiress of Eudo la Zouche, answered for half a Knight's Fee in Bingley, at the rate of 20/-. In 1315, he was returned lord of the manor of Bingley. From him is lineally descended His Grace the Most Rev. Edward Vernon Harcourt, Archbishop of York (1807-47), whose grandson is the eminent statesman, Sir Wm. Harcourt, late Liberal leader of the House of Commons. In 1325, William de Harcourt, at the age of 26, succeeded his father to the manorial title, as appears by a royal grant obtained by an inquisition, dated 19th Edward II.,* taken at Bingley before Simon de Grymmesby, the King's escheator. It then appeared that the manor of Bingley was held of the King in chief by knight service: to wit by homage, fealty, and scutage, when it happens for half a knight's fee for all service. It was also stated that the said manor was then worth per annum in all issues according to the true value 100 shillings. It will be remembered that the revenue of the manor, exclusive of the church, in 1273 amounted to upwards of £23; but in the interval up to the date of above grant, 1325, there had been the disastrous inroads of the Scots, following the victory at Bannockburn in 1314.

These predatory incursions brought ruin and loss of revenue on many Yorkshire parishes; Craven was terribly

* In 1324 this monarch probably passed through Bingley *en route* to Skipton Castle (*see* MORTON).

harried, and Bingley did not escape. The canons of Bolton Abbey, we are told, took refuge in Skipton Castle, though the town was reduced to ashes. The raiders drove away the cattle, pillaged the churches, destroyed the granges, and committed other enormities. Bradford, Guiseley, Knaresborough, and other towns were sacked, and at Ripon they were paid 1,000 marks to save the town from burning. In 1320, Bolton Abbey was again pillaged, and the story we hear in many places is, "There are no tenants, the cottages have been burnt." It was useless sowing corn. In 1325, the lord's dues at Bingley were declared to be worth, "in all issues," 100 shillings, while a few years before (1318), the King having authorised an enquiry to be made as to the amount of damage done by the Scottish raiders, with the object of ascertaining the value of church livings, it was found that Bingley had suffered considerably, and that the living, which in 1291 had been fixed as worth £30 per annum, was now declared to be worth only 22 marks, or £14 13s. 4d. Keighley remained the same as in 1291, viz., £8. Was this spared because the church was supposed to have been dedicated to St. Andrew? The value of the soke must have seriously declined, and this may have been let out to farm, as it was not unusual for the King to grant away a demesne manor, and retain not only the exclusive soke (*i.e.* the soke over the pleas of the Crown), but also the common soke in his hand; while, on the other hand, a great man may by purchase acquire soke within his own manor or over land not his own (*vide Leg. Henr.* 20 §2).

Bingley was held by the Harcourts only till the close of the 14th century, when Elizabeth, daughter and heir of Richard Harcourt, married Sir Thomas Astley, Kt. For more than two centuries the manor was held by this old Staffordshire family.* In 39-40th Elizabeth (1596-7) the manor, with appurtenances, was sold by Thos. Astley, Esq., and Margery, his wife, to Anthony Walker for the sum of £400 sterling. This transfer I shall refer to again in the chapter on CHRONICLES OF THE SIXTEENTH CENTURY.

* *See Astley Family Collections*, including 20 pedigrees, &c.

Richard I. reviewing the Crusaders at Vezelai, in 1190.

BINGLEY DURING THE CRUSADES.

THE importance of Bingley as a centre of religious life before the Conquest (a subject I have discussed on another page) was fully sustained by the interest it afterwards took in the prosecution of the Crusades to the Holy Land. Extensive possessions in our parish were given at a very early date in support of that object. Some gifts were apparently made even before the Priors of Drax obtained the church property within fifty years after the accession of William the Norman. Many of these gifts are of such antiquity that it is now impossible to say how the bulk of the possessions of the Crusaders came to be held by them, and their tenures in many other places besides Bingley go back before the time of the monasteries, though hardly a charter exists to prove when or how they became possessed of their fees. But in the multiplied subinfeudations which took place in the 11th and 12th centuries (a practice afterwards restrained by statute) it was not uncommon for the knights to grant out their lands to laymen, who gave them once more to the religious houses in their respective localities. (*See* Whitaker's *Craven*, 3rd ed., page 28.) The Priory of Bolton-in-Wharfedale held many estates by this tenure, and in Bingley the brethren of the Hospital of St. John received an annual rent of one shilling for a piece of land lying on the south side of the church, between the road and river Aire, which had been given to the canons of Drax by Richard de Castelhay.

These Crusades to the Holy Land, so far as they relate to Yorkshire, are amongst the most remarkable episodes in the history of the county. From the period of the institution of the Knights Hospitallers of St. John of Jerusalem, some forty years after the Conquest, up to about the year 1260, when Richard Plantagenet, Earl of Cornwall, founded Knaresborough Priory for the purpose of redeeming Christians taken captive during the Crusades, hundreds of thousands of pounds had been expended and hundreds of thousands of lives had been lost in the effort to rescue Palestine from the infidels, which, however, finally fell into their hands in 1291. In the time of Richard, Cœur de Lion, when public enthusiasm for the salvation of the East reached its zenith, there was hardly a man of substance who was not willing to give away even his last acre, or lay down his life for the cause which all had at heart. It is said that in response to the King's call to arms, thousands mustered under the banners of their respective knights, and swore they were ready to "penetrate mountains and walls of brass," should they (the lords of the soil) but give a nod! Many a wealthy Yorkshire knight, including many an ancestor of old Bingley families, such as the Gaunts, Cantilupes, Harcourts, Ferrands, &c., made the difficult pilgrimage to the Holy Land, returning, mayhap, with the blunted battle-axe or scars of conflict upon them, and with many a story of strange adventure upon their lips.

It was largely the warlike tendencies of the age; the desire to satisfy the military ardour for fresh conquests and glory after the settlement of the Norman Conquest, when peace reigned in the land, that brought about these great Crusades. Churches and monasteries were everywhere being rebuilt or established, and the people were daily listening to the story of Our Saviour's sufferings in the Holy Land, and the wrongs and sacrileges which had been perpetrated by the infidels in places specially sacred to the Christians. Without enquiring too closely into the theological aspects of the question, they felt themselves wronged, and thus the whole world of Christians ultimately rose in one grand corps to wreak vengeance on the violators in that remote clime. It was a gigantic craze; a wild craze; a Craze with a capital C. Hallam speaks of it as an "epidemical frenzy"; but it was an epidemic of no short duration, continuing as it did, with more or less severity, for more than two centuries. The Mohammedans were just as firm believers in their own light as the Christians were, and they greatly out-numbered them.

They were, too, a turbulent, hardy, warlike race. Both they and the Christians believed, though differently, in a future Paradise, and both thought the certain way to it was by death in battle with an Unbeliever. It was Greek fighting Greek.

The first Crusade took place in 1096, when it is computed that from 800,000 to 1,000,000 Christians lost their lives. The western armies were not only ignorant of the character of the country, but were totally unacquainted with the cruel artifices of the barbarous and cunning Mohammedans. Such means of destruction they had never before seen or heard of, and they found themselves unable to cope with the difficulties that surrounded them on all sides. Showers of a fearful consuming liquid, called Greek Fire, met them whenever they got within range of the enemy. The infidels also played many tricks in order to lure the Christians to destruction. On one occasion, a contemporary chronicler tells us, as the two armies were encamped on either side of a river, a Christian observed a large water-melon floating in the water not far from the shore bordering upon the Christian camp. He jumped in, thinking to obtain a prize, when to the consternation of the onlookers he was seen to be dragged rapidly to the opposite bank. The water-melon had been scooped out so as to admit the insertion of the head of a stalwart infidel, who was an expert swimmer, and he dragged his man away to be mercilessly crucified, within sight of his comrades, in the enemy's camp. The suffering, cruelty, and miseries undergone in this single campaign would, one would have thought, have been sufficient to quell the ardour of any further enterprises in the same direction. But otherwise. All who died in the cause were accounted martyrs, and the promise of eternal bliss was vouchsafed to them. Incited by the priests, there was a universal cry for vengeance on the whole race of Mohammed, and so once again men began to array themselves in "the armour of God."

In the meantime there was called into existence an order of military monks, whose chief duty was to shelter and attend upon sick and way-worn pilgrims journeying to and from the Holy Land. They were known as the

Knights Hospitallers of St. John of Jerusalem, but this St. John was not the Evangelist, nor yet the Baptist, but a certain Cyprist, surnamed the Charitable, who had been patriarch of Alexandria. Shortly afterwards, about A.D. 1120, a second and somewhat similar order was established, called the Knights Templars, or Soldiers of the Red Cross, because on their habit of white, which was worn over a suit of mail, there was displayed a blood-red cross, this being the symbol of martyrdom. The principal duty of the Templars was to take charge of the highways, and by protecting the pilgrims through the difficult and little-known passes that led to the Holy Land thus minimise the dangers of the road. They also took the field, and were in the van at all the great battles against the Saracens, including those of Gaza, Jaffa, and Ramleh, as well as at the relentless sieges of Jerusalem, and the still more terrible one of that at Acre, when some hundreds of thousands of human lives were sacrificed, and the country and rivers ran with blood.

These two great military orders rose rapidly in favour; the people of Bingley, or rather their over-lords, rejoicing in the cause, and within a comparatively short period both the Hospitallers and Templars were in possession of enormous wealth. Between them, it is computed, they owned 28,000 manors and farms, about 19,000 of these belonging to the older order of Knights Hospitallers. In Yorkshire they had extensive properties, and in Bingley some of their possessions can to this day be identified by the stone lanterns and double crosses still preserved on the buildings appertaining thereto. All this vast wealth, amounting to millions of pounds sterling per annum, was squandered in these gigantic and for the most part fruitless expeditions to the East.

In 1147, a second Crusade was undertaken, in which the Emperor Conrad III. and Louis VII. of France took part, each with 70,000 cavalry, and an immense number on foot, but nearly everyone perished in the campaign. Then came the third great Crusade, commenced in 1190, in which the flower and chivalry of Europe were engaged, with the three principal European potentates at the head, namely, the Roman Emperor, Frederick II.; King Philip Augustus of France; and Richard, Cœur de Lion, King of England, the latter of whom was absent four years, including 14 months spent in prison. The deeds and exploits of this gigantic expedition exceed anything that happened before, and may be compared with anything that is most astonishing and illustrious in the records of history or romance. The chroniclers of the period tell us that the renown of this expedition spread so quickly that tens of thousands of pilgrims, including men of all ages—the greybeard and the youth in his teens—besides numberless women and children, flocked under the banners of the knights, and prayed to be allowed to accompany the armies in so glorious an enterprise. Monks and priests quitted the cloister for the camp, and exchanging the cowl for the sword, wished to prove themselves truly Christ's soldiers. When in the spring of 1190 the united armies assembled on the field of Vezelai (*see* illustration on page 114), the spectacle was one of unexampled greatness and splendour. Representing the chivalry and blazonry of three empires, there appeared thousands of mounted warriors, each bearing lance and battle-axe, and upon his shield was pictured the arms or device of his family, while the spears and lances of 200,000 foot-men glittered in the brilliant sun! Never since in the history of warfare has such vast multitudes been gathered together, united as they were in one common bond, and determined to perish or retrieve the insult that had been given to their guiding Light and Master.

Meanwhile Saladin had mustered a vast army of trained warriors, together with the forces of all Asia, from the Tigris as far as India, as well as from the parts between the Tigris and Euphrates. Thence and from the southern districts there came hundreds of thousands of swarthy sling-men inured to the hardships of war, followed by troupes of women and their families, even to the babe, bearing and trailing cuffs and chains wherewith to bind the Christians captive, so reckoned they on victory. From Africa, too, there came countless tribes, the Getulians, Nadaburi, and Numidians, who came dancing to war to the spirit-rousing strains of cymbals and pipes; while from the scorching south streamed hordes of black Moors, or Mawritians, with their bows of bamboo and poisoned arrows. The earth, it is said, trembled under the vast hordes. Thus it was the two great Mahommedan divisions of the globe attacked the third and only one which acknowledged the name of Christ.

Into the details of this mighty conflict I have not space, nor is it needful, to enter; sufficient if I make some brief allusions to those Yorkshire families, and particularly to those identified with this district, who participated in it. There was the famous Roger de Mowbray, who was taken prisoner at the desperate battle of Tiberias; Ralph de Glanville, whose heiress founded Coverham Abbey (he fell at Acre); Robert Trussebut, a kinsman of the founder of the Preceptory at Ribston; the De Stutevilles, owners of the Forest of Knaresboro'; the De Courtenays and Albemarles, with the knights in their pay; and Roger de Harcourt, who distinguished himself bravely at the victory in Cyprus. From the chronicles of an eye-witness, Geoffrey de Vinsauf, we learn many particulars of the heroic conduct of the French and English knights, and of the dangers and hardships they suffered in their marches and contests against the Saracens. At the siege of Acre, when an attempt was made to storm the city by a single desperate onslaught of 12,000 fearless Danes—not a hundred of whom returned alive—we are told of a remarkable incident that happened during the confusion of the Christians that followed. A knight named Ferrand, who had been wielding his battle-axe with great vigour, got hemmed in by a band of Saracens, and was so badly bladed and pierced that he fell, and was left for dead among the heaps of slain. But in the night-time this strong man rallied, and managed with difficulty to reach the camp. But his face was so cut that it hung in shreds, and his body so much gashed and covered with blood that he could not be recognised, and it was some time before the guards accepted him as one of their side and allowed him to pass. Whether this Ferrand was any ancestor or ally of the Ferrands of Skipton and Bingley I do not know, but the Ferrands became janitors, or guards-men, of Skipton

Castle under the Earls of Albemarle, and bear for their crest a cubit arm wielding a Crusader's axe.

In this part of Yorkshire the Templars were represented by three houses, namely, Temple Hurst, founded by the Hastings family in 1152; Temple Newsham, founded in 1181; and Ribston, of the foundation of Robert de Ros, in 1217. In the organisation which the order attained the country was divided into a number of balliæ, and in every place where they had considerable possessions they established superintendents, called in this country *preceptors* (receivers), and in foreign countries more commonly *commendatores*, whence commanders and commanderies. The Knights Hospitallers were also similarly organised, and wherever they had large properties they held their courts and had similar receiving-houses. In and about Bingley they had, as I have said, many estates, and the courts of the manors of Bingley, Crosley, and Pudsey were sometimes held at Bingley and sometimes at the preceptory at Newland, near Wakefield. Portions of this ancient court-house of the Crusaders still remain attached to the present Newland Hall, which, with some 800 acres of land, was purchased in 1860 by the late Mr. Locke from the trustees of Sir Matthew Dodsworth, Bart. About fifty years ago the chapel attached to the preceptory was taken down, and some of its old glass bearing coats of arms was removed to Thornton Watlass.

Both the Hospitallers and Templars enjoyed many privileges, immunities, and revenues from various sources, such as the right to hold markets, multure from wind and water-mills, tributes of poultry, eggs, and swine, and services of so many days in a year for ploughing, harrowing, hay-making, sheep-washing and shearing, mending ditches, leading stones, and so on. They were exempt from aids and various kinds of taxes, from stallage and pontage, and from all forced labour on royal parks, castles, or palaces, with right to take timber and essart woods which they possessed within the limits of royal forests, without leave of the royal bailiffs. Their houses also enjoyed the great privilege of sanctuary, by which anyone who had committed a felony or misdemeanour of whatsoever kind was, with certain reservations, safe from harm. This remarkable custom, which is first prescribed by the laws of Ina (*ca.* A.D. 690), was abolished by King James I. in 1625.

From early times all who lived on lands that had been granted to the Crusaders were obliged under a penalty to erect a stone or stones in the form of a double cross upon their houses, or in some conspicuous place in the walls enclosing their domains. This was proof visible of their identity with the Knights of the Cross, and of exemption from such suits and services as I have enumerated. As early as 1345 I find that at the Court of Bingley the Prior of Drax was mulcted in the heavy fine of 3s. 4d. "because he has not erected the cross." As late as the reign of Elizabeth it was still penal to neglect the erection of the cross. Thus at the Court of Bingley held in 1600 it was enforced:

> That everie man that houldeth any land of this manor shall sett a double crosse of his house or ground at or before the 25th day of March next in the most viewe to be seene that hath not one already, on payne XLs. every man.

Such double crosses may still be seen on buildings at Cottingley, St. Ives, and Greenhill, and formerly at Eldwick, &c. Although some of the immunities claimed have become obsolete by an altered state of life, yet some of them are still in force; never having been annulled by the dissolution of their houses, with the monasteries, in the time of Henry VIII. Many interesting facts concerning these old local properties of the Crusaders are preserved among the records at St. Ives. Thus going back five and a half centuries we learn something of the then tenants of Greenhill, which from its name and documentary evidence must have been cultivated grass-land, amid heathery moors, soon after the Conquest. In 1388, John Heyr acknowledges rent per annum 4d., with arrears for two years of tenements in Greenhill, therefore to levy of the aforesaid John for 8d. for these arrears. The same John also acknowledged rent per annum 2d. for tenements which belonged to Alice, who was wife of John Millison, in Greenhill, with arrears for five years, &c. There had been a steady decline in rents from the time of the wars with

Scotland, as I have explained a few pages back, and there was no genuine return of prosperity for fully a century and a half afterwards. In 1338, Ralph, son of Symon, *clerk*, came to Bingley, and shewed a certain charter, by which he purchased his tenement in the Leys, namely, the Hospital Rode, which contains 6 acres of land, of Hugh le Marshall, but he knows not what estate the aforesaid Hugh has in the said tenement, therefore he places in respect to the next, if the same Ralph had any estate, the aforesaid Hugh held the same.

Then in the same year, 1338, we have an inquisition taken by Robert le Longe, William, son of Hugh, Walter of Ravenrode, William, son of John of the Leyes, jurors, who say upon their oath that John of Paris brews contrary to the Assize, therefore he is amerced 6d. Also William atte Kyrksteyel brews and bakes contrary to the Assize, therefore in amercement 5d. William, son of Alan Barkar, brews and is a rogue, contrary to the Assize, therefore is amerced 5d. Again, they say that Roger, son of Richard de Stanbyry, struck and other enormities committed on Ralph, son of Symon, *clerk*, tenant of the Hospital, therefore he is summoned by letters of citation. In 1345, William of Paris and his wife were fined 6d. for brewing and selling ale contrary to the Assize of the manor. In 1415, Robert Smyth and his wife are similarly fined 4d. for brewing beer and baking bread, whilst Robt. Watson, of Keighley, is fined 2d. for receiving the same.

These indictments against Bingley brewers have reference to the precautions that were taken in every manor and in every town and village throughout the country to prevent the adulteration of drink with peony seed, garlic, salt, and other provocatives to thirst, and the ale-house keepers were forbidden to tap their ale until they had given notice to the official ale-taster that they had ale on sale, and until he had certified that it was pure and of proper age *(see Fourth Report of Comm. Hist. MSS.)*. Ale, as I have before said, formed an important constituent in the daily dietary at this time, when few other drinks were known. Tea and coffee had not been heard of. The law also obliged every ale-house keeper to hang a lantern at his door, which was to be lighted in the dark days until nine every evening, when it was to be put out and the inn closed. Specimens of the old tavern lanterns, cut in stone, may be seen on the farm at Beckfoot, and also on Harden Hall.

At the Court of the Prior of the Hospital of Saint John of Jerusalem held at the Commandery of Newland, in 1482, an inquisition concerning certain tenants in Bingley was taken on the oaths of Walter Bayldon, Robert Wodde, John Wood, and Robert Champynot, jurors. They say that William Stede, Richard Wilkinson, Richard Rawson, John Heton, Christopher Morevill, and Thomas Cromoke owe suit to the Court; but they came not, therefore each of them is amerced 2d. It is also ordered that each tenant erect a cross upon his land, under pain for each cross not erected 6s. 8d.

At the court held 26th August, 42nd Elizabeth (1600), the Jury found that the Probate of all Testaments and the granting of all administrations of all and every person and persons dying under the cross, or upon any lands belonging to the Hospital of St. John of Jerusalem, doth of right belong to Her Majesty. And that Her Majesty's Steward of the same possessions for the time being hath used "tyme out of mynd of man" to prove the wills and grant the administrations after the death as well of all Her Majesty's free tenants as of all others dying under the cross, &c. The Jury further say that Her Majesty ought to have, after the death or change of every of her free tenants, a "releyf certayne," which is two years' rent. Furthermore, a pain was laid that every tenant belonging to the manor of Cottingley, within Bingley, do from henceforth grind all their corn at Her Majesty's mill in Cottingley growing upon his grounds in his occupation upon pain of every default 6s. 8d. It was also ordered that Thomas Dixon and Walter Kighley do bring in their milner at the next court to be sworn, and that his moulter-dish be tried, and his strike and peck likewise be tried, upon pain of 20s. This was a requirement of the manorial courts for a long period.

At the court held at Cottingley, April 3rd, 1616, the Jury present that William Long, Edmund Fairburne, William Scott, William Wright, and John Symson "be common typlers and ale-house keepers," and that they have not kept the Assize of Ale, but sold contrary to the statute in that case provided. Therefore they are amerced as in the statute. The Jury lay further in pain that the administrators, executors, or dealers with the goods and chattels of Richd. Jowet, late of Helwicke, deceased, who died under the cross at Helwicke aforesaid, shall make their appearance here at the next court, and then prove the will of the deceased or take administration of his goods upon pain of 30s.

In 1617, at the court held at Cottingley, with William Baildon as foreman, the jurors find that William Francke made affray and drew blood upon William Lange, of Cottingley, and they amerce him 10s.; viz., 6s. 8d. for the blood, and 3s. 4d. for the affray. They further find that the said William Francke made affray and drew blood upon Steven Francke, his father, therefore 10s.

Further, Abraham Willman be amerced 3s. 4d. "for playing football upon the Sabbath."

They also find that certain inhabitants of Cottingley have suffered their swine to go unyoked, as it is presented to them, viz.: Stephen Franck, three; Robert Lister, four; William Long, two; and John Wright, one; and therefore they are amerced for every swine 6d. All these records reflect the customs and manors of the times. Football, for example, had been a national sport from at least the time of Edward III., and it had been played on the Sabbath; but pulpit admonitions against the declared profanation of the Lord's Day ultimately led to some restrictions being put upon the practice of this and other games. It is evident they were strictly applied in the Bingley district up to the time of King James' proclamation, published 24th May, 1618, whereby it was ordered that "after divine service our good people be not disturbed, letted, or discouraged from any lawful recreation, such as dauncing, either for men or women, archery for men, leaping, vaulting, or any other such harmless recreation." During the Commonwealth this order was revoked, and the King's declaration burned by the common hangman.

In 1619 we have an account, in the form of rents and hereditaments accruing to Richd. Sunderland, Esq., of Coley Hall, of certain houses and farms in Bingley lately belonging to the Knights of St. John of Jerusalem. In this rental appears Marley Hall, in the occupation of Wm. Currer, Esq., for which John Rishworth, gent., acknowledges 1s. 6d. The same John Rishworth pays 6d. for a tenement in Thwaites occupied by Robt. Francis Wilkinson, and in Thwaites another tenement, late the lands of Sir Thomas Fairfax, Kt., is paid for by Christ. Hall, 6d. John Rawson has a tenement in Greenhill, for which he pays 5s., and he acknowledges also for parcel of certain lands and tenements called Roide Field, the old farm above Marley, belonging to Mr. Ferrand, where is a stone bearing the initials and date: I·PW·H·I·H·R·1660, Wm. Whitley pays 1s. for a tenement at Greenhill, and there are a number of free rents at Cottingley, &c., paid by the Rawsons and Morvells, of Beckfoot, &c. Also Wm. Baildon pays for one tenement and certain lands in Baildon called Temple Roide *als* Temple Rode-ynge and Temple Croft, as tenants-at-will the sum of 4s.

Richard Sunderland died in 1638, and appointed his sons Samuel and Peter executors of his will. Samuel came to reside at Hill End, Harden, and his brother Peter at Fairweather Green. A long list of tenants within the manor of Bingley at this time is interesting, as supplying us with the names of those local families who occupied the lands and houses once belonging to the old Crusaders. It is as follows:—

An Abstract of the Ffynes and Amercements within the Manor of Bingley from 1631 to 1638.

John Savil, gent. for not doeinge his suyte and service for May 1631, xiid; and for not comeinge to doe his fealty and pay his releife xs; 2th Decr. 1631 for the like xis; 24th April 1632 xiid; 17th April 1633 xis; 2th May 1634 xiid; 22th Aprill 1635 xiid, in all... ... ... £1 16 0

Lewes Sheffeild, gent. for not doeing his suyte and service for May 1631 xiid; 2th Dec. 1631 for the like xiid,

	£	s	d
24th Aprill 1632 for ye like xiid, 17 April 1633 for the like xiid	0	4	0
Willm. ffranke, gent. for not comeinge to p'forme the last will of his father for May 1631 xs; 2th Dec. 1631 for the like xs; 17th Aprill 1633 for the like xs, and for not doeinge his suyte xiid, 22th Apr. 1635 for ye like xiid	1	12	0
Thomas Brooke for not doeinge his suyte for May 1631 iiijd, 24th April 1637 for the like iiijd	0	0	8
Willm. Rawson for not doeinge his suyte for May 1631 iiijd, 24th of Aprill 1637 for the like iiijd	0	0	8
Robt. Emott for not doeing his suyte for May 1631 4d, 2th Dec. 1631 for the like 4d, 24th Aprill 1632 for ye like 4d, 2th May, 1634, for the like 4d, 24th Aprill 1637 for the like 4d, 18th April 1638 for the like 4d	0	2	0
Jonas Lister for not doeinge his suyte for May 1631 4d for not comeinge to make his accompts xs; 2th Dec. 1631 for the like xs; 22nd April 1635 for not doeinge his suite 4d, 24th Aprill 1637 4d, 18th Aprill 1638 4d. ...	1	1	4
The following are charged "for not doeinge suite."			
John Whitley 1s 8d; Sam Longbothome 2s; Henry Lambe 1s 4d; Thomas Townend 2s 4d; Thomas ffirth 1s 4d; Lawrence Taylor 1s 4d; Anthoney Whitley 1s 8d; John Barber 4d; Abra. Bines 1s 4d; James Beane 4d; Stephen Dobson 8d; James Walker 8d; John Bairstowe 8d; Lawrence ffarrer 4d; Richard Hogg 4d; Willm. ffisher 4d; Thomas Angram 1s; John Crabtree 8d; John Hudson 4d; Robt. Hardcastle 4d; Thomas Holdsworth 4d; Robert Keighley 4d; Humfrey Hartley 1s 8d; Willm. Hartley 1s; Thomas Morvell 1s 4d; Walter Taylor 8d; Leonard Exley 8d; the execr. of Willm. Baildon gent. 2s; Stephen Slater 4d; John Rawson 8d; Robt. Hall 4d; John Hustler 4d; Jonas Illingworth 1s; Robt. Blakey 4d; Stephen Piggells 4d; Samuel Tennant 4d; ffrancis Leach 4d; Symeon Collier 4d; Richard Snawden 4d; George Beane 4d; ffrancis Wilkinson 4d; *in all*	1	12	4
Thomas Mitton of Baildon and Jno. Mitton of Hawkesworth for not comeinge to make their accompts according to a payne laid, for May 1631 10s; 2th Dec. for ye like 10s; 24th Apr. 1632 20s; 17 Apr. 1633 10s	2	10	0
James Sagar and Willm. Rawson for a ffine for haveinge the adm. of the goods of John Rawson deceased graunted unto them 18th of Aprill 1638	0	10	0
Jennett Midgley, for a ffine of adm. of the goods of Willm. Midgley her late husband deceased, 18 April 1638 ...	0	5	0
Sum of Bingley Estreats...	£9	14	0

Beckfoot Farm, formerly belonging to the Knights Crusaders.

Although the residences of the tenants are not stated, many of them may be identified, such as the Saviles of Marley. It was John Savile who built Marley Hall in 1627, and it was his wife apparently who died there, and was buried at Keighley in 1688. But he is stated to have died at Marley a widower in 1629, and left an only son, Robert, "a wastrel," who squandered his patrimony, and disposed of his inheritance to the above Samuel Sunderland in 1666. The Sheffields were akin to the Fairfaxes, of Thwaites and Denton; Mary, daughter of Edmund Sheffield, Earl of Mulgrave, having married Ferdinando (*ob.* 1648), father of Thomas, Lord Fairfax, of Civil War fame. The Franks were long resident at Cottingley Hall; Stephen Slater and John Hudson also lived at Cottingley. Anthony Whitley was of Rishworth Hall, and died there in 1639. Jonas Lister lived at Lees in the Hospital Royd; Sam. Longbottom was living at Eldwick "under the cross" in 1619, and in 1684 John Rawson was living at Greenhill, and Wm. Midgley at Marchcote.

The Rawsons also lived at the picturesque old farm at Beckfoot, which, according to a date over the doorway, was built in 1617. It was also a property of the Knights of St. John of Jerusalem, whose symbol of proprietorship is still indicated by the stone lanterns at the gable corners. In the cow-house opposite are some remains of what has been conjectured to be a pre-Reformation chapel, but the masonry has every appearance of later date. A large pointed arch of substantial masonry occupies the east end, the supporting columns being mortised evidently for the reception of a cross-beam or screen. The walls and roof have been altered and partly rebuilt this century, and only a portion of the north wall is original. It has a doorway (now blocked), and close to it and the "chancel-arch" is an aperture with a basin bottom, which looks not unlike a stoup for holy water. There are no records, nor any traditions, respecting the origin of the building; but a field at the end of Beckfoot Lane, adjoining Cottingley Bridge, has been known from time immemorial as Chapel Close.

BINGLEY IN THE FOURTEENTH CENTURY.

BINGLEY had never before reached such a high state of prosperity as it did towards the close of the 13th century; but this was soon afterwards followed by a shocking period of decline. The "victory" at Bannockburn in 1314 put back the dial-hand of civilisation fully two centuries. The Scots invaded Yorkshire, sacked Bingley, destroyed the church (*see* page 113), no doubt after it had served as a refuge for the people, and, like many another northern edifice of the kind, as a fold for cattle and sheep. The King, Edward II., visited Airedale in 1323-4, obtaining quarter in Skipton Castle, and it must have been with bitter reflections that he viewed the scenes of universal desolation and depopulation that followed these savage inroads on our beautiful and erst prosperous valley. The churches were pillaged and then burnt, villages and houses were abandoned, and the land all over was going out of cultivation. People for a time were wandering about like beggars, and there was poverty and sickness in the land. Bad as things were, David, King of Scotland in 1347 again invaded England, and Yorkshire was ravaged and burnt as far as the city of York. This verily put an end to hope!

Famine was now abroad, and the cruel monster Plague also showed his blackened hand in almost every parish! Up to 1350 this "Black Death" carried off the people, sparing neither high nor low, and in Yorkshire, we are told, fully half the clergy died from its effects. In 1365 we have the first mention by name of that terrible malady the "small-pox," which played havoc at that time of imperfect sanitation and medical science.

The Scottish war-scare having subsided, the people began to concentrate themselves in fresh efforts to recover their former prosperity, but they were sadly hampered by heavy taxation. In the second volume of the *Thoresby Society's Publications* is a list of Bingley families who contributed to the war-taxes of Edward III., *ca.* 1380; but a good idea of the population of this district at the time may be gathered from the Poll Tax returns of 1378-9, although their value is as important in other ways as that of a census of the place. They furnish us with the actual names, and in some instances with the callings, of the families then resident here, many of whose descendants, it is interesting to note, are still living in the parish. A comparison with the published lists of other West-Riding towns shows that Bingley was then much more populous than either Leeds, Bradford, or Halifax, and that the tax it paid exceeded double the amounts contributed by either of these towns. At that period Pontefract, Doncaster, Sheffield, and Selby appear to have been the principal centres of population in the Riding. The following is the Bingley return :—

Nicholaus de Stansfeld, ffranklan, & ux. (wife), 3s. 4d. ; Johannes Lowcok, hostiler, & ux., 12d. ; Johannes Chartres, hostiler, & ux., 12d. ; Thomas Collyngworth, talour, & ux., 6d. ; Willelmus de Wyke, carpenter, & ux., 6d. ; Thomas Bosell, sutor, & ux., 6d. ; Nicholaus de Ilton, talour, & ux., 6d.

The following married men paid 4d. each :

Ricardus del Grange, Johannes Coke, Willelmus Lyster, Willelmus de Rowlay, Johannes Kytson, Adam Wade, Johannes de Ledes, Ricardus Walker, Adam Wilson, Jordanus Thorneton, Willelmus Turnour, Hugo filius Hugonis, Adam Balle, Johannes de Collyng, Johannes de Newerke, Ricardus Talour, Henricus Suter, Johannes Smyth, Johannes Milner, Johannes Vylan, Johannes Yole, Ricardus Lang, Willelmus de Ilkelay, Johannes Judson, Johannes Huetson, Johannes Wade, Johannes Curtays, Henricus Couper, Henricus de Stubbyng, Thomas de Parys, Johannes ffouler, Ricardus Wyn, Johannes Ilkelay, Johannes de Bowland, Petrus Studehird, Thomas Grenehill, Thomas de Brunlay, Johannes Yarkar, Symon del Wode, Johannes Dykehouse, Adam Myryman, Johannes Diconson, Johannes Hanneson, Robertus Ibbotson, Willelmus Dyconson, Adam ffydcok, Johannes ffydcok, Henricus Capiman, Rogerus Webster, Johannes Collyngworth, Thomas fflecher, Robertus Gybson, Johannes Elysson, Ricardus Millner, Willelmus Turnour, Johannes filius Rogeri, Willelmus fferson, Adam del Wode, Johannes ffiecher, Ricardus Hunt, Johannes Kytson, Thomas de Crosselay, Willelmus Sugden, Johannes del Rodes, Johannes del Syke, Willelmus Wyllesden, Thomas de Rode, Johannes Couper, Johannes Dobson, Adam de Rauenrod', Nicholaus de Cottyngley, Johannes de Parys, Henricus del Cote.

The following single persons paid 4d. each :

Anabilla Collyng, Matilda Blawer, Matilda Costyne, Isabella Balle, Johannes Wade, Cecilia filia Johannis, Johannes Huetson,

Matilda Cosyn, Margaret Newerk, Matilda filia Johannis, Cecilia Milner, Johannes seruiens Johannis, Isabella seruiens Thome, Johanna de Scheplay, Matilda Mylan, Agnes del Wode, Alicia de Northall, Alicia ffouler, Johannes ffouler, Matilda de Ilkelay, Matilda de Parys, Juliana Bonet, Ricardus Wyndhill, Rogerous Wade, Hugo Rylyng, Agnes Couper, Willelmus Diconson, Johannes Symson, Willelmus de Pillesworth, Ricardus seruiens Vicarii, Alicia de Preston, Thomas seruiens Vicarii, Alicia de Wyndhill, Rogerus seruiens Johannis, Johannes filius Willelmi, Johanna de Helwyk, Agnes de Claton, Anabilla Blolk, Elisabet de Knapton, Willelmus filius Willelmi, Adam filius Ade, Johannes filius Willelmi, Juliana de Haworth, Agnes del Syke, Matilda Milner, Cecilia de Parys.

Married couples, 80; single persons, 46. Sum 47s.

Whether Bingley actually paid the whole or part of this levy is open to question, as we gather that many towns and districts were utterly incapable of meeting the call through sheer want, brought about by recurring plague and famine, and that remissions were granted to such impoverished places. But the above represents the amount due as by law enacted, which obliged every householder (married couples counting as one) and individual above the age of 16, (notorious and privileged beggars excepted), to contribute their quota of the tax. The clergy and monastic orders do not appear in these lists, which include only the lay gentry, tradespeople, and agricultural classes. It will be seen that in Bingley there were two *hostilers*, or licensed innkeepers, two tailors, a shoemaker, and a carpenter, but no one followed the important vocation of blacksmith, although the name of Smyth appears, but this person is taxed at the agricultural rate. The bulk of the population, it is plain, worked upon the land. A quarter of wheat at this time I may say sold for 5s.

The tax had been imposed by Richard II. to carry on the costly wars with France, but we may be sure that the people of Bingley, and the north generally, were little in favour of these wars, and cared little whether Calais belonged to the French or to the English. What with plague and famine and the ravages of the Scots, they were pressed unto death, and it is not surprising that there was a widespread revolt among the peasantry and poorer classes. When work could be paid for, they were thankful to earn 1½d. or even 1d. per day. Again the war-call forced in 1381 another tax on the starving people, when the sturdy, independent character of the Yorkshire folk was especially felt. The clergy, too, were in thorough sympathy with them, for they had been taxed at a higher rate than the laity, and many a priest and ill-paid curate was as badly off as the working classes. Wheat was also at famine price, and it was impossible to till and work the land properly. Hundreds set out to the county capital to aid the insurrection there, when the King commanded the sergeant-at-arms to proceed at once to York, and bring to the Council in London the heads of twenty-four of the rioters. Then the people rose *en masse*, and thousands of famished men and women gathered excitedly under Wat Tyler, who led them to London; their constant cry and motto being, "We will never be slaves!" Hundreds, alas! fell and died from want and exhaustion on the way; Tyler lost his life in a violent squabble with the royal escort at the abbey of St. Bartholomew, and when the Bloody Assize came on many of those unfortunate beings whose names appear in the Poll Tax lists were laid "shorter by the head," or otherwise put to death.

It may be noted that many of the families recorded in the Bingley list of 1378-9 are found among the tenants of the dissolved order of St. John of Jerusalem in the local court-rolls for the year 1838 and 1848, cited in the last chapter.

CHRONICLES OF THE SIXTEENTH AND SUCCEEDING CENTURIES.

WHETHER any Bingley men took part in the celebrated battle of Flodden Field, A.D. 1513, when

> "Shivered was fair Scotland's spear
> And broken was her shield,"

we have no means of ascertaining, as in the manuscript list of Lord Clifford's followers, preserved among the Household Books at Bolton Abbey, Bingley is not mentioned. though Morton Banks is put down as contributing 11 men. Nicholson, the Bingley poet, in his *Lyre of Ebor*, introduces some of the stalwart heroes of Craven as follows :—

> Old Giggleswick beneath her craggy scar
> Had fifty sons, who bravely fought in war
> Stackhouse and Preston, with good bow and bill,
> Fought with the Brayshaws on old Flodden hill;
> The Summerscales from Settle cut their way
> Through files of Scots on that eventful day;
> And Keighley's warriors, led by Smith and Hall,
> Unparted fought, and made the Northerns fall.

Among the 47 Keighley men appear many names common to this district, as Butterfield, Hanson, Shackylton, Hartley, Sharppe, Beanlands, &c. But it is to the *Letters and Papers of Henry VIII.*, some years after Flodden, that we must turn before finding the actual names of Bingley men who were liable to be called to action. In a muster taken at Wyke, near Harewood, 26th March, 1538, before Sir Wm. Gascoigne, &c. *(vide Thoresby Soc. Pub.)*, there appears the following "abyl persons" in the township of Bingley :—

George Pasloo, horse and harness, a sperman, abyll person. [By the Statute of Winchester, A.D. 1284, which was repealed in 1553, every man was bound to provide and keep armour and weapons according to his estate or goods.]

Thes be archers, abill men, horsid and harnessed: John Beyne, Henry Wylkynson, John Long, John Tomlyngson, John Markytrod, John Wood, Christofer Stansfeld, John Wylson.

Thes be archers, abyl men, parcell harnassed and horsed: John Rawson, a horse, Willm Hollyngrake, a horse, John Laycoke, a horse.

Thes be billmen, abyll persons, horsed and harnassed: Antony Foster, John Beyne, Thomas Lyster, John Mylner, John Harvye, Thomas Leth, Wm. Beyn, Gyles Beyn, Richard Kyghley, Thomas Moberley, John More, John Hollyngrake.

The "abyl men" of Morton are likewise given.

This was the stormy period of the Reformation. In 1536 Henry VIII. dissolved more than 300 of the lesser religious houses whose incomes did not exceed £200 a year, and this was followed by the suppression of the larger monasteries, and the appropriation of an immense revenue. The dissolution came as a hard blow, especially upon the poorer agricultural classes, who were largely dependant upon the monasteries. Thousands found themselves without any kind of employment, and the roads became filled with freebooters, sham pedlars, gipsies, &c., while many endeavoured to eke out a subsistence as wandering minstrels, pipers, &c. These became so numerous and troublesome that it was ultimately necessary to pass an Act whereby "all tinkers, gipsies, pipers, and fiddlers wandering abroad" were to be apprehended by the constables and watchmen and taken before the nearest magistrate, to be dealt with according to law. In the Bingley Parish Registers for April 18th, 1595, appears the baptism of Isabel, daughter of Raulphe, the piper, and in 1608 is Robert Hodgson, a piper, buried. In the Leeds Parish Registers, under date July 29th, 1592, is the burial entry of John Morvell, fidler, of Bynglay, doubtless one of the Cottingley Morvells. At the back of the *White Horse* inn, Bingley, is a piece of land known as "Piper Acre," which may have something to do with events of this period.

There were no monasteries at Bingley, but the monks and canons of various religious houses had large properties in the parish. Queen Mary in the 4th year of her reign, 1557, also revived the old order of Knights Hospitallers, and endowed it with lands in this neighbourhood that had never been sold, including the manor of Cottingley and lands in Baildon, Harden, Bingley, &c. Little progress, however, was made around Bingley in the way of house building until the very close of Elizabeth's reign, and the poor must then have lived in wretched hovels. To remedy matters—but, unfortunately, it had often the opposite effect—it was enacted that no cottage was to be built unless "four acres of ground at the least" be appurtenant to it, and this old law survived until comparatively recent times (*see* Jacob's *Court Keeper's Guide*, p. 35).

The following laymen in the township of Bingley contributed to the levy laid by the despot King Hal in 1523:—

Thomas Magelay, for goods, 20s.; John Bene, for goods, 5s.; Antony Eltoftes, gent., for lands, 10s.; Thomas Eltoftes, labor, 4d.; Chrystofer Rauson, for lands, 1s.; Thomas Morgatroyt, for lands, 1s.; Roger Thornton, for goods, 1s.; Ric. Wilkynson, for goods, 1s.; Edward Fether, lab., 4d.; John Elyngpage, lab., 4d.; William Bristo, lab., 4d.; Robert Bygheley, lab., 4d.; John Martlay, lab., 4d.; John Ferandes, lab., 4d.; Henry Magelay, lab., 4d.; Antony Foster, lab., 4d.; William Long, lab., 4d.; John Morgatrowyd, for lab., 4d.; Hugh Glover, lab., 4d.

We do not gather what was the amount of the rate, but it was a percentage on the movable possessions of the tax-payer, as also in some instances on lands, and in others on the value of a man's labour. There was little chance of escape indeed for anything that could be taxed.

The ashes of disaffection continued to smoulder for generations after the Reformation; indeed, the dissolution of monasteries by Henry VIII. upset the peace of England for fully 150 years. The great contest between King Charles and his Parliament was fundamentally a religious war. The Puritan party dreaded any reassertion of the Roman Catholic autocracy, and so it was largely the desire to uphold and strengthen the Protestant religion that led to the peoples' revolting against their lawful King, who was perforce a High Churchman. When

The Civil War

broke out Bingley sided with the Parliament, although there were not a few who honestly liked the King and his indulgent ways, who loved feasts and mirth better than fasts and psalmody; who, as we have seen in our court-rolls for this period, revelled in field games and the fun of May Day and in sports which the stern soul of

Puritanism was fain to repress. But over the moors in Wharfedale there lived the great Ferdinando, Lord Fairfax, a sedate, austere, but able and zealous Puritan, and it was to his nod that the people bowed. He was a property owner in this neighbourhood, and, singularly, was one of the very few noblemen in the north who rose in arms against the King. When it became known that he was to lead the Parliamentary army in the north, men in this district, and in the Aire valley generally, between Keighley and Bradford especially, gathered round him, for everyone had faith in his ability and experience. His family was blazoned with martial achievements, and had a fine old military fame; his grandfather, Sir Thomas Fairfax, was with Bourbon at the sack of Rome, in 1527, and his son, Thomas, was knighted for valour before Rouen. Lord Fairfax enlisted under him the Currers of Kildwick, Gawthorpe, and Marley, the Drakes of Coates, the Lamberts of Malham, the Listers of Thornton, and other heads of leading houses in these parts. His son Thomas, who succeeded to the title on his father's death in 1648, was made a Captain of Horse, and subsequently this adroit and valorous soldier rose to high distinction, becoming eventually General of the Parliamentary forces throughout England.

At this time Henry, Earl of Cumberland, of Skipton Castle, was Lord-Lieutenant of Yorkshire, and to him there fell the onerous duty of rallying his Majesty's forces for the defence of the country, and for the "repression of the enemies of his Majesty's peace." On the issue of his proclamation, he was loyally supported by the flower of the nobility in the north. Abraham Sunderland, elder brother of Samuel Sunderland, of Harden, whose monument is in the tower of Bingley Church, joined the Royalist forces, and died in the siege of Pontefract Castle, March 25th, 1644, leaving a son and heir, Langdale Sunderland. The latter was a Captain of Horse under Marmaduke, Lord Langdale, and on the accession of the Commonwealth paid dearly for the part he took on the side of the King.

The war, so far as it affected this district, really opened at Bradford, in December, 1642, when, as Joseph Lister, the historian of the Siege of Bradford (who at one time lived at Bingley), tells us that a number of horsemen on the approach of the enemy were at once "despatched to Halifax, Bingley, and the small towns about, who came with all speed with such arms as they had, and did much service." Captain Hodgson, of Halifax, came to their aid, "a man of military skill, who instructed us in the best manner possible how to guard and fortify ourselves." The Royalists had pitched their tents "on that part of the common called Hundercliffe, in three separate bodies, where they entrenched themselves." They next approached Barker End, some 300 paces from the church, and raised a battery against it; but the steeple had been protected with wool-packs, and garrisoned by some of the best marksmen, one of whom succeeded in killing one of the enemy's canoneers. Then they made a rush on the enemy's camp, and there was a hand-to-hand fight, the defenders of the town being mostly armed with clubs, scythes, spits, flails, sickles fastened to long poles, and such like rustic weapons. It was a deadly struggle, in which victory hung in the balance until a furious onslaught of Bingley club-men dealt so severe a blow that the Royalists, crushed and defeated, were compelled to fall back on their trenches.

While this was going on at Bradford, the castle at Skipton had been garrisoned with a force of 300 men, under Sir John Mallory and his lieutenant, Major Hughes. Subsequently there was a good deal of skirmishing from Skipton in different directions, and in the Keighley Parish Registers for 1643 to 1645 are various burial entries of soldiers slain on the moors, &c. On February 17th, 1645, a party of about 150 horse from the Skipton garrison, led by Major Hughes, fell suddenly upon the Parliamentary quarters at Keighley. They had learnt of Colonel Brandling's absence, and entering the town took about a hundred prisoners, sixty horse, and other plunder. But Colonel Lambert, hearing of the attack, was soon on the spot, and after a severe encounter succeeded in recovering the prisoners and most of the booty. The conflict is believed to have taken place on the old Corn Mill Bridge; Guard House being the site of the Parliamentary camp, where sometime since a lead cannon-ball was found.

Major Hughes in this encounter was badly wounded, and his burial is recorded in the Skipton registers for Feb. 19th, with the encomium, "a most valiant souldier." During the siege of Skipton Castle, which continued for fully three years (1642 to 1645), the forces of the Parliament were much harassed by sallies from the Royalist garrison. It is very probable that the traditional battle of Harden Moor took place at this time, but there appears to be no documentary evidence whatever of any encounter here. There are, however, traces of a line of excavation a little to the west of the Druids' Altar road, which has been always known as "Fairfax Entrenchment." It extends southwards as far as the long Pan Hole cave, which some think is part of the entrenchment covered in. Also in the fir wood adjoining, a short distance beyond the high wall, are a number of mounds, lying east and west, which are reputed to be the graves of about a hundred soldiers, slain perhaps during a night attack of the King's forces. When this piece of ground was planted by the late Mr. Ferrand, about sixty years ago, he gave orders that the mounds, which were then very distinct, were not to be disturbed; the space was therefore kept open, and the graves are now much concealed by an overgrowth of grass and heather. Perhaps some day a little investigation may be made of the ground to ascertain the truth of the tradition. At the corner of a wall on the moor is the stump of the old "Fairfax Pinnacle," erected as a memorial of the battle.

While the Roundheads remained on Harden Moor, Lord Fairfax or his son lodged at Harden Hall, and an old stone table in the garden is said to have been used for writing despatches upon. It is octagonal in form, and is now in the summer-house at St. Ives, and bears this inscription upon a brass plate: "*This table was at Harden Hall when the troops under General Fairfax were encamped at Harden Moor, MDCXLII.*" Some years ago a bullet was found in a rhododendron bed at St. Ives, near the scene of the traditional conflict, and in 1890 a sword with recurved blade, 36in. long, and iron hand-guard, was found partly embedded in turf on the moor between Morton and Ilkley.

The great turning point in the events of this horrible warfare was the decisive battle of Marston Moor, when 50,000 men of one blood, one tongue, servants of one realm, including the flower of the gentlemen of Yorkshire, and the best bone and sinew of her hardiest sons, drew swords upon each other in mortal combat.* Having collected a force in Lancashire, Prince Rupert hurried through Craven by way of Skipton and Bolton Bridge towards York, taking with him some of the garrison from the Craven stronghold. The writer has an old sword, with wooden handle and iron hand-guard, which is said to have been used by one of his ancestors at this fatal conflict. The man, named John Moorhouse, was one of the Skipton garrison, and a member of an old Craven family, which had been settled in Skipton parish from at least the time of Bannockburn. He appears to have gone north and returned with the Earl of Newcastle's army in 1642. His sword was kept by the Moorhouses at the family home at Skibden, near Skipton, from the time of the war till 1747, when they removed to Elslack, and the sword remained there, with other coeval relics, till about 1870, when the present writer obtained them from his great-uncle, John Moorhouse. The latter's grandfather, John Moorhouse, was born at Skibden in 1729, and died at Elslack in 1807. He had two sons, Thomas and John, and a daughter, Nancy. The latter married Richard Ayrton, of Scale House, Rylston, whose daughter Ellen married Wm. England, of Bingley Corn Mills, and from whom descend the present families of England of Bingley. A daughter of John Moorhouse married James Haggas, of Keighley, from whom the present family of Haggas of Keighley descend. Thomas, the elder brother, had a daughter, Nancy, who is the present writer's grandmother. She

* Mr. Ferrand, of St. Ives, has a copy of a MS. that belonged to the late Mr. Wm. Murgatroyd, which appeared to be a fragment of an original Order Book of the Council of the Northern Parliamentary Army. It had formerly belonged to Captain Ibbetson, of Bradford, who left it, with other valuable manuscripts, to two maiden sisters, and by them the whole were destroyed, except the remnant copied, which fills about 20 folio pages of Mr. Ferrand's MS. volume. There is, however, nothing in it appertaining to this neighbourhood.

married John Aldersley, of the family of Aldersley of Lothersdale, owners of the limestone quarries and barytes mines, inherited by the Spencers through marriage with the daughters of Peter Aldersley, of Raygill. (*See* the author's *Airedale*, page 215.)

After the battle of Marston, which was fought on the 2nd of July, 1644, some of the Royalist army fell back upon York, and others returned to Skipton. Prince Rupert's hot-headedness is acknowledged to have lost the day. His men were led immediately into action after the fatigues of a hot summer day's march, and many of them succumbed as much from exhaustion as from their wounds. The wells at Marston, it is said, were drunk dry. Many of the men who managed to struggle back into quarters died soon afterwards. The parish registers at Skipton record the burial of the above John Moorhouse on July 27th, 1644, or twenty-five days after the battle. He is described as a "soldier," while the Parliamentary men in these registers are invariably described as "rebels." Cromwell returned by way of Otley to Skipton, either through Morton and Bingley, where his friends were numerous, or by the road through Addingham.

The Bingley registers do not contain many evidences of the conflict. In 1647 there are two entries of soldiers buried, but this was after the King was a prisoner of the Parliament. The Parish Books also contain items of payment to lame or wounded soldiers in Bingley during the time of the Commonwealth.

But alas! for the short-lived Puritan rule. The speedy restoration of the monarchy under Charles II. showed that the Government which preceded it was not suited to the spirit of the times. The people still clung to the old ways, they loved their feasts and May-games; so when it came to pass that the King was proclaimed, joy-bells pealed from tower and steeple throughout the land as augurs of happier times, and the old parish accounts show that Bingley shared in the national hope and rejoicing. Before the 29th of May, 1660, when the streets of London were carpeted with evergreens and flowers, and many an old English village was gaily decorated with May-bloom and posies, even the grave Lord Fairfax rode out of Wharfedale to smile benignantly upon the King. He submissively asked, we are told, pardon for all his offences, kissed the royal hand, and presented him with a beautiful horse from his own stud, upon which the King deigned to ride gaily to his coronation.

I should state that at the close of the Civil War, and up to the year 1672, there was a scarcity of copper coinage in England, and certain tradespeople were permitted to issue their own pence and half-pence. Several persons did so at Bingley, including a certain " John Tomson, shoomaker," whose half-penny, dated 1668, is figured in Bowman's *Yorkshire Tokens*. The respected chairman of the Bingley Free Library Committee (Mr. Jesse Thompson, bootmaker, in the Main Street) tells me that this was probably an ancestor of his, as his family have been shoemakers in the district for many generations past. Mr. Thompson also informs me that he has seen another copper trade-token of one Thomas Smith, of Bingley, dated, he thinks, 1666, but I have failed to discover any further information about it.

A remarkable method of raising money for imperial purposes at this time was the obnoxious Hearth Tax, which was a charge of 2s. on every hearth or stove in all dwelling-houses except cottages. It was first imposed in 1662, and repealed after the revolution of 1688. In the Thoresby Society's Publications (vol. I. pages 186-7) is a list of those who paid the tax in Bingley, amounting in 1672 to 434 hearths.

I have said, on page 118, that the manor of Bingley belonged to the Walkers, of Gawthorpe Hall. The transfer in 1596-7 included 12 messuages, 12 tofts, 12 cottages, 12 barns, one water-mill for corn [the old mill mentioned in 1273], one fulling-mill [these mills were erected by statute in 1376, as no woollen cloth was to be exported before it was fulled], 12 gardens, — orchards, 140 acres of land, 50 acres of meadow, 100 acres of pasture, 20 acres of wood, 1,000 acres of furze and heath, — acres of moor, 500 acres of turbary [peats for fuel], 500 acres of mossy ground, and 100 solidates of rent, with appurtenances in Bingley, Micklethwaite, Gilstead, &c. It was probably this Anthony

Walker who rebuilt the old house at Gawthorpe, which continued for a century and half afterwards to be the residence of the lords of the manor.

The above description of the manorial property more than bears out the assertion that one-third of the whole of England was moor and waste in the time of Queen Elizabeth. At Bingley the proportion of moor and moss to the cultivated area looks excessive, but the population it is obvious was proportionately small, as appears by the number of messuages and cottages. There must then have been a fair reach of woodland on the Priesthorpe side of the town, and a small vestige of this old forest tract still remains. Fish in the river and game on the moors must have been plentiful at this time. Doubtless a good many sheep were maintained on the wastes, too, as wool was in great demand locally; many neighbouring towns, such as Leeds, Halifax, Bradford, and Wakefield, were at this time, Leland tells us, "standing by clothing." There were several thousand acres of moorland, and the heather probably at one time descended nearer the town than it does at present. A small patch still exists near the park gates. May this bright spot of golden furze and purple heather of Nature's planting long continue here as a reminder of Bingley in the olden days!

Before the Civil War the manor had been acquired by Hugh Currer, Esq., of Marley, a connection of the family of Currer who purchased the manor of Kildwick in 1558. His cousin, Henry Currer, of Holling Hall, co. York, left a family of two sons and two daughters; the younger of the latter was Elizabeth, who married Nicholas Walker, of Gawthorpe Hall. Anthony Walker died in 1629, and there was a Nicholas Walker, apparently his son, who died before him in 1617, and was buried at Bolton Abbey. During the Commonwealth Henry Currer, grandson of Hugh, was living at Gawthorpe Hall. He sold the manor of Bingley in 1668 to Robert Benson, father of the first Lord Bingley, who had purchased the manor of Elslack shortly before.

When the Treaty of Seville had been completed in 1729, the roads in England, we are told, were full of disbanded soldiers. John Walker was at this time Recorder of Leeds. Thoresby mentions that he was the son of John Walker, of Headingley, who was descended from "a very ancient family formerly residing at Gawthorpe Hall, Bingley." If the family was "very ancient" in Thoresby's time, it must have been of some standing long before the Reformation and the date of parish registers.

The Bensons were living at Red Hall, near Wakefield, when they purchased the manor of Bingley, and Robert Benson, son of the purchaser, was a gentleman who occupied a prominent position in the State. He was some time Chancellor of the Exchequer, and was raised to the peerage in 1713 by the title of Baron Bingley, of Bingley, co. York. He built the mansion at Bramham Park, and established the famous pack of fox-hounds. Occasionally he came to Bingley and resided at Gawthorpe Hall. He died in 1731, and was interred with much honour in Westminster Abbey. His wife, Dorothy, was a daughter of Toby Jenkins, Esq., of Grimston, by his wife Ann Wickham; whose granddaughter, Mary Jenkins, married at York, in 1707, Sir Henry Goodricke, of Ribston. His son, Sir John Goodricke, M.P. for Ripon, who died in 1789, aged 81, held through his wife, Mary, a natural daughter of Lord Bingley, the Bingley estates for life. The same Sir John Goodricke, by warrant dated 6th Oct., 1773, appointed James Willoughby, of Guiseley, one of his gamekeepers within his manor of Bingley. (*See Publications of the Harleian Socy.*, vol. 38, for pedigree of Lord Bingley; also C. A. Goodricke's *History of the Goodricke Family*).

Lord Bingley's daughter, Harriet, married in 1731 George Lane Fox, Esq., who was elevated to the peerage in 1762 by the title of Baron Bingley, of Bingley, co. York. He left an only son (described in the Wakefield Sessions Records for July, 1765, as the "Hon. Robert Lane, Esq., lord of the manor of Bingley"), who dying in 1768, without issue, the estates descended to his cousin, James Lane Fox, Esq., of Bramham. His grandson, the late George Lane Fox, Esq., the popular sporting squire of Bramham, succeeded to the lordship of Bingley, &c., in

1848. He retained the old manor house at Gawthorpe until 1854, when it was sold to the late Mr. John Horsfall. Mr. Fox died in October, 1896, aged 79. He had at different times disposed of extensive properties at Bingley, and in 1882 the Bingley Improvement Commissioners bought from him the market rights for the sum of £800.

Mr. Fox occupied in many respects a unique position in Yorkshire country life, and the following abstract from the *Field* for Nov. 7th, 1896, will be read with interest:—

Mr. George Lane Fox, who was born in the year 1816, was the only son of Mr. George Lane Fox, of Bramham, his mother being a daughter of Mr. Edmund P. Buckley, of Hampshire. The deceased gentleman was educated at Eton, afterwards going up to Christ Church, Oxford, where he followed, as frequently as opportunities allowed, one or other of the packs which hunt almost up to the gates of that city; and at Oxford it was that he gained his first experience of mastership, for he was master of the "House" pack. At that time stage coaching was about at its best, and Joe Tollitt, who died some years ago, used to speak of Mr. Lane Fox and Lord Macclesfield as two of the best pupils he or Will Bowers (commonly known as "Black Will") ever had in the undergraduate population of the University. Will Bowers was one of the heavy division, Tollitt was a light man, while Mr. Lane Fox exceeded them in weight as much as he over-towered them in height. He was one of the early members of the Four-in-Hand Driving Club, and in years gone by used to bring his coach to town for the season, when he frequently turned out in the Park with his club, while for a long time he never missed driving his team from Bramham to Doncaster during the St. Ledger meeting. On the box he sat as gracefully as he did in the saddle, and, in the days when he used to go, no more elegant rider for so big a man was ever seen in the hunting field, either in Yorkshire or anywhere else. In 1837 he married Katherine, daughter of Mr. E. Stein, M.P. She died in 1873, and since that day the master of Bramham never exchanged the black coat he then donned in the field for the pink which he had previously worn.

A countryman born and bred, Mr. Lane Fox was an admirable landlord, and no service of plate that ever yet formed the subject of a testimonial spoke so eloquently of success as the fact that about the year 1856 the whole body of Mr. Lane Fox's tenantry came forward and offered to raise their rents for him. That complimentary offer was declined in kindly and grateful words, but the tenants, with their hearts full, presented Mrs. Lane Fox with a portrait (by Sir Francis Grant) of her husband mounted on his fine horse Courtier, together with an address. This was surely a compliment of which any man might be proud.*

* Portraits of Mr. Fox appeared in the *Illustrated London News* and *Black and White* for Nov. 14th, 1896.

View of Harden Grange (old St. Ives) from Beckfoot Lane.

THE PARISH CHURCH.

"Ye everlasting piles!
Types of the spiritual Church which God hath reared."
Wordsworth.

"DRIHTEN God mildsa thu saulum ussa leoda" [Lord God, have mercy on the souls of our people], was the dying utterance of the Christian King Oswald as he fell in battle against the heathen King Penda, A.D. 642. It is the first recorded cry of a Saxon Christian, and became a household prayer in Northumbria long afterwards. Penda fell at Winwæd (Whinmoor), near Leeds, in 650, and with him fell paganism in Yorkshire for ever. Christianity, as I have previously related, then most likely reached this district. Twelve monasteries were founded in Northumbria in commemoration of the event, and of these the house of St. Heiv (Ive), at Healaugh, near Tadcaster, exercised its ministry over a wide area of the surrounding dominion. St. Heiv, as Bede tells us, was really the first woman in Northumbria who embraced the monastic life. She was a woman of considerable influence in the work of Christianising the heathen population of Yorkshire, and founded the monastery at Heruteu (Hartlepool) before A.D. 649. Anxious to extend her sphere of usefulness in the west, she established herself at Healaugh (Heiu-lagh?), and was succeeded at Hartlepool by the celebrated St. Hilda.

St. Heiv's Monastery.

From what I have said of the Celtic occupation of Bingley, and the boundaries then fixed and determined by the edict of A.D. 680,* and retained ever afterwards as the limit, civil and ecclesiastical, of the parish, deanery, and wapentake, it is more than probable that St. Heiv had established a cell from her monastery at Healaugh on the verge of the now Christian province of Elmet. This would be the old St. Ive's, in the territory of Harden

* *See Newman's ed. of Fleury*, vol. I., p. 51.

(perhaps *Hilda's bounds*; but *see* page 64) within Elmet, which extended, as already explained, from near Sherburn and Tadcaster to the western boundary of the parish of Bingley. But in the quest of our monastery at St. Ive's we have in truth to grope through a valley obscured in the densest mist of mediæval ages, and to try and make the light shine where all is darkness. But we must not despair! There are several aids to our endeavour; the stories to wit of contemporary chroniclers, the precious but barbarously used rune-stone now in the church, and the ancient name of St. Ives, a name full of meaning, apparently little corrupted, which still clings to the locality.

Nennius, who lived in the 8th century, tells us that Ceretic was the British King of Elmet, and that Edwin, the Christian King of Deira, expelled him, and annexed his kingdom to his own, which included Yorkshire, *ca.* A.D. 620. The annexation was fruitful of good alike to civil and religious progress, and never before had this territory enjoyed such happiness and freedom from the danger of enemies as during this good King's reign. A woman with her new-born babe, it is said, might have walked from one extremity of his dominion to the other without fear of molestation (*see* also the author's *Richmondshire*, page 358). This annexation took place during the archiepiscopate of the venerable St. Lawrence, and the motive appears to have been revenge for the treacherous death of Edwin's nephew, Hereric, who had been poisoned by order of Ceretic while sojourning in Elmet, whereof Bingley was part. Hereric was the father of St. Hilda, the successor to St. Heiv at the monastery of Hartlepool, and afterwards at Whitby. St. Hilda died in 680, and Mr. Holmes thinks she has left her name in the Bingley Harden, which in *Domesday* is spelled Hateltun.* Of St. Heiv locally we know but little. In the year 1842 an ancient and peculiarly sculptured stone cross was dug up in Healaugh churchyard, bearing the name MADUG (a Celtic priest) on the dexter side of the stem and HEIV

* Harden, in the parish of Clapham, in Yorkshire, is in *Domesday* suggestively spelled Heldetune, *i.e. Hilda's town.*

on the sinister side. As the synod of Whitby in 664 did away with the Celtic priesthood, the stone is doubtless of an age anterior to this date.

Accepting, therefore, these facts of the establishment of Christianity by St. Heiv in these parts, the monastery, or cell, at Bingley must prior to 664, when the Romish principle was adopted, have been built and reared on the old British Christian methods. During the latter part of this same century the Northumbrian Church was, as Dr. Bright justly observes, conspicuously the backbone of the Church of England. But now let us turn to

THE BINGLEY RUNE STONE,

which Professor Stevens, of Copenhagen, bravely maintains is an Anglo-Saxon font, and which the Rev. D. H. Haigh as stoutly asserts is the base of a memorial cross. I am sorry I can agree with neither of these conclusions, and briefly for the following reasons :—(1) The remarkable variance in the reading of the inscription by these two authorities; (2) the absence of any evidence as to the existence of such like fonts of the age of this stone; (3) because the hole in it is of later date, having been driven horizontally at one end right through the interlacing pattern, which was thereby damaged and partly broken away. Is it likely that if the hole was coeval with the inscription and ornament that this "labour of love" would be so ruthlessly spoilt? (4) that it is not the base of a cross because of the internal shape of the stone, its sides sloping inwards; (5) because of the rebate round the brim of the aperture, as if a lid, which I contend has fitted it, and (note) there are no traces of fastenings; (6) because both fonts and memorial-stones of the character implied by the authorities named are absolutely unknown. The latter, however, is not a fatal objection, as we possess so very few objects in stone of this period that it would be unwise to reject them wholly on this ground. But we learn from Bede (who died in 735) that stone fonts were not used in his time. Professor Stephens, however, reads the inscription as follows :—

EADBIERHT, KING, HOTE [ordered] TO HEW THIS DIP STONE FOR US. BID [pray thou] FOR HIS SOUL.

Runic Inscription at Bingley.

Whereas Father Haigh's rendering is :

EADBERHT SON OF EATTA KING UTTERED A GRACIOUS BAN. ONGUS VISITED BINGLEY.

Thus it will be seen that they agree only in respect to the first word of the inscription, which, with all due respect to their special knowledge, means that the remaining portion might be construed to mean anything else. The fact is the inscription appears to be hopelessly lost, being so far obliterated that "the best men may differ, and widely differ, as to its meaning." (*Vide* Stephens.) It is a pity that Professor Stephens has neglected to reproduce in an engraving the actual inscription itself, while he furnishes (*vide* "Runic Monuments") engravings of his own and Father Haigh's renderings.*

Eadberht, who was King of Northumbria, reigned from 737 to 758, when he abdicated for pure love of religion, and became a canon in his brother Egbert's metropolitan church at York. It may thus be argued that Bingley being an important centre of Christian missionary work at this period (which no doubt it was), the King, with the consent of the Archbishop, ordered this "dip-stone" to be made, with the view to promote the rite of baptism in his dominion. But, as I have said, fonts of this pattern were at that time unknown, all those which were made down to the Norman Conquest being capacious enough to admit of total immersion, according to the canon of the Church. The laws of Ine (A.D. 690) certainly ordain the baptism of infants within thirty nights from birth ; but this was done by the administrator in the open bath, nor have we any certain knowledge of baptism by sprinkling from the small font until after the erection of the new churches in Norman times. In the seventh century thousands were baptised in the open rivers.

Father Haigh's reading, I agree, fits admirably with the history of the time, but the shape of the stone strongly opposes his theory with regard to its use as the socket of a cross. At the rune end the external measurement at the top is 32½ inches, and internal 17¼ inches, while at the opposite end it is 25 and 15½ inches respectively ; thus the

* His omission is provided for by the illustration opposite.

irregular slope of the cavity, with its sloping interior, is quite unsuited to hold the upright shaft of a cross. Moreover, the rebate round the edge of the cavity has, I do not doubt, been made to receive a cover; and as there are no indications of fastenings such as the protection of holy water would require, I shall venture the opinion that it was no font, but nothing else than a *relic chest*, and that the inscription has not been correctly read. There were, of course, other Eadberhts and Eatas besides those suggested by Father Haigh. There was an Eadberht, Bishop of Lindisfarne when the twelve northern monasteries I have mentioned were founded (*ca.* 650). He it was who caused the tomb of St. Cuthbert to be opened, and the body to be re-laid in a new shroud in a wooden chest, and set above the pavement as a shrine. Eata was also Bishop of Lindisfarne (the oldest of the Northumbrian monasteries) when the seat of the northern episcopate was removed to York, where it remained till A.D. 678. Eata received from the King of Deira (in which province Bingley was situate) an estate of 30 or 40 hides at Ripon for the erection of a monastery, afterwards held by the sainted Wilfrid. Wilfrid visited Rome in 679, knelt at many shrines, and viewed the venerated cist holding the precious relics of the Christian martyr, St. Lawrence. Many relics he brought back with him, together with many other things "for the adornment of the house of God," including a *privilegium* for the monastery at Ripon. Again he visited Rome in 704, and brought back "a store of relics duly catalogued." He was a zealous, able, and active churchman, "riding about incessantly to baptize and confirm, holding ordinations, and forming new church settlements," as we learn from the venerable Eddi, the contemporary biographer of Wilfrid.

In the face of these facts, and of the actual object itself, I hazard the conjecture that the Bingley stone was a relic-chest, or stone shrine, holding the holy things of some worthy saint, of whom we now know nothing, or, perhaps, belongings of the venerable St. Lawrence himself, whose name was preserved in the dedication of the new church at Bingley in Norman times, and whose festival is still commemorated here by the chief annual fair or feast. Every church at this time, be it remembered, had its reliquary, or relic-chest, either in wood or stone, and when of the latter material, as at Bingley, the cover would be fitted in the rebate and cemented down, that no sacrilegious hands might molest the sacred contents. Such an inscribed sarcophagus, containing the relics of St. Innocent (from the catacombs at Rome), is preserved at the altar in the beautiful church of St. Paulinus, at Brough, near Richmond, in Yorkshire. (*See* the author's *Richmondshire*, page 140.)

Still, for whatever purpose the Bingley stone may have been intended, or whatever may be its inscription, there can be no doubt that it is a Christian memorial of early Saxon times, probably unique, and as such ought to be respected and carefully preserved. As the very basis of the Christian church in Bingley, carrying us far beyond the Norman centuries, when the faint but cheering light of Holy Scripture spread from the little chapel in the wood —like, indeed, unto the inscription on one of the Bingley bells: "*Ring out the darkness of the land; ring in the Christ that is to be*,"—this age-worn monument of piety, with more than eleven hundred years of history upon it, is an heritage from the past, valuable as it is rare. I can only express the hope that it may ere long find a suitable and safe resting-place in the present restored church as an object of Christian interest, and which perhaps a more enlightened knowledge in the future may adequately explain.

At the Norman Conquest a great many wooden churches were burnt or destroyed, while many that remained were neglected, and went to ruin; and being of no value, were not mentioned in the survey of A.D. 1086. The church at Bingley was refounded (when peace was restored) by the new lord of the manor, William Paganel, who gave it, with other possessions of his, to Drax Priory in the time of Archbishop Thurstan (A.D. 1119 to 1140). The church was apparently at this time

DEDICATED TO ST. LAWRENCE,

but whether this was a resumption of an older dedication,

or what may have been the actuating motive for this ascription, we have not sufficient authority for stating. It was retained by one of the chapels in the later church dedicated to All Saints, and the church at Eldwick has been happily dedicated to St. Lawrence also. The parish church was sometimes dedicated after the name of the principal patron, or one who had greatly assisted or contributed to the erection of the building; but most frequently it was dedicated to the saint of the day when

BURYING "LAWRENCE" BY TORCHLIGHT AT BINGLEY.

the church was consecrated. This was probably the case at Bingley. St. Lawrence, whose anniversary day is the 10th of August,* was a very popular saint in England. He was martyred in Rome, A.D. 259, by roasting on a large gridiron. The instrument of his martyrdom was long preserved in the temple erected at Rome in his honour. At the Reformation of the Church in England by

* The Parish Feast is regulated by it, the method of reckoning from August 22nd being due to the 12 days added by the alteration in dating last century.

Henry VIII., a very large number of early Christian relics were torn from their caskets, exposed, and destroyed; amongst them were many fragments of coal which were traditionally believed to have roasted St. Lawrence. It was probably after the restoration or rebuilding of the Norman structure, which had been plundered and so much injured by the invading Scots after Bannockburn, that the church at Bingley was re-consecrated to All Saints.

In this district "Lawrence" used to have a bad name, but I have found some difficulty in allying this circumstance with the old guardian saint of the parish. An idle person, or vagabond, is said to be as bad as Lawrence! "I see Leng Lawrence has getten howd on tha," is said of any person who has got into loose or idle ways. Some sixty or seventy years ago, when things were not very prosperous at Bingley, the local wool-combers vowed that Lawrence was at the bottom of this evil time, and so they decided to revenge themselves. A wooden coffin was made, an effigy of the supposed offender was put into it, and at night a procession was formed, which proceeded by torchlight to Bailey Hills, when amid the bitter remonstrances of the whole company poor Lawrence was consigned to earth. Mr. Thomas Longbottom (aged 80) tells me he well remembers as a boy following the mock cortége to the site of the present cemetery, and amid the strange glare of the torches seeing the coffin lowered with all the solemnity of a real funeral. I cannot, as I have said, get properly at the root or meaning of this custom, but at Nun Monkton (*see* the author's *Nidderdale*) I find a similar feeling towards the patron saint of that village prevailed. Every annual feast-day a wooden image of St. Peter was placed in a box coffin and carried in procession, and buried with proper ceremony beneath a large sycamore tree on May Pole Hill. This performance was always spoken of as "Burying Peter," and the image, rudely dressed in any odd manner, lay undisturbed until the ensuing "Little Feast Day," that is the Saturday before the 29th of June, when a procession of villagers, usually led by a fiddler, marched to the spot and the ceremony of "Rising Peter" took place.

Parish Church, Bingley, before the Restoration, 1870-1.

Description of the Church.

The old Norman church was doubtless so utterly despoiled by the invading Scots after the battle of Bannockburn in 1314 that its re-erection in a later style would be necessary, as was the case at Bradford and many other places during this era. This building was, again, removed early in the reign of Henry VIII., when the fabric now existing was erected. The upper portion of the tower was added in 1787. During the restoration made in 1870-1 several bases and capitals of Norman pillars were discovered, which were utilised for the foundations and repair of the pillars. A fragment of a Saxon cross, with interlacing pattern, in addition to the Runic-stone, already described, has been also preserved. As affording some idea of the character of Paganel's building, it may be stated that one of the original capitals, which now rests under the centre pillar of the Busfeild Chapel, measures at its narrowest part 31 inches, consequently these Norman pillars must have been very large and massive. The choir was erected in 1518, at the cost of the Rev. Richard Wylson, Prior of Drax, and Suffragan Bishop of Negropont, afterwards Bishop of Meath, Ireland, who is believed to be a native of Bingley, and if so he is the only bishop, Catholic or Protestant, known to have been born within the deanery of Craven. Dodsworth, in 1621, noted a Latin inscription in the east window, with twelve coats of arms, including those of Paslew, *arg. a fess between three pierced mullets, sa ;* Marthley, *arg, three squirrels, sej. gu. ;* Eltofte, *arg. three chess rooks, sa ;* Maude, *arg. a lion rampant, sa. over all two bars, sa ;* also Ryshworth, Kighley, Warde, &c. The following was the inscription translated:—

> Pray for the good estate of the Most Reverend Father in Christ, Richard Wylson, Bishop of Negropont, Suffragan of York, Prior of Drax, and for the souls of his parents, who caused this choir and window to be made, in the year of our Lord, 1518, and the 26th day of the month of March.

In the account of Bishop Wylson in Wood's *Athenæ Oxon.* it is stated that " 'tis probable he was born at Bingley, but when he died appears not." A copy of the original inscription is now to be seen in the west window of the tower, with the arms of the Bishop and those of Paslew of Riddlesden, Mohaut (Maude) of West Riddlesden, Eltofte of Ryshworth, and Marthley of Marley; also those of Mr. Johnson Atkinson Busfeild, by whom these arms were restored in 1847, the originals having been lost or destroyed. Several of these arms, cut in stone, but now much defaced, appear on the outside of the west entrance.

A thorough restoration of the church took place in 1870-1, when the west gallery and organ-loft were removed and the tower arch and west window opened to the nave. The roof of the latter is of simple but massive oak, while additions of beautifully pannelled oak were made to the roofs of the chancel and aisles. The old square pews were replaced by commodious oak benches, and provision for warming with hot air introduced. The handsome memorial font to Mrs. Emily Busfeild, with its richly-carved canopy, and the beautiful pulpit presented by George Alderson Smith, Esq., as a memorial to his late wife, were also provided. The Ryshworth Chapel, on the north side of the chancel, and the Riddlesden Chapel, on the south side, are doubtless coeval with the church. There is also a private chapel of late date belonging to St. Ives in the centre of the north aisle, above the vestry. The South Chapel, dedicated to St. Lawrence, is now occupied by the organ-loft, and the north, dedicated to Our Lady, was the ancient burial-place of the Eltoftes, from which family it was purchased in 1591 by Edward Bynns. In 1672 Abram Bynns, J.P., of Ryshworth Hall, sold the same to William Busfeild, of Leeds, merchant, and it is still the property of his family, now represented here by Mr. Ferrand, of St. Ives. This chapel was greatly improved and beautified by the late Mr. Busfeild, of Upwood, at the general restoration in 1870-1. Upon the handsome oak screen, which divides the chapel from the chancel, the following inscription is carved in old English characters :—

In pious remembrance of his ancestors this chapel was restored by Johnson Atkinson Busfeild, A.D. 1870.

The south entrance is by a substantial stone porch,

built at the same time in place of an old, dilapidated one. The windows have all been renovated with the exception of the one at the east end of the south aisle, which retains its original stone-work. The short buttress under the great east window is curious, and I know of no similar instance of a buttress in this position save the one at Whalley Church, in Lancashire, which ancient edifice had originally a five-light east window.

Within the church is some good stained glass, including a window in the Busfeild Chapel, designed by Sir E. Burne-Jones, and executed by Morris; and there are numerous mural monuments and inscriptions, details of which are recorded in the third edition of Whitaker's *History of Craven*. At the restoration an exact account was taken of those memorials on the floor which it was necessary to cover in, while some of them were erected against the walls of the tower. The principal families commemorated are Ferrand, Busfeild, Sunderland, Leach, Currer, Rishworth, Lamplugh, Stansfield, Hartley, Hudson, &c. Formerly there were two tattered banners hanging in the church, one of which remains. They were the colours of a local corps of volunteers, which on being disbanded were, as usual, placed in the parish church.

Many thousands of interments have taken place in the churchyard, which is crowded with memorials of old Bingley families. Formerly all poor people who received town's pay were buried on the north side of the yard, unless their friends came forward and paid the funeral expenses. A pauper's coffin, it may be added, cost a century ago from 4s. to 5s. But, then, what of that? The magnificence of the pall is no certain introduction to heaven. The world will always keep many poor, but God knows where to look for a soul! Amongst the interesting memorials is a table-stone to the Airedale poet, John Nicholson, which was erected at the cost of the late Mr. Geo. Lane Fox, lord of the manor of Bingley.

Another stone commemorates Hezekiah Briggs, a noted bell-ringer, who died in 1844, and who was sexton for 43 years, during which period he interred, as is recorded on his tombstone, upwards of 7,000 bodies.

A list of the vicars of Bingley from A.D. 1275 is printed from Torre in Whitaker's *Craven*. To these I may add two others, viz.: Jordan de Bingley, collated to Gisburne in 1228, and Gilbert de Bingley, collated to Thornhill in 1234 (*vide* Archbishop Gray's *Register*, 1215-1255). Probably others may be found in the chartulary of Drax Priory, in whose presentation the church remained from the 12th to the 16th century. At the dissolution of monasteries, the appointments were made by the Crown up to 1837, and from that time by the Bishop of the diocese. The benefice is declared in Pope Nicholas' *Taxation* (A.D. 1291) to be worth £30 per annum; in the *New Taxation* (1318) £14 13s. 4d.; in the *Liber Regis* (Henry VIII., A.D. 1539) £7 6s. 8d.; and in the *Parliamentary Survey*, vol. XVIII., page 343, it is stated: "Vicarage, £26 per annum. A thousand communicants."

The following account of the tithes is copied from an old paper addressed by Mr. Currer, of Kildwick, to Benj. Ferrand, dated 28th April, 1772:—

The Rectory of Bingley and the tythes of that parish were parcel the possessions of the Priory of Drax, and upon the 20th May (3rd James I. (1604-5) were conveyed by Sir Thomas Sherley of Whiston in Sussex, Kt., and from others (who probably were grantees of the Crown after the Dissolution of Monasteries) to Richd. Sunderland of Coley Hall, Anthony Wade of King's Cross, Wm. Currer of Marley, Abm. Binns of Rishworth, and John Oldfield of Gilstead, subject to a yearly fee farm rent of £22, payable to the King, his heirs, and successors. Wade, Currer, Binns, and Oldfield some time afterwards conveyed their share of this Rectory and tythes to the same Mr. Sunderland. Which Mr. Sunderland, or some of his family, at different times conveyed the greatest part of the tythes of the parish of Bingley to the owners of estates there in order to make them tythe free.

In one of the conveycs. above mentioned, Rd. Sunderland in 1608 grants "all the tythes of sheaves, grain, grass, wool, flax, hemp, and lambs, which shall arise from the purchaser's estate, and it is supposed that most of his other grants of tythes are in the same words. In some, small rents or modus's are reserved, in others none. It has been said that John Sunderland of Purston, gent., a descdt. of Rd. Sunderland above mentd., in or about the year 1712, conveyed all the tythes of the parish of Bingley, which had not before been granted to the proprietors of lands there, and also the modus's or rents reserved by those grants to James Roberts, Clerk,—And that Mr. Roberts conveyed them to Thomas Fell, Esq., 3rd Nov. 1721, under which title Mr. Solomon Fell, as heir or devisee, has claimed either the tythes or modus's out of several estates within that parish.

Within the important period of the last sixty years the extension of trade, the increased number of houses, and consequent development of religious work among all sects in the parish has been most marked. When the Rev. James Cheadle, M.A., was instituted to the living of Bingley in the year of the Queen's accession, 1837, the parish church had to suffice for the spiritual needs of the whole parish, which at that time had a population of about 17,000, of which about 10,000 were in Bingley-with-Micklethwaite. There were schools in Bingley only, and there was no

THE REV. JAMES CHEADLE, M.A.

proper vicarage-house. Mr. Cheadle's predecessor, Dr. Hartley, had, there is no doubt, centred his attention on the Grammar School, of which he was headmaster, and consequently the large parish was much in need of organization, and additional schools and churches. His being the first appointment by the Bishop, special interest was taken in the event, and it was soon seen that Mr. Cheadle was the "right man in the right place." He entered upon his new labours with a devotion and energy which only terminated with his death, after 25 years of fruitful service. During this time the church, parsonage, and schools were erected at Morton; the church at Riddlesden and the church and schools at Cullingworth were likewise built. Mr. Cheadle also turned his energies towards obtaining an adequate residence, and this was in due course granted him, and completed in 1841. He had previously resided at the Grammar School House. The Grammar School was also rebuilt. A new organ was put in the parish church; in 1856 a new clock was placed in the tower in place of the old one erected in 1704,* and the interior of the fabric was partly re-pewed. Additions were also made to the churchyard, which was now railed off, and the wall built alongside Bellman Row. Previously the sacred enclosure had been open all round and used for various purposes; not the least objectionable was as a drying-ground for clothes, &c.

Mr. Cheadle also took an active share in almost every public movement for the welfare of the town and parish. He took a great interest in the Mechanics' Institute; and the Temperance Society should revere his memory for the splendid service he rendered in reforming the very widespread drinking habits that then prevailed. During the harassing period of the Chartist excitement he likewise did good work quietly and persistently, sometimes addressing large gatherings on the moors, and he was always listened to with respect, and was never, I think, molested. He was very fertile in argument, and ever had a pithy answer. On one occasion, I am told, when he was presiding at a local entertainment, a stranger in the audience got up to express his interest in what had been said, remarking on the progress Bingley had made, but adding, "I really do not know whether I should now call the place a *village* or a *town*." Mr. Cheadle promptly replied, "We pride ourselves, sir, that Bingley is a market *town*." Mere dimensions could not upset this historic fact. The audience naturally smiled at the aptness of the reply.

* *See* "The Old Church Clock's Petition" in the *Bingley Chronicle* for Jan. 11th, 1895.

Here is another anecdote of Mr. Cheadle told by Wallet, "the Queen's Jester," who once came to Bingley with a travelling theatre. He says :—

Our next stand was at Bingley, where a very pleasant circumstance occurred. We were erecting the large booth, when the vicar came up, and addressing me, inquired, "What are you doing here?" "I am erecting a large portable theatre, sir." "Oh, indeed! have you any ladies with you?" "Oh yes, sir, we have at least twenty." "Dear me," said he, "I hope you don't represent anything immoral." I assured him we did not. I did not know at the moment who he was; but as he bade me good morning, he shook me kindly by the hand, and said, "I shall come and see you, and, in return, you must come and see me on Sunday; I'm the vicar." I promised to do so, and we both kept our words. The worthy vicar was a frequent attendant at our theatre, and, I think, never had cause to regret the countenance he gave us. We made up a large party, and on the first Sunday visited the old parish church. The subject of the sermon was the value of a good name. Valuable on earth, he said, even supposing, as infidels would make out, that there was no world to come. I must tell you that our party had been ushered into the large scarlet-cushioned pew belonging to the minister's family, where, of course, we were the "observed of all observers," and immediately under the preacher's eye. In the course of his sermon, he quoted the entire passage from Shakespeare, commencing, "A good name is the immediate jewel of my soul," delivering it with admirable emphasis. At its conclusion, he looked down upon us with a peculiar expression of face, as if to say, "I, too, am a disciple of Shakespeare, and there's a sop for you in your own element." After the service, we waited for the reverend gentleman, to thank him for his kind invitation and the accommodation afforded, and also for the high intellectual treat we had enjoyed. This was one of the pleasantest episodes of my life.

For the first fifteen years of his vicariate Mr. Cheadle had no curate, with the exception of the first few years when he was responsible for services at Morton and Morton Banks, and though at times feeling the active work of this large parish too much to sustain, he managed to take three full services every Sunday, together with all marriages, baptisms, and funerals. He was a widely-read and accomplished scholar, and when graduating at Cambridge, in 1881, he took the high position of 18th wrangler out of 800. He was devoted to history and literature, and on one occasion lectured to a large audience on Bingley history. He was also regarded as an authority on ecclesiastical law, and was often asked for counsel and advice by the clergy in the diocese. Overwork had partly undermined a naturally vigorous constitution, and he died Feb. 2nd, 1862, at the comparatively early age of 52. He was a native of Nottingham, and had been previous to his coming to Bingley incumbent of Colne. The accompanying portrait was taken shortly before his death. His son, Dr. W. B. Cheadle, of London, married Anne, daughter of

The Rev. A. P. Irwine, M.A.

Wm. Murgatroyd, Esq., of Bankfield, Bingley. She died in 1889, and to her memory there is a beautiful stained glass window in the church.

His successor, the Rev. Arthur Parke Irwine, M.A., found ample scope in still further extending religious work in the neighbourhood. Within six years of his appointment as vicar of the parish, he had the pleasure to see the large and handsome church of the Holy Trinity, in Bingley, erected and opened. Largely through his efforts, too, the important restoration of the parish church, in 1870-1, took place, which cost upwards of £2,500, raised by subscription. Mr. Irwine was also instrumental for good in other directions. He established Church services at Harden, in a room licensed by the Bishop, and raised a large sum of money towards the erection of a church there. The Bingley National Schools were enlarged and improved, and Cottage Meetings were begun at Eldwick. In 1875 Mr. Irwine was appointed Rural Dean of South Craven. He was also chaplain to the Volunteer Corps (Duke of Wellington's), and was chairman of the Bingley Grammar School. After a long illness, Mr. Irwine died on the 14th of September, 1889, aged 75. Before coming to Bingley, he had been curate of Prestbury for two years, and left to take up the appointment of first organising secretary to the Pastoral Aid Society, which office he filled with success for about twenty years.

The Rev. Charles Edwards, M.A., Honorary Canon of Ripon, succeeded Mr. Irwine as vicar of Bingley and Rural Dean, and during the short two years of his ministry made himself exceedingly popular with all classes. He was a thorough Churchman, and an assiduous worker. For 25 years before his appearance in Bingley he had served, and served well, the populous parish of Holy Trinity, Bradford, and greatly did his parishioners regret his removal; he being their first vicar. They presented him with a handsome testimonial of the value of about £500. In most practical questions relating to the well-being of the community he took a prominent part. Among other activities, he had associated himself with the various temperance movements in Bradford, especially of the Church of England Temperance Society, of which he was president. He was also a director of the Bradford Coffee Tavern Company, and chaplain of the 2nd West York Artillery Volunteers. He was also on the committee of the Rawdon Convalescent Home, the Society for the Propagation of the Gospel in Foreign Parts, the Blind Institute, and was one of the stewards of the West Riding Charitable Society. He took a great interest in the subject of education, and from 1876 to 1882 sat as a member of the Bradford School Board. Canon Edwards died on the 29th March, 1892, aged 55; his death being greatly regretted in this parish. During his brief residence here his natural activity and love of work were productive of much good.

He was succeeded by the Rev. Francis Chas. Kilner, M.A., the present vicar, and previously vicar of St. Martin's,

THE REV. CANON EDWARDS, M.A.

Potternewton, Leeds. He is a son of the Rev. Jas. M. Kilner, chaplain of Chester Castle, and was born in June, 1851. Mr. Kilner, who was educated at Rugby, Keble College, Oxford, and Cuddesdon Theological College, was ordained by the Bishop of Chester, deacon in 1874 and priest in 1875. He was curate of Christ Church, Bootle, Liverpool, up to 1879, when he was appointed Wilberforce Missioner for the diocese of Winchester. On his appointment to the vicarage of Bingley in 1892 he became also Rural Dean, and on September 29th, 1896, he was instituted at Ripon Cathedral Archdeacon of Craven, vacant by the death of Archdeacon Bardsley, vicar of Bradford.

Under Archdeacon Kilner church work in the parish has made good progress; many improvements have been effected in the parish church, and two beautiful new churches, at Harden and Eldwick, have been erected and opened for public service. Little comment is necessary on what is still going on, but of the vicar's ability and interest in his work there is ample evidence in the crowded congregations at the parish church. He is ably assisted by his two curates, the Rev. S. Rogerson, M.A., and the Rev. M. Power, B.A. The previous curate, the Rev. Emil B. Smith, it should be added, accomplished a great deal of excellent work during his residence in Bingley, and on March 9th, 1896, received a handsome testimonial of the respect in which he was held by the parishioners on his appointment to the living of Kippax, near Leeds, where he is now vicar.

From old wills and other documents much information might be given respecting earlier vicars and their work and actions in times past. Thus I find that in 1415 Robert Emsey, who was instituted to the living in 1399, took on a lease of ten years a close called Wadecroft, an acre of land lying at Wythcrosseyat, in a certain parcel of meadow called Moseyeng, paying to the lord of the manor of Bingley, Thomas de Astelay, annually 6s. 8d., and he gives to the lord as fine for entry 6s. 8d. It would be interesting to locate these lands now. Again, of the Rev. Saml. Oley, vicar of Bingley, who died in 1618, we learn that he left to the poor of the town and parish the sum of 40s., "if the inhabitants of Bingley p'sh will pay my adms. or exors. within three months of my death the xii£ I spent for the schoole and poore there." He also mentions his son, Samuel, and his married daughters, Jane Wright, Rebecca Whitley, and Sara, wife of Edward Shackleton, of Morton Banks, &c.

Parish registers were first ordered in 1538, but there are none at Bingley earlier than 1577. They are for the most part in good condition. As the original order provided that the register-book was to be taken out of the parish chest only every Sunday, and all christenings, weddings, and burials of the week before then entered, we cannot be certain that strict accuracy in the matter of

THE VEN. ARCHDEACON KILNER, M.A.

dates was always ensured. For example, the vicar of Barkston, in Leicestershire, entered in his register: "1689, Ellen, the daughter of Bryan and Ellen Dun, was baptised April 23rd." But the entry may have been made weeks after the event, and his memory had probably failed him, for he adds the following apologetic note: "Lord, pardon me, if I am guilty of any error in registering Ellen

Dun's name." In the Rotherby registers appear some allusions to a crisis in which Bingley also was closely concerned: "1643. War! 1644. War! 1645. War! Interruption. Persecution!" During part of the Commonwealth the Bingley registers appear to have been disregarded; Cromwell having made other provision for parochial registration by his well-known publication.

The old Churchwardens' Books at Bingley are interesting and valuable, as they go back to the period of the Commonwealth, and from them I have drawn much curious and various information, reflecting bygone habits, manners, and customs of the parish, which are referred to throughout this work. Should any additional volume on local history ever be issued, many other items for reflection may be adduced from these interesting collections. The post of churchwarden, procurator, synodsman (or sidesman) is an ancient and honourable office that has existed in the Church of England from time immemorial. Civil obligations, as may be gathered from the Bingley accounts, rested with them in ancient parishes till the legislation of 1894 removed these duties. The churchwarden of the past has, however, not always been regarded with that respect due to the importance of his office, and we are apt to associate him with those ecclesiastical desecrations known as "Churchwardens' Gothic," and to picture him with the long clay pipe and mug of "nut-brown," which he was prone to enjoy whilst discussing the doings or misdoings of his parish. That the churchwarden at Bingley appreciated his pipe and grog is evident from an entry in the accounts for 1788, wherein it is ordered that each member of the committee who attends by rotation be allowed a tankard of ale for his trouble, and those who do not attend to pay 6d., to be spent by those who do; but the discussion of the grog and parish business was wisely ordained to cease at 8 o'clock in the afternoon. It would be interesting to ascertain if the discussions did always terminate at that hour! At Giggleswick, I learn, these wise men actually sold the bell-ropes "to cover their refreshment bill." Pray, let us draw the curtain here!

The members of the committee usually met in the vestry of the church, but sometimes they assembled at one of the inns in the town; thus it was ordered that a general meeting of the committee be called on Wednesday, the 29th April, 1778, to meet at the *White Horse*, by 8 o'clock in the afternoon, "on special business." On Nov. 1st, 1782, I find that it was ordered to receive plans and estimates for a new vestry and a house for the reception of a hearse. The latter was situated in Bellman Row, near the churchyard, where the old bone-house formerly stood. It is now about forty years since the parish hearse was given up. Up to the restoration of 1870 the vestry was in the tower of the church. Payments were ordered for a variety of objects: For crying the fairs, for crying parish matters in the church, for ringing the eight o'clock (curfew) bell, as well as for ringing the bells on certain anniversaries, for ridding the district of a superabundance of foxes, crows, hawks, hedgehogs, badgers, &c., which a century or two ago were very numerous in upper Airedale. "Window money" is also mentioned in the accounts, an obnoxious old tax, which shut out health-giving air and light, and was only repealed in 1851, when a duty was put on certain inhabited houses instead.

It seems to have been a custom in Craven to pay any clergyman who came to preach at a church the sum of one shilling, and there are records of this payment at Giggleswick down to 1846. At Bingley, in 1704, I find it was ordered that "nothing shall be allowed to be spent with strange ministers," and also that nothing shall be allowed for fox-heads, &c. Either a spirit of necessary retrenchment must have prevailed at that period, or that the custom was being openly abused, for example by breeding foxes, &c., in captivity, and claiming the sum allowed per head, and the tippling parson, with his convivial friends, being probably no better in this respect than his Norman or Anglo-Saxon brother elsewhere alluded to.

The settling of poor apprentices upon owners and occupiers in the parish, by rotation, also gave the parish wardens a good deal of work. Payments to the poor was also the heaviest tax on the parish. In 1780, for example, I find a rate of 2s. 8d. in the pound raised the sum of £348 4s. 8½d., apportioned as follows: Bingley £69 10s. 1½d., Micklethwaite £142 6s. 0½d., and Harden £131 8s. 6½d. This was paid by a total of 270 inhabitants, as follows: Bingley 78, Micklethwaite 95, Harden 97. How this contrasts with the improved condition of the working classes at the present time, when the rate for precisely the same purposes is now (1897) 1s. 2d. in the pound, yielding a revenue of £8,500, paid by about 5,500 persons in the same places. Taking the whole of England, the decline in pauperism is similarly marked. In 1858 about 50 persons in each thousand of total population of the country were in receipt of relief, while at the present time there are less than half this number.

The bells of Bingley Church are famous in the history of English campanology. The rich-toned peal of six bells was raised in the tower in 1773; Mr. J. A. Busfeild being the principal benefactor. They bear the following interesting inscriptions:—

1st Bell. Although I am but slight and small,
I will be heard above you all.
2nd Bell. If you have a jealous ear,
You'll own my voice is sweet and clear.
3rd Bell. At proper times our voices we will raise
To our benefactor's praise.
4th Bell. Such wondrous power's to music given
It elevates the soul to heaven.
5th Bell. Ye ringers all, that prize your health and happiness
Be sober, merry, wise, and you'll the same possess.
6th Bell (Tenor). This peal was raised in 1773. Johnson Atkinson
Busfeild, Esq., was the principal benefactor.

Two other bells were added in 1873, the gift of Mr. Walter Dunlop, of Harden Grange, making a peal of eight. Says Mr. T. W. Green in his interesting booklet on the subject: "The excellent natural situation in which they are placed, on the banks of the Aire, amidst hanging woods, and with hills on every side, all combine to give a peculiar sweetness to their tones, and no one could better describe the beautiful effect of their musical echoes than the author (poet) of *Airedale*." The following excerpt from the same little work will be read with interest :—

"Though not the first deserving of notice, the first to record will be a peal that was rung in 1798, on the occasion of William Busfeild, Esq., of Myrtle Grove, attaining his majority. The company on that day rang seven whole peals of 720 changes each, in all 5,040 changes, on the most difficult of known methods, all "Snappers," namely :—Chester, London, Carlisle, Chelsea, Lincoln, Lichfield, Wells.

On Shrove Tuesday, Feb. 7th, 1826, the society met in the tower, and rang without a single breakdown, or a false change, the extraordinary number of 86 twelve scores, in all 8,640 changes, on the following various methods, viz. :—

Oxford, Violet, New London Pleasure, Duke of York, Kent, College Pleasure, College Treble, City Delight, Tulip, Primrose, Oxford Reverse, London Scholars' Pleasure, Morning Exercise, Cambridge, Morning Star, Evening Star, Coventry, Ely, Rochester, Treble Bob Reverse, Morning Pleasure, Symphony, Cheapside, College Delight, Royal Bob, Worcester, Chichester, Durham, York, Bristol, Lichfield, London, Wells, College Exercise, London Delight Evening Exercise.

The ringers on this occasion were stationed in the following manner :—John Briggs, *Treble ;* David Bailey, *Second ;* Hezekiah Briggs, *Third ;* James Lilley, *Fourth ;* Henry Dickinson, *Fifth ;* Isaac Rhodes, *Tenor.* The peals were conducted by Hezekiah Briggs and Isaac Rhodes. Time occupied in ringing, 5 hours and 11 minutes. The above is the greatest number of peals on record rung by one company, all living in the same town; and was acknowledged to be a masterpiece by the best authorities of the time. The performance, so far as is known, is without a parallel in the history of change-ringing.

In this wide field the Bingley Society continued to range, with occasional extra "touches" and red-letter days, which would occupy too much space to enumerate. On the 18th April, 1843, the remains of John Nicholson, the Airedale Poet, were interred in the Bingley Parish Churchyard, and the company rang a solemn slow-beat mourning peal, with the bells muffled on the occasion, in respect to the memory of the bard, who had so often made the bells his theme. The poet was a frequent visitor to the belfry, and a warm friend of the ringers, who have treasured up many of his quaint sayings, when he was enjoying a social chat with them."

The following names compose the society of change-ringers at Bingley, from its institution in 1778 to 1878, when the alterations were made in the peal:—Joseph Longbottom, William Moulding, Henry Moulding, James Tillotson (*Treble*), Hezekiah Briggs, Isaac Rhodes, — Baldwin, William Gott, David Bailey, William Wilkinson, John Smith, John Briggs, Henry Dickinson,

HOLY TRINITY CHURCH, BINGLEY.

James Lilley, Jonas Bailey, Thomas Green, Joseph Dickinson, William Bailey, John Wilkinson, T. Wilkinson Green, Edward Walbank, Thomas Walbank, James Ingham, Jonas Ainsworth (*Treble*), Alfred Anderson (*Treble*), Samuel Green, J. Ainsworth with B. Lightfoot.

A new set of Cambridge chimes was added in 1897, as a Jubilee memorial of Her Majesty's sixty years' reign.

By an order in Council, dated March 17th, 1869, a district chapelry was assigned to Holy Trinity Church (all fees being relinquished by the Mother Church), and it thenceforward became a new vicarage. The foundation stone of the church was laid by Alfred Harris, Esq., of Ryshworth Hall, on May 21st, 1866, and the building was consecrated Oct. 22nd, 1868.* Mr. Harris contributed £1,000 towards the £5,000 required for its erection. As the seats (numbering 700) are all free and unappropriated, the offertory system was from the first introduced, and during the first year yielded about £420, exclusive of £230 at the opening services. In 1870 a new organ, built by Messrs. Radcliffe and Sagar, of Leeds, was placed in the church at a cost of £350, raised by subscription; also a beautiful reredos was presented by Alfred Harris, junr., Esq., from a design by Mr. R. Norman Shaw. In 1880 a substantial Gothic steeple, 170 feet high, was erected over the chancel, at a cost of £1,140, also raised by subscription. In 1884 the church was thoroughly restored, and re-opened on August 5th, by the new Bishop preaching on the occasion his first sermon in the diocese after his consecration as Bishop of Ripon. The services in the church are now well attended, and with the large increase in the number of houses of late years in the parish, the parochial responsibilities have proportionately increased.

The following have been the vicars of Holy Trinity, with the dates of their induction: Oct. 20th, 1868, Albert Hudson, M.A., who died April 11th, 1877, aged 35; Aug. 14th, 1877, Henry Lewis Williams, M.A.; Aug. 7th, 1888, Fred. Wm. Bardsley, M.A., the present vicar.

The schools in connection with the church were opened on Nov. 11th, 1871. In 1879 a new wing was added, including one school-room and three large class-rooms, at a cost of about £800, as a memorial of the late Rev. Albert Hudson. This extra provision was utilized for Day and Sunday Schools, and was much needed. The vicarage was built in 1872. It is proposed to erect a permanent Mission Church at Gilstead in place of the present wooden structure, on a site given by Mr. John Walker, of Gilstead.

* A full description of the church will be found in the *Ripon Diocesan Calendar* for 1869, pp. 163-5.

The Grammar School.

Definite information with respect to the origin of the Grammar School is wanting; but as early as the year 1529 a certain piece of land and some closes in Greenhill, in Bingley parish, had been bequeathed in trust for finding a schoolmaster to teach grammar within the town of Bingley. Also certain messuages, with some lands thereto belonging, within the township of Bingley "had time out of mind been assigned and employed for and towards the maintenance of a schoolmaster, teaching grammar within the town, and that three several rent-charges of 13s. 4d., 13s. 4d., and 6s. 8d. had in the year 1570 been granted out of lands and premises in the parish of Bingley to trustees upon the same trusts. Also by deed of feoffment, dated 19th October, 1602, a house with the appurtenances in Bingley were conveyed to trustees, in trust that the yearly rent and profit should be employed for the maintenance of a schoolmaster." Under the will of William Wooller, dated March 27th, 1597, the rents of certain closes called Buredge Close, Lightfoot Close, Hanging Acre, Mastall, &c., were by indenture, dated 1616, assigned to the use of the poor of Bingley and towards the maintenance of a schoolmaster at Bingley. Michael Broadley, by will dated in 1613, gave to the school the sum of £40, to be disposed at the discretion of his executors, Nicholas Walker and Thomas Howgill, then schoolmaster, and in 1618 vicar of Bingley. Furthermore, in 1691 Samuel Sunderland gave certain lands, &c., in Heaton and Wilsden for the benefit of the school, and lands, &c., in Manningham for the benefit of the poor of Bingley.

In the Report of Endowed Charities for the West Riding of Yorkshire (Parish of Bingley) published in 1894, and from which I have taken the above abridged information, there is a schedule of lands and hereditaments given exclusively to the use of the Free Grammar School at Bingley. It fills four folio pages, and in it there is stated to belong to the school in 1862 the sum of £348 0s. 6d. in stock, and £135 8s. 2d. in the bank, besides £78 15s. from the Sunderland Charity for the benefit of the schoolmaster. This endowment fund continued to increase in value, and in 1891 it amounted to £968 10s. 7d.; but with grants from Government and the County Council, and a few sums from other sources, the total was raised to the handsome sum of £1,212 4s. 9d. This is independent of the boys' and girls' fees, which in the same year amounted to £407.

The following are some of the properties of the school in 1845, with their then tenants at Bingley. The names are curious and interesting, and nearly all can be identified:—Pinfold Acre (site of Olive Terrace), Mastalls, Dubbfield, Croft, Hanging Acre, Louse pasture, Apothecary hill, &c., together about 11 acres, in occupation of Thomas Wetherhead; Lady House Ing, Clover Close, Puggle-field, Square field, the Roughs, &c., together nearly 10 acres, in occupation of Thomas Wild; Six days' work, Four days' work, Three days' work, &c., together 7½ acres arable and 1 acre grass, in occupation of Francis Whitley; three houses and shops, garden, coal-yard, and cottages, occupied by Samuel Atkinson (at corner of Park Road and Main Street); the Grammar School and garden, occupied by Leonard Metcalfe.

The old abandoned school, near the Parish Church, of which I give a view, was built early in the 17th century. Its interior length is 50 feet, and width 21 feet, while the walls are nearly two feet thick. It is a two-storey building. The lower room has been lighted, with four mullioned windows on each of the two long sides; the south gable of this room having a five-light and the chamber above a four-light window, shewing that the school was once open at this end, and looked out on to a pleasant garden. A massive stone fire-place appears in the middle of the east wall of the lower room, while the upper chamber was warmed from a fire-place in the south-east angle. In 1781 it was ordered that all certificates, &c., respecting the town's business "be lodged in the chest in the school chamber." The roof of the building has now fallen in, and the floor is heaped up with debris and a thick growth of dockens and wild flowers.

Though the old school be now in ruins, it must ever be

remembered for the many interesting associations that surround it. Within its now crumbled walls many a Bingley youth received the education that helped him to rise in the world; and some, too, were trained here who achieved no small distinction in after life. Nicholson, the Airedale poet, was educated here; so, too, was Richard Thornton, who went out to Central Africa with Dr. Livingstone, and perished in the effort to extend our knowledge of that wild Land of the Unknown (*see* under

OLD GRAMMAR SCHOOL, BINGLEY.

COTTINGLEY). The late Mr. H. W. Wickham, M.P. for Bradford, and some time Chairman of the Lancashire and Yorkshire Railway Company, went as a boy to this school, I am told, from his home at Cottingley. Canon McCormick, Chaplain in Ordinary to the Queen, and formerly vicar of Holy Trinity, Hull, was never, I am informed, at the Grammar School, but was a private pupil of Mr. Dixon when he was master of the school. Mr. John

Hardy, first M.P. for Bradford, was a pupil of Mr. Hudson, at Bingley, and entered the school at the tender age of seven. Mr. Hardy, who was born in 1773, was father of the Right Hon. the Earl of Cranbrook, ex-Home Secretary, Secretary of State for India, Lord President of the Council, &c. His lordship, who is now in his 84th year, has communicated to me some interesting particulars respecting his father's first introduction to the Bingley schoolmaster. He was then preparing to retire for the night, and saw the tall man in a big wig leaning over his bed. The youngster was so terrified at this, his first strange glimpse of his future mentor, that he ran down stairs and out of the house, and was with difficulty overtaken and brought home on horse-back. Very soon afterwards the master won his affection by his tact and friendship, which was retained as long as Mr. Hudson lived. Mr. Hardy was also always a great friend of the two Hartleys, who succeeded as head masters of the school. Lord Cranbrook, I may add, was well acquainted with Bingley and its neighbourhood in his younger days, when staying with his godfather, Major Walker Ferrand, at Harden Grange. The late Mr. Ferrand, M.P., of St. Ives, was a pupil at the school under Dr. Hartley, and among other of Dr. Hartley's scholars at this time was the late eminent surgeon and naturalist, Dr. George Busk, F.R.S., F.L.S., F.Z.S., &c., who was born at St. Petersburg, in 1808. He was one of the founders of the Microscopical and Anthropological Societies, and for many years was editor of the *Journal* of the first-named society. While at Bingley he had good opportunities for the gratification of his natural history tastes; his love of nature and retiring habits would often estrange him from his school-fellows when bent on some errand of investigation, or in search of objects in the surrounding woods and lanes. His contributions to the publications of the learned societies are very numerous.

When Mr. Hudson died, in 1785, he was succeeded by the Rev. Richard Hartley, whose son, Dr. Hartley, was master of the school for 45 years, and the school then enjoyed a high reputation. He died in 1836, when Mr. Anthony Metcalfe, a native of Marsett, in Semerdale, where he was born in 1797, was appointed. Mr. Metcalfe had been assistant master for some time previously, and although the School Trust required the principal to be a University graduate, Mr. Metcalfe's qualifications were such as to enable him to hold the position for many years with satisfaction to all concerned. His failing health eventually obliged the Governors to appoint the Rev. Thomas Dixon, M.A., of Cambridge, and Mr. Metcalfe continued to assist him until his death in January, 1855. He is interred in the Parish Churchyard.

In 1853 a new school was built, at a cost of about £1,000, but in a few years it had to be abandoned, as it shewed signs of giving way; the site unfortunately being close to the treacherous Bingley Bog, which gave the railway contractors so much trouble. In 1868 another school was erected on a new site belonging to Wooller's Charity, close to the highroad between the town and Crossflatts. Under the provisions of the Endowed Schools Commissioners' Scheme (1878) the benefit of the endowments was extended to the education of girls and the teaching of science, in connection with the Bingley Mechanics' Institute. By this scheme Mr. Dixon, the head master, ceased to hold office, and received an annual pension of £125 for life. This sum has been regularly paid to him, and for many years he has held a chaplaincy at Barcelona, in Spain. Mr. Sutcliffe, the present head master, succeeded Mr. Dixon, and under his management the school has continued to hold a leading position among the educational institutions in the north. His son, Mr. Halliwell Sutcliffe, is a well-known novelist of good repute, being author of *A Man of the Moors* and other works.

The present Governors are:—The Vicar of Bingley, Messrs. John Walker, Robert Clough, William Town, Rev. J. Martin, J. Bedford, Samuel Smith, Thomas Smith, W. Greenwood, William Rhodes, R. Conchar, Henry Dunn (Shipley), Herbert Sharp, Mrs. Edwards, and Mrs. Angus. Head Master; Mr. John Sutcliffe, B.A. Assistant Masters: Messrs. S. C. Hodgson, B.A., and W. Bartley. French Master: Mr. A. Messiaen. Drawing Master: Mr. C. F. Dawson. Clerk: Mr. Alfred Platts.

The National Schools.

The Parish Church Sunday School at Bingley was one of the first established in this part of England. In his *Journal* for Sunday, July 18th, 1784, the Rev. John Wesley mentions that he preached that day in Bingley Church, and before service he stepped into the Sunday School, which, he says, "contains 240 children, taught by several masters, and superintended by the curate." It was then the only school of the kind for a large district, and was shared both by Church people and Dissenters. At first it had paid teachers, but as the movement spread these were abolished, and voluntary workers took their places. Mr. Crompton was one generous helper, and he also opened a school at Esholt about the same time. Subsequently at Bingley there arose some differences respecting forms of prayer, when the several denominations concerned separated, and henceforward carried on the schools at their respective places of worship. The Church party not being satisfied with the education imparted on the Sabbath only, took up the subject of secular education, while at the same time religious teaching was to accompany it. This led to the erection of the National Schools for boys and girls living in the parish.

The schools were erected in 1814, on a site in Park Road belonging to the St. Ives estate. The land was then in the occupation of Messrs. Collier & Hodgson, and for some years before 1840 Mr. Thomas Foulds was the tenant, and he received a ground rent of £2 2s. a year from the trustees. The cost of raising the buildings was about £1,600, towards which the London National School Society gave £300. The rest was contributed by voluntary subscription; amongst the principal donors being Lieutenant-General Twiss £340, Rev. Dr. Hartley £200, Walker Ferrand, Esq., £190, Edward Ferrand, Esq., £166 15s., William Ellis £100, and the York Diocesan Society £50. Subscribers of £5 a year, or £25 to the Building Fund, were to be members of the committee.

The late Mr. William Ellis, of Castlefield, took, perhaps, the most active part in the management of the school for nearly the first thirty years of its existence, and for some years had sole control of the building. On the appointment of Mr. Cheadle to the vicarage of Bingley, in 1837, a committee was formed, consisting of the vicar and six others. A local woolcomber, named William Davey, was appointed to teach writing and accounts at a salary of £4 a year; but in 1840 that method of instruction was given up, and a more qualified master was appointed in the person of Mr. Richardson, who was postmaster of the town from the year 1830 to 1862. In 1870, when the Education Act was passed, the school took its place as a part of the great educational machinery of the country. In 1884 four class-rooms were added; the funds for this provision being raised by means of a bazaar. There are about 450 children now on the books.

The Management Committee consists of the trustees, the churchwardens of the Parish Church, and four other members chosen as representatives of the parents. The present trustees are the Ven. Archdeacon Kilner (vicar), George Lane Fox, William Ferrand, John B. Sharp, Benjamin Broadbent, and Charles W. Dunlop, Esqs.

BINGLEY NONCONFORMISTS.

The Independents.

THE followers of Oliver Heywood and George Fox are doubtless the oldest representatives of the Dissenters in Bingley. Heywood's house, where he lived and died, and wrote nearly all his books, was in a little yard called "Speight's Fold," at Northowram, the home of the present writer's great-grandfather. Heywood began to preach in Airedale about 1650, when a very young man. His first visit to Bingley was in September, 1667, and he stayed at Marley Hall, belonging to Robert Parker, Esq., of Browsholme, but then in the occupation of Joshua Walker. In the evening he preached to a considerable audience, "who were much affected." On the following day he called on his "good friend, Mr. Bentley," who had been compelled by the rigours of the Five Mile Act, of 1665, to fly from Halifax and seek a temporary home in this parish. In 1672 he returned to Halifax, and eventually died there.

Mr. Heywood doubtless made a very good impression on the hearts and minds of his congregation at Bingley, and his exceeding piety and eloquence, and thorough earnestness of purpose quickly bore fruit. His congregation gathered in strength, and in October, 1679, he again passed through the town, on this occasion sojourning with Thomas Leach, Esq., at West Riddlesden Hall, where he preached, tradition says from the staircase facing the spacious entrance hall of this historic mansion. This visit was quickly followed by another in the month of January, 1680, when a numerous congregation assembled at Ryshworth Hall, then the residence of Mr. Joseph Walker. Here he calmly exhorted his hearers to profit by the truth as recorded in his text, taken from the Psalms cxix., 158. In February he was again at West Riddlesden, and other visits followed; his fervent preaching constantly gathering fresh auditors, so that on the passing of the Toleration

Act in 1688 the community at Bingley decided on having an adequate place of meeting for public worship of their own. For a year or two they worshipped in each others houses, which had been licensed for the purpose. Then, it is said, Mr. Walker built the "Old Chapel," as it was latterly called, at Bingley, which became the mother church of the Independents for a wide district until the year 1780, when the Dissenters of Keighley began to worship in a place of their own. But for two long centuries the old Independent Chapel, at the corner of Chapel Lane, Bingley (illustrated on the opposite page), stood as a monument to the persevering evangelism of the great apostle of Independency in this district, the Rev. Oliver Heywood. When he died in 1701 we are told that in some parts of upper Airedale there was a woeful religious relapse, and the people fell back on their old ways, playing football and indulging in other ardent sports on the Sabbath, in which even the clergy joined. It was verily an attempt to revive the days of the "Merry Monarch."

Such a relapse does not appear to have taken place among the Puritans of Bingley, which had really now become a citadel of strength among the Protestant Dissenters in this part of Yorkshire, and whose numbers were greatly augmented at a later period in Bingley by the soul-stirring visits of John Wesley. The Rev. Accepted Lister, son of Joseph Lister, of Thornton, the historian of the Siege of Bradford, was the first resident minister of the newly-founded church at Bingley, and here he preached in 1694, and finally settled in May, 1695; the house and chapel being under the same roof offered a strong inducement to the new minister, who suffered much from physical infirmity. A sketch of his life and family, by Mr. T. T. Empsall, appeared in the *Bradford Antiquary*, vol. II., page 289. He remained at Bingley till 1702, when the Rev. T. Wainman, of Eastwood, near Halifax, succeeded him, efficiently sustaining the good work begun by Mr. Lister. After a faithful pastorate of more than 43 years he died at Bingley, and was buried in the Parish Churchyard, where his tombstone may be seen.

From 1746 to 1758 the congregation was without

settled minister, when the Rev. Thos. Lillie was elected, an account of whom will be found in the *Protestant Magazine* for May, 1882. He died in 1797, aged 77, and was buried in the old chapel, but in 1819 his remains were removed to the new chapel, where a monument describes him as "the diligent, peaceful, useful, and much-respected pastor of the Congregational Church for forty-four years." His successors were the Revs. W. Stephens (1797), Abraham Hudswell (1800), and Abraham Clarkson, the latter

OLD CONGREGATIONAL CHURCH, BINGLEY.

entering on his duties here in the summer of 1817. Largely through his exertions, the new chapel, near the old Market House, was erected, and the building was opened for service on April 29th, 1818. It cost upwards of £1,200. The deeds relating to the chapel property, which have been placed in my hands, go back to the time of Queen Anne. At that time, and up to the building of the chapel in 1818, I find there was a good messuage on the site called Lead House, besides several cottages, an orchard, and a croft. Lead House was the property of Joseph Hammond, and by the Act of Indulgence was licensed for public worship, and was one of the first houses in Bingley so privileged before the erection of the "Old Chapel," in Chapel Lane. In 1708 it became the property of John Hammond, who left two daughters, Anne and Elizabeth, the latter of whom acquired Lead House in 1735. It was subsequently divided into two tenements, one of which in 1773 was occupied by the pastor, Mr. Lillie, and the other by Judith Smith. The ministers continued to reside here till Mr. Clarkson's time.

By indenture made Aug. 3rd, 1773, the Chapel estate (which included all the tenements, cottages, &c., granted and demised in 1740 unto Thos. Dobson, of Vicarage, Bingley, gentleman, by Thos. Law, ropemaker, and Elizabeth, his wife, of Bradford, in mortgage for the term of 500 years, and which in 1768 were assigned to the said John Atkinson in trust for Joseph Atkinson, of Huddersfield, merchant) was by Joseph Atkinson assigned to Joseph Hollings, Thos. Leach, John Coates, Joseph Smith, and Abm. Broadley, or the survivors of them, or the heirs of such survivors, that they with all convenient speed convey the said premises unto nine trustees, with intent that such nine trustees, or the survivors of them, shall pay and apply the rents and profits of the said premises granted and released for and towards the support of an Independent Calvinistic Minister of the Gospel in the Chapel at Bingley, such rents and profits to be collected half-yearly by the said nine trustees.

In 1817 these trustees were: Wm. Wilkinson, Thos. Leach, John Illingworth, David Whitley, Samuel Whitley, Michael Booth, Thos. Bairstow, John Stephenson, and John Hagar.

Mr. Clarkson was very diligent and active in his ministry, and regularly visited the surrounding villages, forming and organising congregations, and, preaching with great earnestness on the necessity of personal duty to God and to His church. Physical affliction obliged him to resign his charge in 1837, and he died, much lamented, in May, 1850. He was succeeded by the Rev. John Protheroe, during whose ministry the chapel at Harden was erected. Next came in 1841 the Rev. Wm. Atherton, a very able and industrious young man, who remained at Bingley till 1848. During his pastorate the chapel and schools were enlarged, and the chapel at Morton was also erected. Mr. Atherton died at Idle, at the early age of 33, in July, 1850. The Rev. Wm. Orgar was his successor at

Bingley, and held the charge about eleven years, when the Rev. E. S. Heron accepted it, and on July 20th, 1862, had the satisfaction of witnessing the laying of the corner-stone of a Memorial Bicentenary School (to commemorate the ejected Two Thousand) by Alderman Brown, of Bradford.

REV. JOSEPH MARTIN.

On the completion of the school, which is at the rear of the chapel, it was opened Nov. 19th, 1862, by a tea party and public meeting, over which Mr. Wm. Murgatroyd, J.P., presided. Mr. Heron removed in 1870 to Knoxville, Tennessee, U.S.A., and died there; his eldest daughter having married Mr. Jas. A. McCampbell, a prosperous farmer in that State. The Rev. J. H. Taylor, of Colne, was the next minister, and after four years service he resigned, and withdrew from the ministry. He was succeeded by the present pastor, the Rev. Joseph Martin, who is a native of Thaxted, in Essex, both his parents being of Huguenot descent. His father, William Martin, was for many years a deacon of the Congregational Church at Thaxted (then known as the "Old Independent Meeting House"), and a superintendent of the Sunday School. The son was put to the business of a corn-miller, which he followed till 1872, when he entered the Countess of Huntingdon's College at Cheshunt, in Hertfordshire. After four years of study there, he took the Soper Theological Scholarship, and he settled at Bingley in October, 1876. Mr. Martin has been an active and faithful servant to the cause at Bingley, and his geniality and liberal views have helped to cement the good feeling between the various denominations in the town. In 1889 extensive alterations and improvements were made in the chapel, necessitating an outlay of about £850. Subsequently a new and more convenient entrance was made to the chapel, which cost about £200. The whole of these charges have been met by subscriptions and the proceeds of a bazaar.

From the erection of the church, about 1690, there have been 12 settled ministers, giving an average ministry of 17½ years to each one, and in an interesting "Manual of the Congregational Church at Bingley," by Mr. Martin, and to which I am indebted for some of the facts here narrated, he observes: "Through the exceeding goodness of God, and the great kindness of His people, the present pastor has been permitted to go beyond that average." This is now the 22nd year of Mr. Martin's pastorate. The present trustees of the church are: Messrs. Jonas Atkinson, James Bailey, Alfred Bolton, Charles Dawson, Edward Foulds, William Foster, Jonas Howgate, Lawrence Lee, Ellis Longbottom, William Parker, Matthew Richardson, Benjamin Stephenson, and Sydney Waddington (secretary).

THE SOCIETY OF FRIENDS.

Although the Society of Friends is now practically extinct in Bingley, it was formerly a rather numerous sect, and there were several local houses in the seventeenth century, notably in Bingley and Crossflatts, where its members assembled for divine worship.* In this district the Society dates from the time of the Commonwealth, and, as befel other dissenting bodies, suffered severe persecution during the reign of religious intolerance that followed. When George Fox, the founder of the sect, visited Skipton in 1658, he held "great meetings," and he tells us that many journeyed from distant places to hear him preach, and became converts.

Around Bingley and Keighley many joined the new sect, and eventually under the Toleration Act a Meeting House was erected in Keighley (1690); one was built at Skipton in 1693, and another at Bradford about 1712. The Bingley Friends were originally included in the Keighley Meeting, and visited the Skipton Preparative Meeting, which continued to be headquarters of this meeting down to 1853, when it was arranged that Skipton, Addingham, and Lothersdale comprise the Skipton Preparative Meeting, and that Keighley be included in this meeting, which was to be held at such times and places as may by the members generally be deemed most desirable. At the same time it was arranged to hold the Monthly Meetings as follows:—Bradford 4, Leeds 3, Brighouse 1, Halifax 1, Huddersfield 1, Settle 1, and Skipton 1. This arrangement is at present in force, with the exception that Bentham takes the place of Skipton, where the Society has died out. Bentham in 1853, I may add, was included in the Settle Preparative Meeting, which embraced also Settle, Airton, and Newton. The Quarterly Meetings are now held at York, Leeds, Bradford, and Sheffield, and the Yearly Meeting in London.

From the old Minute Books at Keighley it appears a general subscription was opened towards the expenses of

* Thus in the Quaker Registers at York I find that the house of one William Frankland, at Bingley was licensed as a meeting-place, and here in 1698, 5 mo. 31 day, a marriage was solemnized between Abraham Grimshaw and Elizabeth Bond, both of Calverley.

building the Leeds Meeting House in 1789, as the former subscriptions had fallen short; the cost having exceeded the estimates considerably. Similarly in 1779 a subscription list was opened towards defraying the expense of building the Meeting House at Otley. The like of other places. On the 24th day, 10th month, 1784, the Skipton Preparative Meeting was favoured by visits from the following Friends, who, with others, had been appointed to visit the several Preparative Meetings, viz.: William Tuke and Esther, his wife, John Hoyland and Elizabeth, his wife, and David Priestman, "which has been to the satisfaction of this meeting." The William Tuke here mentioned was a wealthy and influential Quaker, the founder of the Friends' Schools at York, and of other good works. One of his daughters was the celebrated Quakeress, Mrs. Sarah Grubb, and another, Elizabeth, married in 1795 Joshua Wheeler, of Hitchen, great-grandson of Joshua Wheeler, who was a Quaker prisoner in Bedford Gaol with John Bunyan, "the prating tinker," whose immortal book can now be read in eighty different tongues. Mary, daughter of above Joshua Wheeler, became the wife of another noted Quaker, James Ellis, of Bradford, who was born in 1798, and died in 1869, leaving 3 sons and 2 daughters; the second son being the Rev. Joseph Ellis, who was formerly in business with Mr. Thomas Holmes as worsted manufacturers at Dubb Mill, Bingley. He left the Society of Friends, studied at Cambridge for holy orders, became curate under the vicar of Bradford, and was eventually vicar of Wilsden.

Robert Ellis came to Bingley, and married a Bingley lady. He took the old Dubb corn mills about 1818, and was joined by his elder brother, the above James Ellis, about 1822. James and Robert had another brother, John Ellis, who was M.P. for Leicester, and Chairman of the Midland Railway Company. They were, by the way, not related to the Ellis's of Castlefields, Bingley. Robert Ellis while in Bingley occupied the bay-windowed house off Chapel Lane, now the *Vine Tree* inn, where he had a store for the sale of corn and meal. The ascent by the flight of steps adjoining has since been known as "Quaker

Hill." He and his brother James used generally on Sundays to drive to Bradford to attend the Meeting House there. In 1824 Mr. James Ellis, in conjunction with Messrs. Joshua and Samuel Priestman, took the old soke mills at Bradford, and there carried on the business of corn millers until 1836, when Mr. James Ellis, having left Bingley, went into partnership with his brother-in-law, the late Mr. John Priestman, of Bradford, carrying on the business at the same place, under the name of James Ellis & Co. In 1847 Mr. Ellis retired from the firm, and purchased an estate at Letterfrack, in Connemara, an old Quaker settlement in Ireland. At that time the potato famine was at its height, and thousands had to be fed out of the magistrates' hands, while hundreds of hunger-stricken people died on the moors or on the roads while endeavouring to reach the relief depôts. Many Yorkshire Quakers went out to render what assistance they could by carrying provisions with their own hands to the cabins of those who were too weak to walk. Among these helpers were the Right Hon. W. E. Forster, M.P. for Bradford, then a young man, and the late Mr. James Ellis. Mr. Ellis cultivated his estate in order to benefit the peasantry, and his generous actions among the Friends and others in that lonely Irish settlement will long be remembered.

In the old-Quaker Register preserved at York are recorded the names of many Bingley Quakers, among the oldest being the Shackletons, of Harden dale, whose voluminous history I have compressed into the short account of Shackleton House, in that beautiful and interesting valley. Then there were the Taylors, Lees, Heatons, and Mauds, of Ravenroyd, which during the early part of last century was quite a little metropolis of Quakerism. There was also a pretty numerous family of Maud, of Gawthorpe Hall, Crossflatts, and Castlefield, who were influential Friends in their day. The Friends had a burial-ground at Crossflatts, and used to meet for divine worship in an old house still standing at Crossflatts, shewn in the accompanying engraving. Timothy Maud on his marriage in 1684 lived at Castlefields, and about 1700 removed to Crossflatts. He had a son, Timothy, who was living at Gawthorpe Hall in 1720. William Maud, his orphan nephew, of St. Martin's parish, York, came to reside with him, and they cultivated the Hall farm, and in winter employed their hinds in spinning and weaving; being the first family, I understand, who introduced hand-loom weaving into Bingley. William Maud purchased property on Elm Tree Hill, and resided in his house there before 1760. There was a large garden attached, and a picturesque old summer-house, which possessed a striking feature in an ornamental flower-pot chimney. The

OLD QUAKER MEETING HOUSE, CROSSFLATTS.

windows commanded a fine view down the river, and in the building was a fire-place and a cupboard, the door of which bore the owner's initials and date, "W.M., 1760." The property had belonged to a Mr. Jonathan Casson, who got into financial difficulties, and in order to avoid arrest for debt locked himself in this summer-house, and his wife, I am told, used to bring his meals in a basket, which he pulled up by means of a rope through an upper window.

Elm Tree Hill, Bingley.

On Sundays only dare he walk out, as his arrest on that day could not legally be made. But eventually he gave himself up.

The above William Maud married a Waterhouse, of Hill End, who lived to an advanced age. He had a family of four sons: (1) James, a Quaker, who lived at Spring Head, now Myrtle Grove, which had been licensed for public worship. (2) Abraham, who died unmarried, and is buried in Bingley churchyard. He was apprenticed to Timothy Maud, of Gawthorpe, who in the deed of apprenticeship, dated 1st May, 1746, is described as a stuff weaver. He and his younger brother (3) William were also Quakers. (4) Timothy, the youngest, attended the Parish Church, and occupied the family property on Elm Tree Hill. He married Sarah, the youngest sister of Mr. James Murgatroyd, of Greenhill, and died Jan. 26th, 1822. She died in April, 1848. They left two sons; William, who lived in the old homestead on Elm Tree Hill, and James Murgatroyd Maud. William sold his inheritance at Bingley to Mr. Thomas Jowett about 1847. and settled in America. He married, and left a family of one son, Timothy, who died in Seattle, U.S.A., in 1885, and two daughters, Sarah, the elder, married to Mr. William Moore, and Ann, now living at Seattle. The latter resided at Bingley till she was 24, and has since travelled extensively at home and abroad. In December, 1896, when over 70 years of age, she visited Bingley, when the writer had the pleasure of a few hours' conversation with her; her recollections of old Bingley being most vivid and interesting, and she imparted most of the information I have here given respecting the old Quaker family of Gawthorpe, &c.

It was in the house adjoining the residence of the Mauds on Elm Tree Hill that the Friends met for divine worship. Miss Maud tells me that as a girl she had always heard it spoken of as the old Quaker Meeting House, and in this house she says the Rev. Dr. Hartley, vicar of Bingley (of the Eldwick Hartleys), was born in 1745. Next to it was Mr. Christopher Hanson's house and furniture shop, shewn in the annexed view. The old

Meeting House consisted of one large room, and there was a chamber above it. It was a plain, two-storey building, while the house behind, occupied by the Mauds, consisted of three storeys, owing to its position on the slope of the hill. The lower one was entered by a side door in the yard, while the main entrance was from the hill into the second storey, up a flight of solid stone steps, with a broad landing on the top.

The Meeting House at Crossflatts is one of several 17th century cottages; being the oldest block of houses now standing in this neighbourhood. Sixty years ago these old tenements and the houses at Castlefields were the only buildings existing about Crossflatts. All else has sprung up since then. In deeds belonging to Mr. Joseph Foster, of Crossflatts, the names of the tenants are given in 1825, when the property was conveyed to Mr. William Ellis.

The old Meeting House has a spacious mullion-window (now modernised) and a small side-window, originally a door-hole, which was kept well bolted, and only opened after dark when suspicious persons were about and the inmates could receive a message or parcel without unfastening the main door. Such precautionary openings were common in houses of this period. Upon entering there was a stout stone partition wall separating the entrance from the lower room (pulled down some years ago), and the meeting-room was upstairs, and originally consisted of one large apartment, with a "speaker's stand," or square pedestal, about twenty inches high, placed at one corner at the head of the stairs, and removed from outside observation at the window. Here the few ardent members of this humble society used to meet in bygone days to worship God in their own simple way. Their burial-ground, as I have said, was close by, but I cannot hear that more than four grave-stones have ever been observed, and one of these is inscribed to a William Lister.

Where Mr. Longbottom lives, in the Main Street, next door to Gawthorp's basket shop, seems also to have been occupied by a Quaker family named Walker, and many years ago one or more grave-slabs were dug up in the garden behind the house.

The Wesleyan Methodists.

I have told how the teachings of Oliver Heywood and George Fox roused religious life in this part of Airedale. It was therefore not surprising when wonderful John Wesley visited Bingley during the great Evangelical Revival in the middle of last century that the whole town and neighbourhood flocked to hear him, and so great was the crowd on each repeated visit that the occasion was always spoken of as "Wesley Fair." The active pioneer of Methodism, it is said, paid more turnpike toll than any man who ever lived. He travelled on an average 5,000 miles a year, and during his active life preached more than 40,000 sermons. His fervent oratory, observes Green, the historian, broke the lethargy of the clergy. In Airedale the Church of the Establishment was at a low ebb. Mr. Collins, vicar of Keighley, though suffering from infirmity, refused to employ a curate. At Bingley, under the Hartleys, church work made no progress. At Skipton clergymen joined the populace at football and other sports on the Sabbath.

John Wesley's coming to Bingley was the signal of a religious awakening. He was an Oxford scholar and clergyman of the Church of England, and more than once he preached in the Parish Church at Bingley, which was filled to overflowing. Never had such large congregations been seen in the church for probably a hundred years. This I gather from a remark in his *Journal* for 1776. Wesley visited Bingley in all thirteen times, from his first appearance in May, 1757, to his last in May, 1788. He died three years later. Bingley was to him a haven of happiness, and he was always sure of a hearty welcome whenever he came here. Saviour of man that he was, he had in some towns been pelted with earth and stones; but at Bingley people ran out to meet him with open arms, and literally strewed his path with flowers. On one occasion, in April, 1779, while staying with Mr. Busfeild, at Myrtle Grove, he called the place "a little paradise," and it was all this to him in the spiritual as well as to the bodily sense.

Dr. James Crocker.

Mr. George Severs.

Soon after Wesley's first visit a society was formed at Bingley, and in 1768 we have a list of its then members. They were: Thomas Middlesbrough, John Wildman, Benjamin Wilkinson, John Gott, James Farrah, Sarah Moor, John and Martha Curtiss, Wm. Maud, Wm. and James Whitley, John and Mary Whitaker, Wm. Haughton, Sarah Harrison, Thos. Patrick, Robt. Watson, Ann Dobson, Abraham Hartley, David Binns, Joseph Brown, John Jackson, Christ. Townend, Abm. Mitchell, Grace ——, Eliz. Wood, Robert Walsh, Mary Middlesbrough, Hannah Wild, John Walker, and John Whitley. According to Mr. Ward, their first place of worship was a blacksmith's shop on Elm Tree Hill, near to the entrance of Gott's Yard. The next place appears to have been a large room over a block of buildings which occupied the site where the first chapel was erected. At the Sessions held at Bradford, 15th July, 1762, I find that a certain house called Short's House, facing the Market Place, was certified by John Skirrow and Thomas Middlebrook to be a place of meeting of Protestant Dissenters to preach the Gospel, and that the same was recorded as such pursuant to the statute. This I take to be the Wesleyan Room mentioned by Mr. Ward, who says that John Skirrow and others seceded to the Baptists somewhere between 1760 and 1766. As his name does not appear on the list of Wesleyan members for 1768, he must have joined the Baptists immediately after the license for Short's House was granted. He died in 1785, and was interred in the Baptist Chapel, Bingley.

The old Methodist Chapel in the Main Street appears to have been built about 1790. The principal entrance was close to the old Market House, and there was another at the side on Elm Tree Hill. Mr. Thomas Whitley purchased the property for £800, and when the place was sold in 1817 the following were the trustees: John Moorhouse, Joshua Briggs, Joseph Cryer, John Dean, Matthew Foster, Wm. Whitley, Wm. Foulds, John Wild, David Binns, Josh. Barraclough, and Thomas Nicholson, father of the poet.

Bingley was originally in "Haworth Round," but in 1776 Keighley was made head of a circuit, and it was joined to that. In 1808 Bingley was made head of a circuit, and has since continued as such. Many are the "good men and true" who in the present and the past have laboured for the society in this district. Among the earlier members was John Whitley and his son Francis, of Toils Farm, Eldwick. John died in 1818, aged 90, and his son in 1821, aged 77, as is recorded on their tombstone in the Parish Churchyard. John Wesley, it is said, used to call at the old moorside farm on his journeys between Bingley and Otley. (*See* ELDWICK.)

The following are recorded as among the active local workers in the cause in the early part of this century, many of whose descendants are still living in the neighbourhood: John and Nancy Horner, Susan Bentley, John Moorhouse, John Dean, David Walbank, James Speight, John Cryer, Samuel and Wm. Curtiss, Wm. Cockshott (the last three local preachers), John, Matthew, and Thomas Longbottom, John Smith, John Wilkinson, Stephen Snowden, John Wild, David Binns, steward of the chapel property, &c. Mr. Ward in his little volume recounts the circumstances which led to the erection of the new chapel in 1816. It cost nearly £4,000, and stood where the present station of the Midland Railway now is, having to be removed when the station was built about eight years ago. In 1816 there was scarcely a house, where there are now hundreds, between the chapel and the Dubb.

Among the original trustees of the chapel was Mr. John Sharp, elder brother of William and Jonas Sharp, whose family have been liberal benefactors to the Wesleyan cause in Bingley. Mrs. Paulina Wyrill, a daughter of Mr. John Sharp, died, after a short wedded life, in 1839. Mr. Ward relates how shortly before her death she purchased a writing album, intended principally for contributions from ministers and eminent Christians. The author has this album before him, and it contains a number of beautiful autograph poems from the pens of several well-known Yorkshire and other worthies, including James Montgomery, Hartley Coleridge, Edwin Waugh, "the Lancashire Burns"; George Ackroyd, J.P., of Bradford; William Dearden, the bard of Caldene, &c. Not very long before Edwin Waugh's death in 1898 the author had the pleasure of meeting him at the house of his friend, Mr. George Ackroyd, when this interesting album was produced. From it I quote the following admirable Paraphrase of Psalm 42, verse 5, written nearly forty years ago by Mr. Ackroyd. It bears the date 20th April, 1859:—

"*Why art thou cast down, O my soul?*"

How oft when in distress we mourn,
  And Hope is well-nigh fled;
Some kind and providential turn
  Relieves our souls of dread;
And then how soon our fear departs,
  And we, ashamed to own
Our weakness, wonder that our hearts
  Should ever be cast down.

Could we but more undoubting trust
  Our heavenly Father's care,
We oft should find He loves us most
  When least he seems to spare.
While changes last, dark hours will come,—
  Yet why renew our fears,
Since faith can penetrate the gloom
  The heaviest trial wears?

A little, and our fears forlorn
  Disturbing nature's sight,
Shall vanish with the opening morn
  Of everlasting light;
And then, O rapture! we shall see
  The Lord of Life above;
And chant throughout Eternity
  The wonders of His love!

Mr. Ackroyd is still with us, and his two sons have for many years carried on business at Stanley Mills, Bingley.

The present handsome Wesleyan Chapel in Mornington Road, which has almost the proportions of a cathedral, was erected in 1874, and opened by the Rev. Dr. Punshon, President of the Wesleyan Conference, on September 23rd. It cost more than £13,000, towards which the two brothers, Messrs. Alfred and William Sharp, of Bingley, contributed about £6,000 (including the organ and manse). It has a fine tower, with spire, 160 feet high, which in June, 1897, was improved by the addition of a very useful clock, a Jubilee gift of Mr. Herbert Sharp, as a memorial of his late father, Mr. Alfred Sharp. Mr. Herbert Sharp has also quite recently come forward with the generous offer to erect and fit up at his own cost a new Mission Church for the Wesleyans on a site belonging to the trustees which adjoins York Street and North Street. It is expected to commence the work in June, 1898, on the expiration of the tenancies of the land it will occupy. In addition, the trustees of Mornington Road Church have acquired land adjoining for the erection of Sunday Schools.

The laymen who have sustained the cause of Methodism in Bingley stand out more prominently because of the constant change of ministers. Foremost among those who have been unwearied in their efforts to build up and maintain the cause was the late Mr. Alfred Sharp, of whose services and varied benefactions I shall speak in the chapter devoted to the EXTENSION OF THE TOWN AND TRADE. A remarkable revival, which occurred more than fifty years ago, brought into the church a number of young men, who infused into it fresh life and vigour. Among these were Messrs. Alfred Sharp, William Whitley, Samuel White (who built up the Park Road Leather Works), the sons of Mr. John Craven, of Burrage House, and Mr. Robert Waterhouse. Mr. Francis Butterfield was a popular local preacher for forty years. Others had been "pillars in the church" for many years, as Messrs. William Anderton, Thomas Hodgson, Isaac Smith, and John Harrison. Mr. John Smith, who came from Addingham, and died at Bingley, April 23rd, 1898, aged 78, was a local preacher for fully sixty years, being one of the oldest in England at the time of his death, and a man of marked originality. The tall, stooping figure of "Father" Thomas Longbottom and the burly form of Mr. Samuel Atkinson will also be remembered.

Messrs. William Haigh and Matthew Platts were also staunch supporters to the end. Mr. Platts was of a Derbyshire family, but had been in business in Bingley for a number of years. When quite a young man he joined Mr. William Haigh in a drapery business at Keighley, and subsequently commenced manufacturing at Dubb Mills, Bingley, in partnership with Mr. Field, an arrangement, however, which only continued for a short time. Mr. Platts started on his own account at Peel Mills, and afterwards at Britannia Mills. Eventually the present extensive Albert Mills, on the canal bank, were erected, where the business is still carried on by his sons. Mr. Platts died in June, 1892, aged 68. His family is still strongly attached to the local Wesleyans, and one of his sons, Mr. Henry Platts, is circuit steward, together with Mr. William Thornton, who has been for many years a most useful local preacher and class leader. Mr. Nicholas H. Walbank, the respected secretary of the Bingley Building Society is now, I believe, the oldest local preacher in the circuit, and has been usefully and prominently identified with local Wesleyanism for more than forty years. His literary tastes have been shown by his frequent contributions to the local press and by his valuable public lectures.

Dr. James Crocker has also been a life-long and most valued friend in this body, and has held, and continues to hold, many important offices. He is a native of Wincanton, in Somersetshire, and comes of an old Wesleyan family long resident in that part of the country. As a medical practitioner he settled at Bingley about 1870, having previously resided at Wetherby. He has been a local preacher over forty years, and is widely known and appreciated outside his own church and neighbourhood. He is a member of the District Local Preachers' Committee; also honorary member of the Local Preachers' Mutual Aid Association, and has been chosen as a delegate to their annual congresses. He is a class leader, and has been circuit steward nine years, and during that time has represented the Bingley Wesleyan Circuit at the synods; several times he has been elected by those synods as one of the lay representatives of the Halifax and Bradford Districts at the annual Wesleyan conferences. He is also a trustee of several chapels, schools, and other Wesleyan property in Bingley and elsewhere. As a layman and medical practitioner, holding various public appointments, Dr. Crocker has rendered valuable and self-sacrificing services to the cause of Wesleyan Methodism, and is deservedly one of the most honoured members of the society in this town.

In the old chapel a flourishing day school was carried on in the lower room up to 1861, when the present large and handsome buildings in Hill Street were erected and opened. The first master was Mr. T. J. Reynard, who was followed in 1866 by Mr. George Severs, a Wesleyan by birth, and a native of Ripon, under whose prosperous management the school has been conducted to the present time. Some of his old pupils have won University distinctions, and others are occupying prominent positions in art, science, and medicine in England as well as abroad. Mr. Severs, who is an Undergraduate in Science of London University, introduced the Government teaching of chemical and physical science into the Bingley Mechanics' Institute, and also into the old Mechanics' Institutes of Bradford and Saltaire. The success of these and other classes led eventually to the establishment of Technical Schools and to the teaching of science in the Day Schools.

In addition to his thirty years' connection with the Wesleyan Day Schools at Bingley, Mr. Severs has been from the first closely connected with the Sunday School as teacher of select classes and superintendent, and most of the churches in the town and neighbourhood have made use of him to address their children at their school anniversaries. In church matters, also, he has been indefatigable. As society and circuit steward, and as trustee of various Wesleyan properties, he has been most active and useful in promoting the welfare of Wesleyan Methodism in the town. In Band of Hope work, and as local representative of the Society for the Prevention of Cruelty to Children, he has also rendered invaluable service. His portrait accompanies that of Dr. Crocker on page 196.

I have not space to dwell on the good Christian effort that has been carried on from last century to the present by the numerous ministers and their co-workers in the circuit. Much has already been written on this subject by the Rev. John Ward in his little volume, *Methodism in Bingley*, published in 1868, when he was one of the ministers here. The book also contains brief notices of other places in the circuit.

The following have been the ministers since 1863 :

1864-5 Samuel Taylor, Thomas Waterhouse, William Hawken.
1866 William Lees, William Pritchard, William Hawken.
1867 William Lees, William Pritchard, Matthew C. Pennington.
1868 John Walter, William Pritchard, Matthew C. Pennington.
1869 John Walter, William H. W. Evans, Thomas Hackett.
1870 John Walter, Thomas Hackett.
1871 John Morris, Thomas Hackett.
1872-3 John Morris, Josiah Mee.
1874 Jonathan Henshall, Josiah Mee.
1875-6 Jonathan Henshall, Edward A. Wain.
1877-9 Thomas A. Rayner, Joseph Olphert.
1880-2 John Gunnel, William Kirkman.
1883-5 Abel Wood, George S. Meek.
1886-8 Abraham Pearce, John Nayler.
1889-91 Joseph Charlesworth, Frederick Hunter.
1892-4 W. Norton Milnes, Robert Dixon.
1895-8 Thomas Hepton, Robinson Lang, who remove in August, 1898.

THE BAPTISTS.

As is well known, the Baptists in Yorkshire suffered severe persecution under the Conventicle Act of 1664, but in Bingley they were not a numerous body for a full century after this date, when their first public meeting-place was established. Previously services had been held in the houses of the scattered Baptist families. They, in common with other Yorkshire Baptists, enjoyed the occasional ministrations of the eminent and courageous William Mitchell, who for his "unswerving loyalty to the truth" was twice cast into York prison. Prominent also among those who assisted the cause here was the Rev. John Fawcett, of Bradford, author of the well-known hymn which begins with—

"Blest is the tie that binds
Our hearts in Christian love."

Mr. (afterwards Dr.) Fawcett rose to high distinction among the Baptists in England, and a *Life* of him, written by his son, was published in 1818. In 1759 he married Susannah, daughter of Mr. John Skirrow, of Bingley, who at that time was a principal leader and local preacher among the Wesleyans at Bingley. As I have explained in my account of the Wesleyans, it was in July, 1762 that this John Skirrow obtained from the West Riding magistrates a certificate to preach the Gospel in a house facing the Market Place in Bingley, called Short's House, a name that is not now remembered. It must have been about this time that he seceded from the Wesleyans, and shortly afterwards he was, along with nine others, publicly baptized in the river Aire. Many others joined, and the cause prospered, so that in 1764 a chapel was erected in the Main Street, which until recently stood on the site of the present Co-operative Stores.

A year after the erection of the chapel, a Mr. Butterworth, of Goodshaw, was appointed pastor, and he worked so assiduously that when John Wesley visited Bingley in August, 1766, we find him lamenting "with an heavy heart" that so many Methodists here had gone over to the Anabaptists. John Skirrow died in 1785, aged 74, and was interred in the Baptist Chapel, and many of his descendants lie entombed in the old burial-yard adjoining the former ministers' house in Chapel Lane.

The succeeding ministers were: In 1768, John Dracup; 1779, William Hartley; 1797, Joseph Harrison; 1800, Abraham Greenwood; 1806, John Greenwood. For nine years subsequently the pulpit was supplied by lay preachers, students, and neighbouring ministers. At the end of that term, in 1820, Mr. Bottomley, of Horton College, was ordained pastor, and he laboured for nine years, when he resigned. Mr. McKaeg succeeded, and during his ministry the chapel was enlarged. At one time the church was very generously helped by the Yorkshire Association of Baptist Churches. It, however, lost possession of its manse and burying-ground in Chapel Lane, and must at some period, extending over several years, have buried its dead under the floor of the old chapel, because in 1876, when the place was sold, the remains of more than 60 interments were found in the ground beneath.

The old burial-ground in Chapel Lane is, as stated, no longer used for burials. It contains eight memorial stones to the families of Skirrow, Beck, Leach, Burdett, and Penney, dating from the first interment in 1825 to the year 1856. The Skirrows and Mouldens appear to be the oldest families connected with the Bingley Baptists.

In 1831 the Rev. Mr. Bottomley was invited, after an absence of 21 years, to accept the pastorate again, and he continued to labour with much favour. He was succeeded by the Revs. Rodway, Burton, and Dawson, the latter coming to Bingley from Princes Risborough, subsequently removing to Bishop Burton, and returning to Bingley in 1865, where he died, August 9th, 1870. For some years afterwards the church was without settled pastor; but in the autumn of 1864, as the result of an application to the Rev. C. H. Spurgeon, Mr. J. C. Forth, of the Pastors' College, commenced the ministry, and did much good work during the seven years of his residence at Bingley. In August, 1871, Mr. Forth removed to Wirksworth, Derbyshire, and was succeeded in 1872 by the Rev. Thomas

Rev. F. E. Cossey.

Rev. E. R. Lewis.

Hanson, a native of Lockwood, who died August 14th, 1878, after a brief year's work. But the ministry of Mr. Hanson was, I believe, the true beginning of a better and fuller life in the church. He came to Bingley with excellent credentials, having laboured with marked success at Haworth, West Bromwich, Burton-on-Trent, &c., and he had also been invited to settle at Liverpool, Manchester, and Bradford. Some preparation was made for building a new chapel, and the site in Park Road was purchased, and the pastorate of Mr. Hanson altogether gave the church a position in the denomination which it had not previously attained. The late pastor's widow, Mrs. Hanson, still resides in Bingley.

Mr. Hanson was succeeded in 1875 by the Rev. F. E. Cossey, son of Mr. R. Cossey, of Laxfield, Suffolk, and grandson of the late Rev. Edward Manseur, founder and first pastor of the Baptist Church at Horham, Suffolk, Mr. Cossey in 1868 accepted the pastorate of the first Baptist Church at Shipley, and continued there till 1875, when ill-health obliged him to resign. After a few months' relaxation he accepted an invitation to settle at Bingley, the members of the Baptist Church at that time meeting in the large hall of the Mechanics' Institute; the new chapel in Park Road being then in course of erection. The chapel was opened in 1876, and the entire cost of the building, about £5,000, was largely through Mr. Cossey's efforts paid off within a very few years. In this and other undertakings for the welfare of the church he had the help and hearty sympathy, not only of his own congregation, but generous assistance from members of other denominations, notably from the late Mr. Ferrand, of St. Ives, and the late Mr. Alfred Sharp. Mr. Cossey applied himself energetically to outside work in the villages, and he is said to have preached in more than 80 pulpits in Yorkshire alone. Having laboured here with praiseworthy ability and success for 16 years, Mr. Cossey in 1891 decided to accept a call from the Baptist Church at Eye, in his native county of Suffolk. Thither he departed, bearing with him the esteem and hearty good wishes of his congregation at Bingley.

The new chapel is a large and handsome edifice in the Gothic style, and has seat room for 700 worshippers. There is a commodious school-room, with class-rooms attached, under the chapel, and the cost of the building was about £4500. The foundation-stone was laid on June 20th, 1874, by Mr. Thomas Aked, and the chapel was opened on July 19th, 1876, by the Rev. Arthur Mursell, of London.

The present minister is the Rev. E. R. Lewis, a native of Ystrad, Glamorganshire, where he was born in 1860. He was educated at the Academy, Aberavon, and Manchester Baptist College. Subsequently he became pastor of the Bethesda Church, at Barnoldswick, where by his industry and ability the church was raised to a high degree of spiritual prosperity. He is the author of a history of the Church at Barnoldswick, containing most important discoveries. So far as is known, this church is the oldest Baptist Church in Yorkshire, and the first in the county to possess property in trust for the use of Baptists. Mr. Lewis came from Barnoldswick to Bingley in September, 1893. He has recently opened a Mission Room at Dubb, where there is a flourishing Sunday School, and where service is held every Sabbath evening. There are also a well-attended Sunday School and Christian Endeavour Society connected with the Church, which is at present in a very prosperous state. The present officers of the church are:—Mr. James Roberts, the Knoll, Baildon; Mr. W. Town, J.P., and Mr. W. N. Town, the Hills, Bingley; Messrs. T. Foulds, A. Green, and J. W. Smith, Bingley.

Primitive Methodists.

On the introduction of Primitive Methodism into the West Riding in 1821, some friends in Bingley took up the new doctrine, and very soon afterwards a society was formed, subservient to the one at Silsden, where and at Hull it had first taken root. Mr. John Flesher, said to be a native of Otley, was the founder of the sect in Yorkshire and the bordering districts. By permission of the Editor of the now extinct *Airedale Magazine*, Mr. Flesher's portrait appears on the next page. He was born in 1801, first preached at Silsden in 1821, and lived to be present at the jubilee celebration of the parent society at Silsden, in 1871. He is said to have been one of the best grammarians of his time, and was for several years Connexional Editor.

Silsden for some years continued head of an extensive circuit, and included societies extending from Accrington and Colne in one direction to Settle and Otley in another, while it embraced societies in many places in the Aire valley between Shipley and Malham. As the cause prospered, the Keighley circuit was formed in 1824, and Bingley was ultimately joined to that. From a copy of an old Preachers' Plan, dated 1828, supplied to me by the Rev. T. Baron, formerly of Silsden, I find that in this year there were already societies formed at Cottingley, Cullingworth, and Morton, in addition to Bingley and Ryecroft. It was really from the latter place, in the Harden valley, that the truths of the new sect first found their way to Bingley, and the remote little village has ever since remained one of the strongholds of the society. On April 20th, 1828, I find one Crawshaw preached at Bingley and at Micklewood and at Faweather on June 29th. This Crashaw, or Crawshaw (as it is differently spelt), was once a family of some consequence in this neighbourhood, and particularly numerous in the Wilsden district, where the name is found as early as the reign of Elizabeth. It is, indeed, not improbable that the eminent sacred poet, Richard Crawshaw, author of the "Musical Duel" (one of the finest compositions in the language), was of this family; it having been conjectured he was of Yorkshire descent. He died in 1649. William Crashaw (1572-1626) was another distinguished poet and Puritan divine, and although of undoubted Yorkshire descent, little is known of his ancestry. In 1587 Richard Crashaye, gent., appears as plaintiff concerning purchase of land, &c., in Bawne and Cottingley, and in the same year he is party to fine concerning lands in Oxenhope, Morton, and Helwick. Richard Crawshaw, of Wilsden, married Anne Ferrand, who was born in 1594. (*See* Ferrand pedigree in Whitaker's *Craven*.) John Crawshaw, of Bingley, died in

REV. JOHN FLESHER.

London, Feb. 15th, 1814, aged 85 years. At least one Puritan member of the Crawshaw family, as we have seen, embraced Primitive Methodism on its adoption in Yorkshire in 1821.

Their first meetings at Bingley were held in a room near the *Ring of Bells* inn. This place becoming too small, they secured premises in York Street, at present known as Forresters' Court, where their first Sunday School was formed; the room being rented and generously paid for by the teachers themselves. Their next location was in premises in York Place (the present Liberal Club), which had more the appearance of a chapel than the one at Forresters' Court. The site had been previously occupied by two cottages. But this building in time became too small, and land was purchased in Hill Street by the Rev. J. Parrot, whereon now stands the present chapel. It was built in 1854, at an initial cost of £1,050. Under the able ministry of the Revs. R. Brook, A. McKechnie, J. Snowden, and J. Rumfit, the society continued to prosper until 1865, when it declared its independence, and has since that time become a self-sustaining circuit.

Since 1865 the school-room has been built, with class-rooms at either end, the chapel has been enlarged, and the organ erected, at a further cost of about £2,800. The property is now said to be valued at £4,000. The following places are now attached to the Bingley Circuit, viz. : Ryecroft, East Morton, Denholme Clough, Wilsden, Harecroft, and Crossflatts. The various interests of the society have always been well sustained, and deserving of record are the names of other ministers who have laboured in the cause at Bingley: Revs. R. Davies, D. Tuton, J. McPherson, G. W. Armitage, G. Swindell, J. Clarke, C. Smith, G. Normandale, J. Headley, J. A. Bastow, J. Parrot, J. Simpson, R. Tanfield, H. Crabtree, J. Dodsworth, G. Hutchinson, H. Hatherley, W. Bennett, J. Dodsworth, junr., Thomas Mitchell, R. S. Blackburn, B. Robinson, M. Sullivan, Thomas Shaw, J. Swales, J. Phillips, J. Osbourne, M. Knowlson, J. Hucknall, W. Thoseby, and for many years the Rev. John Maylard (superannuated).

Amongst laymen, now deceased, who occupied prominent positions in connection with the Bingley chapel was Mr. Charles Crabtree, who was, perhaps, the best friend Primitive Methodism ever had in Bingley. He came to Bingley from Keighley in 1857, when Bingley became a branch of the Keighley Circuit. At the time of his death, in 1895, he had been a local preacher for nearly 50 years. For 30 years he was circuit steward for the Bingley Circuit, and to his memory the circuit has erected a memorial tablet in the Bingley chapel. Mr. Crabtree

Mr. Charles Crabtree.

Mr. John D. Fox.

was also a trustee for most of the chapels in the circuit. He was of a kindly, genial disposition, and ever ready to help forward any good work. At one time he was chairman of the Keighley Board of Guardians.

The present circuit steward is Mr. John D. Fox, the oldest local preacher on the plan. Mr. Fox was born at Harden, in February, 1849, and came to Bingley when a boy. For thirteen years he filled the post of secretary and librarian of the Bingley Mechanics' Institute. He has now for many years been engaged in the wholesale drug business; but in spite of his extensive business claims, covering the six northern counties, he finds time to indulge his literary tastes, He has written a considerable number of hymns and poems, and has been a lay preacher for thirty years. He is author of *The Struggles of a Village Lad*, and *The Preachers' Register*, now in its seventh edition, testimony to its usefulness having been expressed by Dean Farrar, the Revs. Mark Guy Pearce, Silas K. Hocking, the Bishop of Ripon, &c. Mr. Fox has also had the honour of receiving a letter of thanks from the Prince and Princess of Wales in recognition of a memorial poem he addressed to them on the sad death of their son, the Duke of Clarence, who was engaged to be married to the Princess May. For ten successive years he has given before large public audiences in Bingley a "Review of the Year," dealing with general and local matters, with special reference to departed worthies. The proceeds of the collections have been for the benefit of the Bingley Cottage Hospital.

The present society stewards are Messrs. Abraham Greenwood, Isaac D. Longbottom, and A. E. Whitehead; and the trustees of the chapel are: Rev. A. McKechnie, Messrs. Abraham Greenwood, James William Crabtree, John D. Fox, Henry Laycock, and Isaac D. Longbottom.

There are still a few living who were members of the first Sunday School, viz.: Mrs. Nancy Parker, Mrs. Bella Bentley, Mrs. Richard Hey, Mr. Robert Hanson and Mr. Mark Robinson. The oldest scholar at present engaged in active work in the Hill Street School is Mr. Samuel Hargreaves.

CHRISTIAN BRETHREN.

That numerous body of workers in Christ's vineyard known as the Christian Brethren, or Independent Methodists, seems to have originated in Lancashire, in the neighbourhoods of Warrington, Oldham, and Stockport. In or near the year 1797 there was a severance from the Wesleyan Church, when various local preachers organised mission services, with the result that an independent, or self-governed church was established, still retaining the faith and worship of the Methodists, but having no paid ministry. In many things they carried out the simplicity of worship and in their personal attire, the manners and ideas of the early Friends, and were in consequence sometimes called "Quaker Methodists." The men wore broad-brimmed hats, and the women close bonnets and severely plain dresses, while they addressed each other by the pronoun "thou." No minister was permitted to use any clerical title, nor were musical instruments allowed in their services. Peter Phillips is credited with being the founder of the sect, and during the half-century of his ministry he is said to have travelled more than 50,000 miles, and to have delivered more than 6,000 sermons. He died in 1853, aged 75, and there is a tablet to his memory in the chapel at Warrington.

At Bingley the society was formed just fifty years ago. It was in 1848, during the momentous struggle of the Chartists, when wages were low and food was dear, that a secession from the Primitive Methodists took place, and the new Free Gospel Society was established. Its principal founders were Messrs. Hartley Greenwood, Secundus Neal, Samuel Cawley, Frank Barker, Christopher Brown, Benjamin Sharp, and Jonathan Wilson. From the Hand Book of the 91st Annual Meeting of the United Churches, held at Bingley, in June, 1896, I take the following particulars of the society's commencement at Bingley :—"The work was begun in a very humble manner in a cottage in Nelson Street; seating accommodation being provided by borrowing the stocks used at that time by hand wool-combers, and the pulpit consisted of an old chair, without back, and *minus* a leg, the deficient corner being propped up with stones. But amidst all these unfavourable surroundings, the cause prospered, so that in about six months the friends had to remove to a much larger house in York Street, which is occupied at present by Mr. G. T. Askey. Here the work

Mr. Charles Sellers.

proceeded with vigour; forms were purchased, a decent pulpit provided, and, the best of all, the people gathered in. During the three years our friends occupied this house they had many blessed seasons together, which some of our older members call to remembrance with pleasure."

What a contrast with the present handsome and commodious chapel these small beginnings present! As the society prospered, it was found necessary in 1852 to erect an adequate place of worship, which was done at a cost of £250. There was a Sunday School in connection with it. The building sufficed for about 16 years, when the present substantial sanctuary in Church Street was erected. The foundation-stone was laid by Mr. Thomas Laycock, of Bingley, and it was opened for public worship in 1868, the following brethren taking part in the opening services:—Mr. William Bamber, of Bolton; Mr. James Greenhalgh, of Manchester; and Mr. John Landless, of Nelson. The original cost of the building, &c., was about £2,000, but many additions and improvements have since been made, so that the present value is set down at £8,000. The interior will seat about 700.

The society has not been without its "ups and downs," but is said now to be in a healthy and flourishing condition. The circuit at present embraces the churches at Bingley, Baildon Green, and Windhill. It has produced many useful and worthy men, who have laboured diligently in the cause of Christ and the church. This is especially true of the late Mr. Charles Sellers, whose honourable example and conduct during twenty years' of faithful service to the church deserves grateful remembrance. Mr. Sellers died in 1895. Mr. Joseph Longbottom has also been a most useful member of the society for three years as president and seventeen years as preacher.

On April 27th, 1881, the chapel was licensed for the solemnization of marriages. A Band of Hope has been formed, and about two years ago a Christian Endeavour Society was organised, which has now about 60 members. In February, 1897, it was resolved to adopt the system of free sittings in the chapel, with collections at each service. The present President of the Church at Bingley is Brother Abraham Dean, who is also superintendent of the school and a preacher. The other local ministers are Messrs. J. Longbottom, C. Myers, and P. D. Bilbrough. The secretary is Mr. John Priestley, 22, Church Street, Bingley.

Roman Catholics.

The Catholic mission at Bingley, which up to 1878 was in the diocese of Beverley, and since then in Leeds diocese, was started about the year 1870, by the Rev. Henry Walker, then priest of Shipley. He served Bingley from Shipley; but as the Shipley mission was large enough in itself to require the whole attention of the priest, it was deemed advisable to cut off Bingley from Shipley, and make it into an independent mission. With that object the building now used as the Liberal Club, at the corner of York Street, was purchased; but in the meantime, while it was being put in order and made suitable for church purposes, mass was said in the club-room of the *Fleece* hotel. The Rev. Edmund De Thury, D.D., was the first resident priest at Bingley. He came in 1873, and during his incumbency the land at Crow Nest was bought, and out of his own patrimony he erected the house now in possession of Major Weatherhead, which was used for some time as a presbytery.

Dr. De Thury removed to St. Joseph's, Hunslet, Leeds, and was succeeded in October, 1878, by the Rev. Aloysius Puissant, who had been assistant priest to Canon Motler, of St. Mary's, Bradford. Father Puissant was untiring in his efforts for the good of the mission during the short two and a half years he was at Bingley, and during this time the present beautiful and commodious School Chapel was built at Crow Nest. It was opened on May 11th, 1880, by an imposing service of solemn high mass; the celebrant being the Very Rev. Provost Brown (St. Ann's Leeds), the deacon and sub-deacon respectively being the Rev. J. Slattery (St. Patrick's, Bradford) and the Rev. Xavier De Vacht. The Bishop of Leeds (the Right Rev. Dr. Cornthwaite) occupied the throne; his assistants being the Very Rev. Canon Scruton (St. Patrick's, Bradford) and the Very Rev. Canon Glover (Shipley). The Bishop preached an impressive sermon, and during the service pronounced the Pontifical benediction; the decree authorising the same having been previously read by Canon Scruton.

The chapel is not in any particular style of architecture, but it is well, if plainly, built. It consists of two stories; the chapel being on the upper and the school beneath, advantage being taken of the natural position of the site for obtaining a level entrance to both. The lower story is devoted to a "mixed" school, under the supervision of

Rev. Canon Puissant, M.R.

Miss M. Fitzpatrick. It is capable of accommodating about 170 children, in addition to which there is a class-room and a room for infants. At present there are about 80 scholars on the books, but this number is sometimes much increased. The upper story, or chapel (the proportions and details of which are extremely pleasing), consists of a nave, chancel, and transepts. The total length of the chapel is 80 feet. On each side are five pointed windows, filled with tinted cathedral glass, while on the wall space between the windows are hung the fourteen "Stations of the Cross." The chapel is dedicated to the Sacred Heart.

Father Puissant removed on June 30th, 1881, to the populous district of St. Anne's, Bradford, and in 1890 was made a member of the Chapter of Canons of the Leeds diocese, and in 1892, when he received a very handsome testimonial from his congregation of St. Anne's, he received from the Bishop the still further honour of M.R. He was succeeded at Bingley by the Rev. Alfred Watson, who came from St. Joseph's, Brighouse, and who ably administered the parish for about seven years. He built the presbytery, and laid out, in great measure, the grounds attached thereto. He was removed to Middleton (Ilkley), and died there, much regretted, at the age of 53. The Rev. Thomas Parkin, who came from Heckmondwike, was the next to succeed, and he took charge of the mission October 1st, 1889, and left June 14th, 1896. During his residence at Bingley the church, school, and presbytery were put into thorough repair; the church was also much beautified, and a handsome organ and a gallery were erected. Father Parkin found the work of the mission too great a strain upon his strength; the district embraced extending as far as from Cottingley to Morton Banks in one direction and from Eldwick to Cullingworth in another. He exchanged missions with the Rev. Thomas Bradley, of Settle, who is the present active and respected pastor. Great difficulty has been experienced in reducing the long-standing debt upon the church, now amounting to about £1,200, but it is earnestly hoped that this incumbus will not be suffered to continue. The Catholics of the Bingley district number about 700.

Jubilee Procession at Bingley, June 22nd, 1897.

EXTENSION OF THE TOWN AND TRADE.

I HAVE had much to say about Bingley in past centuries, and some words are now necessary on the great changes that have passed over the town during the century that is just closing. The completion of the sixty years' reign of Her Majesty, which was celebrated in Bingley in "Queen's weather" on June 22nd, 1897, was witness to a marvellous advance in the general condition of the people. But a wider contrast still is presented if we go further back in the century. Its opening years saw the dawn of new methods of existence, which to many minds were auguries of disaster to the physical and moral well-being of the country. Dr. Whitaker, when writing of Bingley, did not disguise his feelings in this light. But in spite of all the evils of conjested population and of manifold difficulties which have beset the path of commercial development, comforts and advantages have resulted to the bulk of the people which a purely agricultural life could not have effected.

Bingley at the beginning of this century had still a comparatively large agricultural population. The census returns for 1801 yield the following particulars :—

	Inhabited Houses.	*Males.*	*Females.*	*Engaged in Husbandry.*	*Trades.*
Bingley	306	688	751	77	261
Micklethwaite ..	242	535	576	133	150
Harden	306	778	772	125	281
	854	2001	2099	335	692

Thus it will be seen that in 1801 nearly one-half of the working population was employed on the land. In 1811 there were 931 inhabited houses, and a total population of 4,782, of which 105 families were engaged in farm work and 829 in trade and manufactures. This was a rapid change in ten years. Only about 10 per cent. were then obtaining a livelihood in farming, while in 1821 the number of families employed in trade had increased to 1,085, and in farming to 138. The population was then 6,176, shewing how the agricultural interest had declined in this period, and the manufacturing industries extended.

Prior to the introduction of power-looms, about a century ago, spinning and weaving were done by hand in the cottages of the workers, which were often connected with farm buildings, and here they reeled, spun, and wove the yarn, and delivered the pieces to country merchants. The principal mart for cotton goods was Halifax, whither traders from Manchester proceeded and made purchases. The inmates of the Poor House at Bingley were also obliged to do a certain amount of spinning, &c., and in 1776 I find it ordered that if one Hannah Gregory does not spin 8 hanks a day for the future she shall immediately be sent to the workhouse at Rosendale. In 1778 it was ordered that Joseph Lund be appointed to reel the yarn spun in the House. In 1779 a stocking-frame was ordered to be obtained for the use of the town, and negotiations were to be entered into with John Armistead, of Bradford, for its hire or purchase. At this time cotton spinning and the manufacture of cotton goods was the staple industry about Bingley, and Mr. James Parker, of Great Horton, tells me that several sisters of the name of Clark, who had learnt cotton-spinning at Bingley, removed to Great Horton, and instructed a number of workpeople in the same trade at the mill then lately built by Messrs. John and Benjamin Knight (*see* Wm. Cudworth's *Horton* and James Parker's *The Factory Child's Friend*, published in 1832). In 1780 the first cotton mill ever erected in Yorkshire was begun at Keighley by Messrs. Ramsden, of Halifax; but many years passed before the venture so far prospered as to encourage the adoption of the factory system at Bingley. By and bye came the application of steam to machinery, and what a revolution it has wrought in the capacity for production since the old hand-spinning days! Then one woman could manage only one spindle, while now one girl can tend over a hundred!

In the first decade of the century several cotton mills had been erected and opened at Bingley. Providence

Mill, adjoining the old Grammar School, appears to be the oldest, and it was built by the brothers William, Charles, and Thomas Hartley, cousins of Dr. Hartley, master of the school, and vicar of Bingley. This mill was afterwards taken by Mr. John Sharp, being the first establishment run by the Sharp family in Bingley. Mr. Sharp put down a gas plant about the year 1822, for lighting his own premises only, and this was some years before the town adopted the new illuminant. The mill took fire on November 20th, 1872, doing damage to the extent of about £12,000, and has not since been occupied for mill purposes. Another cotton mill stood at the corner of Park Road and Main Street, and was run by Mr. Whitley; while a third stood over the way, the Elm Tree Mill, started by the Messrs. Gott. This was suspended about 1825, and the mill turned into cottages. The small mill-pond was also filled up. The old mills at Castlefields, and Cottingley were also originally devoted to the production of cotton goods, and also Dowley Gap after the Walkers ceased to run it. It was built for a worsted mill about 1818 by the brothers Matthew and Thomas Walker, and they ran it continuously up to about 1848, when the partnership was dissolved; Matthew retaining the mill premises, which were occupied for a short time by him, when the mill was let to Messrs. Hilton, of Ovenden, who ran it for some years up to 1865. Then it was taken by Mr. Samuel Rushforth and partners, and subsequently by Messrs. Ira Ickringill & Co., now of Keighley. Mr. Matthew Walker died in 1864, and the property, which is now unlet, is still held by his trustees. Thomas died in 1870, aged 79. His son, Mr. John Walker, of Gilstead, is now the oldest trustee of the Bingley Grammar School.

To Castlefields Mill belongs the distinction of being the first factory in Yorkshire that was lighted with gas, shortly before Mr. Sharp adopted it at Providence Mill. In the notice of West Riddlesden Hall I have given some particulars of the Sidgwicks, and it was Mr. James Sidgwick, of Leeds, father of Mr. John Sidgwick (who died in 1791, and was buried in Bingley Church), who was one of the original partners and, I believe, founders of Castlefields Mills. The partners were Wilmer Mackett Willett, James Sidgwick, Joseph Wood, and Johnson Atkinson Busfeild, trading under the name of Sidgwick, Wood & Co. This partnership was dissolved 26th December, 1798, and afterwards carried on by Mr. Willett and Mr. Busfeild only, under the style of W. M. Willett & Co. Subsequently Mr. Lister Ellis took the mill, and had it up to the time of his death in 1829. His son, William Ellis, had the misfortune to labour during the great Chartist agitation, which so seriously affected his own and other trading concerns in the parish. He was a useful man in the town's affairs, and died much respected in 1856. It was he who built the mansion called The Hills, now occupied by Mr. Town. The Ellises were a very respectable family, who came to Bingley from Bolton-by-Bolland, where one of the Ellises married an aunt of the first Lord Ribblesdale. Lister Ellis, his grandson, died in 1780, leaving a son of the same name, who was the first to settle at Bingley. He built Castlefields House, and married a daughter of Thomas Garforth, Esq., of Steeton, and left two sons, James, of Greenhill, Bingley, and above-mentioned William Ellis. The latter married in 1810 Mary, sister of Mr. Chapman, of Gilstead Hall, a retired East Indian officer, and only daughter of the Rev. John Chapman, vicar of Baildon, to whose memory there is a stained-glass window in the church at Baildon. William Ellis had issue five sons and three daughters; the eldest son being William, who was born in 1818, and married in 1845, at Bath, Sophia Charlotte, daughter of James Woodman, Esq., M.D., of Chichester. His younger brother, George, continued at Bingley, and died here a few years ago. The Ellises are a very ancient family, and notices of its various branches from the Conquest to the present time have been published in a volume of 300 pages, collated by William Smith Ellis, Esq., of the Middle Temple.

When the worsted industry began to revive and reached Bingley, Messrs. Ellis used to give out yarn and warp to people living at Harden, Cullingworth, Wilsden, and even as far away as Burley Wood Head. The woolcombers' and weavers' strike of 1825, which continued in and around

Bradford for more than five months, followed by a mutinous opposition to power-looms, seriously interfered with local trade, and it was a long time before things became fairly prosperous again. Within a few years, however, more spacious factories began to be erected. The three brothers, John, Jonas, and William Sharp,* had been worsted spinning at Harden Beckfoot, and Jonas and William came to Bingley, and Jonas built Prospect Mill, in Chapel Lane, and afterwards Airebank Mill was erected by William, and both of these establishments were subsequently owned and run by Jonas Sharp; the premises and business being still used and carried on by his family, under the name of Jonas Sharp & Sons, Limited. Providence Mill, near the Grammar School, was owned and occupied by Mr. David Wilkinson Sharp and his son. The Sharps are an old local family, and appear in documents relating to the parish as far back as the time of Agincourt, A.D. 1415. In that year John Scharp appears at the Court of the Knights of St. John of Jerusalem, held at Bingley, and complains of one Robert Langrode in a plea of trespass. They have taken a useful part in the conduct of the town's affairs, and have been liberal benefactors in most philanthropic movements. Mr. John Sharp married, and left an only son, the above Mr. D. W. Sharp, and two daughters, Mrs. Wyrill (*see* page 198) and Mrs. Hannah Popplewell, of Ilkley, who died January 11th, 1898, in her 90th year. Mr. Jonas Sharp, the youngest of the three brothers, married a daughter of Mr. Bairstow, of the Corn Mill, Steeton, and died March 24th, 1864, leaving a family of nine sons and daughters. The eldest, Edward, died at Gilstead Hall; he married a Miss Park, of Leeds; Fred, the next, married, and died at Ravenroyd, leaving no issue; William died, unmarried, at Myrtle Grove; Alfred married Elizabeth, daughter of George

* The father of the three brothers was presumably James Sharp, of Cowhouse, who died in 1798, aged 49, and his wife, Hannah, died in 1820, aged 68. Their grave is in the Parish Churchyard, under the south windows of the nave, and the stone also records the burial of two infants of John Sharp, of Beckfoot, one of whom, Paulina, died in 1810. Another daughter of John Sharp was also named Paulina (*see* page 198).

Walker, Esq., of Park House, Lindley, near Huddersfield, by whom he leaves a family of six sons and daughters.

Mr. Alfred Sharp died on June 1st, 1896, aged 72, and is buried in Bingley Cemetery. He takes uudoubtedly in

Mr. Alfred Sharp, J.P.

modern times the first place among local benefactors. He held many offices, and his unbounded charity was given without ostentation, and in so many ways that the extent of it can never be known. He was a native of Bingley, having been born at Elm Tree Hill, June 12th, 1823, and as a boy went to the school at the low end of the town kept by Mr. Richardson, the postmaster. Early in life he became a Sunday school teacher in connection with the Wesleyan Methodists, and was prominently identified with that body to the end of his life. He was practically the builder of the Hill Street Wesleyan Schools, for without his help such spacious buildings, which at that time were considered models of their kind, would not have been thought of. The same may be said of the new Wesleyan Chapel, to the erection of which he and his brother contributed, as elsewhere related, several thousands of pounds. For more than thirty years he was circuit steward. In 1881 he was the recipient of a handsome illuminated address from the teachers, scholars, and members of the Wesleyan congregation. From that year up to 1888 he resided at Carr Head, Lothersdale; but having in the meantime purchased the Myrtle Grove estate, he came back to Bingley, and continued to reside at Myrtle Grove up to the time of his death.

Mr. Sharp became a member of the Board of Improvement Commissioners in 1852, eventually becoming chairman of that body, a position which he filled until his retirement from the Board in 1878. He was elected chairman of the newly-formed School Board in 1875, and was president of the Bingley Technical Institute. He was also the principal benefactor on the establishment of the Bingley Free Library, contributing £1,000 towards the purchase of books. The library was opened on April 2nd, 1892. In 1878 Mr. Sharp was made a J.P. of the West Riding, and on the death of Mr. Ferrand in 1891 was chosen to fill his place as Chairman of the Bingley Bench of Magistrates. Mr. Sharp discharged so many and various duties, and gave of his bounty to every deserving cause with such a liberal hand, regardless of sect or creed, that his name must ever remain conspicuously associated with the progress of the town and trade of Bingley.

Other children of Mr. Jonas Sharp are James, who married Sarah, daughter of Thomas Townsend, Esq., of

Attleborough Hall, Nuneaton; Elizabeth, married Count Francis Bagienski, of Warsaw; Martha, the wife of Abraham Ramsden, Esq., of Micklethwaite; John Bairstow, married Elizabeth, daughter of Eagland Bray, Esq., of Halifax; and Sarah, wife of John White, Esq., merchant, of Bradford.

Another early worsted mill was built at Dubb by Messrs. Joseph and Samuel Moulding, who also built the residence adjoining, now occupied by Mr. Lund Thompson. About 1825 Mr. William Anderton came from Cullingworth, and occupied part of Dubb Mill, but shortly began to build premises of his own in Dubb Lane, where combing and spinning were carried on. The buildings were afterwards occupied as a cotton mill by the Ellises of Castlefields, and were subsequently raised and enlarged, and a new mill was erected on the opposite side of the road, now and for some years past owned and run by Messrs. Rushforth. The large mills by the canal side, now occupied by Messrs. Butler, Wood & Co., Gatecliff Bros., Sargeant & Coupe, and Smith & Sons, was built by Mr. Anderton also, and during his occupation suffered from a disastrous fire on March 20th, 1858, when property to the value of £15,000 succumbed to the flames. A melancholy incident is remembered in connection with this fire, when George Anderson, a man in the prime of life, while endeavouring to save some of his master's stock, was crushed by falling timbers, and burnt to death.

Mr. Samuel Rushforth, J.P., who built the new mill above mentioned, was one of Bingley's "popular men." He was born at a house in Carrier's Row, Chapel Lane, on April 16th, 1844, and died at Moorfield, Bingley, June 24th, 1896. He had the misfortune to lose his father and mother when quite a child, and was brought up by his uncle and aunt, Mr. and Mrs. Sam Foster, in Dubb Lane. Mr. Rushforth was in all respects a self-made man. He began his working life as a "doffer" at Anderton's mill, near Dubb Bridge, and eventually became apprenticed to a draper named Pringle, who occupied what are now the *Bingley Chronicle* offices, in Myrtle Place. Afterwards he joined the drapery establishment of Messrs. Brown and

Muff, in Bradford, and in 1865 commenced business as a manufacturer at Dowley Gap in conjunction with Messrs. Walbank and Hudson; the latter gentleman being his brother-in-law. The partnership was dissolved, and he ultimately took the Dubb Mill, which was purchased by him about 1883, and where the business is still carried on by his sons.

Mr. Samuel Rushforth, J.P.

In public matters Mr. Rushforth was an exceedingly useful and busy man; being continuously engaged in the conduct of the town's business during the past eventful twenty-five years of its history. He became a member of the old Board of Commissioners in 1870, and in 1886 was elected its chairman. He was one of the original trustees of the Technical Institute, and for two years was chairman.

When, through the munificence of Mr. Alfred Sharp, the Free Library was established, Mr. Rushforth was made chairman of the first Library Committee. In 1892 he succeeded Mr. William Sugden, of Cold Spring, Cullingworth, as representative of the Bingley district on the West Riding County Council, and in 1895 his name was added to the Commission of the Peace for the West Riding. In church matters he was throughout life a member of the Congregational body, and was a trustee of the church property. He had been a superintendent of the Sunday School, and also a deacon of the church. Mr. Rushforth was of a singularly energetic and happy disposition, and in so many ways was he identified with the public life of the town, that his active and cheerful presence will surely long be missed.

In addition to those already mentioned, a number of other important factories have been erected in more recent times; notably the Britannia Mills of Messrs. D. & R. England; Bowling Green Mills of Messrs. S. Wildman & Son; Albert Mills of Messrs. M. Platts & Co.; Stanley Mills of Mr. George Ackroyd, Junr.; Lilycroft Mill of Mr. James I. Stocks and Messrs. Binns & White; Airedale Mills of Mr. George H. Aked and Messrs. Helliwell & Todd; and Limefield Mills of Messrs. J. & J. Hartley. These and other firms are all engaged in the staple industries which have an outlet in the market at Bradford. There are in addition various other trades carried on in the town; notably the engineering works of Messrs. Carr Foster, Richard Garnett, and Hartley & Petyt; the old-established corn mills of Messrs. William England & Sons; Messrs. Asquith Bros., corn-factors, at the above-mentioned Airedale Mills; the leather business of Messrs. John White & Sons; the wood and saw mills of Mr. Wm. Whitley and Messrs. W. R. & R. Atkinson; the paper mills belonging to Mr. Chas. Crabtree; the malting business of Mr. Benjamin Broadbent; the brewing and malting establishment of Messrs. J. R. Holmes & Sons. There are also several valuable stone quarries in the neighbourhood, as well as brick and sanitary tube works. Bobbin-turning used to be carried on by Mr. Thomas Brown at Beckfoot Mill, and by

Messrs. John Town & Son at Bingley, but both of these works met with disastrous terminations. The first-named was burnt down on Sept. 10th, 1874, the estimated loss being £2,500 ; and the latter, near Park Road, will long be remembered by the terrible boiler explosion which occurred here on June 9th, 1869. Fifteen persons were killed and nearly forty injured. Amongst the former were the wife and daughter of the junior partner in the firm, and several school children who were playing unheedingly in the adjoining school-yard. The sad circumstances were reported at length in the local and other papers.

During the great

CHARTIST AGITATION,

which continued for so many years up to 1852, there were numerous sympathisers, and not a few "physical-force" men, in Bingley. The Reform Act fell far short of general expectation. The cry also for shorter hours in the factories and the general discontent at low wages, which it was said were hardly sufficient to keep body and soul together, completely disorganised society, and caused a fearful amount of suffering and distress in this part of Yorkshire. Thousands of famished men and women gathered under the banners of such leaders as Fergus O'Connor and Thomas Cooper, who declaimed against the whole electoral system, and denounced the tyrannical oppression of the poor "factory slaves" in no measured terms. Richard Oastler engaged Nicholson, the Bingley poet, to write some verses depicting the sufferings and cruel usage of young children in the factories, many of whom were permanently crippled by the rigorous exactions of labour put upon them and long hours. Cobden and Bright stood up as the champions of free bread, and by their voices won the day, and the wheaten loaf became the poor man's daily meal. Oatmeal porridge and potatoes had hitherto formed the principal dietary of the factory operatives. As fuel was dear, porridge was boiled for breakfast in the morning, and if, as frequently happened, there was nothing but porridge again for dinner, it would be poured hot into a bottle, then corked, and placed in the cottagers' beds to be kept warm until they returned at mid-day. Dry oatbread and a pint of mint tea, sweetened with treacle, was the customary evening meal. As to clothing, one marvels at the wonderful changes that have taken place in the raiment of working people in so short a time. The working girl of the present day is as well, or even better dressed than many a princess of less than a century ago. It is little more than forty years since Fergus O'Connor used to rouse his dejected followers by addressing them as "Ye famished beings in rags," while at the head of all his writing paper was printed, "To the fustian jackets, blistered hands, and unshorn chins, I am your father, and you are my children," &c. What would he think now, and what do many think now who have survived the period, at the general appearance and homes of the working classes throughout the country and of their accumulated savings in the banks and building societies? Fergus O'Connor promised every man that was faithful to the cause that he would have "a house of his own and one to let," and really, to use an Irishism, it seems coming to that. In going through the old Bingley Parish Books one is struck by the number of local families who appear in the workhouse accounts, or have been in receipt of parish pay, who have by application and thrift risen to positions of comparative affluence. Forty or fifty years ago nearly everyone wore clogs, and I am told that female teachers at the Sunday Schools in Bingley might often have been seen going to that noble service on the Sabbath morning wearing clogs, cleanly brushed; also clad in the plainest of dresses, and with shawls pinned over the head.

Charlotte Brontë in *Shirley* draws some vivid pictures of life at that stirring period, when the mob, infuriated almost to madness, attempted to stop work by drawing the plugs from the mill boilers in Yorkshire and elsewhere. A wild, hungry crowd of men, old and young, brandishing shillalahs, pitchforks, sticks and bars of wood and iron, anything they could hold, came trooping into Bingley, and every plug was drawn. They did much other mischief, too, and many stories are still rife on the lips of old folk who recall events of that fearful time. The Petty Sessions were then held at the *Brown Cow*, in a room afterwards occupied by Mr. Charles Hogg as a school-room. On the 26th of May, 1848, two of the ringleaders were captured at Bingley, and committed to York, but were rescued as the constables arrived at the station, and after a good deal of trouble were brought back to the magistrates' rooms at the inn above mentioned. Very soon afterwards the crowd infuriated broke open the door, and amid a scene of the greatest disorder secured the two men, and carried them off in triumph. As they were in shackles, the mob, fully armed, took them over Ireland Bridge to Lambert's smithy, opposite the *White Horse*, and the shackles were hammered off, and the men afterwards paraded through the town. Mr. Ferrand, the squire of St. Ives, was the presiding magistrate during these violent proceedings, and there is no doubt he displayed great courage and judgment throughout. The men vowed they would murder him, and actually proceeded to set a price upon his head. "If you murder me," answered Mr. Ferrand firmly, "another will take my place, who will discharge his duties as resolutely as I have done." Later in the day the crowd, determined on revenge, advanced up the Harden road with the object of either assaulting the squire on his way home or of carrying out their deadly design; but Mr. Ferrand went by the Altar road, and so reached home unhurt. The men, however, cut away the lead pipe at the water trough by the road side at Elm Crag in order to make bullets of it; and in the field opposite, near the reservoir, completely stripped of its bark a magnificent and lofty ash tree, said to have been one of the finest in England, which Mr. Ferrand greatly prized, and which, of course, had to be cut down, but the stump still remains.

Jack o' Mark's, who afterwards became a parish constable, was one of the local leaders in this movement, and there are many others in Bingley who openly or secretly aided the insurgents. An incident in connection with the above proceedings may be mentioned. When the prisoners were going to be tried in the Justice Room at the *Brown Cow*, the clerk, named Joseph Neal Thacker, was ordered to fetch the books from the office in Main Street. As he was returning over Ireland Bridge, some of the mob seized him, and were about to throw him and his books into the river when the constable ran up, just in time to stay the vile deed. The clerk, however, ever afterwards bore the euphonious name of "Tommy Tick-tack," on account of his being within a tick-tack of being immersed in the river, or, perhaps, of losing his life. I have been told that on one occasion, when he lived in the house adjoining the old Baptist burial-ground, a woman, who was a stranger, called upon him, and being blissfully ignorant of his real name, politely asked, "Does Mr. Tick-tack live here?" Mr. Thacker promptly told her that his name was not Tick-tack, and unless she showed better respect she had better go about her business. "Tick-tack," however, is not half so peculiar as many a real name borne by old Bingley families; for example, "Paul Croptayl," who takes a messuage and garden and six acres of land in Micklethwaite in the reign of King Henry V.

Meetings were continuously being held to discuss the "situation" and to drill, sometimes on Priesthorpe Green, near the Alms Houses, but more often further out on Gilstead or Bingley Moors. One Lightowler and Ben Rushton were the great "spouters" at these meetings, and to see Ben stand up and pray with his hands in his pockets to Almighty God to intercede on their behalf was a sight never to be forgotten. Many shed tears, while the stronger of the crowd vowed eternal vengeance on the oppressors. Mr. Wellington Tipping, a gentleman of some standing, who lived in Myrtle Place, near the lock-up, and who was a son of Dr. Tipping, of Skipton, though taking no actual part in the demonstrations, expressed strong sympathy with the agitators. It is noteworthy also that Thomas Cooper, the indefatigable Chartist, whose voice had been heard at Bingley, tells that on one occasion he visited the poet Wordsworth at Rydal Mount, and the poet expressed his sincere sympathy with the several demands of the Chartists, but expressed regret at the violent methods they were employing to obtain their ends.

When on April 10th, 1848, Fergus O'Connor rolled his monster petition, drawn up like a coach-wheel, into the House of Commons, signed, it was said, by five and a half million persons,* praying for universal suffrage, no property qualification, and annual Parliaments, London was guarded by troops, and the Bank of England was defended by sappers and miners. The whole country was in a state of tumult. Over a hundred old pensioners were sent down to Bingley from Chelsea, and billetted on the able householders and innkeepers in the town, each innkeeper, &c., taking two soldiers. A number of special constables were also sworn in. I am told that a well-known solicitor in Bingley had received certain fees for "swearing in" the constables, and a certain vigorous Chartist having got wind of this fact, sent the lawyer a letter demanding every penny of such fees under the most fearful threats. The terrified lawyer, thinking his life was imperilled, at once gave up the money, which on being paid over to the Chartist Committee went to the purchase of a number of formidable pikes or javelins for the "physical force" party. Some of these weapons are still preserved in the town.

The opposing forces were commanded by Mr. Ferrand; the pensioners being armed with old flint-lock blunderbusses. Companies were stationed on Park Road Bridge; near Crossflatts on the Keighley road, and at Cottingley Bridge; the approaches to the town being thus admirably defended, and to some extent also barricaded. The railway station platforms were also lined with old pensioners, one of whom, I am told, had a wooden leg. They were all more or less fully armed, though considerable doubt was expressed as to whether half the old matchlocks would really go off properly if required. The men had to put up with a good deal of joking. A riot having occurred at Bingley on Royal Oak Day, 1848, the military were called out, and on May 31st the forces, led by Mr. Ferrand, proceeded to arrest the principal agitators. Many of them were taken while at work in the mills; in all 16 prisoners were taken and committed to York. A special train came to Bingley to convey the prisoners to York, and the station was well guarded with soldiers. There was a good deal of free talking as the train moved away;

* Though actually when counted containing less than two millions.

one man shouted out, "Go tell that blind lad of mine that his father's gone to die a martyr for his country!"

If the subject was serious, the riots were attended with a good many ludicrous incidents. A man called Crabtree, being wanted, escaped up the chimney of his house in Chapel Lane; and while the representatives of the law were puzzled where to find him, the nimble Chartist had fled by the roof. Another named Jack Colly, who lived in Gott's Yard, also escaped up the flue in a similar manner. Isaac Gill, who lived in a house, now Butterfield's fish-shop, in Chapel Lane, was also a notorious character, who took part in many a local broil during the agitation. Mr. Ferrand thought it desirable to have Ike in safe keeping, so he went to the house with some of his pensioners, and secured his man after some little trouble, and he was sent to York with the rest.

Some days after the riot at Bingley, a monster Chartist meeting was held on Toftshaw Moor, and the streets of Bradford were filled with a violent mob, hurling stones and brick-bats at the police and special constables, who were obliged to use their staves and draw their cutlasses, though no serious hurt was done. A body of dragoons presently galloped to the scene of the disturbance, and a simple fellow from Micklethwaite, named Bob Leeming, who was wielding a bludgeon, had an old felt hat that he wore completely cut in half by some expert swordsman. Bob dropped his cudgel, unable to realise for a moment whether it was his head or his hat that had gone; but when on examining his head-gear he found that he had sustained no worse injury than the loss of half his hat, he thought it time to decamp before greater evils happened, and so he hurried back to Bingley. On entering the town, covered with mud, and wearing a crownless hat, he had to put up with a good deal of banter. Poor Bob afterwards got six months in Northallerton gaol.

Another amusing incident is still remembered in connection with these events. A man named Mitchell came hurrying down one Sunday morning to inform the people that a great crowd of Chartists had assembled on Harden Moor. Services in the churches and chapels were at once stopped, bells were rung alarmingly, and soon a great body of men, led by the redoubtable squire of St. Ives, marched to the scene of action. It is said that one of the yeomanry under his command trembled so much that he was unable to load his weapon, and Mr. Ferrand, cowing the man, loaded the gun himself. But imagine the dismay of these British gallants on reaching the moor top to find, instead of an armed mob, a pious Primitive Methodist Camp Meeting, with their aged minister seated upon an old waggon eating his frugal dinner! Many of the brave forthwith set off in search of Mitchell, but he could not be found. The incident was amusingly versified by Mr. John D. Fox, and printed in the *Bingley Chronicle*. Happily in the end no blood was shed during this so-called "Bingley War."

Mr. Ferrand, who received the thanks of Government for his action in the matter, although strongly opposed to the reckless and lawless manner by which the agitators aimed to achieve their ends, sympathised with the operatives in their desire to shorten the hours of labour in factories, and few worked harder than he did to obtain the passing of the Ten Hours Bill. When the Oastler monument was unveiled in Bradford, on May 15th, 1869, by Lord Shaftesbury, Mr. Ferrand delivered a long and admirable speech; in fact, *the* speech of the afternoon. Mr. Ferrand had joined the Young England Party, of which the late Lord Beaconsfield, then Benjamin Disraeli, was a leading member. Mr. Disraeli came, I believe, several times to Bingley, being the guest of Mr. Ferrand, at St. Ives, and his visit was marked by several local incidents of interest. Accompanied by his host and Lord John Manners, he went to the Druids' Altar, and afterwards introduced a description of it in his novel of *Sybil*. Through the instigation of Mr. Ferrand the Cottingley Allotment Gardens were begun, which had the effect of withdrawing a good many men from low pursuits, such as cock-fighting, &c., at that time prevalent, and they have undoubtedly proved a source of profit and interest ever since. Mr. Disraeli and Lord John Manners were present at the opening of them, as reported in the *Leeds Intelligencer* for Oct. 19th, 1844. Some of the finest gooseberries produced in England have been grown in these plots, and the Bingley Gooseberry Society has an excellent reputation, the National Show having been held here.

Mr. Ferrand had been a Captain in the Yorkshire Hussars, and afterwards commanded the Keighley Volunteers. A Sham Fight once took place in the upper park at St. Ives. That was in the autumn of 1862. The corps engaged were the 3rd West York (Bradford with Eccleshill), 25th (Guiseley), 35th (Keighley), and 39th (Bingley), in all nine companies. Some amusing incidents are related of this sham battle.

A notable event in the history of Bingley was the completion of the Thackley to Skipton section of

THE LEEDS AND LIVERPOOL CANAL,

which was opened 21st March, 1774, when great rejoicings took place in Bingley. The church bells were rung, a band of music paraded the district, guns were fired by the local militia, and there was a general holiday. The first boat went down the five-rise locks in 28 minutes, amid the loud huzzas of the spectators. The locks here, as is well known, are unique on the Leeds and Liverpool system, and when they were completed were considered one of the grandest engineering achievements in the world.

The Act authorising the construction of the canal was obtained in May, 1770, and the first meeting was held at the *Black Horse* hotel, Skipton, on June 20th, 1770, and the next at the *Black Bull*, in Burnley, on August 31st following. At the Skipton meeting the attendance was so large that the assembly immediately adjourned to the Castle, where a committee was formed, consisting of 28 gentlemen, nearly all residing in the vicinity of the proposed canal between Leeds and Liverpool. Amongst the members of this committee appear Abraham Balme, gentleman; John Hustler (treasurer), of Undercliffe House (*see Gentleman's Magazine*, 1790), and Thomas Hardcastle, merchants, of Bradford; Thomas Leach, Esq., of Riddlesden; Colonel Henry Wickham, of Cottingley; William Blakey, merchant, of Keighley, &c. The sum subscribed at this meeting was £185,000, and the full amount required, viz., £200,000, was subscribed for at the Burnley meeting. The committee subsequently met at the *White Bear*, Crosshills; at the *Elm Tree* inn and *Queen's Head*, Bingley. On the death of Mr. Brindley, in 1772 (*see* Smiles' *Lives of the Engineers*), Mr. John Longbottom was appointed chief engineer in his place. He prepared the plans for the great five-rise and three-rise locks, as well as for the locks at Dowley Gap and the Seven Arches over

FIVE RISE LOCKS, BINGLEY.

the river Aire. The mason work for the two first-named works was let to John Sugden, of Wilsden, Barnabas Morvil, Jonathan Farrar, and William Wild, masons, of Bingley, while the contract for the locks at Dowley Gap and the Arches aqueduct was let to Jonathan Sykes, of Oulton, and Joseph Smith, of Woodlesford, masons.

The canal, as I have said, was formally opened at Bingley in 1774. The level of the water-way at Skipton, it may be added, was 267½ feet above the Aire at Leeds Bridge, and this height was obtained by 29 locks, 8 of which are at Bingley, representing a rise of 90 feet. An admirable and exhaustive history of the canal, written by Mr. H. F. Killick, appeared in the *Bradford Antiquary* for 1897, to which the present author is indebted for most of these particulars.

From papers lent me by the late Mr. Alfred Newboult, of Bradford, I gather that John Taylor was keeper of the important five-rise locks in the early part of the century. He was appointed in 1807, and remained here till January 30th, 1816. He was a man of more than average intelligence, as one may gather from notes in his own handwriting. One of his daughters married Mr. Joseph Nutter, founder of "Nutter's Orphanage," Bradford; another became the wife of Mr. Clough, the first Borough Accountant of Bradford; and a third, Ann, married Mr. Thomas Newboult, of Bradford, parents of the brothers Joseph, George, Alfred, &c. Taylor records that Henry Moorhouse came to live at the locks on Thursday, January 30th, 1812, and this family is still there. In connection with events which led to Waterloo, he records that after the Treaty of Peace was signed at Paris, on April 30th, 1814, a feast was held at Bingley, on Tuesday, May 31st, at which all above the age of eight years were present, and on the Saturday following the youngsters were entertained to "a feast of cheese, spice-cake, and warm ale, &c., at 5 p.m., in the Bingley Market House." There was also a grand dinner for subscribers with overplus money at Mary Jowett's *(Queen's Head)* on the same day. One might dwell long on these and other local events of this stirring period, but space forbids.

The lime and coal trade was very much increased by the opening of the canal through Bingley. The absence of limestone quarries in the neighbourhood and the difficulty of conveyance hitherto had been a great hindrance both to agriculture and in building operations. Many of the older houses had been mortared with clay and mud. One such remains in the Main Street at the present time; an antique-looking half-timber structure, which appears much more ancient than it actually is. The upper story (shewn in the accompanying illustration) is constructed of lath-work, cemented with a mixture of clay and hair, with not a trace of lime present. A coeval doorway, however, in this chamber is identical in design with doorways still existing in some 17th century houses in the parish, and the probability is that this house was not built until the reign of Queen Elizabeth had closed. The house and premises most probably were erected for the Longbottoms as a "smithy"; this family, as appears from documents in possession of Mr. Ferrand, having resided on the premises for at least 250 years, and during the whole of that period have followed the occupation of blacksmiths. It is supposed the family came here from York, and as affording some evidence of the heredity of trades, I may mention that among the freemen of that city in 1418 appears the name of John Longbotham, *wryght*.

Limestone, as I have said, was not quarried at Bingley, though it was got plentifully from the numerous drift-hills in the neighbourhood, which had been brought down from Craven in the shape of boulders and pebbles during the glacial age. Down to the middle of last century

Lime Burning

formed an important local industry; no sandstone area in Yorkshire probably contained so much drifted limestone as the hills at Bingley. The limestone was dug up and burnt in primitive kilns on the spot. Scores of these old kilns have been discovered in the course of building operations, &c., and many are at present being bared at the excavations in Myrtle Pasture. Two centuries ago lime-burning here was carried on very profitably; so much so that there was a continual influx of poor labourers seeking work from other and distant places, and these men, sometimes with their families, settled in the town, and became a serious charge on the rates. From papers in my possession I find that in 1699 the freeholders and other inhabitants of the town petitioned the West Riding magistrates for relief in this matter, because they say that "for a long tyme there have been and now are great quantityes of Lyme Stones

OLD HOUSE, MAIN STREET, BINGLEY.

gotten promiscuously in Bingley and Micklethwait, but more especially in Bingley, by means whereof the ground is digged upp and very much impaired to the great decay of the yearly value of the same, and alsoe abundance of poor people are drawn to inhabitt the said constablery, soe that the assessments for the poor daily increase to the great burthen and charge of the petitioners," &c. Eventually in 1701 the Justices issued the following order:

Whereas sevall differences have risen amongst ye Inhabs of ye Constably of Bingley in this Ryding touching their assessmts to the constables and poor by reason of an unequal valuation of sev'all p'sons estates within the sd Constably for remedying whereoff for the future. Itt is ordered that Mr. Tho. Dobson, of the Vicaridge, Mr. Jonath. Dobson, Mr. Richd. Longbothom, Tho. Eastburn, Robt. Walker, John Ellison, jun., Edwd. Wood, John Murgatroyd, Robt. Verity, John Smith, James Taylor, James Swainer, Joseph Maud (being good substantial men of the sd Constably), or any nine of them doe forthwith meet together and view and consider the value of all p'sons estates in the sd Constably, and according to their discrecions make an equal and impartial assesst for one month's pay to the poor of the sd Constably, having a due regard to the intrinsic value of each man's estate. And itt is further ordered that such assessmt so made and signed by the p'sons above named, or any nine of them, shall hereafter remain and be a standing rule and guide for the Inhabits of the sd Constably in the making of all assessmts to the Constable and poor, and if any p'ticular p'son or p'sons of the sd Constably shall find him, her, or themselves agrieved by such assessmts such p'son or p'sons may appeal to the Quarter Sessns for relief and redresse.

Towards the close of the century

THE COACHES

brought passengers from Leeds and Bradford, who were taken as far as Micklethwaite Bridge, where the fly-boats were in waiting to convey the passengers by canal to Skipton, Lancashire, and for the north. This sail in the gaily-decorated passenger-boats through the finest parts of the Aire valley must have been greatly enjoyed, and the change from the crowded rattling coach to the open boat must have tempted many a dejected or enfeebled person to take a trip north for the sake of health. Between Bingley and Gargrave it is a pleasant, open, and level run along the edge of the hills, and without locks.

Many coaches passed through Bingley between Leeds, Bradford, Skipton, Kendal, &c., and tales of the old coaching days might fill many pages. The morning coaches usually changed horses at the *King's Head*, and the return (evening) coaches at the *White Horse*. An old clock, with ponderous iron weight, was kept at the *King's Head* in these days, and for many years was used to start the coaches by. "Now, ladies and gem'men," the guard would say as he entered the parlour of the inn, "the good clock tells us time's up, and we must be off," at which the party took their seats, and then with a merry blast of the guard's horn the wheels rattled quickly away down the Main Street. The old coaching clock, now in the possession of Mrs. Lister, is pictured at the end of this chapter. It may be noted that prior to the alterations in the level of the Main Street the coaches were to lower with the aid of ropes down to the *White Horse*, and a conspicuous large glacial boulder, built in near the door of the old "smithy" house (*see* illustration), was originally below the street level, and the house was descended into instead of as now by an ascent of three steps. The ample stabling of the *King's Head* and *White Horse* affords some indication of the amount of travelling there was in the old days through Bingley, which lay on the main road from Leeds and Bradford to Skipton, Lancaster, and Kendal. Frequently the horses used to be taken down to the river to wash from these inns. There were then other inns in the Main Street besides those now existing, such as the *Old Elm Tree*, *Black Swan*, *Royal Archers* (in the New Row), and *Sportsman*, the latter afterwards used for the "No. 1 British Workman Club Rooms." Before the railway was opened the Bingley inns enjoyed a wide repute for their clean and comfortable accommodation and the general excellence of the fare provided. Many commercial travellers from a distance preferred coming to Bingley rather than stay at the inns in Bradford, or even at Leeds. When the cotton industry prevailed at Bingley, the local manufacturers used to attend the Manchester market usually once a month. They generally took the coach or drove to Bradford, and then joined the York coach through to Manchester. The Manchester connection coaches also ran through Bingley parish from Keighley, by way of Hogholes

(Glen Lee), to Halifax, until the new road was made through Hermit Hole and Cross Roads. The old bar-house still stands near the junction of the roads to Long Lee and Hogholes.

THE POST-OFFICE.

At one time, when Bradford was a very small place, letters for Bingley from that town came *via* Leeds. In 1815 the postage of letters from Bradford to Bingley cost 4½d., from Halifax 4½d., Leeds 5½d., Pontefract 7½d., Kettlewell 7½d., Manchester 7½d. There are some yet living who can remember Robinson Greenwood, of Thwaites, carrying the mails on horseback daily between Bradford and Keighley. He left Bradford every morning, Sundays excepted, at 7 o'clock, and returned from Keighley at noon, carrying usually two bags, one slung over each shoulder. The post-office at Keighley was then at the *Black Horse* hotel, while the office at Bingley was in a shop at the corner of Millgate. Sometime before 1822 it was kept by Mrs. Susannah Askew, who had also a private school. In the year named she was succeeded by her daughter, Mary Ann Askew, and at this time there was only one delivery of letters, &c., viz., at 8 a.m., and one despatch daily at 2 p.m. In 1830 Miss Askew was married to Mr. J. Richardson, the first efficient master of the National School, and he then became postmaster, and in that capacity was understood to be of a rather saucy type. Anyone transacting business at the post-office was obliged to stand outside in the street, and receive stamps or hand in their letters, &c., through a window, a pane of which had been specially cut out for the purpose.

The only postman at that time was John Binns, who was also an earthenware and glass and china dealer, tenanting the premises now occupied by Mr. R. Robertshaw, greengrocer, Main Street. He had to cover a wide postal area, his "round" compassing not only the town of Bingley, but all the ground from Cottingley to East Morton and from Eldwick to Harden and Ryecroft. Like many tradesmen of that day, he kept a donkey, which he used sometimes on his rounds; and being reckoned a

King's Court and Old Shops, Main Street, Bingley.

rather superior, self-contained man of business, anybody who happened to quiz him for his lack of speed on these occasions generally got a smart retort for their pains. It is said, for example, if he had a letter to deliver at the *White Horse* inn he would carefully dismount to execute his charge, and then mount again to deliver a letter on the opposite side of the street! Yet, in spite of these amusing traits in his character, he was a diligent and steady worker, whom everybody respected, and his son, Mr. J. Arthur Binns, Official Receiver in Bankruptcy, and a gentleman well-known for his cultured tastes, is at the present time one of Bradford's distinguished citizens. Mr. Binns is a native of Bingley, and his father died here about 1840.

The office was subsequently removed to the house up the steps behind the railings in the Main Street, where the stationmaster now resides, and afterwards to the shop of Mr. Wood, plumber, which stood where a portion of the present premises of the Co-operative Society have been erected in the Main Street. At a later date it was taken to the house now occupied by the Misses Smith, opposite Millgate, and on the appointment of Mr. Jonas Bailey as postmaster, in 1862, the office was removed to a shop in Main Street, just below Park Road corner, and on October 20th, 1893, was raised from a sub-post-office to the rank of a head office. Yet there was then but one delivery of letters, &c., daily. When Mr. Jonas Bailey died in 1878, his brother, Mr. William Bailey, was appointed postmaster, and up to 1882 one portion of the shop was the post-office and the other portion used as a confectioner's shop. There were now two deliveries daily. In 1877 two postmen, named Allen and Whitley, did all the work of delivery for the town, including Beckfoot and Cottingley. Mr. William Bailey died in 1891, and in September of that year was succeeded by Mr. Louis J. Wills, from the Liverpool Post Office, who in February, 1898, was promoted to the office at Ormskirk, in Lancashire; his place at Bingley being taken by Mr. G. B. Stothard.

In 1893 the office was removed to the present commodious premises at the corner of Queen Street and

Main Street, when Mr. Wills was presented with a pleasing souvenir from the post-office officials, consisting of a large picture containing photographs of all the staff and the old and new offices, with an inscription setting forth the purport of the gift. At the present time there are eight postmen employed to deliver in the town, including Beckfoot and Gilstead; Cottingley having a separate postman. During recent years the business of the post-office has very greatly increased. In 1882, for example, the number of letters, &c., received weekly averaged 9,624, while in 1897 the number was 17,677, or about 30,000 in and out; of telegrams 2,851 were received in the year 1882, and 9,579 in 1897, besides 2,379 transmitted through the Bingley office to East Morton and Crossflatts.

The opening of

THE RAILWAY,

with a station at Bingley (on the Midland system), undoubtedly gave an impetus to the extension of the town and trade, although happening in the midst of the great Chartist agitation, its benefits were not immediately felt. It was opened for the public on March 16th, 1846; but a few days previously a trial trip from Bradford to Keighley was undertaken, and never such a cheer had been heard in Bingley since the lowering of the first canal boat down the five-rise locks, some seventy years before, as old folk tell me went forth from at least three thousand throats on that memorable day when the train drew up for a few minutes at the Bingley station, which was then near Park Road corner, not far from the present station. The latter was opened July 24th, 1892. The old station was afterwards removed to the site of the present Goods Yard, opposite the *Fleece* inn. Mr. William Murgatroyd and Mr. John Rand were amongst the gentlemen present on this first trip.

The whole line from Bradford to Keighley was laid and completed in the short space of nine months, and this included the removal of 150,000 cubic yards of rock and earth near Shipley station; a cutting at Hirst Wood, from which about 70,000 cubic yards were dug; several bridges; a tunnel at Bingley 200 yards long; and the filling up of the terrible Bingley Bog, to which more than 100,000 cubic yards of excavation, chiefly of stone, had to be carted and tipped into it. This apparently "bottomless marsh" (*see* page 20) was the greatest difficulty which the contractors, Messrs. George Thompson and Co., had to contend with in the whole course of the railway, and at one time it was thought the idea of traversing the valley at

Old Railway Station, Bingley.

this point would have to be abandoned, and the line carried along the hillside as the canal contractors had done. Ultimately, however, a safe foundation was obtained, and the work was proceeded with.

Two bogs, one on each side of the railway bridge in Park Road, extended southwards to the Dubb and northwards towards Crossflatts, and these primeval swamps were the paradise and feeding-grounds of thousands of toads, frogs, and other creeping things. Whole armies of these creatures used to migrate at certain seasons of the year from one swamp to another, and I am told by persons who have witnessed these migrations that thousands of toads, &c., might have been seen crossing the neck of land separating the two mires. Park Road up to 1863, when the first sod of the park was cut, had always been known for this reason as Toad Lane. Snakes and lizards also abounded on the drier heaths and among the bushes above the banks of the swamp. All land snakes, of course, are good swimmers. The late Mr. John Dobson told me he remembered seeing a snake a full yard long caught near the old Bowling Green, where Messrs. Wildman's mill now stands. Lizards may still occasionally be seen in the Park.

Main Street Alterations.

During the past ten years the old-world character of the town, and especially of the Main Street, has been completely transformed. For many years before the Improvement Commissioners obtained the Provisional Order in 1887 for the compulsory purchase of land and buildings to carry out the much-needed improvements there had been a good deal of discussion on the necessity of these reforms, owing to the continued extension of the town and increased traffic. The old Market House, Butter Cross, and Wesleyan Chapel quite blocked one portion of the chief thoroughfare, rendering the passsage of vehicles, &c., difficult, and not altogether free from danger. Likewise the elevated block of buildings on Elm Tree Hill, of very old standing, facing the Main Street, had grown very much in the way, and the whole of these have been removed. Through the courtesy of Mr. T. W. Goodall, of Bingley, I have been able to engrave the accompanying views of these interesting bygone features of the Main Street, from photographs taken by him shortly before the demolition took place. The characteristic Market House, erected in 1753, when Tuesday was made the market-day, was removed stone by stone, and re-erected at the top of the Park, where it now remains (*see* page 108). The old Butter Cross and Stocks were also removed thither at the same time. Originally the Butter Cross occupied a site nearly opposite the Bradford Old Bank, but about 1820 it was placed in its well-known position close to the Market House, and about the same time the stocks were removed from the side of the churchyard, and placed between the Cross and the Market House. Subsequently the stocks were removed to the position they have since held. In his poem, *A Voice from the Sycamore* (published in 1856), the late Robert Carrick Wildon describes in a spirited strain many incidents of the past, which are supposed to have been witnessed by the old sycamore on Elm Tree Hill.

The very primitive-looking workhouse, with its white-washed walls, in Myrtle Place, was an old house in 1726 when it was taken by the authorities and fitted up for the purpose it so long served. Pages might be written of events that happened under the *regime* of the old parish constables before the inauguration of the present police system. The old workhouse was pulled down in 1860, when the Court House was built on the site.

Up to the year 1857 the district of Bingley, like the rest of the rural districts in the West Riding, had been under the control of the parochial authorities, whose constables exercised an imperfectly organized system of supervision over the various classes of offenders usually found in country districts, references to which I have made from time to time from the old parish books. On the passing of Sir Robert Peel's scheme in 1856 a police force was established in the West Riding, under the able leadership of Colonel Cobbe, and a number of officers and constables were trained and drafted into the country districts of West Yorkshire; Inspector James Kershaw taking charge of the Bingley section in the spring of 1857. In 1858 Keighley had been made the head of a Petty Sessional Division, and Bingley has since been comprised therein. The division has the reputation of being worked by a steady and efficient body of men; the present chief being Superintendent Benjamin Grayson, who resides at the Sessions House, Keighley. The Bingley Town section, including Morton, Crossflatts, and Eldwick, is controlled by 1 inspector, 1 sergeant, and 10 constables, while the

Elm Tree Hill Inn, Bingley.

Wilsden section, including Cottingley, Harden, and Cullingworth, is superintended by 1 sergeant and 4 constables. The inspectors stationed at Bingley since the formation of the force have been these:—April, 1857, James Kershaw; May, 1857, Henry Hey; June, 1860, E. Whitehead; May, 1865, George Sykes; December, 1865, James R. Croft; May, 1871, H. Goodall; March, 1875, T. Greenwood; November, 1878, Henry Booth; December, 1882, S. G. Tebbutt; December, 1890, T. Blanshard; February, 1895, John H. Birkhead. It is gratifying to record that Bingley with the surrounding district has always enjoyed an enviable immunity from crimes of a serious character.* At one period gambling on moorlands and waste grounds used to be extensively practised by gangs of men, who regularly assembled for that purpose; and certain individuals, generally dwelling in isolated places, were commonly credited with being the manufacturers of an excellent quality of home-spun whiskey. A horned sheep or two also occasionally disappeared from amongst the flocks grazing on the moorlands, especially during hard winters, when food was scarce in many families and employment unobtainable. The spread of education, however, and the general improvement in the condition of the bulk of the people have now rendered these species of offences almost as things of the past.

The town is now well provided with works and shops of every description, where almost anything can be purchased from a gas-engine to a halfpenny orange. In spite of occasional depressions, there has been a continued forward movement in trade; many establishments from very small beginnings have expanded with the improved times; such, for example, as the Industrial Co-operative Society, Limited, which from a very humble lodgment in

* It may be creditably recorded that in the returns of the executions at York from the year 1379 to 1860, of all towns and villages in Yorkshire, not a single person from Bingley has suffered the extreme penalty of the law. The first unfortunate record is: January 4th, 1862, James Waller, of Eldwick, executed in the Castle of York for the murder of William Smith, *alias* Davy, gamekeeper to Timothy Horsfall, Esq., of Hawksworth Hall.

a cottage off Chapel Lane has come to be located in the present handsome block of buildings in the Main Street. With the exception of the Leeds Industrial, it is the oldest society of its kind in Airedale. At the house referred to, No. 10, Prospect Street, the first store was opened in 1850; the first manager being Mr. William Moorhouse. In December, 1851, the first secretary, Mr. John Speight, was appointed, and early in 1853 the society moved into larger premises in Chapel Lane, and the house in Prospect Street was given up. In 1861 the first branch was opened at East Morton, and Mr. Speight was appointed manager, and retained that position until 1868, when he met with a serious fall down one of the banks at Morton, which resulted in his death. Two secretaries were appointed in his place, Messrs. Walbank and Gill, and from that time to the present the business has been one of continued progress and expansion. There are besides the head stores now nine branches, with a total membership of about 3000, and a working capital of £60,000. There are also independent societies at Wilsden, Hainworth, New Road Side, Lees, and Cross Roads, having a membership of about 1200. Hainworth, it may be added, has 23 members, and is reputed to be the smallest distributing society in the kingdom. From these particulars, and the fact that on the presentation of the first balance-sheet for the year ending May 30th, 1854, when it was found that the year's sales had produced the sum of £2905, while at present the turn-over is about £120,000 per annum, a good idea may be obtained of the growth and wonderful expansion of industrial life in Bingley during the past fifty years.

Further striking evidence in the same direction is afforded by the annual statistics of the Bingley Building Society, which has now branches at Shipley, Cullingworth, Wilsden, Denholme, Haworth, Keighley, Sutton Mill, and Barnoldswick. The society first saw the light in the year 1851, when most of the large and important societies were established. Although this society has suffered some reverses, yet from the year 1864, when Mr. N. H. Walbank was appointed secretary, its growth and success has been phenomenal. It may safely be asserted that there is not a Building Society in any town or city in England doing the same amount of business, taking population into account. Its turn-over for the year 1897 was £95,360 8s. 8d., and advances on mortgage £37,697 16s. 2d. The balances due to 904 shareholders was £95,152 13s. 4d., giving an average of £105 5s. 0d.; there was due to 910 depositors £118,383 18s. 1d., an average of £130 1s. 10d. each. There was due by 446 borrowers £215,176 12s. 11d. Reserve Fund and undivided profits £2170 6s. 6d. The turn-over since 1851 has been £2,579,354, and the amount advanced to borrowers within that period £992,257 (approaching a million). This society has all the elements of permanency, and stands in the front rank of local institutions for the encouragement of thrift.

The handsome Town Hall, Technical Institute, Cottage Hospital, and other public edifices shew that Bingley is keeping pace with the times. The Public Library (of 7740 volumes) and News Room are also much used; the issues from the library being about 27,000 volumes per annum. The local (weekly) newspaper, the *Bingley Chronicle*, has a large circulation in the town and district, while the *Keighley News* and *Keighley Herald* have each offices in the town, and enjoy a wide circulation.

Old Coach Clock, Bingley.

Old Bingley "Characters."

OLD CHARACTERS.

"Time, like an ever-rolling stream,
Bears all its sons away;
They fly forgotten, as a dream
Dies at the opening day."

TO go back to the days of the old parish constables, Bingley and the neighbourhood literally swarmed with "characters" of the real old type, now rapidly dying out through the equalising efforts of School Boards and the spread of literature. I have often thought what a grand, soul-stirring sight it would be to witness a procession of such old bygones, headed, say, by Jack Lob and the Rumbalds Moor Hermit, and winding up with burly Tom Varley and his bold comrade of "law and order," Jack o' Mark's. Jack, as I have elsewhere remarked, had been a rampant Chartist, and subsequently became assistant constable, and right merrily he wielded the staff of peace. If any "eccentrics" or notorious characters, and there were admirable specimens of both sexes, saw either of these redoubtable guardians of the parish law approaching it was the signal for an immediate retreat down the nearest passage, or else for a very crest-fallen, demure-faced march past, followed by an after-sigh expressive of such a phrase as "O! I'm safe."

In these days there was a coal wharf between Dubb Mill and Ebor House, and it was no uncommon occurrence among a certain section of the community running short of fuel to go down to the place and quietly help themselves. Tom got wind of a certain Sammy somebody who had got quite expert at this job, so he went down and watched unobserved one evening. Presently he heard a slight disturbance among the coal, and a large lump was being gently raised to the wall above. But Tom at this moment just happened to look over, and quietly remarked, "Stop a bit, Sammy, and I'll help tha to give it a lift." The dismay on the man's countenance at being thus nicely caught may be imagined. Big Tom certainly kept the town's peace without much astir, though rumour has it there were certain "characters" who really never felt themselves out of harm's way, so plagued were they with the constable's questionings about wrongs past, present, or to come. Poor Benjamin Laycock—alas, poor Ben! with his orange and fish cart, over which many a joke was cracked as to whether his herrings were mummies from Egypt or genuine articles; but he had always a ready answer, and was *fruitful* in repartee. "Codger" was his by-name, and he managed to keep his horse till one day, on his returning from a mild course of education at the Wakefield College, he found that some ill-natured person had been stoning the animal, which lay in a helpless condition on the Druid's Altar road. A crowd collected, and after much ado the creature sufficiently recovered to enable Mr. Laycock to transact business at Morton the same afternoon. But, unhappily, the horse (not by any means a pedigree animal) died on the way home, and Ben was forthwith summoned on the evidence of certain witnesses of cruelly beating the animal when it would not go. Tender-hearted Ben, however, vowed and declared he did nothing but coax and pet the beast to proceed. But, in spite of a very wordy defence, he had to go back for a month to the same Academy from which he had so lately returned.

I am told that on one occasion, sometime early in the fifties, "Codger," mounted on his gallant mare, ran an important mile race with another mounted veteran named Tom Wood, better known as "Cockle Tom." The stake was 50s., or 25s. a-side, and a well-known character, who went by the musical sobriquet of "Pig Dough," acted as judge. He rode a blind galloway, which had been borrowed for the purpose. The race was timed to be run at a certain hour in the afternoon, on the edge of Rumbalds Moor; but as nearly the whole party, I am told, arrived in a state of inebriation, there was considerable commotion and delay before the "pistol" was fired and the start made. Tom lay with his head caressingly on his animal's head; "Codger," on the other hand, managed to hold himself erect, talking very much all the time, and looked all the more comical dressed, as it was arranged, in a huntsman's suit of red, and his top lip blackened. The race was finally run, the crowd following. It ended, however, in a row, in which "Pig Dough's" horse got a leg broken, and he claimed, I believe, the stakes as damages. Who got the stakes, I think, was never known. But the spectators evidently enjoyed the melée, and a man who had gone up with a gig-cart full of sandwiches sold out, and had to return to Bingley for more.

I have heard some strange tales of these old parish constable days. Few now living remember Sutcliffe, the burly parish constable and workhouse master. He stood 6ft. 2in. in height, and was broad in proportion. A man called Crowther acted as his assistant, and served as night watchman. He paraded the town at all hours of the night, armed with pike and rattle, and cried the hour and state of the weather. Then there was Walker Waddington, who could have told us many an incident and racy tale in his day. There were no railways in Airedale then, and he always drove his culprits to Wakefield in a gig. Joe Green was the last to hold the office up to 1857, when the police system was inaugurated. He was appointed in 1853, and was also pinder and bell-man. He died in 1872, aged 69. He was one of 16 children, and, singularly, he himself had 16 children, and one of his sons, the gallant William Green (who has saved many lives from drowning), is the present pinder and bell-man. The latter has 12 children. Green lived in Illingworth Yard, in the house still occupied by his son, and where the Greens have resided for at least 150 years. To this house prisoners were sometimes brought instead of being taken to the old parish lock-up, in Myrtle Place. The ill-starred beings would prefer to give themselves up to Joe, when they had the chance, rather than to the custodian of the legitimate prison, as in Green's house was a cosy corner and a chair near the fire, where the delinquents were wont to sit, and the iron ring is still attached to the mantel-piece to which they were obliged to be shackled. Many a tale of woe and suffering has been poured into the sensitive ears of Mrs. Green on the chance of getting a buttered muffin or a bit of extra cake, for which dainties the good woman was widely known to such unfortunate, or rather fortunate customers.

Old Job Senior, the Rumbalds Moor Hermit, for many years used to come down to Bingley every Christmas wassailing. He generally hobbled into Morton first, his legs in winter always well wrapped round with hay or straw; his garments being held together with loops of string, and he was never very particular, like the ancient Romans, whether he wore a hat or not. For a lark the lads at the Grammar School would mount him on a cart, or carry him shoulder high into the town. He would then begin "wassailing"; his loud, stentorian voice, mingled with the barking of dogs which the said singing often provoked, attracting crowds of folk anxious to get a glimpse of the strange pilgrim from the moor. When at Bingley he generally slept in the barn at the back of the *White Horse* inn, and was always sure of obtaining some coppers from the boys at the adjoining school, who got rare fun out of him.

Jack Lob, of Cottingley, was another remarkable oddity who used to be a regular visitor at Bingley. He is still remembered as a "bit short" in his understanding, though he well knew the difference between a penny and a halfpenny, and at times was rather smart-witted. One day a stranger, while handing him a penny, remarked, "I think, my man, you are *not all there.*" Jack, after eyeing himself wistfully all over, replied, "Well where's t'other part of me? If ye can find it, you're welcome to it!" So far as I can learn, he never wore at any season either hat or cap, and Mr. Sam Dean, of Cottingley, who remembers both Jack and his father, when they occupied a portion of the Old Hall, tells me that some Cottingley hand-combers got up a subscription for obtaining Jack a complete fustian suit, and although a cap was purchased, he would never wear it. Jack once laid a plan with Jerry Wilkinson, a discharged soldier, and a simple fellow, then living at Gilstead, to rob a woman at Nab Wood; but the stout-hearted woman recognised the would-be felons, and they made off as quickly as their pedal ornaments would allow them. They were afterwards apprehended, and Jerry got "a month," but Jack's wit saved himself. This Jerry had an almost daily habit of praying "that all the lads and lasses might be wed, and have plenty of roast beef and plum pudding."

But to recite the story of all the old Bingley characters would fill a volume. They were of all sorts and conditions. The picture prefacing this chapter represents three old local worthies, who to Bingley people at any rate hardly need describing, as they were all so lately with us. John Steel is shewn standing up propounding politics to Smith, the barber, who occupies the middle seat, and Tom Wood, *alias* "Cockle Tom," who had a shop near where the *Midland* hotel now stands. It is unnecessary to remark on their political colour, for that is apparent by the familiar portrait on the wall. "Old Steel," as he was generally called, died December 7th, 1896, aged 95. He came to Bingley about 1830, and was father of 15 children; his eldest "boy" being 70. Only a short time before he died the writer tried to elicit some information from him about the old Chartist days. "Well, ye knaw," he said, "I nivver took onny pairt i't rumpus 'at wor goin' on; it wor a sad time for Bingley folk, an' I'd allus plenty on my hands wi' lookin' after my awn castle." Tom Smith, *alias* the "Professor," who died December 4th, 1896, had his shop, as is well-known, in Chapel Lane, and if you wanted the latest news on any subject, Tom was just the man to retail it while enjoying your "scrape," or "mow."

Then we have another hearty old "character" in the person of William Midgley, of Eldwick, who is fast approaching the age of an octogenarian, yet still able to walk his thirty miles a day! Mr. Midgley has had a life of very varying vicissitude, yet he has always been abstemious and enjoyed robust health; being a thorough believer in the maxim, "Never drink except when you are thirsty." He has good family traditions, and comes of the family of Midgley who were lords of the manor of Haworth; his father being Richard Midgley, son of David

Midgley, who was born at the Cliff, Harden, and died at Hunter Hill.

The subject of this sketch was in early life a woolcomber, and for some time worked for Messrs. Hartley, at Sutton Mill. Early in the sixties he joined the police force, and was for a time in the B Division

MR. WILLIAM MIDGLEY, OF ELDWICK.

of the Manchester Constabulary. Afterwards he was watchman at Horton Dyeworks, and while there he bought a piece of land at Eldwick, and built the rustic house he now occupies. Four days a week he used to walk backwards and forwards between his home at Girlington and Eldwick while he raised the domicile stone by stone; all the beams used in its construction being, moreover, carried up to Eldwick on his own back from Shipley. Like a policeman, this industrious toiler kept an Occurrence Book, and when the building was finished, and he sat "by his own fireside," he took the book, and found that to accomplish his work he had walked just 8115 miles!

Witchcraft was also much in favour here at one time. We all know about the Ling Bob Witch at Wilsden, who could only be got rid of by shooting her with silver when she appeared in the disguise of a hare; a tradition, by the way, based on an old Scandinavian legend, which can be traced back to the Celts of the Orient. But few persons now living remember anything of the once famous Wilsden fortune-tellers, Nellie Hobb and Harry Mack, or of the celebrated wizard near Keighley, who went by the name of "Wise Robin of Rumbalds Moor." A remarkable incident concerning his divining the consequence of a robbery of a carrier's waggon in 1790 is related in the first volume of Mayhall's *Annals of Yorkshire*. Then there was 'Becca Brigg, a noted fortune-teller, who lived in a cottage at Jackfield, above Bingley.

Old Dolly Jackson, of the Priesthorpe Alms Houses, who died a year ago, past her 80th year, told me many a tale of these bygone times. Dolly herself was a "character," who had seen a good deal of the ups and downs of life. Her grandfather was a famous horse-dealer, and travelled through the country with a valuable entire horse, and many were the experiences she could relate of public-house life, &c., in the last century. The horse was ultimately sold for 200 guineas, and the money put in the Craven Bank, and when the old man died, at the age of 88, Dolly came in for her share. She remembered a man called Henry Dixon, who was her cousin, being put in the Bingley stocks, now about forty-five years ago. He was a nailer by trade, but addicted to the too common habit at that time of gambling. She said she took him a cup of tea while he was sitting in the stocks, and Mr. Slicer, of the *Queen's Head*, over the way, gave him his dinner when he came out. The stocks were last used about 1870.

One might say something of other well-known Bingley characters, worthy men and women who have played their parts in the past history of the old town. I have just mentioned the old *Queen's Head* inn, which earlier in the century was kept by Mrs. Jowett. Everybody knew Mary Jowett. Her husband was in the coal trade, and also had a smithy down the yard. It is said that Mary many a time when he needed help used to strike for him. She was succeeded at the inn by her grandson, the late Mr. George Slicer, a man of strong individuality, albeit punctual and straightforward in all his business affairs, yet one who might be described as an excellent type of landlord of the old school. He died in November, 1894, at the age of 75, having been landlord of the *Queen's Head* from 1846 to 1875. It is worthy of mention that he never opened his house on the Sabbath, even for many years before six-days' licenses were granted.

The late Mr. John Bradley, who died in October, 1897, aged 83, was another well-known Bingley native. He was the son of Jonathan Bradley, blacksmith, whose house and forge stood behind the old *King's Head* inn. John himself for nearly 50 years had a smithy on the site of the new lock-up shops opposite the station, in Park Road; and it might truly be said of him he was very near the prototype of Longfellow's *Village Blacksmith*. His smithy was not far from the National Schools,—

> And children coming home from school
> Look in at the open door;
> They love to see the flaming forge,
> And hear the bellows roar.

He was also a worthy, sober-minded churchman, and for more than seventy years regularly attended the Parish Church.

> He goes on Sunday to the church,
> And sits among the boys,

as the poet describes. One of his sons is now landlord of the old *Queen's Head*, and another, Mr. Tom Bradley, is well-known as the author of *Coaching Days in Yorkshire*, &c.

Mr. Joseph E. Bradley, who died at Bingley about the same time as Mr. John Bradley, was cousin to him.

He was well-known here from his being blind from a boy. As a professional musician of good repute in the town and district, he enjoyed the respect of all who knew him.

In the early part of the century there was an old clique of enthusiastic bell-ringers; amongst them being Hezekiah Briggs (the sexton), Thomas Green, Isaac Rhodes (the old carrier), and Henry Dickinson. The latter died Feb. 6th, 1883, in his 91st year, and was well known for his wise saws, dry humour, and wonderful memory of past events. He used to tell how on one occasion, when the Bingley ringers were returning over Reedshaw Moss from a ringing contest at Colne, at which the Bingley men were victorious, Isaac Rhodes threw up his hat, shouting "Yorkshire for ivver!" A strong breeze carried the hat a considerable distance, and it was not seen to come down; but it was said that Green, the balloonist, discovered it while making an ascent from Halifax a few weeks afterwards! It used to be said of Thomas Green, who died in 1886, in his 81st year, that he had twice given the living of Bingley away, as he had introduced, according to custom as a parishioner, two vicars, Mr. Cheadle in 1837, and Mr. Irwine in 1862, to the church, and instructed them how to toll a bell. His son, Mr. Thomas Wilkinson Green, an old and able bell-ringer, is referred to on page 171.

I might go on noting other deserving characters did space permit. But now I must say, "Farewell," as the poor lad, James Green, exclaimed as he mounted the Druids' Altar road on leaving Bingley to seek his fortune elsewhere in the hard times of a century ago. His leaving the dear old place of his birth and upbringing brought tears to his eyes, and in after years, when the grey hairs were thick upon his head, he never relinquished his love and admiration for old Bingley. Mr. Green was President of the Bradford Benevolent Society. He was also a trustee and liberal supporter of Eastbrook Chapel, Bradford, and when he died in 1858 it is stated that 2,000 persons were present at his funeral sermon. The property in Main Street, Bingley, called "Green's Yard," belonged to and was named after him, and there are at present some 200 or more of his descendants in Bradford and neighbourhood.

FOLK-LORE AND OLD CUSTOMS.

IN this chapter I would fain carry you on the wings of song to those happy realms of tradition and old-time usage, which belong rather to the poet's than to the prose-man's art. But as truth and fact, and not fancy, are what we must aim at in history-writing, I shall have to deal with these still-surviving romances of bygone ages in plain matter-of-fact prose.

Around Bingley there used to be, and perhaps still is among the older inhabitants, a strong belief in the existence of dwarfs and fairies, and this appears to be based on an inherited tradition that a very small race of beings once dwelt here; in fact, the actual aborigines of the Ice Age. The recent discoveries of human remains among glacial debris in a rock-shelter near Schaffhausen, in Switzerland, shew that the district was frequented by a race of true pygmies, and that these diminutive people may be the very representatives of the traditional dwarfs and fairies who are supposed to have haunted the caves and lonely places in our own time. They are particularly associated with caves, which we know were man's first rude dwelling-place. In Gilstead Crags up to quite recently there was an opening in the rocks known from time immemorial as "Fairies' Hole," and here old people say the tiny creatures used to trip and dance and play their merry antics in the bright moonlight. Woe, however, be to anyone who was bold enough to intrude at such a time; he would be instantly deprived of sight. At Harden, in a secluded part of Deep Cliff, the fairies, it is said, could sometimes be heard clanging musical tongs, and what looked like tiny white garments hung out on the trees could be actually seen, I am told, sometimes on bright nights. Sometimes in places where they were supposed to have been dancing a circle of small creamy fungi would spring up, and these were known to the surrounding peasantry as Fairy Rings. I have myself seen such rings in the Harden valley, and though their presence in this peculiar form is now explained scientifically, yet the belief in them being the outcome of the fairies could never be eradicated from the popular mind, and the tradition still remains.

The cult and influence of the Celt has, indeed, never been effaced from this district. For centuries, as I have shewn, the Brython, or true Briton, held uninterrupted sway here, and the old Arthurian legends must have long had a place among the popular beliefs of the people. But at this day I cannot discover a trace of these traditions, so thoroughly have the loom and shuttle and electric light frightened King Arthur and his knights away! The Celt, I should say, was a greater or more devout lover of Nature than either Saxon or Norman. He had a profound reverence for the sublime and mysterious in the natural world. With him it became a passion, a worship, appealing to and feeding his imagination as nothing else could. The advances of mere material civilization brought him no peace, and gave no satisfaction to the aspirations of his soul. He marvelled at the all-beneficent sun, the wandering moon, the glitter of the far-off stars, and the vastness and mystery of them all moved him to believe that his own little world around him was also full of a mysterious existence; thus the bare hills and the solitudes of the deep woods he delighted to people with all kinds of strange imaginings, which his children's children imbibed in the spirit of actual experience, and out of which grew the traditions of after ages. But modern science surely is gradually driving away these myths of the unknown.

The Celtic child romped on the grass, played in the heather, and joined in the games as our children may do to-day. The easily-remembered game of counting out,—

> "Ickerty, pickerty, pise a-rickety,
> Pomp, alarum, jig!"

is none other than a childish survival of the ancient Celtic numerals prevailing in this district, which I have mentioned on page 52; while another old local game, "tiggery, tiggery, touchwood," has come down to us from the ancient Scandinavian dwellers at Bingley, the formers of the wapentakes; *taeg*, or touch-sword, the well-known origin of which needs no explaining.

One local Scandinavian tradition is particularly interesting. No one seems to know why every autumn fair the school-children at Bingley have holiday, and large numbers of parkin pigs are made, sold, and eaten to commemorate the occasion. Why at these times are not parkin dogs, horses, &c., made instead of the perpetual pig? This parkin pig, indeed, is nothing else but a counterfeit presentment of the sacred boar, or Golden-bristles, of the ancient Teutonic nations. As the Celt had worshipped the sun from his Druids' Altar, and had offered a sacrifice to the all-giving life of the sun (a rite preserved by our harvest thanksgivings), so the Northmen celebrated by an annual feast, in which the boar appeared as the leading dish, the great sun-god of Freyr, the symbol of love, beauty and fertility. The custom of annually dining off boar's head was once universal, and prevailed among all classes. Aubrey, writing in 1678, remarks that "before the last civil wars, in gentlemen's houses at Christmas, the first dish that was brought to the table was a boar's head, with a lemon in his mouth." Even so far back as A.D. 1170, among the State records of Henry II. there appears the written fact that upon the young Prince's coronation, the King "served his son at table as a sewer, bringing up the boar's head, with trumpets before it, according to the manner." By the phrase, "according to the manner," we may infer it was an old custom then. Dugdale also alludes to the same custom. In some districts the much-despised, though truly poetical pig, even yet takes the leading part in masquerading processions at Christmas, though the reason whereof may not now be fully understood. A sucking-pig is also served with an apple or orange in its mouth. At Queen's College, Oxford, the Boar's Head Dinner, served with much eclât, at Christmas, is still one of the great events of the year. The boar's head, decorated with laurel and rosemary, and borne on a silver platter, is heralded with songs and music.

According to the *Edda*, or the great Norse Scripture, the

bristling-boar, or solar deity, is every day boiled and served to the gods, yet every evening he appears whole again. He is the symbol of perpetual food and life. Without him we could not exist; therefore we make thank-offerings to him, and yearly glory in his beneficence by a feast given in his honour.

At Bingley this has come to be celebrated by an annual school holiday at the October Fair, and the making of the humble confection, the parkin-pig. And may the good people of Bingley continue to make the parkin-pig, thus commemorating a rare old historic feast which has had an existence in this district for fully a thousand years ! *

Barguest, guytrash, and such hob-goblins were once pretty common in the district, and certain shady dells and lonely places were their well-known haunts. I have heard stories of clanging chains, hair-breadth escapes, &c., which are too long to detail here. His Satanic Majesty, spitting blue-fire, also once appeared on Wilsden Hill; the strange circumstances being fully related in the *Wilsden Almanac* for 1890. Many persons bolted for very life, but learnt afterwards it was a huge joke. In the Town's Book at Yeadon, it is worth noting, there are entries of sums paid for "boggard-catching." They appear to have been so troublesome in that locality as to have rendered necessary a call upon the public purse for their suppression.

Many other local traditions and customs might be mentioned had I space to dwell upon them. Some of these may be taken briefly. The practice of ringing the Parish Church bell at 8 o'clock every evening is the survival of a custom older than the historic curfew-bell of William the Conqueror. At Oxford, for example, Alfred the Great ordered the inhabitants to cover their fires, put out their lights, and go to bed on the ringing of a bell at Carfax every night at 8 o'clock. The houses were then, and in many places long after the Conquest, constructed

* Doubtless the old Vikings at Bingley celebrated the Feast of the Boar in orthodox fashion by dining of the genuine article. Some years ago, while digging a grave in the cemetery, about 40 yards south-west of the church (*see* page 49), there was found a portion of a boar's skull, which had evidently received careful burial; being covered by a flat stone, 8 feet by 2 feet 6 inches.

largely of wood and thatch, and some precautions against fires were necessary for the general safety of property. The pains and penalties of transgressing the edicts of curfew were withdrawn by Henry II. in 1110, though the time-honoured custom of ringing the 8 o'clock bell has been retained in many ancient parishes, including Bingley, even to this day. In the Parish Books, from the middle of the 17th century forward, are entries of sums paid for ringing the 8 o'clock bell. The towers of churches, however, were not intended solely for the bells as we use them now, but were originally built for places of refuge and safety in times of war and peril, and they also served as beacons, or way-marks, directing travellers, who often got lost or benighted in early times, to places of human habitation. The towers were generally lighted on the darkest nights.

The old custom of ringing "Pancake Bell," which is still practised at Bingley, Dewsbury, Malton, Richmond, and a few other places in Yorkshire, is an interesting local event. Shrove Tuesday, which was the day in Catholic times when people were shriven, or absolved from sin (the bell calling them for that purpose), was a day of general rejoicing and liberation. At Bingley, at 11 o'clock in the forenoon, the bells were rung, and the children let loose from school, while all the parish apprentices left their work and claimed a thirteen hours' holiday, and freedom from the oversight of their masters till the clock struck the hour of midnight. Pancakes formed the chief dish of the day.

Pilgrimages to holy wells were at one time common, and there are a number of such springs in and about the parish which no doubt were formerly in good repute for their healing virtues, either of body or of soul. One of these is the Druids' Well, below the Altar, but nothing is remembered now of its ancient repute. Our Lady's Well, near Lady House Farm (an old pre-Reformation property of Bingley Grammar School), is another, and it doubtless gave name to the adjoining Lady Lane, beside the Park. St. Anthony's Well and St. Ives Well, at Harden, are also traditionally credited as holy wells. St. Anthony was the protector of the lower animals, and especially of pigs, and it is not surprising that the name of this saint is preserved in this district, where, as I have already explained, the sacred boar was so much reverenced, and is commemorated at Bingley to this day. At Rome, Madrid, &c., nearly everyone who has a pig, a horse, or an ass, sends it on the saint's day to St. Anthony's Well to be sprinkled with holy-water, and thus placed under the protection of the saint.

Spa Well, Bingley.

Goff Well, close to the road on Harden Moor leading to Hainworth, has given name to a neighbouring farm, but the purpose or virtues of this water are not now known. It used to be a famous resort of gipsies. Then there is the ever-full Abbey Well, near Wilsden, on an old property once belonging to Kirkstall Abbey, and at Norr is another well of peculiar soft water, which, it is said, is an infallible cure for gravel. Jennet's Well, on Black Hill, near

Keighley, has an old repute, though no one seems to know why. It was formerly a very common protest, or habit of confirmation, of the district folk to swear "By Jen!" and the name of Jennet, or Janet, was at one time locally very much in favour as a name for girls. There is a Janet's Cave at Malham, in upper Airedale, and she is supposed in that district to have been Queen of the Fairies. I have spoken of the fairies of Gilstead Crags, and a little below their traditional haunt in Priesthorpe is a beautiful spring —once much resorted to—long known as Janet's Well. The two or three iron springs called Redman Spa (Rumbalds Moor), Jackfield (Marley Brow), and in Spa Lane (below the Park), used to have a well-deserved repute as mineral springs, and the last-named is still much frequented. The water is usually beautifully clear, and is considered to be an excellent tonic. In 1871 a substantial stone cavity, with basin, was erected to receive the water by Mr. Thomas Garnett, of the adjoining estate of Oakwood. Close to this spring is the old Pinfold, which up to about 1825 stood on the site of Olive Terrace, in Chapel Lane, still remembered as Pinfold Hill.

There were also other famous wells, still remembered for their copious supply of wholesome water, or for some particular quality. Bingley at one time derived its whole supply from such wells. One of the best known was on Watering Well Hill, below Myrtle Place, which was lost some years ago when certain alterations in connection with the pumping apparatus of Messrs. Sharp were being made. A curious old trough was found here some three feet below the surface. The two ends were formed of unhewn boulders, and the sides and bottom of flagstones, the whole being well cemented together with very fine clay. Another well-known spring was Ailsa Well, which still remains by the Goit side, near Bingley Corn Mills. It got its name from a woman, one Alice Hird, long resident in an adjoining cottage. The water was uncommonly hard, probably from its percolating through the adjacent limestone gravels, but was accounted an excellent water for cooking vegetables, and was frequently fetched for that purpose. There is also a copious well of beautifully-soft water by the public road in Priesthorpe, which used to be much in favour for brewing tea, &c. A little below is Janet's Well. There are copious springs in the Park which are known for their great purity and coldness, resembling the Ilkley Wells waters in this respect.

The Bingley waters also possessed "curative" properties in other respects. Bingley had its Ducking Stool, though I have not been able to make out whereabouts this old-time instrument of punishment was fixed. It was used as a reformatory for scolds, both men and women, married and single, who had committed certain offences, such as

DUCKING A SCOLD.

backsliding, brawling, or disturbing the peace. The culprit was securely fastened in the ducking-chair, then lowered and lifted in and out of the water see-saw fashion, amid the jeers and ridicule of the usual crowd of onlookers. When the stool was last used at Bingley I have not ascertained. It is mentioned in the old Parish Books. In the accounts of one John Whitley, who was deputy constable for Widow Bothomley, there appears under date December 6th, 1787, an item of 9s. for the Ducking Stool, which the overseers "think too extravagant, and refer it to a further examination."

The practice of punishing culprits guilty of felony by fastening them to the back end of a cart, and then flogging them bare-back through the town, was also in force at Bingley. Mr. Thomas Longbottom (aged 82) tells me he remembers perhaps the last time that this method of punishment was carried out, now more than 70 years since. A man was apprehended for stealing fruit from Mr. Hulbert's orchard at the Old Vicarage, and ordered to be flogged in the usual manner until the body was bloody by reason of such flogging. An official from Wakefield came and carried out the sentence; the culprit being publicly whipped from the Market Cross to the top of the Main Street.*

Many kinds of sports and games were indulged in at Bingley which are now almost things of the past. Bull-baiting, for example, even up to living memory, provided an enlivening kind of "roaratorio" to certain classes of the community in this neighbourhood. The bull-ring was attached to a large flag opposite Gawthrop's basket shop, in the Main Street, and hither the unfortunate animals were brought, and tethered to a chain some twelve or fifteen yards in length. It was a brutal sight. When a crowd had collected, specially-trained bull-dogs were let loose upon the bull; they then attempted to pin him by the nose to the ground; but alack! often enough the infuriated beast with a savage turn would gore and toss the first dog he met, high up even on to a neighbouring roof, the bleeding animal rolling down again to draw its last breath on the pavement below. Again and again the attempt was made to "muzzle" the bull, until the latter, worn out and exhausted by the repeated assaults, sank prostrate to the ground. Old William Hird, *alias* "Tanner" Hird, of Bingley, now in his 74th year, tells me he can just remember as a youngster the last bull-baiting in Bingley, and he has often heard his father tell of the crowds that collected and the scenes he had witnessed on these "festive" occasions. The exhibitions

* Mr. James Parker, of Great Horton, informs me that his grandmother (*née* Clark, of Bingley), who died in 1864, told him of the same incident.

became less frequent this century, and were finally abolished in England about the year 1828.

Cock-fighting was a very common sport in the district formerly, and there used to be an old cock-pit at Harden, at the top of Longbottom Fold; the site being now occupied by the grocer's shop opposite the Independent Chapel.

In this district the customs appertaining to Christmas, Valentine's Day, Palm Sunday, Easter, Royal Oak Day, Whitsuntide, Plot Day (November 5th), &c., are still carried out in much the same manner as in other places. The mummers on New Year's Eve go round with faces blackened to sweep out the old year and make way for the new. The facial disguise and lacking speech may be taken to mean that we are not to know what the coming year will be like, but must remain content with the presence of the mummers, and by an offering of money or of victuals we are naturally to expect that good luck will attend us in the coming year. The Peace Egg, or Sword Dancers, used to come at Christmas, too, attired in party-coloured clothes, paper hats, trimmed with gaudy ribbons and feathers, and each one carrying a sword. They went through a performance, in which the hero, who was supposed to be invincible, slew one of the leaders of the company. This is undoubtedly another representation of those ancient Scandinavian beliefs which had their origin in the creed of Odin, whose matchless sword was the dread and death of every opponent. Its edge was of such marvellous temper that an assailant did not know he had been cut until shaking himself he fell in pieces to the ground! King Athelstan, too, whom I have mentioned in connection with Anglian Bingley, had a foster-son, Hacon, who possessed a sword of such remarkable power that he was able with it to cleave a quern to the centre eye! In the ancient possessors of these magical weapons are no doubt to be recognised the prototypes of the mimic sword-dancers of recent times.

Old people tell me there used to be great fun on the occasion of local weddings, especially from outlying places of the parish, whence the parties, attended by their friends and invited guests, came to the Parish Church. Sometimes they walked in procession, in couples, arm-in-arm, headed by a fiddler, or, if the distance was far, farm-horses would be requisitioned; the men mounted in front and the women on pillions behind. Both people and horses were gaily decorated with various coloured ribbons. After the wedding, the party usually adjourned to one of the town "publics," and potations were freely imbibed. By and bye the return journey was made, and as the wedding party was usually well primed, a good deal of joking and talk followed, no little amusement being got out of the behaviour of the gaunt and gallant farm-steeds on which some of the party mayhap were mounted. When within about half-a-mile of the bride's home, two of the male members were matched to run a race, and he who reached the bride's house first was rewarded by her with a ribbon, obtained specially for the purpose, and which he handed to his sweetheart (if he had one) or proudly wore himself, and treasured for many a long day afterwards. These country weddings usually ended with a supper and a dance, to the accompaniment of a fiddle.

> "This carol they began that hour,
> With a hey, and a ho, and a hey nonino,
> How that a life was but a flower
> In springtime, the only pretty ring time,
> When birds do sing, hey ding a ding, ding;
> Sweet lovers love the spring."

On May Day the scarlet-coated drivers and guards of the coaches came into Bingley with their horses decked with ribbons and rosettes, and with bright-coloured ribbons also flaunting from their whips and horns. At one time nearly every old town and village had its May Pole, but of this local relic of the past nothing is now known. But at Laycock, only a few miles away, dancing round the May Pole was kept up annually until about fifty years ago. At Bingley, however, May Day was not forgotten, for people used to sport a bit of green or flower, and decorate their horses, &c., while certain games were indulged in. Some people made it a holiday, and the schools always so, the children going into the woods and lanes to gather primroses and other wild flowers, with which they covered their hats, &c. I am told that a number of couples have even started from the top of the Main Street and gone round by Beckfoot Lane, and back by Ireland Bridge, playing "duck-under-water-kit" most part of the way:

"The eye is formed; the couple in the rear
Stand wide apart, their clasped hands in the air.
This arch or eye the foremost swift pass through,
And all the living thread behind them drew."

A similar fête takes place annually in May at the little Cornish town of Helston, when a number of couples, headed by the Mayor and a fair partner, dance through the town to the music of a quaint old tune. The event is known as "Furry Day," a corruption doubtless of Flora Day, intended to commemorate the return of sunshine and flowers, in honour of the goddess Flora.

Holy Thursday, generally spoken of as Hallow Thursday, was also the occasion of a school holiday; the boys at the Grammar School usually went up to the Altar and played various games, in which they were joined by others, and on returning mulled ale and spice-cake were served.

Riverside, near Ravenroyd.

PLEASANT WALKS AND PLACES OF PUBLIC RESORT.

**Poets and painters have praised thee much, thou dear old
"Throstle Nest,"
And I would fain invoke the Muse, or I wear not the crest;
Tell we the world where grandeur lies, then we must speak of thee,
Talk we of nature's queenly sights, then praise we thee, Bingley.
In search of bonny nooks and crags, hills, dales, and waterfalls,
Eager we scan our books, and leave our cots and stately halls;
Called we to beauty's sacred shrine, already known or not,
Rich, rare, untiring, unsurpassed, is one dear hallowed spot;
A gem among a thousand more, a little one I ween,
But one that shines brightest of all the gems, the seas between;
'Tis where our children play, and where the big ones love to roam,
Right loyally beloved by all, for it is home, sweet home;
Entice ye great majestic sights of other lands at will,
Entwined around our loving hearts is dear old Bingley still.**

John D. Fox.

IN the manufacturing districts of the West Riding there is no place more pleasantly situated than Bingley, and none which affords a greater variety of interesting walks within easy compass of the town. From Bingley Bridge, which is 256 feet above sea-level, we may within a distance of two or three miles reach the moorland solitudes, and there enjoy the sweet invigorating air and fresh breezes that sweep over miles of blooming heather, at an altitude of more than 1,000 feet above the town. To the lover of prehistoric antiquities and to the naturalist the district teems with interest, as may be gathered from a perusal of the opening chapters of this work.

One of the most popular walks is that from Bingley Bridge by the Altar Lane to

THE DRUIDS' ALTAR

(one mile), or to make it less of a climb, take the familiar river-side path by Ravenroyd (where there have been houses for a thousand years), and ascend by the well-known path through Marley. To write fully about the Druids' Altar

RAVENROYD, NEAR BINGLEY.

would fill a small volume. It commands a wide and lovely view, and it is particularly grand at evening's close to stand beside the rock and watch the day's glory wane; or in the suggestive words of Mr. George Ackroyd:

To mark the glorious orb of parting day
Wrap all in golden fire, as if to burn
All meanness from the earth and soul away!

On the night of Her Majesty's Jubilee, June 22nd, 1897, there was a large gathering of people to witness the huge bonfire blaze on the projection of ground overhanging the

Druids' Altar, Bingley.

valley about 100 yards south-east of the Altar Rock. There was another large fire on Gilstead Crags on the opposite side of the valley. From the Druids' Altar the present writer on the occasion counted nearly a score fires, some shining like suns, others gleaming like mere stars on the distant horizon, extending from Idle Hill to Ingleborough and up Wharfedale to the fells of Cracoe and Grassington, a radius of several hundred square miles.

The event is referred to by "Jim o'th Cragg Nook" in some capital lines commemorative of Jubilee Day in Bingley, and concluding as follows :—

At night the town was all ablaze with grand illuminations,
And people came from miles around, to see our decorations.
I heard one Keighley chap remark, "Well, lads, we all must own
That Bingley's scored a try this time, and taken Keighley down."
The last of all, though not the least, our two gigantic fires,
That stood upon our mountain tops, like ornamental spires,
And when the tongues of flame leaped up into the darkening sky,
A thousand prayers went up at once to Him who reigns on high.
Then here's success to England's Queen, the greatest and the best,
And the same to all her subjects in England's "Throstle Nest."

Mr. Disraeli (Lord Beaconsfield) visited the Druids' Altar on the occasion of his visit to Mr. Ferrand, at St. Ives, in 1844, and the description he gives of it in his novel, *Sybil*, has been frequently quoted. Mr. Edward Driver, of Transfield, close by, says :

This strangest work of nature,
So rude, but strongly formed,
Once held the guns of Cromwell,
Which down on Bingley stormed.

That is the local belief, though there is an absence of evidence that any such bombardment ever took place. During the rejoicings that followed the English successes in the Crimea, a procession was formed in Bingley and marched to the Altar, where a large fire was lighted, and watched all night by two of the company named William Umpleby and Tom Leach. Nicholson, the poet, says the Altar Rock is "deeply marked with the fire of sacrifice" (*see* page 51), and W. O. Geller, the distinguished artist and engraver, has depicted in a fine engraving a scene at the Altar described in Nicholson's *Airedale*. It may be noted that the Altar stone, which belongs to the Rough Rock, or topmost bed of the Millstone Grit series, is at the surface very coarse, quartzose, and much burnt, while the underlying bed, at 20 feet from the surface, consists of a rather fine sandstone. The rocks are much broken and undermined by the "gnawing tooth of Time" and the action of storms; and not long ago a slight subsidence took place, and a large block fell away. Early this century many massive blocks of this hard Rough Rock in the vicinity of the Altar were obtained, and transported by canal from Bingley to Liverpool, and were used in the construction of the docks there. A small box was found here some years ago by Mr. O. Mitchell, of Morton, containing a number of Scotch coins, which are believed to have been lost by some soldier in the Pretender's army that crossed Harden Moor *en route* to Preston in 1745.

THE CEMETERY

is one of the most popular places of resort, and is justly accounted one of the prettiest and most attractive places of the kind in England. It is especially noteworthy for the choice variety of rare Alpines, a delightfully instructive and handsome display, largely due to the fostering care of the late registrar, Mr. Timothy Lister.

The ground for the cemetery, situated on the historic, or rather prehistoric Bailey Hills (*see* page 47), was purchased in 1869, and covers an area of about ten acres, apportioned into 7,086 grave-spaces. The church portion occupies about half of the eastern side of the cemetery, and was consecrated by the Bishop of Ripon on August 1st, 1870, while the unconsecrated portion lies on the west side. The first interment, a child named Walter Greenwood, took place on Aug. 2nd, 1870, in the consecrated portion. There are two beautiful stone buildings, a church and a chapel, for the reception of funerals, and the grounds, which gently undulate, are interspersed with well-kept gravel walks and paths, bordered with various trees: some of the evergreens being particularly noticeable for their beautiful and luxuriant growth. The mezereons, lilacs, roses, and flower-beds generally also present in season a fine and varied show. But to lovers of botanical treasures the extensive range of rockery, which bears hundreds of curious and beautiful Alpine plants, will prove the chief attraction. Here may be found growing some species even in greater luxuriance than in their native haunts; types of plants whose originals are to be found in the remote regions of the Swiss and Norwegian Alps, the Pyrenees, Himalayas, New Zealand, &c., sometimes even far above the line of eternal snow. There are about a score kinds of primroses, many beautiful varieties of anemones, and more than half-a-hundred species of mountain saxifrages, besides numerous rare British wild plants. The display, indeed, is one that attracts botanists and lovers of Nature's beauty from all parts.

Many of the monuments in the cemetery, I may say, are beautifully designed and wrought; while some of the

THE CEMETERY, BINGLEY.

inscriptions are singularly apt and touching. Here is one over the grave of a child:—

If I go to Jesus,
Happy I shall be,
He is ever calling
Little ones like me.

Another, too, upon a little child:—

He shall gather the lambs in His arms, and carry them in His bosom.

While a third says:—

Thou lovely, priceless little gem,
Placed in the Saviour's diadem.

Another, over the grave of one of Bingley's leading townsmen :—

To live in hearts we leave behind is not to die.

Leaving the monuments, a pleasant shady path has been made down towards the river, and the latter as it flows gently and ever onward seems to remind us of the constancy of Nature and of the fleeting passage of human life :—

"Men may come, and men may go,
But I go on for ever."

Up to December 31st, 1897, there have been 3,562 interments in the consecrated portion, and 3,291 in the unconsecrated portion, together 6,853.

The late registrar of the cemetery, Mr. Timothy Lister, will always be remembered for the constant interest he took in maintaining the beautiful character of this hallowed spot. He succeeded the first clerk and registrar, Mr. William D. Cochrane (an excellent botanist*), in July, 1876, and held the position up to the time of his death, which took place on February 2nd, 1897, when he was in the 60th year of his age. Mr. Lister was widely-known and respected, not only in connection with the Bingley Cemetery, but also in many other ways. He was a practical horticulturist ; being one of the most useful members of the old Bingley Horticultural Society, and was for some time its treasurer. In his youth, while working as a woolsorter for Messrs. Jonas Sharp & Sons, he cultivated one of the Cottingley Bridge allotments ; and being specially interested in berry culture, both he and his father (Mr. William Lister) succeeded in taking prizes at the Gooseberry Show held at Bingley so long ago as 1854. The annual National Show of this society was held at Bingley in 1895, when Mr. Lister opened the proceedings with an instructive speech.

He was also well-known and admired for his indefatigable and time-honoured work for the Bingley district Oddfellows. For the long period of thirty-six years he was the painstaking secretary of the "Victoria

* An able article on the Fungi of the Bingley district was contributed by Mr. Cochrane to the *Keighley News* of Oct. 4th, 1873.

Lodge" of the Manchester Unity of Oddfellows, which in its early days met at the old *Queen's Head*, then kept by Mary Jowett. During his connection with the Lodge, it is said he paid out nearly £10,000 in benefits. In 1885 he held the position of Deputy-Provincial Grand Master, and the following year was elected P.G.M. In October, 1896, he was presented with a beautiful tea and coffee service, and also with a gold albert and the P.P.G.M. gold jewel,

Mr. Timothy Lister.

in recognition of his long and valuable services to the Lodge. Mr. Lister was married, and leaves a widow and family. His son, Mr. Tom Lister, was for a short time secretary of the Bradford Mechanics' Institute, but met with a painful accident to his knee, which terminated fatally in June, 1896, at the early age of 27.

The present clerk and registrar of the cemetery is Mr. John Greaves, who succeeded Mr. Lister in February, 1897, having been previously gardener to Mr. John B. Sharp, of Parkfield, Bingley.

The Park.

Among the ancient local properties of Drax Abbey were several places bearing the name of park; such as Calve Park, Over Park, Cote Park, &c., and there was also a Deer Park at Greenhill. But the park under notice was up to quite recent times an unenclosed tract of shaggy moor, covered with brackens and heather, and occupying a fine inclination on the eastern side of the valley, commanding a wide view. From time immemorial this old moorland slope has been called Brown Hill, not from any person so named, but from the ancient British (Cym. Celtic) *brón*, a hill slope, like the similarly-situated Brown Hill at Cullingworth (*see* page 58) and Brown Hill at Morton. I have previously referred to indications of an ancient entrenchment at the north-west side of the park, the character of which has been greatly altered by the tippings into it from the disused stone-quarry close by. In the depression is a low subterranean cavity, or passage, called "Robin Hood's Cave," made, I am told, many years ago by a man infected with the craze of the Rumbalds Moor Hermit, and who intended to establish himself here as the Hermit of Brown Hill.

Formerly, before the park was laid out and the paths made, a well-defined bank of earth extended from the entrenchment for some distance parallel with the principal gravel walk from the park gates towards the north. From these indications and from the name of the hill, I have suggested that it was occupied by the Welsh Britons on the Anglian irruption in the fifth century, and prior to the ultimate British withdrawal to Eldwick and Wilsden, or Wealhas-den, the valley of (Celtic) Welshmen.

The park embraces an area of 18 acres, 10 of which were vested in the churchwardens and overseers of Bingley by the Enclosure Commissioners (on the enclosure of Gilstead Moor in 1860) for the benefit of the public, and the remaining eight acres were purchased by public subscription. The first sod was cut on March 10th, 1863, by the late Mr. Ferrand, M.P., of St. Ives; this being the Prince of Wales' wedding-day. There was a general holiday in Bingley, and a procession was formed to the park; the day's proceedings ending with a public tea, &c., in the National Schools. In honour of the event, it was called Prince of Wales Park, and His Royal Highness sent two beautiful pine-trees from Sandringham for planting in

IN THE PARK, BINGLEY.

the new park. One of them stands on the right side of the path diverging from the main walk near the drinking fountain. As if to celebrate Her Majesty's sixty years' glorious reign, a pair of throstles built their nest in the tree in the spring of 1897, and often during that season did the present writer listen to the male bird piping his roundelay of goodwill from the tree to the tune, shall I say, of "Old England"?

The park was formally opened on June 6th, 1865. It is admirably designed, and considering the rugged and hilly nature of the ground, the results must be regarded as extremely satisfactory. To many people, however, the very steep character of the ground is a fatal objection as a place of frequent resort; but the paths have been laid at as easy gradients as could be efficiently obtained, and they are amply provided with seats. From the terrace (600 ft.) there is a beautiful view over the valley, extending from the heights of Wilsden northwards to the Cononley fells; the Victoria Tower, erected in 1887, being a conspicuous feature on the ridge above Steeton. Opposite us appear the time-hoary rocks of the Druids' Altar, which often on fine evenings catch the rosy glow of the descending sun, while the woodland tract beneath is bathed in deep shadow. Pleasant it is to be here in the calm of a summer's eve, listening to the songs of many birds, while the ever-active bees fly among the sweetly-scented flowers, as you watch the majestic sun go down in his rosy setting. Then the heavens are afire with a divine glow, changing and paling every moment, until the iridescent splendours have faded away, even like unto our worldly hopes and imaginings, which vanish in the tranquility of decay!

Gawthorpe Hall.

SOME HISTORIC MANSIONS.

Gawthorpe Hall.

THERE are about a dozen places still known by this name in Yorkshire and Lincolnshire; but the only one mentioned in *Domesday* is Geutorp, *als.* Gheuetorp, now Gowthorpe, in the wapentake of Harthill, in the East Riding. I have explained the meaning of this name in the section dealing with the Scandinavian occupation of Bingley, and good illustrations of the same are also to be found in the *Njalls Saga*. That these places have been named, as some imagine, from the Islandic *gouk*, a cuckoo, a wandering bird, is to me incredible. The cuckoo would more often seek the woodland glades on the opposite side of the valley than the open and heathery wastes about Gawthorpe Hall. I would as soon believe that the adjoining heathery slopes of Brown Hill (now the park) were named after some imaginary John Brown (*see* page 287). Moreover, the Teutonic races were very superstitious about the cuckoo, and they would never have allocated it to a position in the north—Gawthorpe Hall being due north of Bingley—because the voice of the cuckoo coming from that quarter was ever considered a potent of sorrow and ill-luck.

The old house at Gawthorpe may, indeed, have been the "Hall" mentioned in the Subsidy Roll of Edward III., *ca.* 1346; called the North Hall in the Bingley Poll Tax of A.D. 1378, and presumably a possession of the canons of Drax, the owners of Priesthorpe as well as of the Parish Church.* It is significant that the name Gawthorpe does not occur

* Five tenements in Bingley belonging to the canons of Drax were granted by Queen Mary to the Knights of St. John of Jerusalem on her revival of that order in 1557. These may have been parcel of the grant of 40 acres, &c., in Bingley made by Maurice de Gaunt to the Knights in 1211. In the Poll Tax returns for 1378 for the Forest of Knaresbro' occur the names of Robert Goukeman, Agnes de Goukthorp (which may refer to the Harewood Gawthorp), along with names of a local or neighbouring origin, such as Henry de Wyndill, Thomas de Farnhill, &c.

in the coucher-books of Drax Priory, neither in the local court-rolls of the Knights of St. John of Jerusalem, nor in any documents I have met with before the reign of Elizabeth, when the place, so-called, was in the occupation of a family named Lee, but whether as tenants or servants I do not know.

The opinion, however, may be hazarded that soon after the Norman Conquest, when Bingley was chiefly colonized by Danes, the name of Priesthorpe arose from the fact of its having become the residence of the priests of Drax serving the church at Bingley, and that the habitations of the older Gawthorpe became absorbed in this manor of Priesthorpe when it was bestowed on the canons of Drax by William de Paganel, and confirmed by Osbert de Baiocis. This is one of the oldest local grants we possess, and it is defined as comprising the whole vill of Priesthorpe, namely, one carucate, extending from Del Dunple stream in one direction, and Merstall [Mastalls] as far as the road leading from Priesthorpe to Gilstead, that is the old road, elsewhere explained, passing through Crow Nest. Thus from the Mastalls in the valley (the old boundary-stone in Dubb Lane, separating it from Mickletwaite, is still remembered) up to the road leading to Gilstead measures about 550 yards, or say eight acres wide, while north and south it may extend from 1,000 to 1,100 yards, or 15 acres, or say a total of 120 acres, comprising the carucate, which is a Danish term for such measurement of land.† This area would, of course, take in Gawthorpe, but if the Del Dunple, *als.* Dimple,‡ is the dell on Morton Beck, below Morton village, still called Dimple, the area would be partly bounded by this stream, which descends past Ryshworth Hall (*see* Burton's *Mon. Ebor*, and *Thoresby Soc. Pub.*, II., 188). I have, however, sometimes thought that the above-mentioned old house

† This is the usual area, but there are instances of the carucate containing 200 or even 240 acres (*vide* Seebohm's *Vill. Com.*, page 37, &c.).

‡ What may this mean? There is a Dumple Street in Scarborough, which is mentioned in a grant of the Knights of St. John of Jerusalem in A.D. 1300.

(North Hall) may have been one of the messuages in Bingley purchased by the Gascoignes of Gawthorpe, in the parish of Harewood (*see* fines 1554, &c.), and for this reason the place may have then acquired and retained the distinctive title of Gawthorpe from its belonging to this well-known family (*see* also page 78). But without the actual aid of documents I shall offer no further premise.

In 1565, or before the rebuilding of Gawthorpe Hall in its present form, there was a "capital messuage called New Hall" in Bingley, the location of which I have not been able to fix, though it was apparently in Priesthorpe. Proceedings in Chancery were entered in the above year by Gilbert, son and heir of Thomas Astley, lord of the manor of Bingley, for the recovery of the capital messuage, which it was stated had descended as of right to John Beeston, son and heir of Robert Beeston, of Priesthorpe, and that Stephen Tempest, John Morvell, and Robert Banes were tenants at will of the said premises, and were receiving the issues and profits therefrom. The abstracts of proceedings are too long for quotation, but going back to the 12th century I find (but do not vouch for the connection) that Hugh, son of Roger de Newhall, quit-claimed 18 acres of land and four tofts in Priesthorpe, and also gave an annuity of 8s. to be paid by Robert, son of William de Alwodeley, out of one oxgang of land with a toft here. In the 24th Edward I. (1295) Roger de Aldwodeley held one messuage in Newhall of the annual value of 5s., and three bovates and seven acres of land worth annually 12s. 10d., and he held 18 penny rents in Newhall by service of paying yearly 8s. 2d. to the manor of Harewood. This may be the Newhall near Otley. Alice, the eldest daughter and co-heir of above Roger de Alwodeley, became the wife of William, son and heir of Robert Franke, an influential family, long owners of the manor of Cottingley, near Bingley. Agnes, daughter of Nicholas Franke, married William Gascoigne, Esq., of Gawthorpe Hall, Harewood, and Anthony, son and heir of William Franke, married Rosamund, daughter of Nicholas Tempest (*temp.* Queen Eliz.). This Nicholas Tempest was third son of Sir Richard Tempest (of Flodden Field fame), by Rosamund, his wife, who in 1540 had property at Wilsden and at Mytholme, adjoining Harden Beck, and also a moiety of the manor of Hainworth (*see* Cudworth's *Bowling*, page 156). A daughter of Sir Richard married one of the Gascoignes, of Shipley, who were lords of the manor of Shipley, at that time. Ralph Gascoigne held lands at Bingley in 1554, and Sir John Tempest sold lands in Bingley and Hainworth to Richard Sunderland in 1563. The Ferrands also held land in Priesthorpe in the time of Queen Mary, and George Ferrand died at Priesthorpe in 1738, aged 31, and his wife, Elizabeth, died in 1752, aged 45.

I have elsewhere stated that the lords of the manor of Bingley were non-resident at Bingley up to the end of the 16th century. There was no proper manor-house here, although Gawthorpe Hall, after its purchase with the manor by Anthony Walker, in 1596, became the property of the lords of the manor, as well as for a long time their residence, down to its sale in 1854 by the late Mr. George Lane Fox to Mr. Horsfall.

The Walkers were an old local family, and had been living at Bingley from at least the time of Edward III. They had been gradually acquiring property at Bingley before the manorial rights were purchased by them in 1596. It was most likely in the life-time of Anthony Walker that the present Gawthorpe Hall was built. He married in 1580 Agnes Wooller, a connection, doubtless, of the William Wooller, who in 1597 left £50 for the purchase of an estate in Bingley for the benefit of the poor. In 1576, I find that a Walter Wooller purchased from the Paslewes certain lands, &c., in Bingley.

There was also an Anthony Walker, of Gilstead, *clerke*, who died in 1607. The Walkers were living at Gawthorpe Hall in 1634, and they sold the estate and manor to Henry Currer, Esq. (grandson of Hugh Currer, of Marley), who resided at Gawthorpe in 1654, if not up to its sale in 1668* to Robert Benson, father of the first Lord of Bingley.

Lord Bingley was an eminent public servant. He was

* In 1661 Mary Currer, of Gawthorpe, was party to an agreement concerning a messuage and land at Frizinghall (*vide* Cudworth's *History of Manningham*, &c., page 266.)

an active member of the Legislature, and was for some years Chancellor of the Exchequer. He died in 1781, and was buried in Westminster Abbey. I was informed by the late Mr. Lane Fox that he occasionally resided at Gawthorpe Hall, Bingley; but the mansion which he built at Bramham Park became the family seat, as it remains to this time. His daughter, Harriet, married into the Fox family, as previously explained, and Gawthorpe Hall remained their property until its sale in 1854 to Mr. John Horsfall. The latter re-sold it in 1870 to Mr. David Salmond, J.P., and he again sold it in the spring of 1890 to the late Mr. Samuel Weatherhead, whose family are the present owners and occupants of the mansion.

For many years, up to about the middle of last century, the Mauds, a Quaker family, (*see* page 190), tenanted the Hall on Lord Bingley leaving it, and they were followed by the Heatons, also Quakers, who were long resident here. Subsequently, Mr. Thomas Whitley, a prominent local Wesleyan, resided at the Hall, and here the Rev. Dr. Beaumont, on his retirement from the circuit about 1828, spent a considerable time as the guest of Mr. and Mrs. Whitley. Next followed the Scotts, who were children of Christopher Scott, by his wife Mary Wood, of Morton, whose sister Dorothy Wood married Thomas Hulbert of the Old Vicarage. Christopher Scott left a family of thirteen; John, the eldest, was born December 20th, 1792, and died, unmarried at Gawthorpe Hall in 1849; Thomas, the third son, also lived at Gawthorpe up to his marriage, when he resided in Leeds. Jacob, the next son, went into the malting business at Goole, but died at Gawthorpe Hall in 1857. The other sons were William, Jeremiah, and James Wood. Of the daughters, their names were Ann, who married James Garnet, of Luddenden; Jane and Mary died at Gawthorpe unmarried; Eliza died unmarried; Sarah, married John Wood, of Morton, father of Mr. Horatio Scott Wood; and Rebecca, twin, died in infancy.

Christopher Scott was a maltster, living in the house now occupied by Dr. Crocker. He was drowned in the canal in November, 1828, and was interred in the Parish Churchyard. He had several brothers and sisters. One of his brothers, William, was a distiller in London; another, John, was a tanner at Horsforth; and a third, Jeremiah, was a maltster at Wortley, and died in 1799. The latter had a son, William, who took over from his cousin, William Scott, son of Christopher, the brewery at Skipton-in-Craven, which is still owned by his descendants. Another son of Jeremiah was John Scott, of Potternewton, who married Margaret, daughter of the above Thomas Hulbert, of Bingley. She died in 1871, aged 75. This John Scott inherited the largest part of a fortune of £90,000, left by a William Bellhouse, his cousin, who was a corn-factor in Leeds, and whose mother was a sister of Christopher Scott, of Bingley. He died Nov. 5th, 1838.

Singularly, not a penny of this large fortune went to his father's family, the Bellhouses, but entirely to the Scotts and their immediate connections and friends. Edward Bellhouse, of Leeds, was said to have been a near relative. His son, William Bellhouse, married in 1825 Jane Mellin, whose sister, Elizabeth Mellin, married Benjamin Speight, of Halifax, the author's grandfather. Sums ranging from £250 to £10,000 were left to about forty members of the Scott family; John Scott, of Potternewton, cousin of John Scott, of Gawthorpe Hall, being one of the executors and residuary legatee. Elizabeth, wife of Jonas Whitaker, of Burley, near Otley, received £1,000; the testator's late wife's niece, Mary Ann Thompson, daughter of Benjamin Thompson, gent., of Park Gate, Guiseley, a like sum. Currer Fothergill Busfeild, of Bradford, chief constable, received £500, and Thomas Cooper, apothecary, of Bingley, the same. Old Dr. Cooper is still remembered in Bingley. He was the Scotts' family doctor.

Jeremiah Scott, son of Christopher, is also well remembered as the Bingley "huntsman." A pack of hounds was kept in the town in the early part of the century. They were what is known as "trencher fed," that is, each person maintained his own dog. "Jer Scott," as he was familarly called, used to come down into the Main Street, and with several blasts of his horn call the hounds together for a merry spin over the moors. Some of these runs were famous, and have been well described by R. C. Wildon in his *Voice from the Sycamore.*

There are indications that the present hall, erected in the time of James I., absorbed portions of an older and much stronger building that stood on the site. Immediately upon entering by the east front there was a wall on the right fully six feet thick, continuous with a wall of equal thickness which led to the kitchen. This wall has been removed, and the space left open to the library. Marks of ancient iron staples in the jambs of the doorways also point to the entrances having been altered or enlarged at different periods. When Mr. Horsfall purchased the property he effected many alterations about the house, both internally and externally. Formerly the grounds on the north-east side extended further than they do at present, and there was no wall separating them from the adjoining field. This was all open, and a portion of the site was occupied by the old stank, or fish-pond, which is now drained. The description of Gawthorpe Hall, Harewood, in 1656 would almost apply to the Bingley property, excepting that the Harewood Gawthorpe had "a parke in former tymes stored with deere." There is, however, at Greenhill, a little above Gawthorpe Hall, an ancient enclosure still known as "Deer Park," which at one time formed part of the Ryshworth Hall estate.

Close to the present turnstile leading up to Greenhill was the pinfold, which was removed further on the lane to its present position behind the spa well. There is an old dove-cote in the field, about one hundred yards west of the Hall, which has been renovated, the roofs having got very dilapidated. Its internal arrangements, however, remain the same. In conclusion, it must be remarked that the situation of the Hall is beautiful in the extreme; from its terrace commanding a lovely distant view of the valley, while the luxuriant woods below the Druids' Altar form a charming background.

The Old Vicarage, Bingley.

THE OLD VICARAGE.

MR. Henry W. Hardcastle, of Priesthorpe Hall, is now the owner of this ancient and pleasantly-situated homestead. It has evidently derived its name from having been the residence of the vicars of Bingley in former times, although the present house does not appear to have been occupied for such purpose since its erection early in the 17th century. Doubtless it stands on the site of a much older house, which was the residence of the priests at the time Bingley Church was a possession of Drax Priory. The canons of Drax, as stated in the preceding chapter, obtained early in the 12th century the whole township of Priesthorpe, in which the Old Vicarage* is situated.

From a charter of "Robert, son of Ralph, villayn of Bingley," we learn that the said Robert ordered his body to be interred in the Priory at Drax, and he gave to the *Canons residing at Priesthorpe* two acres of arable land in the territory of Bingley, of which one abuts upon Brigflat on the one part and Brerilands on the other. The other acre lies in Northfield; all which Simon, his son, confirmed. These lands can still be identified between Bingley and Cottingley Bridge. It is, moreover, evident from this ancient bequest that the vicars were then living at Priesthorpe, and apparently they continued to do so up to the Reformation, when their house was occupied by the last vicar of Bingley whom the canons appointed before the dissolution of monasteries. The following interesting deed is a copy from the original in the British Museum:—

This indenture made at Bingley, Sept. 20th, in ye 28th yeare of ye reigne of our Sufferande Ld. the Kinge Henry ye 8th, 1536, between Sir [*i.e.* Rev.] John Long, the vicar of Bingley, in county of Yorke, on one parte, and George Passlow, of Marlow, gent., on the other part, witnesseth that Sir John hath demised and to farme, lett to George and his assigns the Church of Bingley for the terme of three years next ensuing, with all tythes, profits, commodities, &c., paying yearly to the said vicar £10 at the Feast of St. Martin in

* It may be stated that "*Old* Vicarage" is only a modern appellation to distinguish it from the present Vicarage. Formerly it was called Vicarage only.

winter and St. Mark by even portions, within the space of 20 days, &c. And the vicar shall pay all duties, ordinary and extraordinary, to the churche of Yorke and to the Kinge, and also to discharge the cure of the said church as he will answer to it, to God, and to man. And the said George shall lay no claim to the Vicarage House nor the ground thereto belonging to the canons right, which is £3 of money, and six acres of land lying in Bingley Field and Micklethwaite Field, &c. Witnesses:

Walter Passlow, Esq., Miles Hartley, Joe Dobson, and others.

George Passlow, the lessee, and Walter Passlow, witness to the deed, were brothers; the former residing at Marley and the latter at Riddlesden (*see post*, Riddlesden Hall). Vicar Long is stated to have died in 1586, so that he must have died soon after the completion of this agreement, although his successor, the Rev. John Scholay, is recorded to have been instituted to the living on June 15th, 1586. Whether the Priesthorpe vicarage continued to be occupied by the vicars of Bingley subsequent to this period I have not ascertained. Some of the vicars combined the office of masters of the Grammar School, and resided at the Grammar School House until the present vicarage was built in 1837. There was, however, a very old thatched building in Bailey Fold, on the site of the Midland Railway Goods Yard, which old inhabitants used to speak of as the vicarage house. Possibly it may have been occupied by some of the vicars before the School House became their residence. It was pulled down when the railway was made in 1847.

Early in the 17th century the Priesthorpe Vicarage was in the occupation of an old local family of good standing named Dobson. Among the wills of this family proved at York is one dated May 2nd, 1635, of Elizabeth, widow of Michael Dobson, of Priesthorpe; and another dated February 9th, 1639, of Thomas Dobson, of Priesthorpe, whose son Thomas was constable of Bingley in 1664-5, and his son's baptism (another Thomas) is recorded in the church registers for 1666:

Thomas, son of Thomas Dobson, of Vicarage.

The father died in 1704, and the son in 1747. A monument in the church records that by his marriage with Ann, daughter of William Beaumont, Esq., of Darton, he had three children, viz.: John, who died a student at Lincoln's Inn, 1782; Martha, married to Miles Staveley, Esq., of North Stainley [descended from a family that traces its lineage back to the heroes of the Conquest]; and Sarah, married (1) in 1728 to Benjamin Ferrand, Esq., of St. Ives, and (2) in 1787 to Gregory Rhodes, Esq., of Ripon.

This Sarah Rhodes inherited the vicarage property from her father, and shortly before her death in 1785 she left by will a rent-charge of £15 a year upon the estate towards the maintenance of five poor widows in the almshouses then lately established by her in Priesthorpe, which are still maintained. In 1765 Dr. Johnson Atkinson, afterwards of Myrtle Grove, resided at the vicarage, and a few years later the family of Hulbert became the tenants, and continued to reside there until the death of Miss Ann Hulbert in 1888, aged 84 (*see* page 296). There is a fine old "grandfather's clock" kept at the vicarage, which was provided by Mr. James Hulbert, who died here in 1799. The clock is dated 1772.

The vicarage property was sold in 1879; Mr. Joseph Hardcastle being the purchaser.* After the death of Miss Hulbert the house was occupied by Mr. David Binns England, and subsequently by Captain Boulton. Mr. Thomas Orchardson is the present tenant, and he is a cousin of the distinguished artist, Mr. W. Q. Orchardson, R.A.

The oldest part of the present residence is of early 17th century date, while the south front appears to have been erected during the tenancy of James Hulbert, who was interred at Guiseley Church in 1799. The old-fashioned gardens about the house are nicely and attractively planted, and there are several aged yew trees, in all probability planted by the monastic owners of the estate before the Reformation. A large circular bed on the lawn is completely filled with a single rhododendron tree, now in fine foliage, and measuring 118 feet in circumference. Near the gardens is a spacious old tithe-barn, supported by massive oak props, &c.

* For pedigree of Hardcastle of Fewston, Bingley, &c., *see* the author's *Nidderdale*, pages 406-7.

Ryshworth Hall.

RYSHWORTH HALL.

THE family of Ryshworth, or Rishworth, was at a very early period connected with the Ryshworth Hall estate, and was also of such consequence as to possess a private chapel, which went by their name, on the north side of the Parish Church. In this and the neighbouring parishes the Rishworths have continued to the present time. A descendant of the old line, one Ellen Rishworth, died about 1640, and in her will she requests that her body be laid "in the queere of Bingley Church, which was once her deare and lovinge father's." A family of this name, supposed to have sprung from the same stock, was living at Gillgrange (Howden Gill) more than two centuries ago, and a son of William Rishworth, of Gillgrange, settled at Thwaites, and died at an advanced age in 1772. In 1779 Thomas Rishworth leased from Mr. Ferrand, of St. Ives, the farm called Roydfield, above Marley. Thomas Rishworth died at Thwaites House in 1809, aged 70.

The estate at Ryshworth eventually came to the Eltoftes, who appear as property owners at "Mylnewro," Bingley [is this Mill Row, near the Corn Mill?], in the year of Agincourt (1415), and Christopher Eltofte possessed Ryshworth in 1519.* It was by them sold in 1591 to Edward Bynns, in whose family it remained till 1672, when Abraham Bynnes, J.P., sold the house and lands to William Busfeild, merchant, of Leeds. This William Busfeild was Mayor of Leeds in 1673, and died in 1675. He left an only son, William, then an infant, and his widow, who was a daughter of Hugh Currer, Esq., of Kildwick,† married, in 1685, Robert Ferrand, Esq., of

* The manor of Farnhill, Kildwick parish, came to the Eltoftes through the marriage of an Eltofte to Margaret, daughter of John de Coplay, who was lord of Farnhill in 1385-6, and it remained with the Eltoftes till 1636 (*see* also page 158).

† Hugh Currer formerly lived at Paper Hall, Bradford, afterwards (1720) bought by Robert Stansfield, who married a daughter of William Busfeild, of Ryshworth Hall (*see* Mr. Wroot's paper in the *Bradford Antiquary* for 1896, pages 60-63).

Harden Grange, by whom she had an only son, Robert Ferrand, who died unmarried in 1742. In the meanwhile Ryshworth had been let to Mr. Joseph Walker, a local friend of Oliver Heywood, the Puritan divine, and he continued at the Hall until a short time before 1700, when it was let to Richard Appleyard, of Halifax, whose brother, Jonas Appleyard, was then living at Harden Grange. Robert, eldest son of Richard Appleyard, who was born at Ryshworth in 1703, had a son also named Robert, who was married in 1764, and was secretary to the Lord Chancellor.

William Busfeild, on reaching manhood, settled at Ryshworth, and it continued the family residence until the death of Thomas Busfeild in 1772, when the estate passed to his niece, Elizabeth, wife of Johnson Atkinson, of Myrtle Grove, who thereupon assumed the name and arms of Busfeild. In 1803 it was sold by Johnson Atkinson Busfeild to Peter Garforth, Esq., of Skipton (the friend of Wesley, and one of the founders of Skipton Wesleyanism), for £12,000, reserving the Rishworth Chapel. In 1815 Mr. Garforth's son and successor again sold it to the Ferrands of St. Ives, by whom it is still possessed.

Mr. Timothy Horsfall, of Hawksworth Hall, resided at Ryshworth for several years before Mr. Frederick Greenwood took the Hall in 1828. The Greenwoods lived here about twenty years, and subsequently settled at Norton Conyers and in Nidderdale (*see* the author's *Nidderdale*, pages 394-7. Mr. Fred. Greenwood was brother to Mrs. Sidgwick, who lived for many years at West Riddlesden Hall, and was a cousin of the late Mr. John Greenwood Sugden, of Eastwood House, Keighley, and Steeton Hall, the father-in-law of Mr. Charles W. Dunlop, a subsequent tenant of Ryshworth Hall. After the Greenwoods the Hall was occupied for some years by Mr. Johnson Atkinson Busfeild, father of the present Mr. Ferrand, of St. Ives. Then in 1854 Mr. Alfred Harris (whose elder brother, Henry Harris, lived at Longwood, Bingley, up to the time of his death in 1872), one of the proprietors of Harris & Co., now the Bradford Old Bank, Limited (founded by Mr. Edmund Peckover in 1803), occupied the Hall for about twelve years, when it was taken by Mr. W. Middleton (a former mayor of Norwich), who came to Yorkshire and established himself as a manufacturer at Cononley, near Skipton, and his firm, Messrs. Middleton, Ainsworth, & Co., had also a warehouse in Bradford. He resided at Ryshworth for three years prior to 1870, when Mr. Dunlop took over his lease. Mr. Dunlop, now of Embsay Kirk, near Skipton, retained the Hall for more than 25 years, leaving it in 1896. Mr. Charles E. Sugden is the present tenant.

The Hall, which is situated about a mile out of Bingley, on the Keighley road, is a picturesque old mansion, combining various styles. It has an open prospect towards the Altar crags, and is surrounded with pleasant gardens, and in ancient times there was a large park attached. The Deer Park at Greenhill has also at one time formed part of the Ryshworth Hall estate. In the Warburton Collections in the British Museum is a south view of the original Hall as it appeared about the end of the 17th century. At that time the highroad passed before the south front of the Hall; the road having been diverted when the turnpike was made in the middle of last century, now passes at the back of the house. The west wing was erected about 1750 by Mr. Thomas Busfeild, but the chimneys were rebuilt about fifty years ago. The additions on the north side were made about 1884, but the east end still retains its old-fashioned character, having sturdy, ivy-covered walls, with antique leaden gutters, and small leaded windows. The walls are nowhere more than two feet thick. Some alterations and additions have been made, and the bays in front of the house, shewn in the illustration, are also additions made in the early part of this century.

In the spacious yard adjoining the highway is a magnificent old lime-tree (the finest in the district), which presents a very luxuriant and lofty crown of foliage. The trunk spreads at the base, and measures 35 feet round, while at four feet from this ground measurement it is 19 feet in circumference. The tree appears to be still vigorous and flowers annually.

East Riddlesden Hall.

EAST RIDDLESDEN HALL.

I HAVE elsewhere spoken of the importance of the old Anglian settlement at Bingley, and of the determined onslaught and ultimate annexation of it by the Viking invaders in the ninth century, and it is noteworthy that Riddlesden defines almost the exact boundary of the Norse and Anglo-Saxon place-names in Airedale. Lower down the valley, or east of Riddlesden, there are no Norse names, if we except Micklethwaite, close by, which I have explained was probably the original Norse settlement in the parish. Is it possible that the mound, or eminence, above the river, on which East Riddlesden Hall stands, was the place of meeting, assembly, or Council of the Anglo-Saxons and invading Northmen, called by them Danes, which is, moreover, on the division of the two Dane-made wapentakes of Skyrack and Staincliffe? From Dr. Bosworth, author of the well-known Anglo-Saxon dictionary, I gather that *raedels* (counsel) and *Den* (Dane) would mean the place of counsel of or with the Danes. At any rate, I can offer no better explanation of the meaning of this name. The *red earth* theory and the *red lion's den* (in allusion to the arms of Maude) interpretation seem to me untenable, especially the latter, which is not old enough.

The site was chosen at a very early date for a residence of considerable consequence, and was the home for some centuries of families occupying the highest position in the parish of Bingley. Riddlesden is even mentioned in *Domesday* as a manor that had belonged to the Dane, Ardulf (*see* page 78), but at that time (A.D. 1086) was held by the King. It was said to be then worth 16s. Although the King had deprived Ardulf of his possession, he in all probability continued as tenant, or under-lord of the estate, for a little later we find his kinsman, Simon de Monte Alto, or Montalte, in possession as feudal lord of the manor. He was most probably a grandson of Gospatric, son of Gospatric, lord of Bingley in 1066, and was living in 1165. If this be the case, and there is no evidence to disprove it, we have the remarkable instance of an estate having been but once sold in the course of nearly a thousand years. This Simon is said to have been a younger brother of Robert de Montalte, who held the lordship of Hawarden, in Flintshire, a place that is interesting at the present time as the home of the late Prime Minister (Mr. Gladstone). Burke derives the descent of the present Earl de Montalt, Viscount Hawarden, from these Montaltes of the Bingley Riddlesden.

Some little time after the Conquest the manors of Morton and Riddlesden were granted to the Romilles, lords of the honour of Skipton, and henceforward continued to form a part of the Skipton Fee. For more than two and a half centuries the Montaltes, *alias* Mohautes, now Maude, continued to hold the undivided manor of Riddlesden. But towards the close of the 14th century a change took place. Simon Montalte, or Mohaute, died, leaving a family of daughters, but no son, and the eldest of these, Elizabeth, married in 1402 Robert Paslew, sometime Master of the Rolls. He succeeded to a portion of the lands, which included East Riddlesden Hall, while the remainder, or West Riddlesden, was bestowed on Robert Montalte, or Mohaute, who was son of a younger brother of Richard, father of Simon, last lord of the whole patrimony, and consequently was cousin of the last-named. From this Robert the Maudes of West Riddlesden derive their descent.

The Paslews now continued as lords of East Riddlesden for the ensuing two centuries. They were an old family of good standing, long resident at Potternewton, in the parish of Leeds, and when they settled at Riddlesden they attended the Parish Churches both at Bingley and Keighley, in each of which they had a chapel of their own. In 1341 John Paslew was a free tenant at Leeds Woodhouse, holding there a messuage and two oxgangs of land. Robert Paslew was a Baron of Exchequer in the time of Henry III (*vide* Maddock's *Exchequer*), Robert Paslew, "de Ledys," was vicar of Leeds in 1408. Thomas Paslew was a monk in Bolton Priory in 1379, and Thomas Paslew was Abbot of Fountains in 1484.

Alexander Paslew, of Riddlesden, was interred in the choir of St. Lawrence, at the east end of the south aisle of Bingley Church, in 1518, and one of the supervisors of his will was the celebrated but unfortunate Abbot of Whalley, Sir John Paslew, who was hanged before the walls of his own Abbey for the brave part he took in the Pilgrimage of Grace. He was of the same family as the Riddlesden Paslews, and bore the same coat-of-arms as they, with a crescent for difference. In 1540, or shortly after the suppression of Drax Priory, Walter Paslew, son of above Alexander, obtained a grant from the King of the manor of Harden, and in 1566-7 his son, Francis, who had married a daughter of Sir William Calverley,* disposed of the manors of Harden and Riddlesden and certain lands in Bingley, Marley, and Priesthorpe apparently for political purposes. His family were staunch Catholics—one of them, as we have seen, being principal of one of the largest religious houses in the north,—and they naturally felt the effects of the hard reforming hand very bitterly. Walter Paslew, son of Francis, of Riddlesden, seems to have joined the crusade against the downthrow of the monasteries, which, however, so far as he was concerned, ended with his lodgment in the Tower of London. An old inscription on the walls of the Beauchamp Tower reads: "Walter Paslew, 1569," along with the motto: "Extrema anchora Christus, 1570," and the figure of an anchor. It has been doubted whether this actually refers to the imprisonment here of Walter Paslew, of Riddlesden, but from what we know of the family there is a strong probability that it does.

This Walter Paslew married a daughter of Richard Clapham, of Beamsley, and left a son (who died young) and two daughters. Ellen, the eldest, married John Rishworth, and to this family the East Riddlesden estate came. His son, John Rishworth, turned out a spendthrift, and according to the Rev. Oliver Heywood, died miserably poor at Keighley. During the time of the Civil War the Hall and appurtenances were sold to the Murgatroyds, of

* In the Bingley Parish Registers, under date, 1579, April 12th, is an entry of the baptism of Thomas, son of Francis Paslewe.

p [illegible]
L [illegible]
C [illegible]
n [illegible]
o [illegible]
h [illegible]
la [illegible]
1 [illegible]
ti [illegible]
P [illegible]
in [illegible]

B [illegible]
l [illegible]
a [illegible]
n [illegible]
o [illegible]
r [illegible]
L [illegible]

li [illegible]
T [illegible]
b [illegible]
1 [illegible]
W [illegible]
n [illegible]
o [illegible]
p [illegible]
h [illegible]
th [illegible]

w [illegible]
P [illegible]
([illegible]
r [illegible]
t [illegible]

c [illegible]
Z [illegible]

Starkie, the Hall ceased to be their family residence.* Madam Starkie is remembered as a woman of very masculine habits, who could fire a gun or ride to hounds with the best sportsman in the field; while woe betide the person who raised her tantrums! A story is told of how on one occasion while hunting she had failed to clear a fence, and in the fall had dislocated her ankle-joint. Her husband, hearing she had fallen upon her head, bounded up, and on learning the full extent of the injury, exclaimed with an oath: "It's the wrong joint!"

Nicholas Starkie left two daughters, who married gentlemen living at a distance, and the Hall has since been let to tenants, and is now a farm-house. Our illustration, reproduced from a recent photograph by Mr. Whitaker, depicts the west front, with its handsome rose window and battlemented roof. The gardens in front are doubtless as old as the original homestead of pre-Reformation times, while the spacious fish-pond at the rear of the buildings retains in all probability the same place and dimensions as it did in the time of the second Edward, when it is mentioned in the domestic accounts of Bolton Priory. In the gardens at the north end there are some old but specially well-built peacock-houses, a very unusual adjunct of a family residence in this part of the country; shewing, at any rate, the elegant style in which the family then lived.

The ancient corn-mill at Riddlesden is interesting as in former times all tenants within the manor were obliged to grind their corn here, but whether they were compelled to bake their bread at the manor-oven, as was the case in Bingley, no evidence is forthcoming. About 1150 Simon de Montalte gave the tithes of the mill here to Bingley Church, and he also gave the same tithes of all bees within the manor. Mead made from honey was a favourite drink of the old Danes in England, and it seems at this time that bee-keeping was a local industry of some value.

* More detailed information respecting the various owners I have named appear in an interesting paper on East Riddelsden, contributed by Mr. W. A. Brigg to the *Bradford Antiquary* in 1892, and to which I must express my indebtedness.

West Riddlesden Hall.

WEST RIDDLESDEN HALL.

THERE is no evidence to shew that any house of importance stood here before the partition of the Riddlesden estate about A.D. 1400 (*see* page 308), when West Riddlesden came to Robert Montalte, or Mohaute, in whose family it remained till the 17th century. Most of the present mansion is of the latter date, having been built in 1687 by Thomas, son of John Leach, who married in 1684 the heiress of the Mohautes, or Maudes, of West Riddlesden. On a beam of black oak in the roof of the hall are cut the initials and date, T.L., 1687, which agrees with the statement of the Rev. Oliver Heywood that Thomas Leach rebuilt the house in that year. Heywood preached here in 1679, 1680, and again he preached and slept here on Thursday, May 25th, 1682. The old broad oak staircase, however, with the window and the north wing, appear to be part of a previous homestead. A quarry of ancient stained glass in the window bears a coat-of-arms, a crescent on a chevron between four mullets, three and one, with the partially obliterated name, Arthur de Mohaut. This Arthur Maude made his will in the year 1584, and gave 20s. to purchase a bell for the church of *St. Andrew*, Keighley (*see* page 118).

The Leach family had been settled at Bingley long before they acquired West Riddlesden. Some memorial tablets of them may be seen in the Parish Church. They parted with Riddlesden to John Greenwood, Esq., of the Knowle, Keighley, in 1809; but one portion of the Hall continued in the occupation of the Leach's till 1854, when by the death of William Leach the family here became extinct. Captain Greenwood, of Swarcliffe Hall, Nidderdale, is the present owner of the estate, and James Nicholson Clarkson, Esq., the tenant.

The Hall occupies a pleasant and well-sheltered position on the north side of the valley above the canal, about a mile from Keighley Station and three miles from Bingley. The south front, of three pointed gables, commands a wide and beautiful prospect. The porch-tower and bay-window at the west end are additions made after the purchase of the Hall by the Greenwoods. The ancient gardens enclosing the Hall contain a variety of choice shrubs and flowers. On the west side is a handsome acacia tree; this tree being a native of North America, and it was not known in England till the 17th century. At the bottom of the vegetable garden is a large old mulberry-tree.

A year or two after the death of Mr. Leach, in 1854, the Hall was let to Mr. John Benson Sidgwick, of Stonegappe, Lothersdale (called Stangap in 1840; *vide* Glusburn Charters in *Coll. Top. et Gen.*, Pt. xxiii.), and on his decease in May, 1872, it continued the home of his widow, Mrs. Sidgwick (who was a daughter of Mr. John Greenwood, of the Knowle, Keighley), until her death on Dec. 27th, 1887. I may note in passing that when at Stonegappe Mrs. Sidgwick employed the afterwards distinguished novelist, Charlotte Brontë, as governess to her children for a short time, from May to July, 1839. The Brontës were then living at Haworth, only a few miles distant, and Charlotte had left Miss Wooller's school some months previous to her going to Stonegappe. Mr. J. B. Sidgwick, I may add, was elder brother of the Rev. William Sidgwick, M.A., master of Skipton Grammar School, who died in 1841, aged 85. His youngest daughter, Mary, married in 1859 the late Right Rev. Edward White Benson, D.D., Archbishop of Canterbury. The Archbishop's grandfather, Captain White Benson, who died in 1806, had a sister, Ann Benson, wife of William Sidgwick, owner of the High Mills, Skipton, who was father of the above Mr. J. B. Sidgwick and Rev. William Sidgwick. William Sidgwick's father, John Sidgwick, lived at Bingley, where he died August 15th, 1791, aged 75, and was buried, with his wife, in the nave of the Parish Church (*see* also page 228).

Mr. Arthur Christopher Benson, eldest surviving son of the Archbishop,* kindly supplies the following interesting account of his visit to West Riddlesden when a boy:—

* For other particulars of the late Archbishop Benson's Bingley ancestry *see* Hill End, Harden.

In the summer of 1874, just before I went to Eton, my father, then Chancellor of Lincoln, took Martin, my elder brother, and myself to visit our relations in the North. We went first to West Riddlesden Hall, near Keighley, where my great aunt, Mrs. John Sidgwick, then lived. It was an old manor house, with quiet spacious gardens, bordered by a canal, with the moors behind. I remember the stained glass, with the arms of the Montaltes, in the great staircase window, and a long low room with an alcove formed by a little projection over the porch where we slept; my uncle, John Benson Sidgwick, had been dead some time, and my only knowledge of him was derived from a photograph, which represented him sitting at ease in an armchair, with a black velvet skull cap on his head, and his patriarchal snowy beard growing over his chest. My great aunt Sarah, a Greenwood of Swarcliffe, was a little woman with a sweet face, who received us with gentle cordiality, and won our hearts at once; I remember her telling us that she used to call my father "the little Bishop" when he was a boy. My cousin, Charles Sidgwick, was master of the house, and there was also there "Tiffy" Drury, his sister, with her children; we fished for crawfish in the canal, and paid a visit to Old Riddlesden, a stately old house, now a farm, with large monastic barns.

I am told that on one of the last visits of the Archbishop to Yorkshire he called, as usual, at Riddlesden Hall, and was descending the old oaken staircase previously referred to, when he remarked with a pleasant smile: "Ah! I wonder what the Rev. Oliver Heywood would think if he knew that the Archbishop of Canterbury was occupying the very place where Nonconformity was preached by him with so much fervour?" an observation which may in turn be humorously contrasted with possible events in the future. Who can tell, for is it not a truism that history often repeats itself?

Marley Hall.

MARLEY HALL.

MARLEY, or Mardelei, as it is written in the *Domesday* record, is another of those pre-Conquest places afterwards embraced within the soke of Bingley, which gave name to a family of some consequence in the Norman period. They appear to have been under-tenants of the Montaltes, or Maudes, one of whom, Thomas de Mohaut, held six bovates of land, with appurtenances, in Marley in 1209. Alice, daughter and co-heiress of Simon de Montalte (living in 1254), married Thomas de Martheley (Marley), and by this marriage may possibly have brought Marley to this family. In the *Nomina Villarum* (1325) Prior (Peter) de Martheley and Ralph de Ilkton are returned as joint lords of the neighbouring manor of Morton. John and Richard de Marthele were jurors at the inq. of George de Cantelupe in 1273 (*see* page 110), and a Margareta de Marlay appears in the Poll Tax of 1378 for Newsholme, in Keighley parish. The Marley estate, at any rate, was afterwards held by the name of Maude.

A capital messuage has undoubtedly existed at Marley from Norman times, probably on the site of the existing Hall. It is described in the *Patent Roll*, 4th and 5th Philip and Mary (1556-7), as producing a rent of 1s. 6d. annually due to the Knights of St. John of Jerusalem, as parcel of their possessions attached to the late Preceptory of Newlands, and late of Walter Paslew, Esq. William Martheley was one of 12 jurors sworn at the Court of the Knights held at Bingley in the year of Agincourt (1415) to determine whether a certain "garthraw lying between the field of Priesthorp and the meadow of the lord of Bynglay, called Ryckyeng," was the property of the Prior of Drax or of Thomas de Astley, lord of Bingley, and they decided in favour of the Prior, excepting that three ash trees growing there and another ash tree of ancient growth belonged to the said lord.* In a particular of all the manors, rents, &c., of Richard Sunderland, Esq., of Coley Hall, in A.D. 1619, lately belonging to the dissolved Priory

* Court Rolls, Pt. 211, No. 18.

of St. John of Jerusalem, appears the rent of 1s. 6d. due from Mr. John Rishworth for one tenement called Marley Hall; he being the owner, although the Hall was then in the occupation of William Currer, Esq. This John Rishworth had married Ellen, daughter and co-heir of Walter Paslew, Esq., who is thought to have been one of the Reformation insurrectionists imprisoned in the Tower of London, A.D. 1569 (*see* page 309).

Early in the reign of Elizabeth, William Currer was owner of the Hall estate, apparently by marriage with a daughter of Christopher Maude, and in 1572 a fine was entered between Christopher Wade and Thomas Hudson, plaintiffs, and Walter Paslew, son and heir of Francis Paslew, Esq., and William Currer, deforciants, respecting the "messuage called Marley Hall, with lands in Marley and Bingley, which Francis Paslew, aforesaid, and Alexander Paslew, brother of the said Walter, hold for their lives." William Currer (brother of Henry Currer, of Kildwick, whose wife was a daughter of Christopher Wade) was then living at Marley Hall, which was after the year 1600 occupied by his son, the before-mentioned William. William Currer removed to Farnhill about 1610, and subsequently to Stainton Cotes, in the parish of Gargrave, where he died in 1622. Hugh Currer, of Marley, purchased, as elsewhere related, the manor of Bingley from the Walkers, and his grandson, Henry Currer, of Gawthorpe Hall, sold the same to the Bensons in 1668.

The Hall estate was sold to John Savile, Esq., whose family had held lands and tenements in Marley and in Bingley for nearly a century previous. In 1606 "Miss Savile, of Marley," was married at Keighley to a son of the Rev. Richard Dean, of Saltonstall, who was Bishop of Ossory, in Ireland, in 1611. John Savile, soon after his purchase of the estate, rebuilt the Hall in its present form, A.D. 1627. It is stated that he died at Marley in 1629, apparently a widower, leaving a son, Robert, and two daughters, Isabel and Ann.* But there was a John Savile, evidently of Marley, who was fined for not doing suit and service at the court (ordained by the dissolved order of the

* *See Bradford Antiquary*, 1898, page 167.

Knights Hospitallers) between the years 1631 and 1635. In the year 1638 the wife of John Savile was buried at Keighley; presumably the wife of Mr. Savile, of Marley.

The Saviles lived in great style at Marley, and kept their own fool, hal, or jester, who is still traditionally remembered in the neighbourhood as "Sil o' Marley," and of whom many laughable anecdotes are related. The office of "jester" was in ancient times of no mean importance, and was often held by gentlemen wits of good family or education. Will Somers, Court fool to Henry VIII., was a man of standing, and his portrait is preserved at Hampton Court; while going back even to the days of the Norman we read of one, Berdic, *joculator* to William the Conqueror, receiving a gift of three towns and five carucates in Gloucestershire. Sil o' Marley, however, was never so lucky, and probably died in the service of his master.

Marley passed from the Saviles to the Sunderlands, and from the latter to their kinsfolk, the Parkers, of Browsholme. Edward Parker, who died in 1667, married a daughter of Richard Sunderland, sister of the above Samuel Sunderland, lord of the manor of Harden with Marley, and his son, Robert Parker, who died in 1718, resided at Marley Hall; the estate remaining in the family until 1842, when Mr. Parker, of Browsholme, sold it to Mrs. Sarah Ferrand, of St. Ives, and it still forms part of the St. Ives estate.

The Hall, built, as stated, in 1627, is an interesting many-gabled building, occupying an elevated site on the west side of the railway between Bingley and Keighley. It is now a farm-house. The interior has some carved Jacobean oaken doors, and an ornamental plaster ceiling deserving of notice, such having become fashionable in the mansions of the gentry since the preceding century. Over the front entrance are carved the arms of Savile, *three owls on a bend*, which also appear in a window in stained glass. Below the Hall is the old pinfold. The accompanying view of the picturesque old homestead is from a recent sketch made for this work by Miss Preston, of Littlebeck Hall, Gilstead.

MYRTLE GROVE.

IN 1765 Mr. Johnson Atkinson, M.D., married the heiress of the Busfeilds, a lady then in her 18th year, and possessed of a fine property of nearly 1,000 acres at Crosby, in the North Riding; an estate at Bordley, in Craven, part of which the family had possessed for two centuries; the Ryshworth and Myrtle Grove estates, besides others at Harden, Marley, Halifax, Shelf, Cayton, Poole, Brotherton, &c. For a few years after their marriage they lived at the Old Vicarage. In 1767 Mr. Atkinson purchased the Myrtle Grove estate, at that time consisting of a farm, with homestead, called Spring Head—an old meeting-house of the Society of Friends—which he pulled down, and erected the present spacious mansion on its site. The name was then changed to Myrtle Grove. In 1772 his wife's uncle, Mr. Thomas Busfeild, died, and left them the Ryshworth Hall estate. Dr. Atkinson then assumed the name of Busfeild, but continued to reside at Myrtle Grove, and was exceedingly popular in the neighbourhood. It is recorded in the Yorkshire newspapers that his son's majority was celebrated with every demonstration of joy and every expression of good-will from both friends and neighbours. There was a very animated public fête at Myrtle Grove; an ox being roasted whole in the park, which, with hogsheads of ale, was distributed among the people, and this was followed by a grand ball in the evening. This son, William Busfeild, lived to represent the borough of Bradford in Parliament from 1837 up to the time of his death in 1851.

Mr. Johnson Atkinson Busfeild when he purchased Myrtle Grove in 1767 intended it to be his principal residence, and to erect a family mausoleum within the grounds. In 1781 a site for the purpose was marked out and consecrated by the Archbishop of York, the Most Rev. William Markham, D.D. (whose granddaughter,

Lucy Markham, married Henry L. Wickham, Esq., of Cottingley), then on a visit to Myrtle Grove. But the building was never commenced. A small upright stone, 20in. by 16in., may still be seen in the Myrtle Pasture (now being built upon), about 80 yards south of the wall bordering the highway, and inscribed as follows :—

This ground was consecrated for a burial-ground in 1781.

When in 1805 Mr. Birch purchased Myrtle Grove for £10,500, Mr. Busfeild removed to Cononley Hall, and

MYRTLE GROVE, BINGLEY.

died there in 1817. His remains were brought to Bingley, and interred in the Busfeild Chapel in the Parish Church. During the greater part of his life he was, as I have remarked, very popular, and he possessed, moreover, unquestionable abilities. He commenced his career by taking a high wranglership at Cambridge, and upon quitting the University was destined for the profession of medicine, but his marriage to affluence rendered the pursuit of a profession unnecessary. For nearly forty years he fulfilled the duties of a magistrate at a period when these officials were "few and far between." For many years he was Colonel of the Bradford Volunteers, and the manner in which he was elected in 1809 by the freeholders of the West Riding, when in his 70th year, as Registrar of the Riding, in opposition to the great influence of the Fawkes family, shews the esteem in which he was publicly held.

In 1810 the property was sold by Mr. Birch to General Twiss, Colonel Commandant of the Royal Engineers, an English officer who had experienced half-a-century of active service in various countries, but chiefly in the American wars. He was in advanced life when he and his wife and daughter took up their residence at this pleasant and retired corner of rural Bingley. During the twenty years of his well-earned ease at Myrtle Grove he had the character of being a gentleman of wealth and consequence. When outside the grounds, which were extensive and beautifully kept, he almost invariably rode in a sedan chair, carried by two men in livery. At one time he employed eight gardeners, and both gardens and glass-houses contained a very large and choice assortment of flowers and fruits. His only daughter, Catherine, married Walker Ferrand, Esq., M.P., of Harden Grange, and the General died there in 1827, aged 82. His widow died in 1835, at the great age of 94. They were both buried in Bingley Church, where a tablet is placed to their memory. Mr. Walker Ferrand inherited the entire fortune of General Twiss, amounting from £7000 to £8000 per annum. He died in 1835, shortly after the death of Mrs. Twiss.

In 1874 the estate was disposed of by the trustees under Mr. Walker Ferrand's will, and Mr. Alfred Sharp, J.P., became the purchaser for £13,500. The Allotment Gardens, however, which formed part of the estate, comprising twenty acres, with the river boundary of 500 yards, and a frontage to the road extending from Cottingley Bridge to Holy Trinity vicarage, were afterwards purchased from Mr. Sharp by Mr. William Busfeild (the present Mr. Ferrand, of St. Ives). Mrs. Alfred Sharp has continued to reside at Myrtle Grove since her husband's death in 1896.

The mansion, of which I give a view, is a large, plain building in the Georgian style, and the room in which the great preacher, John Wesley, slept is still shewn. Wesley, who was the guest of Mr. Busfeild in April, 1779, was charmed with the place, and describes it in his diary as a "little paradise." The situation is certainly beautiful, looking over rich and ample grounds, while from the back of the premises there is a superb and truly Highland prospect of the lofty forest-clothed Bell Bank. A fine avenue of beeches extends from the house towards the river, and at the foot a retired and lovely landscape is revealed of the quietly-flowing river and ascending woods. The grounds, as I have said, are well laid out, and there are numerous large glacial boulders, used for ornamental purposes, taken from the hill of glacial drift on which the house is built.

MILNER FIELD.

AT the old upland hamlet of Gilstead there are one or two ancient houses of some interest, and Gilstead Hall has doubtless been the capital mansion of the place. Gilstead gave name to a local family, of whom John de Gildestede is mentioned on page 110 as living in 1273. Another notable homestead was Milner Field, which is shewn in the annexed view, copied from the original, in possession of Mr. John Walker, of Gilstead. The old house was pulled down in 1869, when the palatial residence of the Salts, which was visited by the Prince and Princess of Wales in 1882, was erected on the site. It was a roomy old place, the ground floor consisting of only two compartments, with a decidedly Tudor look about them. The large hall had a gallery running round it in the old Elizabethan style, one side of which gave access to the bedrooms, while another small part was raised as if it had been intended to serve the purpose of a rostrum from which to address those assembled around or below.

The place at an early date belonged to the old Bingley family of Mylner, or Milner, who were settled here in the time of Richard II., if not before, and some early wills of the family are now at York. At the south end of the house was a stone bearing the initials and date, I.M., 1608. Subsequently the Oldfields possessed Milner Field. One branch of the family lived at Roydfield, Bingley, and they had acquired lands at Gilstead, according to the fines, in 1554, and in 1608 John Oldfield, of Gilstead, released to Richard Sunderland, of Coley Hall, all claims to tithes belonging to the rectory of Bingley and arising out of certain lands, the inheritance of William Whitley, of Greenhill. The will of John Oldfield, of Bingley is dated Feb. 27th, 1564, and another of Sarah Oldfield, widow, of Gilstead, is dated Sept. 2nd, 1643.

Next we find an old Bingley family named Fell living at Milner Field, and their initials and date D. F. M. 1702, appeared at the east end of the house. David Fell was then living here. In 1712 Thomas Fell, of Milner Field, leased to Thomas Milner, the elder, of Jack Field, three closes of land, arable, meadow, and pasture, situate at Royd Field, called East Close, Nether Close, and Thompson Close, containing by estimation eleven days' ploughing. The lease was for seven years, at a yearly rent of £5 5s.; the lessee not to cut down or lop oak, ash, or elm, nor cut the quickwood hedges, &c., save at reasonable times for

Old Milner Field, Gilstead.

repairing fences. About this time a Thomas Fell, of East Morton, removed to Flansill Hall, near Wakefield, and in the Parish Church of Bingley there is a commemorative tablet to one Thomas Fell, gent., of East Morton, who died in 1697.

The last of the Fells who resided at Milner Field* was Mrs. Elizabeth Fell, who died in June, 1811, aged 87.

* The wood along the river side at the bottom of Milner Field from Seven Arches is still known as Fell Wood.

She was a devoted member of the Wesleyan body, and was very well-known for her deep sympathies and benevolence in any good object. Mr. Ward pays the following kindly tribute to her Christian character. He says :—

At Christmas she always sent seasonable presents to the necessitous. The fine orchard and gardens at Milner Field yielded abundant fruit, and they were cultivated by this excellent woman principally for the sick and poor around her. Her name is almost forgotten amongst men, but her record is on high; and in the last grand adjudication of all things she will receive the full reward of her doings from Him who has said that a cup of cold water given to one of His disciples shall not go unrewarded.

From a rubbing in my possession I find that each of the initials I.M. (1608) are followed by a small letter o, doubtless for John Oldfield and his wife, who were living here in 1624. In 1834 the property was purchased from Mr. William Penny (who married the heiress of the Fells*) by Mr. J. Wilmer Field, of Heaton Hall, who left two daughters, co-heiresses; the elder married to Lord Oxmantown, afterwards Earl of Rosse, and the other to the Hon. Arthur Duncombe. The latter for her portion obtained Milner Field, and in 1869 this estate was sold by Admiral Duncombe to the late Mr. Titus Salt, for the sum, as reported, of £21,000. About 1836 Mr. William Busfeild, Jun. (*see* page 365), resided at Milner Field; afterwards Mr. Joseph Ellis (*see* page 182) took it; and then Mr. Benjamin B. Popplewell occupied the old house up to its sale and subsequent demolition in 1869-70.

The old name was retained when the present large and elegant mansion was built, which is now occupied by Mrs. Salt. Previously there had been another homestead in the vicinity of Milner Field called Stubbing House, which was pulled down about the same time. It stood on the right side of the tree-shaded lane going down towards Saltaire, and about thirty yards from the top gate. The material from this old house was used in making additions to Broadstones House (New Scarbro'), the well-known picnic place above Shipley Glen, which for the past twenty-seven years has been in the occupation of Mr. William Denby.

* On page 203 I mention Mylnewro (date 1415), and in 1652 Anthony Fell purchased lands at Gilstead described as Milner-wrose (Cym.-Celt *rhos*, a moor) and Breary, doubtless the same.

GREENHILL HALL.

OVERLOOKING the valley to the north of Bingley stands this picturesque homestead, charmingly situated in the shelter of a rocky hill, partially screened from observation by a grove of trees. The present residence dates only from last century; the former Hall, which is close by, being now occupied as a farm-house. The latter was built by John Murgatroyd, of the family of East Riddlesden, in 1692; but when the heir of the Greenhill Murgatroyds married into the Carter family the lady, it is said, declined to live in the old house, and so the new Hall was built. Tradition says she was a lady of rather eccentric habits, and kept a part of the house entirely to her own use. The last of this family who lived here was James, only son of John Murgatroyd, whose youngest sister, Sarah Murgatroyd, married Timothy Maud, of Elm Tree Hill, who died in 1822. She died in 1848. James Murgatroyd died without issue, and the Greenhill property was bequeathed to his niece, Mercy Carter, daughter of his second sister, Betsy. Mercy Carter became the wife of Richard Hodgson, of Keighley, but they left no family, and the property was willed to Mrs. Hodgson's youngest brother, the Rev. John Carter, vicar of Saxton, in whose family it is still vested.

Mr. and Mrs. Hodgson left Greenhill about 1830, and went to live at Arthington, when the Hall was rented by Mr. Thomas Whitley. Afterwards Mr. Jacob Passevant became the tenant, and in 1855 he was succeeded by the late Mr. George H. Leather, who made it his home for more than forty years up to his death in Nov., 1897, aged 81.

Greenhill Grange, close to the road above the Hall, is an old Crusaders' property (referred to on page 122), and the double-cross symbol of the Knights of St. John of Jerusalem may still be seen on the gable-end of the house. One or two ancient querns have been found here. A Thomas de Greenhill was living in Bingley, probably at Greenhill, in A.D. 1379.

Morton Bridge.

PART IV.

BRIEF NOTICES OF SURROUNDING PLACES.

MORTON.

THE scenery of Morton, extending from its ancient verdant enclosures overhanging the valley to the lofty sweeps of Rumbalds Moor, presents many striking and interesting features. I have shewn how the Norwegian rovers came down Airedale from the west and north in the 10th century, how Bingley was annexed, how Micklethwaite* was cleared by them for cultivation, and Morton, close by, became another of their important settlements in the parish. Old traditions, such as "Guytrash," and the well-remembered "Hob of Elam," still lurk in the neighbourhood, and their counterparts are to be found in the ancient myths of Scandinavian legend. In 1086 Morton, East and West, was in two separate manors retained by the King; but in the reign of the Confessor they had belonged to two noble thanes of Viking descent, named Archil and Ardulf, who may have continued as under-tenants. Archil and Ardulf were probably brothers, and are said to have been sons of Ulf, but in this case Archil could not have been the great Northumbrian chief who rebelled against the Conqueror, as explained on page 78.

The principal highway through the township was that which, as at present, connects Keighley and Otley, and crosses Morton Beck by a picturesque stone bridge, shewn in the accompanying illustration. Before its improvement

* Kirkstall Abbey held various lands in the parish of Bingley, and it has been stated by Shaw and others that they had a Grange at Micklethwaite, near Bingley, but this is incorrect. It should be Micklethwaite on the Wharfe, near Wetherby.

some fifty years ago it was a mere pack-horse bridge, only wide enough for a single cart to pass; so narrow, indeed, that we might almost say of it: "Twa wheelbarrows trembled when they met." Early this century Mr. James Greenwood (now in his 82nd year) tells me that a couple of two-horse wains used to come this way to Otley from Haworth corn-mill every Monday morning; returning in the afternoon laden with "shellings" (oat-groats). The waggoners generally called at the old *Hare and Hounds* (now the *Busfeild Arms*), which sixty years ago was kept by a man named James Barber.

In April, 1768, it was ordered that Mr. John Watson do view the bridge, and report to the next Easter Sessions, which was held at Pontefract, on April 3rd, 1768, when the following order was passed:—

Whereas the Inhabitants of the Township of Morton in the said Riding have been indicted at the General Quarter Sessions of the Peace held for the sd. Riding for not repairing a certain common public Bridge called Morton Bridge situate over a rivulet called Morton Beck in the parish of Bingley in the highway leading from Keighley to Otley in the Riding aforesd. and have submitted to the sd. Indictment and confessed themselves on record legally chargeable with the repair of the sd. Bridge. And whereas it appears to this Court as well upon the representation of the said Inhabitants of Morton as by the report of Mr. John Watson one of the Surveyors of the Riding Bridges upon his own proper knowledge and view of the sd. Bridge that the arch is 24 feet by 12 feet, that the foundations are laid five feet deep with strong stones and that all is set across the Beck with large strong stones piled and cramped together to prevent the water from undermining the work, the whole of which might cost the sd. Inhabitants about forty pounds, now at the prayer and on consideration of the expense the sd. Inhabitants of the Township of Morton aforesd. have been at in rebuilding the sd. bridge. It is ordered that the Treasurer of the sd. Riding do on notice of this order pay or cause to be paid unto the said Inhabitants the sum of twenty pounds as a gratuity out of the Riding's stock.

Perhaps it was by this old road through Morton that the unhappy King, Edward II., travelled on his way from Pontefract to Skipton Castle (1324), viewing the devastations of the Scots. He had also been at Skipton in the previous year, and may have ridden with his escort by way of Otley, or through Bingley by the Beckfoot route (*see* page 75).

Morton (there are at least six places of this name in Yorkshire) gave name to a local family, of which Richard de Morton was living here in 1379, and in the same year Alice de Morton was living in the neighbouring township of Steeton. The Poll Tax of this year (*see* page 131) enumerates about a score families in the township engaged in agricultural pursuits. Not a single artisan is mentioned. A Radulph, "of the Hall," appears, and probably East Riddlesden is meant, as West Riddlesden Hall was not built then. The squire of Riddlesden, Robert Paslew, is entered as the largest contributor to the Poll Tax in Leeds.

An old property, consisting of a tenement and certain lands, which had been given to Fountains Abbey by Simon de Montalte in the 12th century, was granted by Henry VIII. in 1543 to Richard Androys (Andrews), and was then in the tenure of William Rogerson.*

Among other old Morton families are the Montaltes, or Maudes, Rishforths, Fells, Butlers, Butterfields, Dobsons, Shackletons, Fullers, Rawsons, and Beanlands (all these were living at Morton before the Reformation). Towler, Ickeringill, and Smith appear *temp.* Charles I. William Woode was a tanner, of Smithfield, Morton, who died in 1648. Christopher, youngest son of John Clapham, of Exley, bought land in West Morton, called Moor Ing and Moor Close, in 1621. This Christopher Clapham appears in the subsidy roll for Morton, A.D. 1627. Ann Elizabeth Clapham was married in 1632 to Bryan Longfellow, of East Morton, who died in 1647, and his daughter, Ann Longfellow, married Francis Clapham in 1670 (*see* Margerison's *Calverley Registers*). It is not at all improbable that these Longfellows were connected with the Longfellows of Horsforth, which is about 10 miles from Bingley, and from whom descended the distinguished American poet, Henry Wadsworth Longfellow (*see* the author's *Airedale*, pages 94-95). A pedigree of Clapham, printed in *Yorkshire Notes and Queries*, 1888, shews that Mr. John Arthur Clapham, born at Burley Hall, in Wharfedale (where the Longfellows were also numerous), and now residing at Gilstead, Bingley, is lineally descended from the above Francis Clapham and Ann Longfellow.

* In the fines for 1571-2 a water-mill and fulling-mill are mentioned as then existing in Morton and Riddlesden.

The Rev. Samuel Clapham, M.A., was their great-grandson. He was born at Leeds in 1755, and after serving some time the curacy at Yarm, in Yorkshire, became vicar of Bingley in 1791. An account of him will be found in Taylor's *Leeds Worthies*. He died in 1830.

About 1788 Abraham Dewhurst, who is described as a weaver, of Morton Banks, removed higher up the dale to Skipton. He had a family, one of whom, Abraham, returned to Morton Banks about 1830, and claimed to be

OLD THATCHED HOUSE, MORTON.

related to the Dewhursts, of Skipton, founders of the large cotton mills in that town. Mr. James Ambler, father of the founder of the firm of Thomas Ambler and Sons, worsted spinners, Bradford, was also a native of Morton.

Morton was constituted a chapelry by order in Council dated August 8th, 1845, and is now a vicarage in the patronage of the Crown and Bishop alternately. Before the church was built in 1850-1 services were held in a picturesque thatched cottage, near the present Riddlesden

Church, shewn in the accompanying view. The old house is still standing, and is also interesting as being, I believe, the only thatched house now to be seen in the old parish of Bingley. Mr. Cheadle was the first to establish mission services in this building, and it was also used as a Sunday School for some time. Mr. Frost took the services until the Rev. William Fawcett, M.A., was appointed vicar in October, 1845, and Mr. Fawcett remained at Morton until 1876, when he resigned and removed to Warwick. He was succeeded by the Rev. Francis Marriner, B.A., son of the late Canon Marriner, of Clapham. He resigned in 1883, and the vacancy was filled by the Rev. Joseph Weedow, F.R.G.S., formerly curate of Holy Trinity, Bingley, who died September 16th, 1892, and on February 5th, 1893, the Rev. William H. S. Hartley, M.A., late curate of Wyke and Ilkley, was given the parochial charge, and is still vicar.

The church (St. Luke's) is a beautiful edifice, and was consecrated March 23rd, 1851. In the year 1878 it was lighted with gas. In 1880 the vestry was converted into an organ-chamber, and the organ repaired and enlarged. In 1888 the church was renovated at a cost of nearly £200, under the care of Mr. Thomas Bottomley, of Crosshills. A handsome chancel screen was added, and the members of the Morton Branch of the Girls' Friendly Society presented a beautiful brass altar cross, similar in design to the one in the Lady Chapel of Manchester Cathedral. Other suitable gifts have also been made, including, in 1897, a handsome brass eagle lectern, "in grateful commemoration of the sixty years' reign of Queen Victoria." In 1895 a new organ, built by Messrs. Forster & Andrews, Hull, and costing over £600, was formally opened by the Archdeacon of London. Two bells and a stained glass window were at the same time added by Miss and Mr. Garritt to commemorate the jubilee year of the formation of the ecclesiastical district of Morton. Two stained windows in the south aisle were erected in 1866, one in memory of Harriet, wife of Alfred Harris, Junr., Esq., of Ashfield, Bingley, and the other by H. Booker, Esq., Castlefields, Bingley, as a "thank-offering."

Riddlesden Church (St. Mary's) was erected in 1847. Up to December, 1874, it had been in the parish of Morton. It was then constituted a separate parish, and a population of about 700 assigned to it. There is a memorial window in the nave to the late Mr. J. B. Sidgwick, of Riddlesden Hall. In 1873 the chancel was greatly improved, and a handsome east window and oak reredos placed in it, in memory of the late Frederick Greenwood, Esq., of Norton Conyers, and formerly of Ryshworth Hall, Bingley. In the same year a new Infant School was erected at a cost of £870, and in 1886 the Church Schools were enlarged at a cost of over £500, defrayed by public subscription, &c.

These are the names of the vicars, with the dates of their institution :—

February 5th, 1875—John Fisher. Died 1877.
1877—Samuel Sandberg, B.A. To Langcliffe.
March, 1880—F. A. Colbatch-Share, M.A. To Linton.
1891—David Cowling. To Gildersome.
1895—H. A. Claxton, M.A. From Gildersome.
March 15th, 1897—Charles Edward Wannop, B.A.

Upwood, for many years the seat of the Busfeild family, is in Morton township, and is pleasantly situated on elevated ground adjoining the road which crosses the moor between Keighley and Ilkley. The Roman road to Ilkley lay close by Upwood, and portions of it were removed by the late Mr. William Busfeild, M.P., who died in 1851 (*see* page 58). Upwood was subsequently, about the year 1854, occupied by Mr. Johnson Atkinson Busfeild, previously of Ryshworth, and he enlarged and greatly improved the house and estate. Though not in the ordinary sense a public man, he was an active magistrate, and regularly attended the Bench at Bingley, and occasionally at Keighley. He was an accomplished antiquary ; being especially interested in local history, and compiled several beautiful manuscript volumes, sumptuously adorned with numerous coloured and other plates, including portraits, coats-of-arms, &c., which are now in the possession of his son, Mr. Ferrand, of St. Ives. Mr. Busfeild died on September 19th, 1882, aged 68, and was interred in the family vault in Bingley Parish Churchyard.

In the picturesque glen which ascends from Morton for a considerable distance towards the moor are several commercial works; that at Dimples, a worsted-mill, the property of Messrs. H. & J. W. Wright, being now in ruins, caused by a fire on October 28th, 1871, when damage was sustained to the extent of £7,000. Messrs. Wright run the paper-mill higher up the stream, and above this, and close to the Morton Beck Bridge, is Messrs. Hastings' paper-mill. The old-established Holroyd Mill stands on the beck below Dimples Mill, and is now tenanted by Messrs. Shackleton as a worsted-mill. Worsted spinning and manufacturing were also carried on at Morton sixty years ago by Messrs. James Whitley, George Walker, and William and Samuel Nichols.

Another important paper-factory was erected over sixty years ago in Sunnydale, near the head of the glen, by Mr. John Smith, who had also a place in Leeds. The Morton mill was worked by a stupendous water-wheel, said to have been the largest water-wheel in the United Kingdom, the famous one at Laxey, in the Isle of Man, alone excepted. Subsequently Mr. Thomas Scott took this mill for a short time, when it passed into the hands of Mr. William Hastings for a few years. For about twenty years it has not been worked, and has lapsed into ruin. A portion, however, has been fit up for a picnic-place, and a large room is used for dancing, &c. The monster water-wheel was taken down, and disposed of at the price of old iron to Messrs. Chapman & Co., of Keighley.

In 1788 an Act for enclosing common lands at Riddlesden and Morton was obtained. When the proposal was mooted to make the moor above Morton into a military camp Mr. Busfeild, of Upwood, entertained a number of the officers, &c., including the Duke of Cambridge and Lord Halifax. They went over the ground, and much was said in favour of the site, which, however, was ultimately abandoned. The bridge over the beck at Upwood has been known ever since as the Duke's Bridge. Considerable excitement prevailed in the neighbourhood at the time, and many plans were suggested, including a railway to the camp across the moor from Guiseley.

ELDWICK.

HELGUIC, as this place is written in *Domesday Book*, A.D. 1086, had been occupied some centuries before this time by the Welsh Britons (*see* page 52), and at the Norman Conquest retained its pure British name, as above. It comes from the Cymric-Celt, *hel* (a hollow) and *guic* (an abode, or dwelling-place), cognate with the Sansc. *veca*, Teut. *wic*, *wyk*, Scand. *wick*, &c. The pre-Conquest settlement was probably on or near the same site as it now occupies, in the *hollow* by the beck. It is a pity that its ancient name has suffered the very recent corruption to its present form, which is misleading, most people supposing the name to be derived from the Anglo-Saxon *eald* (old) and *wic* or *wick*, a village; but for seven centuries at least—from the Conquest down to about 1800—it is spelled in local and other deeds and in the parish registers, Helwick, Elwic, and the like.

My already much-extended volume prevents me from making little more than bare mention of the British occupation of Eldwick, as well as of the adjacent *Domesday* township of Baildon. Numerous urn-bearing tumuli, marked stones, &c., on the surrounding moors attest the former presence of the Celt. In medieval times a good deal of poor coal has been won on the same moors, and there are numerous circular cavities still visible here, which many believe to be the remains of ancient British pit-dwellings, but which in all probability are the partially filled-up old coal-shafts. Iron, too, has been worked here in early times. On this subject I will quote what Mr. John Brigg, now M.P., says in his useful little manual on the *Industrial Geology of Bradford* (1874):—

The remains of ancient bloomeries, or iron-smelting furnaces, which are found on the slopes of the Aire valley, and also in the Calder district, point to a time when steam engines were unknown, and when labour was so cheap that the extraction of a small portion of the metal contained in the ore was a sufficient recompense for the trouble of building a furnace and waiting for a favourable wind to blow the fire. Heaps of slag and cinders mark the sites of these ancient "bloomeries." Although usually spoken of as the work of the Romans, they are considered by the best authorities to have been in use within two hundred years of the present time. The supply of ore has in some instances been derived from modules of ironstone washed out of beds of shale, and left in the water-courses.

In the Eldwick and Baildon beck-courses ironstone nodules and pieces of slag may even yet occasionally be picked up. I have found in searching the Wakefield Sessions records that the adjoining coal-workings on the moor had been abandoned in Charles I. time, and that the surface holes were then a hindrance and source of peril to those who had occasion to traverse the moors. In 1638 a paine was laid at Pontefract that "Sr. Richard Hawkesworth, Kt., Wm. Vavasour, Esq., and George Tempest, Esq., should sufficiently fill upp the Colepitts uppon the wastes of Baildon and Baildon Moore." But as the said wastes were declared to be within the liberties of the Archbishop of York, the above defendants are exonerated, and the "paine" is to be laid in the Sessions of the said Lord Archbishop. This seems to solve the long-contended origin of the supposed "British pit-dwellings" on the Baildon moors.

At an early period lands at Eldwick were given to the Knights of St. John of Jerusalem, the rents of which were devoted to the expenses of the extraordinary Crusades to the Holy Land (*see* page 115). The Eltofts of Ryshworth held their Eldwick property at the dissolution of monasteries, and when Queen Mary revived the Order in 1557 she gave them back "one our rent of 12d. issuing out of a tenement in Helwyke, late of Thomas Eltoft." The Longbottoms, Brears, and Jowetts were among the tenants of the Order at Eldwick.

Eldwick Hall, belonging to the Stansfield family, of Esholt Hall, is the most notable old house here, and is passed on the familiar walk from Eldwick Beck up to the moor by "Dick Hudson's." It contains a fine mantel-shelf, flanked by two arched doorways, and the shelf extends the whole width of the room, 18 feet. In the centre is a shield of arms. The house was built, according to an inscription over the south doorway, in

1696, a date that is accompanied by the initials R.L., probably a Longbottom. Among the deeds at Esholt is one concerning a Richard Longbottom, dated 1730, and the parish registers record the death in November, 1696, of Ann Longbottom, and in July, 1700, of Jonathan Longbottom, all of Eldwick. In the Skipton parish registers, it may also be noted, is the marriage entry, dated June 15th, 1650, of Richard Longbottom and Margaret Bowes, of Bingley.

An old foundation-stone of the garden-wall close by bears some defaced letters and the date 1677. In the east wall, fronting the road, is also a stone inscribed I.H.S., 1716, which was brought from an out-building and placed here some years ago by Mr. William Wildman, of Eldwick High Crag. The family of Hartley, which had long previously been living at Eldwick, was at this time residing at the Hall. John Hartley, of Eldwick, had a family of several children, and one of his sons, William, who was born March 7th, 1683-4, was father of the Rev. Richard Hartley, B.D., vicar of Bingley. He was born at Eldwick Hall in 1714, and died in 1789. He was twice married, and by his second wife had a son, the Rev. Richard Hartley, D.D., who was Head Master of the Grammar School, and also vicar of Bingley. He died in 1836, aged 72.

Thomas Hartley, who died at Keighley, May 25th, 1852, and was buried in Keighley Parish Churchyard, is believed to be a member of the same stock. His only daughter, Nancy Ann, born November 7th, 1820, married in 1848 Joseph Holmes, J.P., son of Thorpe Holmes, who was a brother of Joseph Henry Henden Holmes, F.S.A., described as advocate at the Bar of Demarara, Proctor of Vice-Admiralty, and Judge Advocate to the Forces of Demarara and Essequibo. He died at Demarara in 1831. He was a noted man in many ways, and as a scientist was joint inventor with Sir Humphrey Davy of the famous safety-lamp. Before going abroad he resided at Newcastle-on-Tyne, and married a daughter of Stephen Pemberton, Esq., of that city. One of Thomas Hartley's grandsons is Colonel Holmes, son of above Joseph Holmes, and now Deputy Adjutant General of Manitoba.

There was also a Jonathan Hartley living at Eldwick Beck early last century, and one of his sons was the Rev. James Hartley, born in 1742, and in 1771 appointed Head Master of Otley Grammar School and curate of Otley, at a salary of £30 per annum. In May, 1775, he was inducted to the rectory of Staveley, Yorkshire. In the latter part of last century John Hartley, of Eldwick Hall, kept a pack of harriers. Lieutenant-Colonel Joseph Hartley, of Hartley, Kent, claims lineal descent from him.

At the foot of this chapter will be found a small sketch of Toils Farm, another old homestead at Eldwick, which has been in the occupation of the Greenwood family for nearly a century and a half. In its mullioned window at the front of the house is a pane of glass containing a clever portrait of the eminent divine, the Rev. John Wesley, and below it is some out-of-date shorthand, terminating with the date 1675. In the next pane to it appears the following verse:—

Man, thy years are ever sliding,
Brightest hours have no abiding;
Use the golden moments well;
Life is wasting,
Death is hasting,—
Death consigns to heaven or hell.
[shorthand] Octr., 1776.
Prepare to meet thy God.

When Wesley visited Bingley (*see* page 191) he generally went on to Otley by way of Eldwick, and called at Toils Farm. The above lines are commonly attributed to him, but even if they merited that distinction the date recorded,—October, does not agree with the actual time of Wesley's visit to Bingley in 1776, which was in May. On February 20th of this year Martha, wife of John Whitley, the friend of Wesley, died.

Below this farm was a house, now pulled down, which for a long time was occupied by the Whitley family. John Whitley, who died in 1813, aged 90, was a prominent Methodist, and through the influence of Mr. Wesley he became an acceptable local preacher. His son, Francis, was also a Methodist preacher for nearly half-a-century. He died in 1821, aged 77. One of his daughters became the wife of Thomas Nicholson, father of the Airedale poet, and here at Eldwick John Nicholson, the poet, spent the happy days of his childhood. He grew up in love with the wild moors and beautiful scenery that surrounded his early home, and to which he remained fondly attached to the day of his death. A large rock, on which he had carved his name, near the present reservoir, is still known as "Nicholson's Rock." It was while endeavouring to reach these beloved scenes of his youth on the evening of Good Friday, 1843, that he lost his life while attempting to ford the flooded river at Dixon's Mill, now Saltaire.

The Wesleyan Chapel at Eldwick was originally built in 1832, and, it is said, cost under £10; the bulk of the work involved in its erection being contributed gratuitously. The present handsome chapel, the foundation-stones of which were laid on March 30th, 1888, by Mr. Ralph Fawcett (Bingley), Miss White (Gilstead Hall), and Mr. Henry Platts (Bingley), was constructed from plans prepared by Mr. John Bruce, of Eldwick, and the building, &c., cost £700. It was opened in the following October.

The foundation-stone of the beautiful Mission Church at Eldwick was laid by Mrs. Ferrand, of St. Ives, on June 10th, 1893, and it was dedicated on October 28th by the Bishop of Ripon. The plans of the church, which is in the Gothic style, were prepared by Messrs. Armistead & Parkinson, of Bingley and Bradford. The building has accommodation for about 150, and consists of chancel and nave, with a vestry on the south side of the chancel. There is a small saddle-backed bell-turret over the west gable. The cost, exclusive of furnishing, was £600, covered principally by the proceeds of a bazaar. There is a flourishing Mutual Improvement Society at Eldwick, the members of which give lectures and entertainments in the Board School weekly during the winter season. The secretary is Mr. Joseph Walbank.

In addition to its having nourished the muse of Nicholson, the bracing air of Eldwick has given inspiration to another not less notable writer. Mr. Ben. Preston, who was born at Bradford, in 1819, settled here in 1865, in the house built and still occupied by him above the beck.

Mr. Benjamin Preston.

His dialect and other writings, both in prose and verse, are the undoubted products of a vigorous mind, and evidence a wealth of thought and power of expression much above the average. The late Edwin Waugh, "the Lancashire Burns," characterised him as the ablest Yorkshire poet of his time, while the Rev. S. Baring-Gould, in speaking of an hour with Preston's collected poems, says it is to him "an hour of unclouded happiness, like many more I have spent on the Yorkshire moors, with the scent of whins in the air and the larks singing overhead." The accompanying recent portrait of Mr. Preston is from a photograph specially taken for this work by Mr. George Whitaker, of Bingley, and shows the veteran author seated in his garden, with his familiar walking-stick and "churchwarden," though the latter has been only the solace of his old age. A well-grown mountain-ash tree, planted when a sapling by Mr. Preston, near the garden gate, presents in the autumn, when laden with the brightest of berries, a beautiful picture.

The late Mr. John Preston, of Littlebeck Hall, Gilstead, was the poet's younger brother. He was a man of many talents, though best known as a painter of landscape who knew how to interpret Nature with the feelings and skill of a poet and artist. He was highly successful in imaginative art, and many of his idealizations of passages in the poets have been admirably conceived, and perhaps in this class of art he has never been excelled.* Mr. Preston died in 1888, leaving an only son, Mr. John Emanuel Preston, who with his wife and family continues to reside at Littlebeck. He has inherited the talent and tastes of his father; is a skilful painter and accomplished antiquary; being well known for his local archæological researches and collections of prehistoric relics from the Eldwick and surrounding moors. Mr. Preston is also a well-known collector for collectors, possessing a considerable knowledge of Art, ancient and modern, in its various branches, and his judgment and services have often been requisitioned

* A sketch of John Preston's life and work appeared in the *Bradford Antiquary* for 1895, from the pen of Mr. Butler Wood, chief librarian of the Bradford Public Libraries.

in the formation of public and private collections. Unfortunately, from early life he has suffered from acute deafness, a circumstance which has greatly interfered with his activities as a "man of the world."

To his accomplished daughter, Miss Nannie Preston, the present writer is indebted for many of the beautiful drawings which have been executed and engraved specially for this work.

In 1874 Mr. Abraham Holroyd came to reside at Eldwick. He was well known in Yorkshire literary circles, and during his long and unselfish devotion to the cause of local literature wrote much himself, and published many meritorious works of others, including the Rev. Patrick Brontë's *Cottage in the Wood; Poems and Songs of Ben Preston; A Garland of Poetry by Yorkshire Authors*, &c. Mr. Holroyd died at Shipley, on New Year's Day, 1888, aged 72, and was interred in Clayton Churchyard. In 1893 a beautiful memorial-stone was placed over his grave by his literary friends, and a *Souvenir* of the event, consisting of a neat illustrated brochure of thirty pages, dedicated to Mr. Holroyd's old friend, Mr. George Ackroyd, J.P., was written by Mrs. F. C. Galloway, of West Bowling, and printed for private circulation. The scenery of Eldwick has been well described by Mr. Holroyd, and with his words we will conclude :—

And now, farewell! ye dear delightful shades!
Eldwick! awhile, adieu, thy sylvan glades!
Full oft my tempted feet shall hither roam,
When cares bow down, and weighty troubles come;
When hard the world against my bosom beats,
And seek sweet peace within thy green retreats.

Cottingley Hall.

COTTINGLEY.

THE pleasant village of Cottingley was one of the *Domesday* manors included in the ancient parish of Bingley. Thoresby, referring to the Cottingley, near Beeston,* offers the following opinion on its name:—

Whether from *cot-land*, as belonging to and occupied by the *cotarii or cotmanni*, a sort of under-tenants, so called from their *cotes*, or sheds, which with certain parcels of land adjoining were originally assigned them in respect of their services, or from the British *coit*, wood, I shall not determine, though I incline to the latter.

I feel little hesitation, however, in saying that its origin is in the Anglo-Saxon *Goding*, *Goting*, a family or tribal name, and *ley*, *leah*, a cultivated district (*see* page 102). The site of the Old Hall is entrenched, and this may have formed part of the original defences of the Teutonic settlers. It is now much filled up and obscure, though very distinct evidences remain on the west side, where the moat-like excavation extends for about one hundred yards towards the deeply-channelled Cottingley Beck, which has protected the south and south-east sides of the enclosure, the space bounded by the entrenchment and the beck measuring about two hundred by one hundred yards. Beside the beck is the Old Hall Well.

The Old Hall stood at the top of the village; being the last house on leaving it in this direction. It was a picturesque Jacobean building, but much decayed, and had been long divided into cottages when it was pulled down in 1872. It bore the double cross, and also an initialed and dated stone, R.F.A.F., 1659; the initials being those of Robert and Anne Ferrand, of Harden Grange. Doubtless it occupied the site of a much older building, for the Franks, who had very honourable family connections, resided at Cottingley Hall long before the Reformation. William Gascoigne, of Gawthorpe, son and heir of William Gascoigne, married Agnes, daughter and heir of Nicholas

* It is singular that Beeston, like Bingley, has both a Cottingley and Crossflatts. Cottingley Hall, Beeston, was an old home of the Claphams, &c.

Frank, and had issue, Sir William Gascoigne, Chief Justice of England. Stephen, son of William Frank, gent., was living at Cottingley early in the reign of Elizabeth, and had several sons and daughters, the eldest of whom, William, was born at Cottingley in 1581. Stephen died in 1620, and in his will, which is dated 29th March, 1617, he mentions his son and heir, William, who it would appear was something of a vagabond and spendthrift. It is ordered that unless he "live frugally and thriftily," a certain sum of money is to be left in trust to Alice, daughter of Stephen, who was wife of Thomas Leach, for the benefit of her children absolutely. It is doubtless the same William Franke who was fined in 1617 for what seems to have been unprovoked assaults on his father and another Cottingley man (*see* page 125).

When Queen Mary in 1557 revived the Order of the Knights of St. John of Jerusalem there was issuing out of the manor of Cottingley the sum of 6s. 8d. and service, then or late of the heirs of William Franke. At the court held at Cottingley, on April 6th, 1621, a copy of an ancient deed was presented, shewing that the Prior of St. John and Henry Walrush had entered into an agreement whereby on the death of a tenant of the Order the lord of the manor claimed heriot, or the best chattel in the possession of the tenant at the time of his death. Thus the court sought the executors of the above Stephen Frank to compound with the lord of the manor "for the bed whereon he dyed, or deliver ye same to ye said lord." Whether the bed was actually delivered or compounded for is not stated.

In 1567 a fine was entered touching the manor of Cottingley and 8 messuages, 4 cottages, and a water-mill, with lands in the same. The plaintiff was Brian Bayles, Esq., and the deforciants Anthony Francke, gent., and William Francke, his son and heir apparent. In 1590 another fine appears concerning the manor, &c., wherein Stephen Franck and others are plaintiffs, and John Thornhaghe, sen., and others are deforciants. The manor was subsequently, about 1620, acquired by the Sunderlands, and in 1669 it was in possession of the Dobson family, of the Vicarage, Bingley. Thomas Dobson, Esq., of Cottingley House, in 1723 devised the same to his only child, who marrying in 1737 the Rev. William Lamplugh, carried the estate to that family. The issue of this marriage was again an only daughter, Elizabeth Lamplugh, married in 1761, at Bingley, to Henry Wickham, Esq., J.P., after whose death in 1804 the property was sold to the trustees under the will of Benjamin Ferrand, Esq., and added to the settled family estates.

Cottingley House, now known as Cottingley Hall, is a handsome old mansion, standing pleasantly amidst "tall ancestral trees," close to the village. The original building consists of three stories, the principal entrance to it, which was obliterated by the wing built by the Wickhams, having been at the west end. Over the front door is carved a buck's head; being the crest of the Wickhams. The old portion is now luxuriantly covered with ivy and creepers, and its lofty and spacious front presents an imposing and very picturesque aspect. Attractive and well-kept gardens delight the eye on this side of the mansion, while the whole is enclosed by an extensive park. Formerly the coaches passed through the park, and emerged on the road by the archway (now blocked) opposite the Town Well, continuing upwards past the *Sun* inn (the bridge then not being built), and ascending the hill through Cottingley. The gardens in front of Cottingley Grange were then only half their present width. There was a private bath-house close behind the old toll-bar house, and from the Hall down to the fish-pond, beside the highway, there was a long, shaded walk by an avenue of stately old trees. The walk continued to the river-side, where the Wickhams had also a boat-house. The aspects at that time were beautifully wooded and retired.

The Wickhams were a distinguished family, intimately associated with Royalty, and one of whose ancestors was the eminent William Wickham, D.D., Bishop of Lincoln, and afterwards Bishop of Winchester in the reign of Elizabeth. Henry Wickham, Lieutenant-Colonel Foot Guards, who was born in 1731, married, as stated above, Elizabeth, daughter and heiress of the Rev. William Lamplugh. Colonel Wickham died at Cottingley in 1804. He lived in great style at Cottingley Hall, and it is said usually drove to Bingley Church in a coach with four horses and postilion. His eldest son, William Wickham, M.P., who was born at Cottingley in 1761, was Under Secretary of State in 1798, Envoy to the Swiss Cantons, a Privy Councillor, and Lord Treasurer in 1806. He died at Brighton in 1840, and was buried there.* He married a daughter of M. Louis Bertrand, of Geneva, and had issue a son, Henry Lewis, of Binsted, Wyck, Southants., barrister-at-law, who married, at Aberford, Lucy, daughter of William Markham, of Becca, and they had issue: William, of Binsted, M.P., who married Sophia Emma, daughter of H. F. Shaw-Lefevre; Henry Lamplugh, Captain of Rifle Brigade, of Wootton, co. Warwick, who married a daughter of Lord Arundell, of Wardour, widow of Sir Alfred Joseph Tichborne, Bart.; and Leonora Emma, wife of Herbert Crompton Herries, Esq. Colonel Wickham's second son, Lamplugh Wickham, of Low Moor House, Bradford, was born in 1768, and married at Guiseley in 1795, Sarah Elizabeth, daughter of Richard Hird, of Rawdon, and he took the name of Hird on his marriage. He was father of Henry Wickham Hird (who retook the name of Wickham on his father's death in 1848), for some years Chairman of the Lancashire and Yorkshire Railway Company, and in 1852 M.P. for Bradford.

After the death of Colonel Wickham in 1804, Cottingley House was occupied by Mrs. Sarah Ferrand, and upon her leaving it in 1819, the old mansion remained untenanted for a number of years. It was then leased, about 1835, by Mr. Richard Thornton, of Bradford, who for some time up to his death in 1843 was clerk to the old Court of Requests in that town. He was a gentleman of literary tastes, and was one of the founders of the Bradford Library. He was a member of a younger branch of the Thorntons of

* *See The Correspondence of the Rt. Hon. Wm. Wickham* (with portrait) *from the Year 1794*; edited by his grandson, Wm. Wickham, M.A. (1870), 2 vols.

Tyersall,* and had property about Bowling. His grandfather, Jeremiah Thornton, and also his father, Joseph, who died in 1825, aged 80, owned and lived at Thorntree House, Thornton Lane, Horton. Joseph had ten children, of whom six died in infancy. Richard, of Cottingley, was the youngest, and he married in 1821, at Askrigg, Eliza Hastwell, whose family belonged an estate at Askrigg, which included the beautiful glen and

MR. RICHARD THORNTON.

waterfall known as Mill Gill. Twelve children were born of this marriage; the eleventh child being Richard Thornton, the gifted friend and companion of Livingstone on his explorations of the unknown regions of Africa. He was born at Cottingley Hall, April 5th, 1838, and was

* For pedigree *see* J. W. Clay's *Additions to Dugdale's Visitation*, pages 133-6.

barely 20 years of age when he left England with Livingstone for the hitherto unexplored tracts of the Zambesi. After five years of unwearied effort as geologist of the party, during which period he brought to bear a skill, a knowledge, and an interpretation of the varied phenomena of that mysterious country, that evoked the praise and admiration of the most eminent geographers then living, young Thornton fell a victim to malaria, and died in the heart of Africa in the prime of his career, at the early age of 25. Sir Roderick Murchison, who was at that time Director General of the Geological Survey, and President of the Royal Geographical Society, speaking of Richard Thornton in his anniversary address, in May, 1864, remarked that " so gifted and rising an explorer, had he lived, his indomitable zeal and his great acquirements would have surely placed him in the front rank of men of science."

Failing health compelled him for a time to separate himself from the Zambesi expedition, and in the interval he joined the eminent German explorer, Baron von der Decken, in his first survey of the wild and untrodden region of the Kilimandjaro mountains. These two intrepid travellers were the first Europeans who were able to settle by actual observation the question of snow-capped peaks in equatorial Africa. The Baron, who communicated the important results of this expedition to the German Government, wrote in high admiration of the labours and able assistance of this indefatigable young Bingley man.

On February 18th, 1863, Thornton went on alone to visit the " Universities' Mission," and found that district suffering from famine, and the whole population in a most pitiable state. The commiserating young traveller, in conjunction with the Rev. Henry Rowley, volunteered to undertake a journey overland to Tété to purchase sheep, a distance of about 80 miles. The privations and exposure which he had to undergo on his toilsome march through a barbarous, hot and swampy fever-stricken country, returning with about 100 head of sheep and goats, told heavily upon a constitution already weakened by previous over-exertion. They reached the mission-station on

April 2nd, and on the 11th Thornton, then in a very weakly state, was with Livingstone on board the "Pioneer," when he was suddenly taken ill with dysentery, and died on April 22nd, 1863. On the 25th Dr. Livingstone communicated the intelligence of Thornton's death to Sir Roderick Murchison, stating that he was buried about 500 yards from the foot of the first cataract, and on the right bank of the Shiré.

MR. RICHARD THORNTON'S BURIAL PLACE IN CENTRAL AFRICA.

By the courtesy of the explorer's surviving sisters, I am privileged to present his portrait, and also the scene of his place of burial in "darkest Africa," from a picture sent to the family soon after his interment. The tree, bearing his name upon the device of a Christian cross, is known as the *baobab*, and is the characteristic tree of these parts. It is a species of cork, and grows very rapidly, and may possibly not be in existence now. I am also permitted to print the following hitherto unpublished letter of Dr. Livingstone addressed to young Thornton a few weeks before the expedition to the Zambesi. The steamer, it may be added, left Liverpool on March 10th, 1858 :—

50, Albemarle Street,
2nd Feby., 1858.

Dear Sir,

We must have all ready to start in the "Pearl" from Liverpool on the 15th of this month.

I submitted your list to Captain Washington, but it cannot be approved until further enquiry. Prof. Ramsay seems to have forgotten that a man is no geologist without his tools. Now you are to be the geologist of the expedition; your pay is now running on, and that up to the day of sailing; he should, I suppose, supply you with all needful implements, they would then be your own. I shall try and get everything possible for you, but it may be a little more graceful to curtail the list. We bogled at a binocular telescope, a sextant, "Murchison's Siluria," &c.

I have taken strong tin boxes, japanned, about the size of railway trunks, as being safe from insects.

Rifles are provided for the Kroomen only, and the expenses of the expedition are limited to a certain sum.

Yours, &c.,
D. Livingstone.

Mr. Thornton.

P.S.—You will get half-a-year's pay in advance.

Richard Thornton, and also his brother Hastwell, went to Bingley Grammar School. The latter brother became a doctor of medicine, and died in Canada. Richard, on leaving Bingley, was a pupil at the Bradford Grammar School, and subsequently received a scientific training in London, at the School of Mines. I may also add that while the Thorntons resided at Cottingley Hall the distinguished novelist, Charlotte Brontë, applied there for a situation as governess, but as Miss Brontë could not undertake to give music lessons to Mrs. Thornton's children, she was not engaged.

Cottingley Hall was subsequently occupied by the several families of Lupton, Firth, Smith, and Stansfield. In 1887 it was taken by the late Mr. Charles H. Priestley, whose widow still resides there. Mr. Priestley died Feb. 19th, 1893, and a very beautiful monument was erected to his memory in the Bingley Cemetery, where he is interred. Mr. Priestley left the sum of £5,000, free of legacy duty, for charitable purposes, particulars of which were announced at the time.

Cottingley Grange, opposite the ancient *Sun* inn, is another old homestead, the property of the Hollings family, and at one time their residence. A stone on an out-building is inscribed I.H., M.H., 1671, G.H., and in front of the house appears the double cross, indicating that it was formerly a possession of the Hospital of St. John of Jerusalem. In the yard behind is an old bakehouse, with spacious fire-place, once used as a drying-room for leather. A number of tan-pits formerly existed near an old homestead close by, appropriately named Bark House (now pulled down), and the business of leather-dressing has been carried on at Cottingley for a long period. The Lister family were engaged in the trade here in the time of the Civil Wars, and a century ago the same business was carried on by some of the Hollings. This family has been connected with Cottingley from at least the reign of Henry VIII., but is not now resident here.

Before the adoption of steam power most of the villagers at Cottingley were engaged in combing and spinning by hand, and for many years up to his death in 1838, Mr. Edward Berwick kept nearly half the inhabitants so employed. He resided at the old Grange, and in the building in the yard adjoining he used to store his wool before weighing out to the hand-combers. He ran the old Dixon's Mill, at Saltaire, for nearly twenty years, and he also farmed the land afterwards owned by Mr. Thomas Baines, as well as that included in the property of the late Mr. Henry Mason, of Bankfield. Mr. Berwick is remembered as a capable and considerate employer, and was well known in the trade and greatly respected. In middle life he had the misfortune to meet with an accident, which necessitated the amputation of one of his legs. The operation was performed at his residence at Cottingley, and it is said he bore the trial with remarkable fortitude; chloroform being at that time not used. He left a family of ten sons and daughters; one of the latter, Sarah, was wife of the late Mr. Isaac Skirrow Smith, who resided in the house adjoining, afterwards occupied by Major Edward

Stephenson ; another, Ann, married Mr. Benjamin Stephenson, father of Mr. Alfred Stephenson, of Bolton Grange, Bradford; a third, Grace, married, and is the mother of Mr. Reuben Williamson, of Huddersfield. Mr. Berwick's son, John, succeeded to the business at Cottingley, but afterwards took the Junction Mill, at Shipley, and went to reside there. All the other children left Cottingley, except William, who took the farm at Cottingley Bridge, now occupied by Mrs. Waddington. The old grange is now divided into two separate dwellings, and for the past thirty years occupied by Mr. Samuel Dean and his son.

The worsted business was carried on at Cottingley Mill for many years by the late Mr. Thomas Baines, who on acquiring the property made considerable alterations and enlargements in the premises, formerly tenanted as a leather works by Mr. Michael Horner. On Mr. Baines giving up business, the mills were taken over by the Cottingley Manufacturing Company, and in 1895 they were sold to Mr. Walter R. Kay, who now occupies a portion of the mill for wool-combing; the other portion being appropriated for weaving purposes by Mr. Thomas Smith.

The old *Sun* inn, above mentioned, where the coaches used sometimes to stop before the new road was made and the toll-bar erected in 1825, is the only "public" in the village, and has doubtless been an inn for centuries. In the old parish constable days, and before the erection of the Town Hall, cases used to be tried in an upstairs room, and meetings were usually held here for the transaction of public business. The inn a century or more ago was kept by a man well known to the drivers of the coaches as Joss Smith, whose widow, Jane Smith, continued in the house until her death at an advanced age in 1812. It was then taken by the Fosters, who had it for forty years. Joseph Foster died in 1832, and his widow, Hannah, in 1852, when their son-in-law, James Moore, continued the occupancy. Mrs. Foster—good old body—knew the requirements of a country inn, and her house enjoyed a good reputation. She was mother to another veteran innkeeper, Mrs. Slicer, of the old *Queen's Head*, Bingley.

The Church of St. Michael and All Angels was

consecrated by the Bishop of Ripon on September 29th, 1886. The building had been erected in 1877 as a mission church of the parish of Holy Trinity, Bingley. In 1881 a large school-room was added by the liberality of Mr. Henry Mason, of Bankfield, and early in 1886 Mr. Mason offered a sum of £1,500 towards the endowment of an independent parish church. A district comprising 985 acres was assigned by the Ecclesiastical Commissioners out of the parish of Holy Trinity, and the Rev. John Simpson, M.A., from Grasmere, who had been nine years curate-in-charge, was appointed first incumbent of the new parish, and is still vicar.

Bankfield, the residence of the late Mr. Henry Mason, was built in 1848 by Mr. William Murgatroyd, mayor of Bradford, in a beautiful position some little distance from the highroad between Cottingley and Bingley. It is a handsome erection in the Tudor style, and has a frontage to the road 120 feet long. It is noted for its large and valuable collection of paintings, acquired by Mr. Mason, and including choice examples of the works of J. M. W. Turner, Sir J. E. Millais, L. Alma Tadema, J. Constable, David Roberts, Holman Hunt, David Cox, and other well-known artists. Mr. Mason died June 11th, 1898, aged 77.

The picturesque house at Cottingley Bridge, now occupied by Mr. W. Middleton, steward of the St. Ives estates, was from 1805 to 1825 the residence of Mr. and Mrs. C. F. Busfeild (*see* page 364). At that time it was a delightful place, with its pretty nut-grove and lovely walks along the banks of the river; the latter clear as crystal, and abounding with fish. When the road was improved in 1825 a considerable encroachment was made on the lawn in front of the house, and a magnificent oak-tree, whose branches extended entirely across the highway, was cut down. On April 24th, 1820, the house had a narrow escape of being destroyed by fire; and on the night of April 16th, 1825, a daring attempt at robbery was made at the house, but Mr. Busfeild, who had been watching one of the men carefully unfasten a bedroom window, and as soon as it was sufficiently opened, pushed the burglar backwards, and he fell into a holly-bush in the garden below and escaped.

St. Ives, Bingley.

HARDEN.

"A LOVELY road as e'er the foot of minstrel strode," is that which runs through the picturesque Harden valley from Ireland Bridge to the borders of Wilsden and Cullingworth. Beautiful and many-tinted woods extend high up to the horizon, and beyond to the north are wide, breezy moors, on the eastern edge of which, overlooking the Aire valley, stands the far-famed Druids' Altar. Various interesting plants and flowers grow by the road-sides, as well as in the tangled and luxuriant woods on either hand; while from the crannies in the old lichen-stained and moss-covered walls—how rich in places these old walls look, clothed as with velvet-pile in their bright green drapery of living moss!—spring wild geraniums, stitchworts, violets, strawberries, and blue veronica, which many think is the true forget-me-not. In one pasture primroses also grow in some profusion, and cowslips, too, and it is well they appear on forbidden ground, otherwise it is to be feared their presence would be of short duration. Here, too, in a truly wild state, is the home of the uncommon odorous violet, and proud ought all lovers of Nature to be of the fact; indeed, as the vale of Furness Abbey is known as the "Glen of Deadly Nightshade," well might we describe our beautiful Harden dale as the "Valley of the Sweet Violet."

Rich in historic memories, too, is this delightfully sequestered little valley, upon which, had space permitted, a hundred instead of a dozen pages might well have been written. Almost every house is a shrine of interest, associated with many great and good names. The monks of Rievaulx for centuries were absolute owners of the vale, and must often have sojourned at the old Grange.* But it was doubtless hallowed ground long before their day, for,

* Rievaulx Abbey had also a Grange at Faweather, on Rumbalds Moor, valued at the Dissolution at £4 13s. 4d., and they had also iron-mines in the same locality. Doubtless the cinder heaps and iron scoriæ found about Harden Hall are the result of their old smelting-works here.

as I have elsewhere explained, the first voice of Christian prayer in the parish in all probability emanated from the monastery here of St. Heiv's. In after centuries it was the home of the Ferrands, the present owners and occupiers of the estate, and at their mansion, long known as St. Ives, many distinguished people have been entertained, including the ex-Premier, Benjamin Disraeli, afterwards Earl of Beaconsfield; Gathorne Hardy, now Earl of Cranbrook; Lord John Manners, now the venerable Duke of Rutland; and many others. John Ruskin and Dante Gabriel Rossetti have also paced the woodland walks of the Harden valley, while Charlotte Brontë and her gifted sisters were likewise familiar with the neighbourhood. Richard Shackleton, the friend of Burke, came from Shackleton House, and the Sunderlands, whose family took part in the disastrous Civil Wars, lived close by at Hill End. At this house, too, lived the maternal ancestors of the late eminent Churchman, Dr. Edward White Benson, Primate of All England, of whom I shall speak presently. Dr. Benson took an especial delight in his Yorkshire homes, and was a regular visitor to this district.

The manor of Harden, as I have said, anciently belonged to Rievaulx Abbey. Early in the 13th century it was granted to this monastery by Thomas de Birkin "for the safety of his soul and of all his parents and posterities." The following is an extract from the charter:—

To all, &c., know ye that I, Thomas de Birkin, do give, grant, and by this my present deed confirm to God and the blessed Mary, and to the monks of Rivax, all my lands and all my wood, which is called Harden, between Hadelson [*see* page 64] and Cullingworth, without any retentions by these divisions following: Even from that place where the divisions begin between Hadelson and Harden, above the highroad which goes from Haworth to Bingley, and then by the same division even to Harden Head, and then by Harden Brook even to the place where Harden Brook falls into Wilsden Brook, and from thence by Wilsden Brook even to Cullingworth Brook, and then by Cullingworth Brook even to Cullingworth Mill, and then by the Mill Dam even to Hainworth Shaw, and then by Hainworth Shaw even to the above-mentioned highroad that goes from Haworth to Bingley, and then in a straight line by the same road towards the north, even to the place where the afore-mentioned divisions begin between Hadelson and Harden.

This charter was attested by John, Abbot of Fountains, Stephen, Abbot of Sallay, Richard, Abbot of Selby, and many others.* In 1267 we have an interesting record of a disturbance that arose from some of the Abbot of Rievaulx' cattle, which were pasturing at Harden, having strayed to the other side of the beck, and were consequently in the parish of Bradford. Some men of Bradford were ordered to impound the cattle, but a number of the Abbot's men from the Grange, including the forester of Harden, went down to prevent this being done, when a free fight seems to have taken place. During the melée one, William Chirichek, raised his bow and deliberately shot the Harden forester, who a few weeks afterwards died. Chirichek went to the house of John Bullok, at Gilstead, but on hearing of Adam, the forester's death, he absconded, and he was therefore ordered to be outlawed.† This happened in 1267, and if the deed took place in Bingley, which is doubtful, it is the only record of a murder committed within the parish of Bingley up to 1862 (*see* page 253).

The manor of Harden was retained by Rievaulx Abbey until the suppression of monasteries. Then in 1540—Harden Grange at that time being tenanted by John Milner‡—it was granted to Walter Paslew, of Riddlesden (*see* page 309), and by fine dated Easter Term, 16th Eliz. (1573), it passed from the Paslews to Martin Birkhead, gent., whose son, Nathaniel Birkhead, in 1636 sold the Grange estate to Robert Ferrand. The latter made the Grange his residence, placing the family arms over the entrance, with the following quaint inscription, which still exists, as shewn in the accompanying plate :—

If thou a house shalt finde
Built to thy mynde,
And that without thy cost ;
Serve thou the more
God and the poore,
And then my labour is not loste.

* From the *Rievaulx Chartulary* it appears that the canons of Bolton Priory had held one bovate of land in Harden, of the gift of Adam, son of Peter de Birkin, which was afterwards absorbed in the local possessions of Rievaulx.

† *See Yorks. Archl. Journal* (Record Series), xvii., 177.

‡ *See Bradford Antiquary*, 1896, page 23.

Old Harden Grange (near the present St. Ives).

These lines by George Herbert were placed over the doorway probably in compliment to the Lady Anne Clifford, who married in 1630 Phillip Herbert, Earl of Pembroke and Montgomery; the poet being his kinsman and chaplain. For their loyalty to the house of Clifford the Ferrands owed their advancement; the family arms having been ratified and confirmed in 1586 at the request of Francis, Lord Clifford, afterwards Earl of Cumberland. Their arms are: *Argent*, on a chief, *gules*, two crosses flory, *vair*, a cinquefoil *azure*, for difference; crest: on a wreath of the colours, a cubit arm, *vair*, charged with a cinquefoil, *gules*, in the hand a battle-axe proper.

One of the Ferrands, referred to on page 120, displayed great bravery during the Crusade against the Saracens in 1190. He was probably a knight in the pay of the Earls of Albemarle, who on their accession to the manor of Skipton about this time made Hugh Ferrand janitor, or custodian, of the gate of Skipton Castle, an important post, which continued hereditary with the Ferrands for several centuries afterwards. William de Fortibus, Earl of Albemarle, died in 1195, and his grandson in 1280 contested the right of Hugo Ferrand to this office, but it was confirmed to the latter. So late as 1616 a Thomas Ferrand is mentioned as "steward of Skipton Castle."

The Ferrands of Bingley are descended from this family, and have been resident in this parish from about the middle of the sixteenth century; but the first who is mentioned as of St. Ives is Benjamin Ferrand, who was born in 1676, and died in 1731. The manor of Harden, however, is but a recent acquisition of the family; having been purchased, with the Marley Hall estate, in 1841 from Thomas G. Parker, Esq., for the sum of £17,300.

On the death of the above-mentioned Robert Ferrand, in 1712, his son, Benjamin Ferrand, removed to St. Ives (now Harden Grange), in the valley below, and his successors continued to reside there. Major Walker Ferrand, M.P. for Tralee, who was born in 1780, and who resided thirty years at Harden Grange, expended large sums upon ornamental grounds and additions to the house, so that when his nephew, Mr. William Busfeild-Ferrand, succeeded to the estates in 1854, he determined to make it again the family seat. With that view he, too, added considerably to the place, and completed the handsome front elevation the house now presents. The name of St. Ives was at the same time substituted for that of Harden Grange. Of the original St. Ives mansion, which formed the residence of Benjamin Ferrand, who died in 1731, not a trace exists. His only son, Benjamin Ferrand (1730—1803), rebuilt the house in 1759; this date and his initials being retained over a modern porch at the present mansion. There is a remarkable story remembered of this Benjamin Ferrand, who was a Major of Militia for the West Riding. On account of ill-health he went to Buxton, and after remaining there some time, being sufficiently recovered, he decided to return home. As he was riding over the Buxton Moors he was suddenly taken ill, and had to be removed to the well-known hostelry, the *Cat and Fiddle*, reputed to be the highest inn in England, where he passed away. On the night of his death, October 20th, 1803, as some servants of Dr. Hartley were walking from Harden homewards they perceived the familiar figure of the Major, mounted on his white pony, at the entrance to St. Ives, and they ran to open the gates for him. On their reaching the school-house, they told their master that the Major had returned home, and nothing was thought of the matter until some days afterwards, when it transpired that the old Major had died that very night! The incident was a good deal talked about at the time, and the venerable Earl of Cranbrook, who used to visit St. Ives when a boy, tells me that the ghost of Major Ferrand was at that day well remembered.

The old house (St. Ives) was taken down in 1859, with the exception of that portion which formed the domestic offices. This was permitted to stand, with a view to its being converted into a homestead for the tenant of the land, and for a few years as such it was occupied. The house is beautifully situated upon an elevated site, enclosed in a fine park, and commanding a lovely view of the valley (*see* page 146). Mr. Walter Dunlop, a Bradford merchant, proposed to take the place upon lease, provided a suitable house was erected incorporating the old remaining portion of the previous building. This was agreed to by the owner, and resulted in the handsome residence which now exists, called Harden Grange, and where Mr. Dunlop, who is a magistrate of the West Riding, has continued to reside now for more than thirty years.

The present mansion of St. Ives, which adjoins the old Harden Grange above referred to, is a large rectangular mansion of stone, having a frontage to the east of 196 feet, while on the west it measures 157 feet, and on the south 86 feet. (*See* the illustration prefacing this chapter.) The extensive prospect of wood and dale from some parts of the grounds is extremely beautiful, and seen in its summer luxuriance is certainly not surpassed by any Yorkshire landscape. The interior of the mansion contains many handsome rooms, beautifully furnished, and adorned with numerous family portraits and other works of art. The gardens and conservatories adjoining contain a choice variety of plants; the whole being kept in admirable order. A park of considerable extent surrounds the mansion; some of the trees, notably the beeches, being conspicuous for their noble proportions and luxuriant foliage. On the north side, at the top of the park, bounded by bracken-covered fells and margined with trees and rocks, is a fine sweep of lake, fed by natural springs, yet nowhere more than ten feet deep. The water is deliciously clear and bright, and is the haunt of various wild fowl, including teal, coot, heron, and wild duck. Close by is a small enclosed reservoir, which supplies the house with water. At the west end of the mansion towers a fine Lombardy poplar, and near it is a summer-house (shewn in the illustration), which contains the stone table referred to on page 139. A large bell nearly two centuries old is kept here. It is inscribed: "Robert Farrand, 1705." At the west end of the garden is a singularly-formed receptacle, hewn out of the solid rock, and in shape like a coffin, six feet long and three feet deep. Stone coffins went out of use towards the end of the 15th century, but the monks of Rievaulx Abbey held the estate and had the adjoining Grange, as already stated, from about A.D. 1200 to 1536.

On the death of Benjamin Ferrand in 1803, his kinsman, Edward Ferrand, who was born at Barnard Castle in 1777, succeeded to the family estates. He was a man of singularly amiable character, distinguished through life by his kind acts and gentleness of temper. He died in 1837, leaving an only daughter, Frances, who married in 1840 R. Paul Amphlett, Esq., Q.C., J.P., and D.L., of Wychbold Hall, Worcestershire. He was M.P. for East Worcestershire in 1868; appointed a Baron of the Court of Exchequer in January, 1874; and knighted by the Queen in January, 1875. Their only child, William Ferrand Amphlett, died in infancy. On the death of her brothers, Edward and Walker Ferrand, without male issue, Sarah, widow of Currer Fothergill Busfeild, of Cottingley Bridge, brother of William Busfeild, M.P. for Bradford, succeeded to the family estates, and assumed by sign manual her paternal name and arms of Ferrand, in compliance with the testamentary injunction of her relative, Benjamin Ferrand. She died in 1854, and was the last of the Ferrands to reside at the old St. Ives.

William Busfeild, Esq., her eldest son, who was born at Cottingley Bridge, 26th April, 1809, succeeded to the property, and in 1839 assumed by sign manual the surname and arms of Ferrand, in addition to those of Busfeild. The arms of Busfeild are these:—

Argent, a chevron invected *gules*, *gutté d'eau*, between three fleurs-de-lis *vert*. In the centre chief point a saltire couped of the second. Crest, on a wreath of the colours, a cubit arm in armour, proper, charged with a saltire as in the arms, holding in the hand, proper, a fleur-de-lis within an annulet, or.*

Mr. Ferrand at the time of his mother's death was living at Harden Grange, and was well-known through his long and prominent connection with this district. To a former generation he is best remembered by the name of Busfeild-Ferrand, and as a young man he was known as Mr. Busfeild, Jun., by way of distinction from his uncle, Mr. William Busfeild, of Upwood. He was endowed with

* This does not correspond exactly with the arms of Busfeild on the old hatchment in the Parish Church, but the above is the authorised coat.

a more than ordinarily vigorous constitution, and was conspicuously energetic in most things that he took up. I have spoken of the active part he took in suppressing the Chartist riots, and in various other ways he distinguished himself by his wise counsel and firm ruling. For many years, until the infirmity of deafness, with which he was afflicted during his later years, caused him to retire, he

Mr. William Busfeild-Ferrand.

was chairman of the Bingley Bench of Magistrates. Besides being a J.P. and D.L., he in 1841 obtained a seat in Parliament, as colleague of Mr. Andrew Lawson in the representation of Knaresborough. He took an active part in support of the Ten Hours Factory Bill, and assisted in carrying it through the House of Commons. He also brought under notice the iniquities of the Truck system, and a stringent law was passed to compel the payment of wages in the current coin of the realm. He vigorously exposed the harsh clauses of the new Poor Law until they were removed from the statute book, and he was the firm denouncer of all corruption among public men. Three times he unsuccessfully contested Devonport, in 1859, and two bye-elections in the same year. On a fourth occasion, however, he was more successful, gaining the seat in 1863. He was again returned at the election of 1865, but was unseated on petition, in consequence of his agent, without his knowledge and against his express wishes, having paid to the dockyards-men who voted, a day's wages in accordance with a custom which had long prevailed. After another unsuccessful effort to regain his seat in 1868, Mr. Ferrand finally retired from the field.

Mr. Ferrand was twice married—(1) in 1831 to Sarah, daughter of John Priestley, Esq., by whom he had issue, a son, William Ferrand, who died unmarried in 1865, and a daughter, Sarah Harriette Lilla, married in 1855 to Edward Hailstone, Esq., F.S.A.; (2) in 1847 Fanny Mary, second daughter of the eleventh Lord Blantyre, by whom he had a son, Hugo Ferrand, who died unmarried in 1877. The last-mentioned Mrs. Ferrand, who died in 1896, was aunt to Mrs. William Henry Gladstone, whose son, William Glynne Charles Gladstone, is heir to the Hawarden estates, so well known as the property and seat of the lately-deceased ex-Premier, the Right Hon. W. E. Gladstone. Mr. Ferrand died on March 31st, 1889, in his 80th year, and was interred in Bingley Cemetery.

His nephew, Mr. William Busfeild, only surviving son of Mr. Johnson Atkinson Busfeild, of Upwood, younger brother of Mr. Ferrand, of St. Ives, on becoming the devisee under his uncle's will, assumed by royal licence, dated March 18th, 1890, the surname and arms of Ferrand, in lieu of Busfeild. Previous to coming to St. Ives he had resided at Morland Hall, Westmorland, and for many years has been a magistrate of that county. He is also a J.P. and D.L. for the West Riding. He married, April 19th, 1865, Emily, youngest daughter of Alfred Harris, Esq., D.L., and J.P., who then resided at Ryshworth Hall, Bingley, and had issue: William Harris Busfeild, now Ferrand, late Lieutenant of the Yorkshire Artillery Militia, who married in 1897 Constance, second daughter of Colonel The Hon. Augustus Murray Cathcart, of Mowbray House, Ripon; Emily Mary, and Guy Ferrand. Mrs. Busfeild died July 16th, 1881, and Mr. Busfeild married, secondly, September 26th, 1883, Florence Annie Letitia, eldest daughter of the Hon. Amias Charles Orde-Powlett, younger brother of the third Lord Bolton, by whom he has issue: Amias William Powlett, Stafford Hubert, Florence Marjorie, and Hermione Monica. Mr. Ferrand regularly attends the Bingley Bench of Magistrates, of which he is chairman, and although taking no active part in the public life of the country, he has always identified himself with most movements for the welfare of the town and neighbourhood; while Mrs. Ferrand has been not less conspicuous for the excellent help she has rendered in many good works for the benefit of the parish, especially in connection with the church. In addition to owning extensive properties in the townships of Bingley and Wilsden, Mr. Ferrand is lord of the manors of Harden, Marley, Cottingley, Crossley, and Allerton-cum-Wilsden. He owns about half the land in the parish of Bingley, his estates comprising an area of about 6,000 acres, and include fine ranges of moorland, woodland, and pasture. Through his kind indulgence the present writer has had access to all portions of the estates, which privilege and the many transcripts he has been courteously permitted to make from the records at St. Ives (*see* page 335) have been invaluable in the preparation of this work.

In addition to the family and other memorials, there are preserved at St. Ives many local and other relics, besides various public and private souvenirs of great interest and beauty. Among them is an exquisitely-designed silver Grecian Vase on pedestal, bearing an inscription that it was presented to W. Ferrand, Esq., of St. Ives, Bingley, by 2,539 contributors of the working-classes of the borough of Devonport and township of East Stonehouse as "a token of their high esteem" to promote their welfare; also a Gold Casket, containing an address, presented to the same Mr. Ferrand by the Dublin Protestant Operatives' Association and Reformation Society in 1844. Another interesting object is a gilt spur, supposed to have been worn by Richard III., found in the land adjoining the court-yard of Middleham Castle, which was left with a number of other curios to the present Mrs. Ferrand by her late great-uncle, Thomas Topham, Esq., of Middleham (*see* the author's *Richmondshire*).

Woodbank.

Leaving St. Ives and Harden Grange, and proceeding a little higher up the valley, we arrive at the picturesque old homestead of Woodbank, which has many interesting associations, including visits from John Ruskin and Dante Gabriel Rossetti. The old house lies in a beautifully sequestered dell, where in the design of the surrounding grounds Nature has lent herself admirably to the hand of Art. Most attractive it is in the early summer when the lawn is a carpet of wild daisies and the rhododendrons are swelling with bloom; the pleasantly-wooded gardens below, watered by a natural stream, which has been utilised in the formation of an ornamental lake, with a luxuriant background on the opposite side of the valley of native woodland, from which the voice of the cuckoo may at this season often be heard, make up a charming picture. In the gardens is a fine peach-tree, about thirty feet high, and of proportionate girth, which bears fruit—an unusual sight in Airedale.

The gardens and grounds were designed and planted by the late Mr. John Aldam Heaton, who took the place in May, 1860. For many years before that time it had been a farmhouse belonging to the St. Ives estate, but on Mr. Heaton entering into possession he was allowed a free hand as regards alterations and improvements both in the house and grounds. Mr. Heaton was an artistic decorator by profession, and several specimens of his skill may be seen in Bradford churches, while his secular work includes the decoration of many large mansions and other residences in Yorkshire and elsewhere. He also designed a great quantity of furniture, wall-papers, carpets, and

Woodbank, Harden.

stained-glass, and in early life he became intimate with some of the pre-Raphaelite leaders, with whose ideas he was largely in sympathy. Dante Gabriel Rossetti in the year 1861 spent a month as his guest at Woodbank, and while there painted Mrs. Heaton's portrait, which is referred to in the second volume of Rossetti's *Letters and Memoir*. It has been several times stated that Rossetti did some decorative painting at Woodbank, including the design and lettering from the *Song of Solomon* in the summer-house; but I have been assured by Mr. Heaton that this is not correct. It was entirely his own.

John Ruskin, the distinguished art critic, also visited Woodbank, as the guest of Mr. Heaton, on April 22nd, 1864. He had been lecturing at Bradford (*see* "Crown of Wild Olive") and stayed two nights with Mr. Alfred Harris, at Ashfield, Bingley. Mr. Heaton remained at Woodbank till 1876, when he removed to London, and carried on his business with much success until the time of his death, which occurred on November 20th, 1897, aged 67. He was the son of Mr. John Heaton, a Leeds merchant, whose father, Benjamin Heaton, came from Haworth. At one time Mr. J. Aldam Heaton was a manufacturer in Bradford, at Beehive Mill, in Thornton Road; but his artistic tastes eventually led him to take up, as stated, the profession of a practical designer and decorator. He was one of the principal promoters of the School of Art Needlework at South Kensington, and was author of several works on the subject of art and decoration. His book on *Furniture Decoration in the Eighteenth Century*, published in two folio volumes (1889), is regarded as the first authority on the subject. He was also a skilful painter in water-colours, and several times his work found a place in the exhibitions at the Royal Academy. One of these was a view in the Harden valley, commanded by St. Ives, which he painted as a present for the late Mrs. Ferrand, and which had the merit of being hung at the Academy nearly on the line. An illustrated article on Mr. Heaton and his work will be found in *The Artist* for March, 1897.

The house is inscribed over the front door with the

letters and date, "S.F., M.F., Bt. 1685," which are the initials of Stephen Ferrand and his wife, Mary, whose maiden name was Walters. The "Bt." stands for "built," the house having been erected especially to receive the newly-wedded pair. After Mr. Heaton left it, the house was occupied by the Flemings, and subsequently by Mr. Herbert Sharp and Mr. Harold Dawson. The present tenant since May, 1896, is Mr. George Bertram Bulmer, of Leeds, who is author of a beautifully-illustrated work entitled *Architectural Studies in Yorkshire* (1887), and also *Historical Notes of the Baronial House of Bulmer*, privately printed.

Long might I dwell in and around the pleasantly-situated village of Harden, narrating the story of its progress from the far-off days of the Conqueror, when it was called Hateltun and Heldetone, which may mean either "battle-place" or "Hilda's-place," as explained on pages 64 and 148. But this volume must perforce end soon.

At Cockroft Fold*, a picturesque cluster of buildings by

* In a release, dated 17th October, 1655, from Henry Paslewe to John Cockroft and others, all claim is ceded by the said Henry Paslewe to the said John Cockroft, &c., of all lands, &c., in Harden then in their peaceable possession. Probably this has reference to the origin of the name Cockroft Fold.

the way-side before we reach the village of Harden, lived the Bowers for nearly two centuries up to 1875. About a century ago this property belonged to Mrs. Sarah Rhodes, and Miles Staveley, Esq., of Stainley (*see* page 301), who leased it to the Bowers, together with about eleven acres of the adjoining land. The Bowers were successful village cobblers, and made boots and shoes for all the country side. What has been said of the shoemakers' craft and their patron saint might aptly be said of them :—

Cobblers from Crispin boast their public spirit,
And all are upright, downright men of merit.

Jonas Bower, father of the brothers John, Jonas, and Thomas Bower, the latter now chairman of the Bingley Burial Board, was born at Cockroft Fold in 1792. His father, John Bower, married Rose Ackroyd, of Haworth, whose sister, "Tabby," was the well-known nurse of the Brontës. John Bower, currier, of Bingley, tells me he well remembers as a boy, now more than sixty years ago, going with his father, Jonas, on a visit to "Aunt Tabby" at the Haworth parsonage. She presented him with a couple of Branwell's linen shirts, which he had out-grown, and which the lad Bower wore with great pride, as they were a cut above the ordinary village wear of that time.

Jonas Bower (1792-1864) married Mary, sister of John Nicholson, the Airedale poet, who in the year 1822 lived at Harden Beck, in Low Fold, in the second house from the road. The old malt-kiln here, the subject of one of Nicholson's poetical efforts, has long ago disappeared. John's brother, William Nicholson, also lived at Harden, and married Elizabeth Bailey. He had several daughters, one of whom, Ann, married Thomas Robinson, who had property at Harden, including the *Fleece* inn and houses adjoining; another, Sarah, married John Pickles, whose daughter, Ellen, married (1) Arthur John C. Watmuff, son of Samuel Watmuff; and (2) John Barron, now of Claremont, Bingley.

The worsted-mill at Harden, for many years run by Messrs. Walter Milligan & Son, was purchased about 1865 by Mr. Samuel Watmuff, who considerably enlarged the premises, carrying on business here for about thirty years, and employing most of the inhabitants. Mr. Watmuff lived in the house at Harden now occupied by Mr. John Haggas, chairman of the Bingley School Board, whose father was elder brother of James Haggas, of Keighley, who died April 28th, 1864, and who in 1825 married Ann Moorhouse (*see* page 140). Messrs. Haggas are the present owners and occupants of Harden Mills.

Mr. Watmuff in 1868 built the large house formerly occupied by Mr. John Gatecliff, which adjoins the old, low-standing farm-house at Low Cliff. The latter was the

Low Cliff, Harden.

home of Jonas Sharp and his brothers, William, &c., in the early part of the century. William Sharp married Mary, daughter of Henry Pickles, of Jackfield. She was a sister of William Pickles, who had the old Cockroft Corn Mill about the year 1845. He afterwards lived at Low Cliff. The old house has the initials H.M. R.M. over the door, and an almost obliterated date, probably 1692—some say 1592. It was built by a Midgley. One of the family, John

Midgley, who died in 1746, aged 82, lived at Ryecroft, where his initials, and the date 1748, may be seen over a barn belonging the picturesque old farm now occupied by Mr. James Clayton. David Midgley, of Low Cliff, married Martha Jennings, of Streamheads, Thornton, and, I am told, received by his marriage a farm at Thornton and one hundred spade guineas. His family was David, Jonas (who settled in Ireland), and a daughter, who died young. David had several sons, one of whom, Richard, was the father of William Midgley, of Eldwick (*see* page 262).

The adjoining picturesque glen, called Deep Cliff, is doubtless the "Cipping Clive" mentioned in the Patent Rolls of 6th Edward III. (1822). The scenery in and around this rugged, well-wooded gorge is very romantic, and from its eastern margin spread fine heather and bilberry moors, forming part of the St. Ives estate.

The beautiful church (St. Saviour's) at Harden was consecrated by the Bishop of Ripon on September 24th, 1892. The site, which adjoins the Haworth road, was given by Mr. Ferrand, of St. Ives, and the cost of the building, exclusive of special gifts, was about £2,800. It is in the Early English style, and has seat room for 250 persons. The Wesleyan Chapel was erected in 1818, mainly through the efforts of the Sharp family, many of whom are buried in the adjoining grave-yard. Services had been previously conducted at Hill End and other houses in the neighbourhood. The chapel has since been enlarged and beautified. The Independents have also a handsome and substantial place of worship in the village; erected in 1865 on the site of a previous one which was built in 1838. The Primitive Methodists have a chapel at Ryecroft, and it is worthy of record that this local body has produced many first-class singers and musicians of no small note. Thomas Windle, who is an octogenarian, still living there, has been leader of the singing choir at Ryecroft for nearly sixty years; while his son, Edward Windle, of Burnley, possesses the musical faculty in a high degree, and has composed the music of numerous well-known hymns and anthems. Robert Holmes, originally a hand-loom weaver, and afterwards a schoolmaster, is a native of Ryecroft, and author of *Heirs of a Farmstead* (1858), a work of considerable merit, and full of local colouring. Mrs. Jane Shackleton was also a local authoress of good repute. Her maiden name was Atkinson, and she was a niece of Mr. William Atkinson, of Ryecroft. Some of her poems are written under the *nom de plume* of "Jenny Wren."

Around Harden there are other old homesteads of interest in addition to those already mentioned. Harden Hall, erected by the Ferrands in 1616, is snugly placed in a charming situation about half-a-mile south of the village. On one of the buildings appear the initials $\text{B.}^{\text{F.}}\text{M.}$ and date 1650. The letters stand for Benjamin and Martha Ferrand, both of whom died in 1699. One of their daughters, Lydia, born 1652, married in 1694 Thomas Whaley, of Winterburn, whose daughter, Abigail, married at Giggleswick, in 1715, Christopher, son of Robert Inman, of the family of Inman, of Trans-Atlantic shipping fame (*see* the author's *Nidderdale*, page 480). She died in 1716, leaving an only child, Michael Inman, of Bewerley, born July 14th, 1716, and died in 1784. His son, Whaley Charles, sold property at Barnoldswick, Carlton, Bingley, &c., which had probably come into the family from the Ferrands of St. Ives. Michael Inman's uncle, Samuel Whaley, is described in his will as of St. Ives, Bingley.

It was at Harden Hall that the officers of Cromwell lodged when the Parliamentary army was encamped on Harden Moor, and the stone table (*see* page 139) on which the despatches were written was removed from here to St. Ives some years ago. Some old stone lanterns, similar to those at Beckfoot, have been placed at the gable corners of the house, implying that it was one of the properties of the Knights of St. John of Jerusalem (*see* page 128). The present house has always belonged to the Ferrands, and in the early part of the century it was tenanted by Joshua Anderson, a genuine specimen of the shrewd, careful, steady-going Yorkshireman, slow to move and sparing in speech. He farmed the adjoining land, and his nephew, generally known as Bill o' t' Beck, kept the *Malt Shovel* inn, afterwards taken by Abraham Foster, whose brother,

Harden Hall.

Joseph, had the *Sun* at Cottingley. Abraham's son, Joseph, had Shackleton House farm, and William, Joseph's brother, lived at and farmed the land attached to Brass Castle. He married Mary Nicholson, a niece of the poet, and his daughter, Elizabeth, is the wife of Mr. James Roberts, of the Knoll, Baildon.

Harden Hall was subsequently occupied by the Deans, and from 1865 to 1870 Mr. Michael Mahony was the tenant, he having previously resided at Goit Stock. He was brother to the Messrs. Mahony, owners of the extensive tweed factories at the well-known village of Blarney, near Cork. He was twice married, and his second wife was Mary, daughter of James Haggas, of Keighley, by his wife Ann Moorhouse, whose aunt, Nancy Moorhouse, married Richard Ayrton, whose daughter, Ellen, married William England, grandfather of Mr. Henry England, of Brass Castle, Harden (*see* page 140). Brass Castle was rebuilt by Benjamin Ferrand a century ago on the site of an older house. It is significant that all the so-called "Brass Castles" are in the vicinity of old Roman highways, and they may originally have been watch-towers or treasure-houses of the Roman legions. There is a Barass near the Roman road over Stainmoor, which may have the same meaning. Above Harden Hall is Ivy House, inscribed S.S., 1676, probably built by Samuel Sunderland, of Hill End.

While Mr. Mahony was at Harden Hall he kept a very fine breed of show pigs, and took many prizes. Harden at one time was famed for the number and excellence of these animals reared both for show and for the market. One of the largest and finest pigs ever seen in England was bred by William Smith, of Harden Beck, in 1797. At thirteen months old this remarkable animal scaled 770lbs., the lard alone weighing 6 stones 9lbs. The owner's son, William, was a butcher at Harden, and died in 1842, aged 75, and his son, Edward, is mentioned on page 51.

From Harden it is a charming walk through Mr. Ferrand's private grounds up the flower-strewn and beautifully tree-shaded Goit Stock valley as far as the waterfall; the latter, however, is not in Bingley, but in the township of Wilsden and old parish of Bradford (*see* WILSDEN). The partly-ruined and romantically-situated mill here was originally built by the Ferrands for Mr. Timothy Horsfall, who carried on cotton-spinning in it in the early part of the century, and lived in the good house adjoining.

Subsequently, about 1865, when the mill was abandoned, it was rented, together with about fifteen acres of land, by Mr. Henry Beldon, the celebrated poultry fancier, and one of the most successful exhibitors of poultry this country has ever known. Among his friends he was generally spoken of as "King Good Stock"; being a play upon the words Goit Stock. Mr. Beldon fit up a portion of the old mill with pens, and during the first twelve years he occupied the place was continuously sending valuable and rare birds to all the principal shows in the home countries, and there is no doubt he won more prizes than any exhibitor then living. He remained at Goit Stock till 1880.* He had been originally located at Gilstead, and bought there a stock of birds belonging to Mr. Job Rawnsley, who was his manager for nearly twelve years at Goit Stock. Mr. Rawnsley then in 1876 started on his own account, at Langley, above Priesthorpe, and for seventeen years he exhibited at all the leading shows, including the Crystal Palace, Birmingham, Leeds, Liverpool, &c., taking in the course of that period many thousands of prizes, and was accounted the most successful exhibitor in England. Mr. Rawnsley also built the Langley Kennels for show dogs. His famous bull-terrier, "Tarquin," won 49 prizes at various shows in three years, and his champion bull-terrier, "White Star," bought from Mr. Mackenzie, of Perth, for £30 when 2½ years old, obtained for Mr. Rawnsley 73 prizes in a little over four years (1884-8). The celebrated pedigree dog, "Langley John Bull," afterwards known as "Monkey Brand," was bred by Mr. Rawnsley at the Langley Kennels, and eventually this magnificent animal sold for £100. These famous kennels since 1894 have been occupied by the Bingley beagle-hounds.

* *See* the *Stock-Keeper* for September 25th, 1880, and February 12th, 1892.

Still ascending the picturesque valley, presently we reach more open ground, where are several other notable old homesteads, such as Hill End, Shackleton House (so-called from an old Quaker family of that name), and the high-perched little monastic hamlet of Ryecroft, which is mentioned in 1312 in a composition made between the monks of Rievaulx and Drax. Coming to Shackleton House first, the view expands as we approach, and looking backward in the summer evening light, how beautiful gleams the richly-forested vale of Harden, while swelling wood, meadow, and hill enclose the upland valley of Wilsden, with its scattered farms and long main street sweeping away to the south from the romantic edge of Birchlands, with its lingering memories of Charlotte Brontë! Shackleton House (long the home of the Fosters) was last tenanted by Mr. Thomas Foster, brother of William, of Brass Castle, and after his death in 1892 the old house was partly taken down for building some adjoining premises. Little is left now to attest its former busy days save the remains of an old stone bake-oven, such as was used in the time of the monasteries. The house has been a substantial Jacobean building, having long mullioned windows, similar to other houses of the same age in the parish. The door was of solid oak, well studded with nails, and there was a stone above it bearing the initials and date, $_{R.}{}^{S.}{}_{E.}$ 166- (figure obliterated). This stone and door in 1892 were given by Mr. Ferrand and removed to Ireland by Mr. George Shackleton, of Lucan, county Dublin, a descendant of the former owners.

The first known member of the family connected with the property was a John Shackleton, living in 1582, but from a very early period the family has been settled in Yorkshire, and the name, which is said to be of ancient Norse origin, is mentioned in *Domesday Book*. Richard Shackylton, of Keighley parish, was a bowman at Flodden Field in 1513. Early in the 17th century the Harden property was owned by a John Shackleton, whose eldest son, Roger, was baptised in Bingley Church in 1638. He inherited it (*see* "Fines," Easter Term, 1656), and settled it in 1675 on his only son, Richard, who was the first of this branch of the family to become a Quaker. Richard Shackleton suffered much both in person and property; being kept a prisoner for more than two years in York Castle for non-attendance at church, &c. Eventually in 1696 his house at Harden was licensed as a meeting-house for Quakers. Richard married Sarah, daughter of Thomas Brigg, of Calversyke Hill and Guard House, Keighley, and by her had several children; the fourth son, Roger, born in 1691, being a man of great character and influence. He prepared an address to the Secretary of State on behalf of the Quakers, which is still preserved in the British Museum, and in 1733 he was elected one of the sheriffs of York, but refusing to take the oath on conscientious grounds was fined £150.

Richard Shackleton's youngest son was Abraham, who was born at Harden, in 1696. He settled at Ballitore, a Quaker colony in Ireland, and founded there in 1726 the well-known classical academy at which so many eminent men were educated, and which is said to have been the means of removing much of the prejudice against the Quakers in Ireland. Abraham's son, Richard, born in 1726, was a man of great talent; being a skilful poet, and conversant with several languages. He was the friend of Edmund Burke, the renowned orator, who was educated at the Ballitore School. An interesting letter written by Burke to the Shackleton family on the death of Richard, in 1792, summarises in few words the character of this wise and good man, of whom many stories are related of his largeness of heart and charity to the poor:—

> I knew him from the boyish days in which we began to love each other. His talents were great, strong, and various; there was no art or science to which they were not sufficient in the contemplative life, nor any employment that they would not more than adequately fill in the active. Though his talents were not without that ambition which generally accompanies great natural endowments, it was kept under restraint by great wisdom and temperance of mind.

In 1748 he married Elizabeth, daughter of Henry Fuller, of Fullers' Court, Ballitore, by Deborah, daughter of John Barcroft, a descendant of the ancient family of Barcroft, of Barcroft Hall, Lancashire, and one of the founders of the village of Ballitore.* By this marriage he had a son, Abraham, born 1752, who succeeded his father in the management of the school. Richard married secondly, Elizabeth, daughter of Joshua Carleton, by whom he had a daughter, Mary, born in 1758, a lady eminent for her talents, and author of several volumes of prose and poetry. Abraham married Lydia, daughter of Ebenezer Mellor, by Margaret, daughter of John Abraham, of Swarthmoor Hall, and descendant of the Martyn Anne, daughter of Sir William Askew, of Kelsey, in Lincolnshire, who was burnt to death in 1546. From this marriage descend the Shackletons in Ireland, Sydenham, Watford, and Tunbridge Wells. Shackleton House continued in possession of the family till 1801, when it was sold to Benjamin Ferrand, Esq., of St. Ives.

A little beyond, on the crest of the road, and commanding a superb view, stands Hill End, which in its palmy days must have been thought a fine, large homestead, prepossessingly and substantially built, and even at this day retaining some traces of former elegance. So many interesting associations cling around this time-stained mansion that it might well have formed the subject of a separate volume. Here in the troubled days of Charles I. and the Commonwealth lived a merchant prince, Samuel Sunderland (*see* page 187), who died here in 1676, aged 76. The story of the great robbery and of the horses' shoes being reversed in order to mislead pursuers, has been so often told that I need not repeat it. In Parson's *History of the District of Leeds* it is erroneously stated to have taken place at Harden Hall instead of at Hill End. Mr. Sunderland's wife was a Waterhouse, but whether of the same family as old Mary Waterhouse, who died here in 1822, aged 103, I do not know.

Following the Sunderlands came a family of the name of Smith, the maternal progenitors of the late Archbishop of Canterbury, Dr. Edward White Benson, of revered memory, whose painfully sudden death on October 11th,

* Burke wrote some lines on Richard Shackleton's marriage. *See* the second volume of the *Annals of Ballitore*, containing chiefly letters from Burke to Shackleton.

Hill End, Harden.

1896, in the church at Hawarden, while on a visit to Mr. Gladstone, aroused the sympathy of the whole nation. I have spoken of the Archbishop's family connections with the Sidgwicks of Riddlesden, &c., and from the Smiths of Hill End he was lineally descended on the mother's side. Christopher Smith died at Hainworth in 1637 (will proved September 18th), and John Smith, late of Hainworth, was living at Hill End in 1708, and in that year bought lands, &c., of Jeremy Craven, of Steeton. James Smith, of Greave House, in the township of Midgley and parish of Halifax, followed him in the occupation of Hill End, and had three daughters: (1) Ann, married (1) the Rev. Henry Norminton and (2) Edward Benson, of Ripon (*see* the author's *Nidderdale*, page 444); (2) Betty, married Richard Hollins, of Ripon, a partner with Edward Benson in his wine business at York, &c.; (3) Mary, married her cousin, the Rev. Thomas Carr, of Bolton Abbey. Ann Smith, born at Hill End, was baptized at Bingley Church, March 23rd, 1741-2, and was married when quite a child, against her wish; being left a widow when barely out of her teens. With her second husband, Edward Benson, she lived happily until her death at York, where she is buried at the east end of St. Saviour's Church, in a vault by the side of her son John. Her eldest son, White Benson, grandfather of the Archbishop, was a Lieutenant in the 6th Royals, Warwickshire Regiment, commanded by Prince William, Duke of Gloucester, and served in the Irish rebellion of 1798. Some account of him will be found in my *History of Nidderdale*. He died in 1806, leaving an only son, Edward White Benson, father of the Archbishop, who was born in 1829, and married Mary Sidgwick.

By his wife Ann, from Hill End, Edward Benson had a family of four sons and three daughters. The eldest of the latter, Ann Dorothea, married, first, Thomas Skepper, attorney-at-law, who died in 1805, leaving one daughter, Ann Skepper, wife of the distinguished poet and author, Bryan Waller Procter ("Barry Cornwall,") whose talented daughter, Adelaide Ann Procter, died when quite young in 1889. Her second husband was Basil Montagu, son of Lord Sandwich, and a Chancery barrister of some note, the editor of Bacon's works, as well as of *Selections* from Taylor, Hooker, &c. The laureate poet Wordsworth was some time tutor to one of their sons.

This old Harden homestead is thus particularly interesting from its distinguished associations with the ancestry of the late Primate of All England, and had space permitted, many things concerning the family's connection with it might have been added. Of Mrs. Edward Benson's (Ann Smith, of Hill End) family much has been written in his usual vein by Thomas Carlyle in his *Reminiscences*.

At the back of Hill End a pleasant path skirts the plantation, passing Hunter Hill farm, and emerges on the open moor at the top of old Dolphin Lane (*see* page 80). Close by is the Catstones quarry, which has been worked for about fifteen years by Mr. Joseph Sunderland, who also rents from Mr. Ferrand the Hunter Hill farm. The Catstones entrenchment, elsewhere referred to, has got much filled up and overgrown with heather and bilberries, but is still well defined on its north and east sides. In outline it appears to have been an irregular quadrangle; on its east side the trench can be followed for about 320 yards, and on the north for 110 yards, where it is crossed by a stone fence, but is traceable for some distance in the grass field beyond. On the south it is obliterated by the quarry.

Dropping down to the picturesque locality of Cowhouse Bridge, we have here an old parcel of the possessions of Rievaulx Abbey, which in 1540, (then called Cowelhouses), was granted to Walter Paslew, of Riddlesden. Hand-spinning was carried on in a small way here in the premises adjoining the farm-house, at present tenanted by Mr. James Jowett. At the Low Fold, early in the century, the Sharps carried on business before they took Harden Mill, afterwards occupied by Messrs. Milligan and Watmuff. The long-established tanning business at Cowhouse was formerly carried on by Mr. Timothy Horsfall, of Goit Stock, who died in 1811, and whose grandson, Mr. John Horsfall, lived at Gawthorpe Hall. The tannery is now occupied by Mr. George Towler.

CULLINGWORTH.

IF large open spaces, high situation, and fresh moorland breezes keep a locality healthy, Cullingworth should be one of the most salubrious places in the whole county of York. Its principal street runs up to about 600 feet above sea-level, and from it looking eastward there is a fine uninterrupted view of the leafy Harden valley, backed by the rugged heights of Gilstead, while westwards and northwards range the grand hills and open moors surrounding the famous little town of Haworth.

I have pictured on page 62 evidence of the early colonization of the district, when the native Britons fled to the hills and moors before the Anglian conquerors, who afterwards amalgamated with them, or left the old Celt to perish in dreary isolation. When the Normans came and made their great survey in 1083-6, Cullingworth then spelled Colingauuorde, was with Hainworth a separate manor, held with the manor of Bingley by Erneis de Burun (*see* page 104), and forming part of the great parish of Bingley, to which it has ever since been attached. It owes its name doubtless to some Anglian settler *(Col)*, who with his family *(ing)* was established on a farm, house, or hall *(worth)* before the Norman inrush. The affix *worth*, equivalent to the Celtic *garad* (a guard or enclosure), is frequent on this side of our parish, as in Oakworth, Hainworth, Haworth, &c., while the tributary dale extending from Keighley to the western moorlands is called Worth Valley, no doubt from its being colonized by the Anglo-Saxons on the Celtic conquest.

At an early period grants of land, &c., in Cullingworth were made to various religious houses, including the Knights of St. John of Jerusalem, the Nunneries of Esholt and Kirklees, but chiefly to the Abbey of Rievaulx, to which Robert de Meynill gave nine bovates of land, with the appurtenances, in Cullingworth, and a moiety of the mill within the township, with the appurtenances, and of his men of the said township, with their families and chattels. Another instance of old Norman serfdom, of the buying and selling of slaves; the lords of the soil having power of disposal over the bodies of their tenants, born and unborn, to be sold or, as at Cullingworth, given away with their moveable goods.

After living in holes,* caves, and mud huts, the people began to build houses of stone, at first unmortared and with roofs of thatch, and it is really surprising how slow progress has been in this respect; what small improvements have been made in the course of centuries in the habitations, especially of the rural poor. Many old houses, single-deckers, dry-walled, or mud-plastered, and rough-thatched, remained in the parish until within present recollection, in striking contrast with the improved, well-furnished, farm-houses and dwellings of the working-classes at the present day.

Besides the sturdy old Hall little now remains to remind one of Cullingworth in ancient times. Improvements and alterations have been many during recent years, and one by one the old landmarks are fast disappearing. Opposite the old Hall just referred to, the street—a very ancient thoroughfare—is being widened, and the accompanying view, from a photograph kindly taken for this work by the Rev. T. Mellodey, the vicar, pictures another lately-bygone fragment of old Cullingworth linking the present with the past. We gather from Mr. Cudworth that there are people still living who can remember Cullingworth containing but thirty-eight habitations, all-told; the village street consisting of eight farm-houses, four on each side, and a few cottages. An Act for enclosing common-land was obtained in 1808, and this gave something of a stimulus to industry, followed by the introduction of the worsted trade into the district, and the consequent increase in the number of houses. From very small beginnings the business of Messrs. Townend increased until extensive and

* At Eller Carr is a large stone covering the entrance to an old cave, called Mootham, but no one knows why. It has probably been a habitation, and the name may be from the A.S. *múth* (a mouth) and *ham*, *heim* (a home or shelter).

well-built mills rose beside the village, a wonderful pile truly, making the old folks look with amazement on this formidable encroachment on the wonted tranquillity of their moorland home. At one time these mills gave employment to fully 800 people. On Messrs. Townend giving up, the mills were worked with marked success for about four years by Mr. Clarendon Willey, and then, eight or ten years ago, Messrs. J. J. Broadbent & Co., Limited, of Great Horton, started operations on a large

Old Houses, Cullingworth.

scale, pulling down old buildings to make way for new, and erecting a large number of dwelling-houses for their workpeople. Other employers in the worsted trade are Messrs. Walker & Greenwood, at Eller Carr Mills, which are most picturesquely situated near the miniature park. There are besides extensive stone-quarries in the village, worked by Mr. J. Clayton, who has also a mill for sawing and dressing stone.

In 1846 Cullingworth was made a separate ecclesiastical parish. A church, dedicated to St. John, was built and consecrated in 1853. The interior has since been thoroughly restored and renovated, and was re-opened on May 10th, 1874. Its structural and decorative features are now in admirable keeping with the rest of the building. It may be noted that the chancel is apsidal in form, after the style of the ancient Roman basilicæ, and it contains some beautiful stained-glass windows, erected to commemorate the Rev. J. H. Mitchell (vicar); Mr. George Henry Townend; Mr. Edward Holmes Hartley and his father and sister. The following have been vicars of the parish, with the dates of their induction :—

August, 1847—John Hollings Mitchell, M.A. Died June 21st, 1873.
7th Aug., 1873—Robert Stansfield. Resigned May 22nd, 1875.
6th July, 1875—Richard Cockrem, B.A. Died March 19th, 1877.
10th July, 1877—Thomas Mellodey, M.A. Present vicar.

The Baptists and Wesleyans have neat edifices here. The chapel of the former was built in 1837, and the Wesleyan Chapel was opened in 1825, and enlarged in 1861. Among the earlier adherents to the Methodist cause were the families of Rhodes, Hollingdrake, Crowther, Ellison, Northrop, Binns, Dixon, &c. The families of Hollingdrake, Ellison, and a few others have been located at Cullingworth for many centuries, and families of the name of Collyngworth also appear in the Poll Tax list of A.D. 1379, printed on page 131. The following are amongst the wills at York of old Cullingworth families, with the dates of probate :—

Dec. 18th, 1433, Hugh Colyngworth; May, 1639, Thomas Ellison: July 11th, 1544, William Fedder; Dec. 18th, 1517, John Hollyngrake; Nov., 1637, John Hollinrake; Sept. 4th, 1527, Jenet Holyngrake; Dec. 10th, 1553, Thomas Margatroyd; Nov. 7th, 1517, Robert Rodeley; Oct. 29th, 1558, Robert Hainworth; May 6th, 1557, William Lacoke; April 17th, 1567, John Threpland; Jan., 1636-7, William Waddington.

The walks and scenery around Cullingworth are extremely varied and picturesque. High moors and beautifully-wooded gills, with here and there an ancient homestead, give abundant interest and variety to a ramble in the district. A very pleasant upland walk is that by way of Brown Hill and Ivestones Bridge, and in the lane approaching Bleak House, the nurseries of Mr. C. Kershaw, is the ancient Castlestead entrenchment, (originally 260 yards in circumference), mentioned on page 62. Another ramble may be enjoyed by taking the lane near the railway-station bridge by way of Fieldhead Farm, an old house bearing the initials and date R.V., 1684, and now in the occupation of Mr. Hugh Ellison. Thence through the fields by Sugden Houses, or through the romantic Sugden Nick to Cross Roads and Haworth. Eastward, the walk by old Hallas Hall is also interesting. The picturesque Hallas Beck, Hallas Bridge, and Hallas Mills are all close by; a locality that has borne the name of Hallas from time immemorial, and which may be a curtailment of Hallows in reference to the monastic ownership previously referred to. In the fines for 1572 it is described as the manor of Hallowes. The Andertons were long associated with this and the adjoining Bents Mill property. The old Hallas Bridge Mill, in a deeply-wooded dell, and the neighbouring cottages were lately the property of Mr. Solomon Brear, who died about a year ago. He came from Doncaster, and was a noted horse-breeder, having sometimes as many as forty pedigree hackneys in his stud at Hallas Mill. The mill was burnt down in the winter of 1895, and subsequently the ponderous water-wheel, weighing about twenty tons, was sold at the price of old iron, and in removing it a man named John Horton, of Calderhebble, near Halifax, met with a shocking death through the wheel setting in motion and catching him between the iron buckets and the front of the pen-trough. Horton was an old soldier, and had fought through the Indian Mutiny and the Crimean War.

At Eller Carr, previously referred to, there has been a substantial farm-house for many centuries. Francis Paslewe demised the house and land to John Wilson, of Woodhouse, and soon after, in 1549, it passed to his brother, William Wilson, a glover, of Harden, who died in 1618. A daughter of this Wilson married Richard Whitaker, whose family afterwards possessed the property. It was then called Elder Carre.

WILSDEN.

ALTHOUGH Wilsden is not in Bingley parish, but in that of Bradford, and formerly in the old chapelry of Thornton, yet it is in so many ways associated with Bingley that a brief notice of it will doubtless be looked for. The picturesque Hallas Wood scenery, with the famous Goit Stock waterfall, are in this township, though generally believed to be in Bingley. Looking round the district, one may feel surprise that Wilsden has not become a popular health resort in these days of tourist development, when so many townsfolk are on the look out for pleasant places of recuperation and rest. The bracing uplands of Wilsden, with their romantic surroundings, are just the places where the city-dweller would be likely to receive most benefit to both body and mind. I have heard it said that a whiff of pure highland air on the grand edge of Birchlands—commanding one of the finest views in Yorkshire—is as exhilarating as a draught of champagne. The village is within three miles of Bingley, five of Haworth, (the home of the Brontës), and the walks in almost every direction possess some interest.

The broken and diversified character of the scenery is due in great measure to several faults or throws and subsidences in the strata, which traverse the district in different directions, and belong to the great system of Pennine faults, which become less frequent as we travel northwards and eastwards to and beyond Bingley. The principal of these local "earth-shocks" is an extension of the Deep Cliff fault, which passes Harden Hall, and then pursuing a south-easterly course runs along the bank, parallel with the road which ascends from Bent's Foot to Wilsden. Evidences of the action of mighty glaciers are also present in the district, and boulders of encrinital and other limestones have been dug out in draining the main street.

The name of Wilsden I have explained on page 63, but the name is erroneously printed Willesden (though in the Poll Tax of A.D. 1379, it is spelled Wyllesden) like the place of that name near London. It should be Wilsedene, an effort apparently on the part of a Norman scribe to interpret the A.S. *Wéalhas*, as Walise (now Wales), a *Domesday*, manor, near Rotherham, and perhaps Wilsenden, an ancient hamlet in the parish of Penistone, now corrupted to Windleden.* There is ample evidence of the pre-Norman occupation of Wilsden, where ancient Briton and Angle have dwelt upon its once wild uplands.

> There hills abound on ev'ry side,
> And moors wide-stretching far—
> Here traits of Romans still abide,
> And signs of long-past war,

as Mr. Æthelbert Binns, an interested and well-known local writer, expresses it. There are prehistoric earthworks at Catstones, Castlestead, and at Moot Hill, near Hewenden (*see* page 65). There is, by the way, an ancient Moot Hill at Birstall, and a Catstones on Pennythorn Hill, Baildon; likewise a Catstones on Burn Moor, between Clapham and Bolland. There is a Burn Moor at Wilsden, and though its original aspects are now long forgotten, I have little doubt that it was the scene of similar earthworks, circles, and tumuli as exist at other places bearing the same name. Places of this name, or compounded with *burn*, I venture to assert, have in Yorkshire nothing to do with the Scottish and Northumbrian word for a stream as always stated. In Scandinavian Yorkshire all streams are *becks*, and the word *burn* is never used in these parts for a stream or brook. Thus it will, I think, invariably be found that these "burns" are associated with prehistoric works, and an illustration is offered in the old line of forts extending possibly from Black*burn* direct north-east by

* In the *Wilsden Almanac* for 1890 a derivation from the personal name *Will* is suggested, but the *Domesday* spelling is an obvious attempt to interpret a *three-syllabled* word, which *Wills-dene* is not. *Will* I may further add, is Anglo-Saxon for *a well*, and had the unrivalled spring at Manywells (in the fines for 1572 spelled Manywelles), Hewenden, been in Wilsden one might easily have explained its meaning by that.

Chat*burn*, Gis*burn* (Castle Howe), Otter*burn* (Howber), to Winter*burn* (Scarnber). Borans, Burwens, and Burrence seem to have the same meaning. Part of the Roman *Colonio* (Colne) is built upon a site called Burwains, and at Elslack is a large mound called Burwens, where I have often heard a tradition of a vanished castle and spectre knight.

Several ancient legends are still current about Wilsden, and one of them, recorded in the *Wilsden Almanac* for 1892, is of a supposed sorceress or witch, who is believed to haunt the steep picturesque lane which descends to Hallas Bridge on the Cullingworth side of the beck. She is traditionally said to be coming down the hill at the cautious pace of *seven stree (straw) breeadths i' t' year*, and when at last she reaches the bridge, woe betide any person or house that may then be upon the hill, for by one magic wave of her hand the hill will vanish, and of course everything upon it!

The Goit Stock waterfall, already mentioned, is situated on the beck a little below Hallas Bridge, in Mr. Ferrand's private grounds. It is a beautiful, retired spot, the white-crested water falling over a hard rocky cliff, about twenty feet high, into a deep pool below, the whole embosomed in a luxuriant and lofty screen of trees, making a perfect fairy dell, which is sometimes lit up by the slanting sunbeams with charming effect. One might say of it in the words of "Jenny Wren," a local poetess:—

> I long to spend the short, bright hours
> Once more where the mellow sunlight pours
> In golden floods, over fairy bowers,
> Where it ripens the fruit and kisses the flowers,
> And the bursting buds.

The lofty banks and rocks around, in a hundred varied hues, are clothed with ferns, lichens, mosses, and expansive sheets of liverwort *(Pellia epiphylla)*, which are kept perpetually moist by the springs of water that are constantly trickling over them.

A delightful walk, especially in that sunny season when the "lark is singing in the blinding sky and the hedges are white with May," is along the well-known

Banks. There is here a massive flat stone called the Orange Rock, where Nicholson, the Airedale poet, wrote much of his "morning" poetry, including those beautiful lines on the *Return of the Swallow*. (*See* my *Airedale*, pages 177-8). Below we come to Bank Bottom and Mytholme, where the aspects are thoroughly rustic and quiescent. Around Hewenden the scenery is also very

GOIT STOCK WATERFALL.

romantic, and the famous Manywell Spring here need only be mentioned as one of the most copious in England. Hewenden viaduct (which the mountain railway from Keighley to Halifax crosses) is pictured at the end of this chapter.

Wilsden gave name to an ancient local family, and at an early period the monks of Byland and Kirkstall held lands in the township; in 1318 the Abbot of Byland being returned as lord of the manor of Allerton-cum-Wilsden, the two townships having been since the Norman Conquest parcels of one ownership. At the hamlet of Norr Green, Wilsden, is a row of cottages called Black Abbey, and a never-failing spring called the Abbey Well, while some Abbey lands comprised Norr Farm, as well as the farm at the top of Sykes' called Clara Mount and a field at the bottom of Coplaw Lane. In 1459 the Wilsden tenants of Kirkstall Abbey were John Threapland, John Wodhall, and John Woodd, as recorded in a rent-roll printed in the *Thoresby Society's Publications*.

The manor of Allerton-cum-Wilsden eventually passed from the Bollings to the Tempests, and in 1648 was mortgaged to and afterwards bought by the Marsdens, owners of the manor of Bradford. In 1795 John Marsden, of Hornby Castle, sold the same to Benjamin Ferrand, of St. Ives, and it now forms part of the family property belonging to Mr. Ferrand, of St. Ives. An old 17th century homestead at the bottom of the village, now occupied by Mr. T. Wilkinson, is known as the Manor House.

Allerton with Wilsden also forms one parish, having been separated from the chapelry of Thornton, in the large parish of Bradford, when the church of St. Matthew's, Wilsden, was built in 1825. It was erected under the "Million Act" at the same time as Shipley Church, and both were designed by the same architect, Mr. J. Oates. While the tower of the church was being built in July, 1825, a very unusual accident happened. A mason named Haughton was bending down at the foot of the tower, when a heavy stone was observed falling from the top; someone called out, and the man immediately stood up, and at the very instant the stone shaved past his head and fell sharply upon his foot, smashing it dreadfully. Believing the whole structure was falling, he leapt, maimed as he was, over an eight-foot fence which had been raised round the building!

The Methodists are an old and numerous body around Wilsden, and met for divine worship in various houses until their chapel was built in 1828. A better chapel was erected in 1847. The Independents date their origin from the year 1793, when a society was formed, and their first minister, the Rev. Joseph Harrison, was appointed. He at that time resided at Harden Beck. In 1795 a small chapel was erected; but a larger building being afterwards required, a new chapel was built in 1816. The Primitive Methodists and the Salvation Army have each neat and well-attended places of public worship in the town.

One of the oldest Temperance Societies in England was formed at Wilsden in 1832. Perhaps the largest meeting in connection with the early movement of the societies in Yorkshire was held at Wilsden, at Easter, in 1836, when the attendance on each of the three days that the proceedings continued averaged about 4,000. In his published *Lecture* (1897) on the history of the Bradford Temperance Society Mr. George Field states that the first Temperance Society in Yorkshire was established by the late Mr. Henry Forbes at Bradford in 1830, and among the original subscribers to the erection of the Bradford Temperance Hall in 1837 were four who are still living, namely, Messrs. Thomas Baines, late of Cottingley; W. S. Nichols, James Dixon, and H. W. Crossley, whose ages average about 87 years each.

One of the staunchest friends the temperance cause at Wilsden ever had was the late Mr. Francis Butterfield, who was born at Wilsden, and died there February 23rd, 1898, aged 86. He was father of the well-known naturalist, Mr. E. P. Butterfield, referred to on page 41. He was one of the originators and promoters of the local Temperance Society, and the friend and helper of many of the early pioneers of the movement. Mr. Butterfield remembered with bitterness the evil effects of village drinking fifty or sixty years ago. He wrote an excellent *Life of Thomas Worsnop*, one of the first temperance heroes, who was born at Hill Top, Low Moor, in 1799, and died in 1869; being buried in the grave-yard of Undercliffe Methodist Chapel. Mr. Butterfield was also the friend of Mr. George Jacob Holyoake, the celebrated advocate of Co-operation, &c. Being of a literary turn and interested in all objects of a progressive character, he made many friends, and corresponded with men and women distinguished in various capacities, and at a time when education was not so widespread nor at the high level it is now. On one occasion he visited Harriet Martineau at her beautiful home in the Lake country, and he had also worked side by side with John Nicholson, the Airedale poet, when he was a wool-sorter at Hewenden Mill. For the self-trained genius of Nicholson he had the profoundest respect, but always lamented the poet's sad drinking habits as having degraded a truly honest and amiable character. He was one of those who induced the poet to sign the

MR. FRANCIS BUTTERFIELD, WILSDEN.

pledge (alas! but too soon broken), and he possessed the old Wilsden Temperance Pledge Book containing Nicholson's signature.

Mr. Butterfield, though never a "physical-force" man, was in strong sympathy with the Chartists (*see* page 231), and there was no one in the neighbourhood of Bingley who entered with greater zest into the activities of their movement for the amelioration of the "poor factory slave." Well does the present writer remember visiting Mr.

Butterfield, now some years ago, and hearing him tell of the events of that disturbed time. Charlotte Brontë, with her famous dog "Floss," walked over from Haworth to Wilsden, the distinguished novelist desiring to consult Mr. Butterfield with respect to a proposed story on the Chartists' agitation. She spent the best part of a long afternoon with him, taking tea at his house, and was dissuaded from engaging in the proposed work, which at that time would only have added a flame to the still smouldering embers of discontent. In the evening Mr. Butterfield accompanied Miss Brontë as far as Birchlands End, and for a moment they stood in rapt admiration of the magnificent scene around them, the sun at that hour lowering over the western moors;—presently they arrived at the old stone stile where the footpath leads down to Hallas Bridge, when the immortal authoress of *Shirley* and *Jane Eyre* said, "I will bring you no further; thank you for your company"; then offering her small white hand, she added, "I shall act upon your advice. Good bye!"

With these words the present author must also close his book, hoping that by his feeble efforts to rescue "chronicles and stories" from the old inhabitant, the ancient homestead, the decaying tomb, and the muniments of bygone centuries, some interest may be awakened in the life of Bingley in the olden time.

ADDENDA AND CORRIGENDA.

Page 13, line 5. *Read* one inch instead of one foot.
" 46. Jack Field, near Druids' Altar; Jack Moor and Jack Lane, near Cowling, evidently from the Cym-Celtic *giac*, a snipe.
" 47. Bailey Hill, near Bradfield (Sheffield) is a noted archæological site.
" 52. "Yan West" came from Greenhow Hill, near Pateley B'dge.
" 109 *et seq.* In the *Plac de quo warranto* (211, 253) are two pleadings of the Prior of Drax claiming sac, soc, tol, them, and *infangtheof* in all his lands at Drax, Waplington and Bingley. He therefore claimed to erect gallows at Bingley.
" 120 *et seq.* Portion of a sleeve of Crusading chain-mail was found on Silsden Moor, near Keighley, and exhibited at York in 1846.

THE BINGLEY ARMS.

The above were adopted as the arms and crest of the town of Bingley in December, 1898, in lieu of the old coat of the Lane-Fox family, lords of the manor of Bingley. ARMS: a shield bearing three trefoils, *sable*, on a bend, *argent*, cotissed, *gules*: the shield being supported on each side by a rampant bear, muzzled. CREST: above a helmet, in profile, a bear's head, erased, muzzled, and collared, *gules*, studded and ringed, *or*. MOTTO: *Opes parit industria* (Wealth comes by industry). The above arms are based on those granted to Robert Benson, first Baron Bingley (A.D. 1713), which peerage became extinct in 1768.

Page 154. At West Witton, in Wensleydale, a custom still lingers of "Burning Bartle" every 24th of August; an effigy of St. Bartholomew (the patron saint of the church) being placed in a hand-cart and wheeled through the village, in procession, to Creskeld End, and there burnt.
" 158. At the restoration of the church in 1870-1, a black-letter inscription was found on the plaster of the east wall of the south aisle, now covered by the organ. An Elizabethan painted text is still visible in a similar position in the old church of St. Mary's, Bubwith, near Selby.
" 294, at bottom. *Read* Lord Bingley, not Lord of Bingley.
" 300. Railway was opened in 1847, (as on page 248.)
" 331. The family of Jane Shore is supposed to have come from Morton. The name also occurs in the Bingley registers.

SUBSCRIPTION LIST.

Subscribers to December 31st, 1897.

The * denotes subscribers to the patrons' edition, and the figures after the names refer to the ordinary edition.

**ACKROYD, GEORGE, J.P., Manningham (2).
*Armistead, R. Bingley.
*Asman, Destin W., Bradford.
*Anderson, Hiram, Bingley.
Ackroyd John, Cullingworth.
Atkinson, W., Bingley.
Atkinson, R., ,,
Aked, George H., ,,
Arundel, Capt. C. E., Leeds.
Ackernley, Rev. F. G., Keighley.
Allen John, Keighley.
Allen, John, Burnley.
Ayrton, William, Liverpool.
*Anderton, H. F., Bolton Royd.
Ackroyd, John, Rodley.
*Atkinson, Herbert W., Bradford.
Atkinson, Jonas, Bingley.
Anderton, Joe, Bradford.
Anderson, Denby, Eldwick.
Arminson, J., Crossflatts.
*Allen, James, Bingley.
*Angus, Dr., ,,
Atkinson, Robert, Bingley.
Atkinson, W. R., ,,
Anderson, Eliza Ann, ,,
Appleyard, Joseph, Keighley.
*Atkinson, Pearson, ,,
*Asquith, Mrs., Priesthorpe.

*BINNS, J. Arthur, Bradford (1).
*Baldwin, Herbert, Bingley.
*Baildon, W. Paley, London.
*Banks, Dr. Charles E., Washington, U.S.A.
*Bethell, William, Hull.
*Bardsley, Rev. F. W., Bingley.
*Broadbent, H. W., Bradford (1).
*Barwick, Mrs., Shipley (1).
*Brigg, W. A., Kildwick Hall.
Bingley, Godfrey, Leeds.
Barwick, John, Bingley.
Bracewell, K., ,,
*Binns, Priestley, ,,
Briggs, Mrs., ,,
Breuninger, William, Bingley.
Brooksbank, William, ,,
*Bower, Thomas, Bingley (1).
Bage, Miss, Bingley.
*Brown, W. H., Keighley.
Brooke, W. H., ,,
Binns, David, ,,
Bottomley, W. H., ,,
Briggs Bros., Silsden.
*Booth, John, ,,
*Beaver, John H., Oxenhope.
Bradley, James W. Keighley.
Brook, F. W. J., ,,
Booth, Lister, ,,
*Beaver, John, ,,
*Barrett, Denis, M.A., ,,
*Bulmer, G. Bertram, Harden.
Bailey, Miss, Bingley.
Binns, Æthelbert, Wilsden (2).
Butterfield, E. P. P., Wilsden.
Burdon, Rev. R. Leeds (2).
Boyes, J. E., Haworth.
Brown, W., Micklethwaite.
Baldwin, Mrs., Burnley.
Bartle, Albert, Wilsden.
Bruce, John, Gilstead.
*Bools, William Edward, London.
Berry, James, J.P., Preston.
*Butterfield Bros., Oldham.
Bailey, J. B. Maryport.
*Beckett, Dr. S. T., Cullingw'th (1).

Bell, Dr., Bradford.
*Boothroyd, W., Brighouse.
Buckley, J., Bradford.
*Beanland, Rev. J., M.A., Calv'ley.
Brooks, Uriah, Bingley.
Browne, George, ,,
Bradley, William, ,,
Bower, John, ,,
Barwick, George, ,,
Broadbent, B., ,,
*Bedford, James, ,,
Birkhead, Inspector, Bingley.
Bairstow, Mr., Bingley.
Brear & Co., Limited, Bradford (6 and 24).
Bailey, Charles, F.L.S., Manchester.
*Banks, Kirby, Beeston Hill (1).
Baynes, Ald. John, Ripon (2).
Bradley, Thos. A., Dewsbury.
*Black, J. W. A., Wibsey.
*Bailey, H. R., J.P., Newcastle.
*Bromley, Charles, Goole.
Bell, George, Laisterdyke.
Brittain, Ald., W. H., J.P., Sheffield.
Bruce, Saml., LL.B., Wakefield.
*Bradford Historical Society.
Bradford Mechanics' Institute.
*Bradford Free Library (10).
Bradford Library and Literary Society.
*Bradford Church Institute.
Blackburn Free Library.
*Bingley Free Library (1).
*Briggs, William, Glasgow.
Bancroft Arthur, Worth Village.
Browne, Rev. A. B., M.A., Bradfield.
Bilbrough, W. R. Leeds.
Ball, George, Healey.
*Butler, J. H., Bingley.
*Beetham, Dr., ,,
Buckle, Fanny E., ,,
Bentley, F., ,,
Bailey, Mr., ,,
Booth, Mr., ,,
Booty, W. E., ,,
Bibbs, E. J., Wolverhampton.
*Brayshaw, Mark, Bradford.
*Brundrett, Frederick, Clayton.
*Barrett, J. H., Horsforth.
*Brogden, J. H., Bradford.
Barker, T. E., ,,
Brown, Arthur, ,,
Brown, J. B., Hebden Bridge.
Brayshaw, Thomas, Settle.
Birtle, R., Bingley.
Bradley, Rev. Thomas, Bingley.
Butterfield, Sharp, ,,
Butterfield, John, ,,
Brentley Robert, East Morton.
Blakey Thomas, Morton Banks.
Bowker, Bracewell, Keighley.
Butterfield, J., ,,
Butterfield, Albert, ,,

*CRANBROOK, RT. HON. THE EARL OF, Hemsted Park.
Cooper, Mrs. Skipton.
Crossland Charles, Halifax.
*Cowburn, W. P., Bingley.
*Clifford, Joseph, ,,
*Cooper, A. J., ,,
*Calvert, Rhodes, Manningham.
*Carter, J. W., ,,
Carter, James, ,,
Camidge, William, York.
Collins, M., Southwark, S.E.
Crowther, Walker, Bingley.
Cryer, Walker, Bingley.
**Cheadle, Dr. W. B., London (4).
**Clapham, J. A., Gilstead (2).
*Conchar, Robert, Bingley.
*Clarkson, J. N., Riddlesden Hall (1).
Crabtree, Charles, Bingley (2).
*Crocker, Dr. James, ,,
Crowther, T., ,,
Clark, Miss A., ,,
Crabtree, S., ,,
Chapman Thomas, Keighley.
*Claridge, W. Bradford.
**Clough Ben, ,, (3).
*Cudworth, W., ,,
Constantine, J., M'chester Baths.
Cross, Ald. H. W., Scarbro'.
Clarke, Rev. A., Steeton.
Cordingley, John R., Bradford.
*Cooper, Richard, Gisburn.

*Clayton, John, Bradford.
Clayton, James, Ryecroft.
*Cossey, Rev. F. E., Uxbridge.
Clapham, John, Bradford.
Cryer, B. G., ,,
Cross, Abraham, ,,
Cox, Mrs., Hong Kong.
Cragg, R. B., Skipton.
Craven, John E., Todmorden (2).
Cunliffe, Walter, London.
*Craven, Fred., Bradford.
Craven Printing Co., Settle (2).
*Chadwick, S. J., Dewsbury.
Collier, Alfred, Bingley.
Crabtree, Miss, ,,
Cockerham, Miss, ,,
*Craig, Dr., ,,
Crowther, T., ,,
Craven, Edward, ,,
Crownbeck, Wm., ,,
Cockshott, E. H., Keighley.
Clayton, Arthur, ,,
Craven, William, Silsden.
Cowling, Harry, ,,
Crown, Thomas, Skelton.
*Chesney, P. K., Bradford.
*Copperthwaite, G. A., Shipley.
*Crabtree, J. W., Shipley.
Charnock, G. F., Bradford.
Crowther, Jos., Burley.

*Dewhurst, J. B., Skipton (1).
*Dyson, Geo., Marsden (1).
*Dodgson, J., Leeds (2).
*Dunlop, Charles W., Embsay Kirk, Skipton.
*Dobson, Benjamin, Bradford.
Denison, R. W., Bradford (2).
Dunlop, James, Bradford.
Darlow, Stephen, Bingley.
*Dawson, Miss, ,,
*Dale, Rev. Bryan, M.A., Bradf'd.
Dale, J. & Co., Ld., Bradford (3 and 6).
*Dodsworth, John S., ,,
Dawson, William, Gilstead.
*Dalton, J. W., L.D.S., Bingley.
*Dawson, Charles F., ,,
Driver, Edward, ,,
*Duxbury, Tom, ,,
Dickinson, John G., Keighley.
Dempster, George, ,,
Darlow, John J., Ashton-on-Mersey.
*Darlington, Latimer, Bradford.
*Dickons, J. Norton, ,,
Dobson, William, Shipley.
Darlington, Edward Pease Public Library.
*Dewsbury Public Library (1).
Drury, Edward, J.P., Halifax.

*Effingham, Rt. Hon. Lord Howard of, Tusmore Park.
*England, Henry, Bingley.
*Emmott, J., Bradford.
Elliott, F. W., ,,
Eales, W. S. Birstall.
Eastham, John, Clitheroe.
Eastwood, John A., Manchester.
Edmondson & Co., Skipton (2).
Earnshaw, Joseph, Bingley.
Edwards, Mrs., ,,
Evans, George, ,,
England, W. E., ,,
Emmott, T. A., Keighley.
Emett, John, ,,
Emmott, Frank, Crossflatts.

**Ferrand, W., J.P., St. Ives.
**Fox, George Lane, Bramham.
*Foster, John, Horton-in-Ribblesdale.
*Fryer, Robert, Crosshills.
*Farrah, John, Harrogate.
*Foster, Abraham, Dewsbury.
Friend, Rev. Hilderic, Tipton.
Fawthrop, Joseph, Bradford.
Firth, J. Crossflatts.
**Fox, J. D. Bingley.
Foulds, Thomas, Bingley.
Foulds, Edward, Bingley (6 and 24).
Foulds, John, Cape Town.
Feather, Michael, Keighley.
France, Hiram, ,,
Foster, Carr, Bingley.
Foster, Harry, Thackley.
Fearnley, F., Bracewell.
Fox, Isaac, Great Horton.

*Fawcett, Edwin, Lidget Green.
*Frankland, M., B.A., Ossett.
*Fenton, Samuel, Bradford (1).
Frear, Robert, Saltaire.
Federer, Charles A., Bradford.
Fitzpatrick, Miss, Bingley.
Freer, Albert, ,,
*"Friend, A," Bradford (1).

*Garnett-Orme, Mrs., Skipton.
*Gerrard, John, Manchester.
**Gomersall, Mrs. Wm., Skipton.
*Glossop, William, Bradford.
*Grayson, Supt. Benj., Keighley.
*Green, Sam, Halifax.
Goodricke, C. A., Upper Norwood.
Gregory, E. E., Bingley.
Green, Arthur, ,,
*Goodall, T. W., ,,
Green, William, ,,
Greenwood, W., Eldwick.
Green, Hannan, Bingley.
Gill, F. G., ,,
Garnett, Richard, ,,
*Greenwood, Pharaoh, Bingley.
Goldsbrough, G. H., Wakefield.
Gomersall, Rev. W. J., London.
*Gunston, J., Bradford.
*Gott, B. S., M.A., Cheltenham.
Gill, H., Bingley.
Green, A., ,,
Green, T. W., ,,
Green, Miss, Priesthorpe.
Green, Bernard, Glusburn.
Greaves, Mrs., Bingley.
Gill, Mrs. Ann, ,,
Gawthorp, Martha, ,,
Green, Herbert, ,,
Geller, Carl, Manchester.
Gill, George William, Shipley.
Grandage, James, Bradford.
Guy, T. A., ,,
Greenwood, Fred, ,,
Grange, Ernest, Crossflatts.
*Graves, Henry, Bradford.
*Grindrod, Arthur, Glen Lee.
*Guest, Ernest, Keighley.
Gill, S. & Son, ,,
*Goodall, William E., Harden.

*Hawkesbury, Rt. Hon. Lord, Kirkham Abbey.
*Hailstone, Mrs., London.
*Holmes, Rev. H. C., Birkby Rectory.
*Hainsworth, L., Farsley (1).
*Hardcastle, William, Scalby.
*Hanson, C. E., Manningham.
Hales, Professor J. W., King's College, London.
Holmes, W. H., B.C.L., Truro, Nova Scotia.
Hick, E., Horsforth.
Horne, Wm., F.G.S., Leyburn.
Hardaker, John, Manningham.
*Howarth, John, Bradford.
*Hill, Thomas R., ,,
*Hodgson, R., ,,
Hopkinson, Geo. H., ,,
Hill, Wm., Philadelphia, U.S.A.
Heaton, James G., Wilsden (2).
Hawkesworth, L., Bradford.
Hiles, R., ,,
Harker, James, Harrogate.
Hansell, Eliz., Cleveland.
*Haggas, Herbert, Keighley.
Haygarth, Thomas, ,,
Hugill, Herbert, ,,
Hartley, Rev. W. H. S., Morton.
Hewgill, Rev. William, Kent.
*Hind, W. Harley, Bradford.
*Hartley, Algernon G., London.
Hartley, Wm. Pickles, Hainworth.
*Hartley, Joseph, J.P., D.L., LL.D., Hartley, Kent (1).
Hartley, John, Bingley.
Hartley, William, ,,
Hartley, Sam., ,,
Hartley, Martha, ,,
Hartley, Wm. (Co-op.), Bingley.
Hepton, H. C. ,,
*Harper, Mrs., ,,
Hemmant, Thomas, ,,
*Hird, Noble, ,,
*Hirst, F., Gilstead (2).
*Heaton, John P., Oxenhope.
Hudson, Frank, Keighley.
Hanson, Charles, ,,
Hoyle, Timothy, ,,

*Helliwell, H., Halifax.
*Hutchinson, John H., Catterick.
Hutchinson, J. Gwynne, Horton.
Holmes, Lionel, Steeton.
Holmes, Mrs. Joseph, Nab Wood.
Hodgson, J., Bradford.
Hodgson, William, Darlington.
**Hardcastle, H. W. Bingley.
*Holt, Mr., „
*Holmes, J. E., „
Hudston, H., „
Howgate, John, „
Hollings, Fred, „
Hargreaves, Samuel. „
Howley, Councillor M., Keighley.
*Howgate, A. „
Holmes, H. Lincoln, „
Huckle, Henry, „
Hooley, John, „
Haigh, William, Harden Beck.
Haley, Charles H., Stanningley.
*Holmes, Mrs. Abm., Ilkley.
Hoyland, Miss E., Wentworth.
Hooper, Wm., Heckmondwike.
*Hill, J. H., Tadcaster.
*Higson, T. S. Shipley.
*Howarth, J. H., Heaton.
Heaton, Mrs., Undercliffe.
Helmsley, Sam, Manningham.
*Handley, H., Shipley.
Halifax Public Library (2).
Harrison, William, Keighley.
Hempsall, John, „
Hopkinson, W. H., „
Hammond, Wm., Stockbridge.
Hammond, Wm., Bradford (2).
Hofmann, George, Bingley.
Hanson, Lowther, „
Hill, Tait, „
Hullah, Geo. H., „
Hird, James, Harden.
Head, Arch., Dolgelly, Wales.

*Illingworth, T., Halifax.
Illingworth, W., Pudsey.
*Industrial Society, Limited, Keighley.

*Johnston, Jas., Manningham.
James, Philip, Brough.
Jowett, James, Cowhouse.
Johnson, S., Bingley.
Jennings, Alex., Keighley.

*Killick, H. F., Rawdon.
*Kershaw, J. A. Saltaire.
*Knowles, T. F., Bingley.
*King, C., „
King, Mrs., „
*Kidson, Francis J., Leeds.
Knubley, Rev. E. P., M.A., Trowbridge.
Kirkwood, Stephen, Bramley.
Knowles, C. H., Harrogate.
Keighley Institute.
Knowles, Jonathan, Bingley.
Kinder, Thomas, „
*King, Thomas, Keighley.

*Liversedge, Fred J., Manningham.
*Lambert Abraham, Harrogate.
*Le Page, Mrs. L. I. W. Bayles, Cheadle.
*Lister, Mrs. Timothy, Bingley.
*Lund, Sam., „
Lund, Frank, „
Lund, William, „
Lund, James, „
Lobley, A., „
Lee, John F., „
Lawson, Tom, „
*Lucy, Charles F., Pickering.
Lofthouse, J. H., Harrogate.
Leach, Arthur, Sheffield.
Law, Robert, F.G.S., Hipperholme.
Longbottom, William, Bingley.
Longbottom, Benjamin, „
Longbottom, Ellis, „
*Longbottom, Thomas „
*Longbottom, David, Silsden.
*Lambert, W. H., Silsden.
Lee, William, Bingley.
Lewis, Hartley, East Morton.
*Lamb, John H., Cullingworth.
Longbottom, A., Graniteville, Mass., U.S.A.
*Laycock, Thomas S., Keighley.
Lamb, W. K., Manningham.
Leggett, T., Bradford.

*Lancaster, Seth, Bradford.
Leeds Church Institute.
*Leeds Free Library (1).
Lord, John Thomas, Barnsley.
Lupton Bros., Burnley (10 and 6).

*MASHAM, RIGHT HON. LORD, Swinton Park.
*Maud, Ann, Washington, U.S.A.
*McCormick, Rev. Canon, D.D., London.
*Maude, William, Manningham.
*Maude, Wm. C., Bournemouth.
Maude, Miss, Ilkley.
Moro, Mrs. Arthur, Hyde Park, W.
*Marriner, W. Lister, Keighley.
*Myers, S. P., Bradford.
*Metcalfe, John, ,,
Metcalfe, James, Barnoldswick.
*Mellodey, Rev. Thomas, M.A., Cullingworth Vicarage.
Midgley, J. W., Keighley.
Marshall, Fred, ,,
Mitchell, Arthur, ,,
Mitchell, Arthur, ,,
Moorhouse, Sam., East Morton.
Middlebrook, L. H., Bingley.
Muggleton, Sam, ,, (2).
Murgatroyd, F., ,,
Maskew, R. B., ,,
*Milnes, Eli, Bradford.
*Mason, Richard, Liverpool.
Mason, Philip B., Burton-on-Trent.
Margerison, Sam., Calverley.
*Manchester Public Library.
Margetts, Rev. W. J., Baildon.
Marriott, C. H., Dewsbury.
Mills, F. W., F.R.M.S., Huddersfield.
Morrell, Geo., Saltaire.
Marsden, Ormerod, Bingley.
Mitchell, William, ,, (2).
Marshall, Miss, Gilstead Hall.
Moulding, T. H., Bingley.
Mitchell, Smith, ,,
Moore, John, ,,
Moorhouse, John, ,,

Matthews & Brooke, Bradford (12 and 36).
*Moulden, W. H., Bingley.

*NAYLOR, EZRA, Bradford (1).
*Newton, William, Laisterdyke.
Nutter, J., Bradford.
Nichol, T. C., Bradford.
*Newton, Arthur, Silsden.
*Newton, George, ,,
Newboult, Alfred, Bradford (2).
Newboult, Alfred, Bingley.
Nunn, Robert, ,,
*Newton, G., ,,
Northrop, Ruth, ,,
Northrop, Harry, ,,
Newton, H. Keighley.
*Nicholson, R. E., Halifax.
Nelson, T., Halifax.
Nunwick, Harry, Ingrow.

*OXFORD, LORD BISHOP OF, Cuddesdon Palace.
Oldfield, Geo. W., M.A., London.
*Orchardson, Thomas, Bingley (1).
Oldham Public Library.
Ogden, Squire, Keighley.
Overend, Alfred, ,,
Ogden, Sam, ,,
Ogden, J. H., Halifax.

*POWELL, SIR FRANCIS SHARP, BART., M.P., Horton.
*Priestley, Mrs. Charles, Cottingley Hall (1).
*Peacock, F. G., Crosshills.
*Parke, Geo. H., F.L.S., &c., Wakefield.
*Parkin, Rev. Thomas, Settle.
Poole, Richard, Bradford.
Patchett, John, ,,
*Pollard, Collingwood, ,,
*Petty, S. Lister, Ulverston.
*Pearson, Rev. Mark, Northowram.
Pearson, Thomas, Heaton.
*Parker, William, Bingley.
Platts, Walter, ,, (2).
Platts, Miss E., ,,
Pratt, Joseph, ,,

Preston, Benjamin, Eldwick.
*Pearson, Joseph, Bingley.
Pitts, Frederick, ,,
Pike, Mr. ,,
Perigo, James, Keighley.
Parker, John, ,,
Preston, Martha A., Keighley.
*Preston, J. E., Gilstead.
*Pawson, A. H., Farnley.
*Pattison, Frank W., London.
Pattison, Edwin, Bingley.
Pickard, Alfred, Wakefield.
*Paget, William, Skipton.
*Paget, James, Bradford.
Pawson, Thomas, ,,
Payne, A. E., Thornbury.
Parker, James, Great Horton.
Parker, Abraham, Bingley.
Pearson, John, ,,
Pashby, J. H., ,,
Pitts, Messrs. A. & E., Bradford.
*Patrick, Walter, Cottingley.
Pickles, Hiram, Harecroft.

*Rhodes, W. V., Cleckheaton.
*Rowntree, W., Scarboro'.
Randall, Joseph, Sheffield.
Ross, Percival, Wibsey.
Rhodes, Joseph, Keighley.
Roberts, George, Lofthouse.
Roebuck, W. Denison, F.L.S., Leeds.
*Robertshaw, S., Bingley.
Rushton, F., ,,
Royston, Samuel, ,,
Rushton, W., Eldwick.
Rotheray, Lister, Skipton.
Read, William H., Draughton.
Richardson, Joseph, Bingley.
Robertshaw, W., ,,
Redman, J. H. Keighley.
*Riley, Edwin, ,,
Riley, James, ,,
Roff, William, ,,
Rhodes, Wm., East Morton.
Robinson, Mr., Pudsey.
Rothera, H., Heckmondwike.
Rochdale Free Library.
Rhodes, John, Silsden.
Rawnsley, W. B., Bradford.
Rawlinson, John, Keighley.
*Robertshaw, William, ,,
Riley Ellis, A.L.C.M., ,,
*Richardson, Arthur, ,,
Russell, G. B., Bradford (3 & 6).

*Salmond, David, Ilkley.
*Salmond, Percy N., Ilkley.
*Shackleton, Henry, M.D., Sydenham (1).
*Shackleton, Rev. Canon T., Hereford.
*Shackleton, Francis R., Torquay.
*Shackleton, E. H., Sydenham.
*Shackleton, Rev. M., M.A., Beechingstroke.
*Shackleton, Geo., Lucan.
Shackleton, Abraham, Dublin.
*Shackleton, Ethel R., Sydenham.
Shackleton, Amy V., Sydenham.
Shackleton, Gertrude A., ,,
Shackleton, William, Chorley.
Shackleton, William Webb, Watford.
Shackleton, George, Bingley.
Shackleton, Matthew, ,,
*Skidmore, Chas., J.P., Bradford.
*Stephenson, Alfred, ,,
*Slicer, J., Idle.
Swire, Henry, Keighley.
*Sharp, Mrs. Alfred, Myrtle Grove.
*Sharp, Miss, Parkfield.
*Smith, Rev. Emill B., Kippax.
*Severs, Dr. George, London.
*Severs, John, ,,
*Stead, John James, Heckmondwike.
Stead, Walter, Heckmondwike.
Senior, Albert, ,,
Speight, T. W., London.
Speight, James, Bingley (2).
*Sutcliffe, Halliwell, ,,
Stoney, William ,,
*Severs, Charles ,, (1).
*Sowden, W. M., Bradford.
*Schofield, John, ,,
Smith, Jonas, ,,

*Stewart, Miss, Exmouth.
Smith, Sam., Crossflatts.
Smith, George, Utley.
*Smith, J. H., Cullingworth (1).
Smith, Thomas, Ingrow.
Smith, Jonas, Thornbury.
Smith, Peter Wilson, East Morton.
*Smith, Mary, Bingley (2).
Smith, Isaac, ,,
Smith, Miss, ,,
Smith, Charles, ,,
Smith, Luther, ,, (6 & 20).
Smith, Mrs., ,,
Smith, C., ,,
Smith, John, Keighley.
Smith, T., ,,
Scott, Miss C. H., Oxford.
Staffurth, Mrs. H. L., Bognor.
Swithenbank, J.A., Heckm'dwike.
Sim, D. A., Draughton.
Stuart, Dr. J. A. Erskine, Batley.
Singleton, James, Leeds.
*Sutcliffe, Frank, Bingley.
Skirrow, J. E., Gilstead.
Stott, John, Bingley (2).
Steel, T., ,,
Smales, T. W., ,,
Scott, Joshua, ,,
Sutcliffe, Mr., ,,
Sharpe, Samuel, ,,
Shuttleworth, J., Keighley.
Spencer, Hugh, ,,
Sugden, H., ,,
*Sellars, J. R., ,,
Simpson, Herbert, Ingrow.
Scarborough & Boyes, Haworth.
*Scott, John, jun., Skipton.
*Stephenson, Joseph, Bath (1).
*Sykes, Arthur F., Bradford.
Sutcliffe, John B., Fremington.
Shuffrey, Rev. W. A., M.A., Arncliffe.
Stockdale, Albert, Huddersfield.
*Sewell, Percy R., Liversedge.
Simpson, William Wroe, Crossflatts.
Stephenson, Mrs., Crow Nest.
Sheard, Michael, Isle of Ely.
Scruton, William, Baildon.
Swire, Tom, Keighley.
Slingsby, Thomas, Keighley.
Salt Schools, Shipley.

*Tempest, Sir Robert, Bart., Tong Hall.
*Trappes, Chas. J. B., Clitheroe.
*Taylor, Rev. R. V., Swaledale.
Towler, George, Cowhouse.
Tait, Mrs. Lawson, Warstock.
Thomas, John W., Bradford.
Thackeray, Chas. W., ,,
Terry, Percival, M.A., ,,
Thompson, Jesse, Bingley.
Thompson, James, ,,
Thoseby, Rev. Wm., ,,
Taylor, J., ,,
Taylor, Benjamin, ,,
Taylor, J., Ship Inn, ,,
Thornton, Jonathan, ,,
Town, Samuel, ,,
Taylor, James G., ,,
Thompson, Lund, ,,
Tetley, Miss S. A., ,,
Tyzack, Mrs., Sheffield.
Turner, Benjamin, Barnsley.
Thrippleton, John, Leeds.
*Thoresby Society, Leeds (presented by John Scott, jun.).
Tetley, T. Wilsden.
Thomson, William, Keighley.
Turley, James, ,,
Tidswell, F., Haworth.

Varley, John, C.E., Skipton.
Varley, W., Wilsden.
Vint, Horsfall, Idle.

*Wilson, Sir Mathew W., Bart., Eshton Hall.
*Weatherhead, Mrs., Gawthorpe Hall, Bingley.
Weatherhead, Miss E. E., Gawthorpe Hall (2).
*Willans, F., Edinburgh.
*Wilson, Bernard, Sedbergh.
*Wilson, J. R. Robinson, Leeds.
*Wright, Samuel, Wyke (1).
Wilkinson, John H., Leeds (2).
Walton, Miss Alice M., Bramley.

Whitham, John, Ripon.
Ward, Thos. F., Middlesbro'.
*Wright, James, Keighley (1).
Wright, Joseph, Crossflatts.
Whitaker, Hartley, Keighley.
Weatherhead, David W., ,,
Walsh, Councillor Jas., ,, (3).
Wade, Charles A., ,,
Wilson, S., ,,
Whitaker, T., ,,
*Wood, Horatio S., Morton.
Wilkinson, P. K., Bingley.
Wood, Ben., ,,
Wood, Robert, ,,
Wood, Edward, ,,
Wood, Joseph, ,,
Walbank, William, ,,
Walbank, Joseph, Eldwick.
Wright, Professor, M.A., Ph.D., Oxford.
Wilkes, Ald. J. K., Darlington.
*Woodcock, Henry B., Low Moor.
*Wurtzburg, John H., Leeds.
Wright, Edwd. H., Queensbury.
*Williamson, Reuben, Huddersfield.
Wilkinson, W., Bis'p. Auckland.
Whiteley, John, Barnoldswick.
Wild, Joseph, ,,
Weatherhead, Miss, Bingley.
Wild, Thomas, ,,
Wild, Roger, ,,
Wild, Herbert, ,,
Whitley, Ernest, ,,
Wilson, Thomas, ,,
*Walker, John, Gilstead.
*Waddington, T. A., Heworth.
Wild, Tom, Crossflatts.
*Wilkinson, Arthur, Bingley (1).
Wilkinson, John, ,,
Whitaker, George, ,,
*West, John, ,,
Whitwham, James, ,,
Walbank, Thomas, ,,
*Walbank, N. H., ,,
*Walsh, William, Paisley.
Walbank, H. W., Urworth.
Walker, S., Shipley.
Wildman, George, Bingley.
Wood, Tom, ,,
Walton, Albert, ,,
Walton, Maudsley, ,,
Watson, Joshua, Saltaire.
Waldby, Joseph, Harrogate.
*West, George, Ravensthorpe.
Wright, James C., Bradford.
Walmsley, William, ,,
Woolley, Alfred, ,,
Wright, A. P., ,,
Wright, Miss, Wilsden.
*Waddington, Sydney, Bingley.
*Waddington, Miss, ,,
Wood, Albert F., ,,
Wild, Joe, ,,
Whitley, James, ,,
Whitfield, A., Cottingley.
Wigglesworth, Miss, Guiseley.
Waterhouse, Whitaker, Eldwick.
Wroot, Herbert E., Bradford.
Walker, Alfred, ,,
Whitehead, J., Halifax.
Whitaker, John, Lees.
Whitley, James, Queensbury.
Watson, Thomas, Leeds (2).
*Wilkinson, Thos., Manningham.
Wilson, S. E., ,,
Whitwell, Wm., F.L.S., Balham.
*Wills, Louis J., Ormskirk.
Willings, Miss, Gilstead Hall.
Wakefield Mechanics' Institute.
Wakefield Book Society.
Wildon, J. T., Bingley (2).
Whitwham, H., ,,
Whitley, Walter, ,,
Whiteley, A., ,,
Whiteley, Mr., Huddersfield.

*Yorkshire Archl. Society (presented by John Scott, jun.).
Yarker, John, West Didsbury.

GENERAL INDEX.

OPINIONS ON THE WORKS OF HARRY SPEIGHT.

The *Times*, in reviewing *Nidderdale*, says: "It must assuredly take high rank as a repository of local history at once popular in form and full of original matter." The *Bradford Observer* says: "It will be a lasting monument to the author's untiring zeal and devotion in the cause of antiquarian research. The printing of the book is admirable."

His works embrace every aspect of Local Topography.

The *Academy* (one of the leading English reviews) says: "Mr. Speight has a happy versatility. He can write with confidence on the history, topography, geology, ecclesiastical antiquities, and ancient customs of those romantic districts in which he has spent his life. Much folk-lore, much family history, and many a streak of native humour lend variety to the pages, which are abundantly illustrated."

THE AUTHOR POSSESSES HUNDREDS OF COMPLIMENTARY LETTERS, AND HIS WORKS HAVE BEEN SUBSCRIBED TO FOR HER MAJESTY'S LIBRARY AT WINDSOR, AND THE LIBRARIES OF THE ARCHBISHOPS OF CANTERBURY AND YORK, AS WELL AS BY THE NOBILITY, CLERGY, AND GENTRY IN YORKSHIRE AND ELSEWHERE.

The *Leeds Mercury* says: "His works are thorough and exhaustive, and in addition have the charm of extreme readableness." The *Naturalist* (the organ of the Yorkshire Naturalists' Union) speaks of "Mr. Speight's unapproachable works," and the *West Yorkshire Pioneer* says "his works are models of accuracy and completeness."

The *Darlington and Stockton Times*, in a lengthy notice of *Richmondshire*, says: "Mr. Speight has added another standard work to the literature of Yorkshire. It is certainly the ablest contribution to the history and antiquities of Richmondshire since the time of Dr. Whitaker." The *Speaker* says: "No aspect of his subject appears to be overlooked." The *Craven Herald*, in a three-column review of *The Craven Highlands*, remarks: "It is no flattery to say that Dr. Whitaker at the beginning and Mr. Speight at the close of the present century stand out as the ablest authorities on this district." The *Bradford Observer* says: "There is nothing at all comparable to it in the wealth of its accumulated fact and research." The *Leeds Mercury* says: "It deals with every aspect of the life and conditions of the country it describes.

Many of the volumes are out of print, and command considerably advanced prices.

To be had from the Publisher:
ELLIOT STOCK, 62, PATERNOSTER ROW, LONDON, E.C.
Or from any bookseller.

Lightning Source UK Ltd.
Milton Keynes UK
UKHW020637131121
393891UK00003B/192

9 780344 039294